INTRODUCTION TO COMPARATIVE LAW

This textbook presents a clear and thought-provoking introduction to the study of comparative law.

The book provides students with in-depth analyses of the major global comparative methodologies and theories. Written in a lively style, it leads the student through debates in comparative legal scholarship, both in the Western world and in the lesser studied jurisdictions, beyond Europe and North America.

The second edition includes a revised structure to help the student understand the subject, an updated introductory chapter, and new material on legal transplants and globalisation. It also explores allied disciplines, including linguistics, history, and post-colonial studies giving students full context of the subject.

Introduction to Comparative Law

Second Edition

Jaakko Husa

·HART·
OXFORD · LONDON · NEW YORK · NEW DELHI · SYDNEY

HART PUBLISHING

Bloomsbury Publishing Plc

Kemp House, Chawley Park, Cumnor Hill, Oxford, OX2 9PH, UK

1385 Broadway, New York, NY 10018, USA

29 Earlsfort Terrace, Dublin 2, Ireland

HART PUBLISHING, the Hart/Stag logo, BLOOMSBURY and the Diana logo are trademarks of Bloomsbury Publishing Plc

First published in Great Britain 2023

Copyright © Jaakko Husa, 2023

Jaakko Husa has asserted his right under the Copyright, Designs and Patents Act 1988 to be identified as Author of this work.

All rights reserved. No part of this publication may be reproduced or transmitted in any form or by any means, electronic or mechanical, including photocopying, recording, or any information storage or retrieval system, without prior permission in writing from the publishers.

While every care has been taken to ensure the accuracy of this work, no responsibility for loss or damage occasioned to any person acting or refraining from action as a result of any statement in it can be accepted by the authors, editors or publishers.

All UK Government legislation and other public sector information used in the work is Crown Copyright ©. All House of Lords and House of Commons information used in the work is Parliamentary Copyright ©. This information is reused under the terms of the Open Government Licence v3.0 (http://www.nationalarchives.gov.uk/doc/open-government-licence/version/3) except where otherwise stated.

All Eur-lex material used in the work is © European Union, http://eur-lex.europa.eu/, 1998–2023.

A catalogue record for this book is available from the British Library.

A catalogue record for this book is available from the Library of Congress.

Library of Congress Control Number: 2023932877

ISBN: PB: 978-1-50996-356-0
ePDF: 978-1-50996-358-4
ePub: 978-1-50996-357-7

Typeset by Compuscript Ltd, Shannon
Printed and bound in Great Britain by CPI Group (UK) Ltd, Croydon CR0 4YY

To find out more about our authors and books visit www.hartpublishing.co.uk. Here you will find extracts, author information, details of forthcoming events and the option to sign up for our newsletters.

Acknowledgements

THIS SECOND EDITION would not have been possible without the help I received from many colleagues and friends. It would be impossible to mention all those names here. Notwithstanding, I would like to acknowledge separately Mark Van Hoecke, Juha Karhu, Pia Letto-Vanamo, Michael Palmer, Heikki Pihlajamäki, Juha Raitio, Geoffrey Samuel and Mathias Siems, who have provided inspiring ideas and feedback over the years. I also thank Claire Banyard for her excellent support with revising the manuscript. Moreover, I would like to thank Hart Publishing for their continued support with this updated and improved edition. Special thanks go, once again, to my family for their encouragement and patience. Finally, I thank my faithful but mostly useless research assistant Yorkshire terrier, Usko, for keeping me on the alert for imaginary threats that were lurking in the stairwell while I was writing and revising.

Jaakko Husa
November 2022

Use of Indented Paragraphs

THE FORMAT OF this book is intended to facilitate comprehension and make the text more reader-friendly. To avoid excessive footnotes with additional information or clarification, the book indents paragraphs that are related to but not an essential part of the main text. These paragraphs refer readers to other sources for examples, clarification and additional information. They enrich the text, guiding readers through the more challenging parts and enabling them to seek additional information independently.

Contents

Acknowledgements .... *v*
Use of Indented Paragraphs .... *vii*

1. **Introduction** 1
    I. About this Book 2
    II. Legal Culture in Focus 3
    III. Structure of the Book 6

2. **Comparative Law as a Discipline – A Short History** 7
    I. History of Comparative Law in a Nutshell 7
    II. Comparative Law in the Twenty-first Century 11

3. **Comparative Law – Definitions and Distinctions** 19
    I. Challenge of Further Definition 20
    II. Comparative Study of Law 22
    III. The Theory of Comparative Law 28

4. **Comparative Law – One of the Legal Disciplines** 33
    I. Part of a Larger Field of Knowledge 33
    II. A Member of the Family of Legal Studies 34
    III. Comparison and Fields of Law 53
    IV. Difficulty of Demarcation 59

5. **Why Compare?** 62
    I. Starting Points – Creating Added Value 63
    II. Comparison as a Cross-border Form of Knowledge
         Acquisition 64
    III. Comparison as Thinking Outside the Box 70
    IV. Basic Knowledge-interests 74
    V. Integrativity and Contradictivity 75
    VI. Practical v Theoretical Approach 90
    VII. Pedagogical – Comparison in Teaching and Learning Law 96

6. **Basic Strategies in Comparison** 100
    I. Introduction 100
    II. Scope – From Macro to Micro 105
    III. In Time and Space – The Time Dimension 108

x Contents

    IV. Quantity 113
    V. The Diversity of Legal Systems – Transnationality 115
    VI. Cultural Dimensions and Overlapping 119
    VII. Methodological Choices of a Theoretical Nature 122
    VIII. Functionality – Functional Comparative Law 122
    IX. Structural Dimension 132
    X. Systemic Approach 138
    XI. Critical Study Approaches – Two Examples 140
    XII. Depth of the Study – Decisiveness of the Knowledge-interest 146
    XIII. Research Ethics 148
    XIV. Comparative Methodology – Heuristics? 151

7. Comparing – Differences and Similarities 153
    I. Need for a Yardstick for Comparison – *Tertium Comparationis* 154
    II. Differences and Similarities... 160
    III. Culture and Explanation 162
    IV. Economic Factors 169
    V. Historical Factors 171
    VI. Geography and Climate 180
    VII. Other Factors 184
    VIII. Differences between Explanatory Factors 186
    IX. The Presumption of Similarity? 188

8. Comparison – Obstacles and Difficulties 194
    I. Comparative Research – Between the Familiar and the Foreign 194
    II. Research Data Related Problems 197
    III. Pitfalls in Research-material Processing and Analysis................. 200
    IV. Side-step to Theory: Comparing Laws but What Laws? 207
    V. Legal Comparison – A Particularly Risky Business?................... 213
    VI. Comparison as a Learning Process 215

9. Macro-comparison 218
    I. Basic Blocks of Macro-comparison 219
    II. Building Macro-constructions 229
    III. Grouping Legal Systems 234
    IV. Macro-constructs and Methodology 246
    V. Finally 251

10. Legal Evolution? 252
    I. Is There Evolution in Law? 254
    II. Problems in Macro-comparison 258
    III. Limits of Legal Evolution? 262

11. Groupings, Classifications, Categories 265
    I.   Technical Criteria 267
    II. General Requirements 269
    III. History-related Factors 271
    IV. Nature of Legal Thinking (Legal Mentality) 273
    V. Factors Related to Ideology 277
    VI. Cultural Factors 280
    VII. Finally 283

12. Conclusion 285

Index *289*

1

Introduction

THIS BOOK IS an advanced introduction to comparative law as a discipline and as a form of legal research. However, the reader should bear in mind that there are no generally accepted theoretical frames, established terminology or aims set in comparative law. Comparative law is a special field of legal study that is dynamic and open to innovation and is not cemented to any particular research approach. On the one hand, this means insecurity caused by the lack of an established research tradition; there is no true paradigm. On the other hand, it gives better opportunities for free research than is possible in a discipline that has been specifically defined. What is more, the scholarly freedom means that comparative law as a field of legal study is open to methods and insights from such neighbouring disciplines as history, linguistics, economics and social science.[1]

Compared to the doctrinal study of law, comparative law allows for much more freedom although it is worth noting that the expression 'anything goes' is not an apt description of comparative law. It cannot be denied that – as Monateri puts it – 'discipline of comparative law is characterized by several different and conflicting projects'.[2] As a result, there are degrees of freedom in comparative law, but all the same it is extremely important to be able to identify what one compares and how and why it is done. One should also be able to express the same to the reader in such a form that the contents of a publication are both comprehensible and as argumentatively persuasive as possible. This clearly exceeds mere description of the similarities and differences between the laws of different countries.

It is fair to note that in the literature on comparative law there are significant differences of opinion about the field. Comparative law, whose roots are in the tradition of German civil law, offers a very different view from the more theoretical comparison that has its roots in French philosophy or critical legal anthropology. Here the reader is offered an extensive view of comparative law and its scope. Where there are differing views this book endeavours to strike a balance. The solutions and examples suggested in the book should not be seen

---

[1] See for more detailed discussion on interdisciplinarity J Husa, *Interdisciplinary Comparative Law* (Cheltenham, Edward Elgar Publishing, 2022).
[2] PG Monateri, *Advanced Introduction to Comparative Legal Methods* (Cheltenham, Edward Elgar, 2021) vii.

as normative methodological rules but rather as new stimuli and helpful heuristic insights. Even though they are just stimuli they give a clear indication about what the field contains and what the typical characteristics are that separate it from the other members of the family of legal disciplines.

In the most extensive way possible, comparative law can be said to be an academic practice that studies large organised human communities and focuses on law as a normative phenomenon. Typical of the discipline is the use of a comparative approach where conclusions about differences and similarities are drawn. The definition seems at first quite clear if the reader conceives law in the way a civil law lawyer would usually grasp it. However, when we look at many expressions in various languages, such as English *law*, German *Recht*, French *droit*, Latin *ius*, Finnish *oikeus*, Greek *δίκαιο* or Chinese fǎ/faat (法), we notice that each concept in its own linguistic and legal cultural context is made up of slightly different content. Here we immediately face the basic epistemic problem: how to understand foreign law that is based on different legal historical and often very subtle legal cultural nuances that result in conceptual and other kinds of confusion. Further, these nuances are not directly revealed from the text of statutory law or the precedents, but instead they have to be deduced from the other materials that are available. So, by introducing the context, parallel description is transformed into comparative research that reaches beyond mere description.

I. ABOUT THIS BOOK

This book is meant to be used as a textbook or to a certain extent as a kind of manual for the methodology of comparative law for advanced Bachelor, Masters and early phase PhD students. The book is not a reference book on foreign law, nor do the examples given have any legal aims. If the reader is interested in foreign law, it is advisable to find updated legal literature on the system or systems in question – preferably in the original language, if possible. The aim of the book is to acquaint the reader with the theoretical and methodological foundations of comparative law. This author's epistemic and legal cultural home base is Nordic, but this book is written in a manner which embraces readers with other kinds of epistemic and legal-cultural backgrounds. The scholarly aspiration is to provide a modern and global view to comparative law without expanding to a thousand pages like Kischel's thick treatise.[3]

This book consists of two main parts: in the first part (chapters two to eight) general questions on the theory and methodology of comparative law are discussed, and in the second part (chapters nine to eleven) the grouping of legal families and cultures and the related problems are dealt with. As there are

---

[3] U Kischel, *Comparative Law* (Oxford, Oxford University Press, 2019).

plenty of online sources and much literature on the legal systems of different countries available, this book concentrates on legal families and their classification in the light of examples. However, it does not aim for complete coverage or a novel taxonomy. Furthermore, the reader should not expect country-specific figures where photo-like presentations on the law in force in each system can adequately sum things up. This book concentrates on the theory and methodology of comparative law instead of the legally detailed description of foreign law.

By and large, there are no extensively detailed references to sources in this book because this is a textbook and not a research monograph. However, when there are direct quotations or the text is directly based on a source, the name of the person and the work quoted are mentioned so that the reader has an opportunity to look for additional information at will. This is also in accordance with research ethics. The text has been divided into the main text and indented text that supports the main text. By reading the main text, it is possible to get a general picture about the topic in question while the indented text contains examples, specifications and additional explanations on topics discussed in the main text. The indented text and the main text support one another in such a way that the indented text enriches and complements the main text.

II. LEGAL CULTURE IN FOCUS

This book gives the reader an updated picture of comparative law as it is at present internationally understood. The focus is often on legal culture, which means that the book's orientation is different from that of many earlier books, and this explains why the first edition of the book was titled *New Introduction*. Even though the epithet 'new' is now abandoned, this book still seeks to encapsulate some of the new mentality and spirit of comparative law as a discipline as it is today. Simply put, the feeling of today is quite different from that of the twentieth century. The modern intellectual history of comparative law is a story of a paradigm shift as depicted by Fekete.[4]

In the 2020s there has so far not been any prominent single new theme or tone that radically differs from the comparative law of the previous century. However, the key focus has changed. As a kind of motto for this book the idea presented by EA Hoebel (1906–93) in his classic on legal anthropology *The Law of Primitive Man* can be mentioned: 'law divorced from its cultural matrix is meaningless'.[5] A second motto could be what Mireille Delmas-Marty (1941–2022) said in her inaugural lecture at the Collège de France: 'comparative studies means to give a preference to a pluralistic internationalisation which does not renounce the

---

[4] B Fekete, *Paradigms in Modern Comparative Law* (Oxford, Hart Publishing, 2021).
[5] EA Hoebel, *The Law of Primitive Man: A Study in Comparative Legal Dynamics* (Cambridge MA, Harvard University Press, 1954) 39.

4 *Introduction*

diversity of systems'.[6] With this in mind, the two key underlying features of modern comparative law are culture and pluralism or diversity.

Legal culture refers to the attempt of comparatists to recognise and accept the significance of legal contexts. Legal culture is a concept that present-day comparatists and legal theorists increasingly refer to; it no longer belongs solely to the vocabulary of legal anthropologists and sociologists. The problem with it though is that no unambiguous definition has been given. Regardless, the notion of legal culture and what it entails is crucial for today's comparative law.

The word culture goes back to the Latin verb *colore*, from which the word *cultura* is derived. Both words refer to cultivation. The rather old-fashioned phrase 'cultivation of the mind' is quite fitting, considering that the meaning of the term cultural has later been extended to cover civilisation and refinement in general. *Cultura* in a way offers a contrast to words that are related to wild (unorganised) nature. It is a question of the human being moving away from the state of nature, which classical legal philosophers (eg Thomas Hobbes) considered the natural state. From the point of view of comparative law, the most important dimension of culture is legal culture because comparative law studies different legal cultures. Recognition of the need to look beyond formal law and to see law in its legal cultural context is an important part of the self-reflective modern comparative law scholarship. Accordingly, rethinking comparative law's intellectual ways means taking the field seriously and accepting that it is essentially an interdisciplinary endeavour.[7] Besides, in practice using the viewpoint of legal culture is challenging and there are certain problems involved although almost all modern comparatists support the basic idea of looking beyond the limits of formal law.

In this book legal culture refers to what legal comparatists usually refer to when they use the concept: it is a question of factors that are outside the formal legal system but are still closely related to the operation of the legal system. In essence, law is put into context. It is a question of established attitudes of a permanent nature to law adopted by jurists in particular (internal legal culture) and more extensively by the society (external legal culture). Legal culture refers to the system-specific way in which values and practices and legal concepts are integrated in the actual operation of the legal system. Law is no longer considered autonomous but intimately connected to its human environment. For a comparative study of law this is an indispensable observation as it underlines the unavoidable need to look also beyond positive law.

Like this book, Siems' thick textbook pays attention to the context of law.[8] Siems places weight on social, political, and economic contexts of law from a comparative

---

[6] 'les études comparatives, c'est exprimer une préférence pour une internationalisation pluraliste qui ne renonce pas à la diversité des systèmes', 'Études juridiques comparatives et internationalisation du droit', leçon inaugurale faite le jeudi 20 mars au Collège de France,: books.openedition.org/cdf/2700.

[7] This argument is made strongly by S Glanert, A Mercescu and G Samuel, *Rethinking Comparative Law* (Cheltenham, Edward Elgar Publishing, 2021).

[8] M Siems, *Comparative Law*, 3rd edn (Cambridge, Cambridge University Press, 2022).

perspective. However, whereas he focuses on socio-legal and numerical approaches, this book underlines hermeneutical, historical, linguistic, and anthropological dimensions. In addition, Siems' book may also be characterised as a 'New Comparative Law' as to its nature. However, the book at hand has a distinct legal cultural and a historical and linguistic emphasis. Another important book, Samuel's introduction to theory and method of comparative law, is designed for postgraduate students. It has a distinct approach which is largely built on certain ideas of the French epistemology of social sciences.[9] Although books by Siems and Samuel are different from this book, it makes sense to note that these three books represent modern comparative law. As pointed out by Van Hoecke, these books are characterised by pluralism both in substance and methodology.[10]

The significance of legal culture is depicted in the fact that almost identical rules or extensive receptions of law produce completely different end-results at the level of legal reality. Reception in its legal meaning refers to the adoption of a system of law that has been created in another state or in a different historical era. It is a question of legally relevant prevailing attitudes according to which law and legal actors are in mutual interaction – void of the superior status of positive law. It is, it would seem, impossible to measure legal culture with scientific accuracy even though its significance is understood. However, the difficulties with the notion of legal culture have not stopped comparatists from developing the notion of legal culture into an analytical tool by splitting it into two main spheres: the institutional structure and the intellectual structure. This means focusing on six key dimensions: conflict resolution, norm production, ideals of justice, legal method, professionalisation and internationalisation.[11]

Therefore, legal culture refers to the contextual factors that produce a different end-result, for example in Switzerland and Turkey, although the codifications of their civil laws are extremely alike. Legal culture explains also why in the Netherlands there are so few civil trials compared to Germany where the formal legal system is very similar. North European legal culture is usually considered pragmatic when compared to its cousins in Continental Europe that are generally considered more formalistic. An explanation for the differences is searched for in history, social factors, attitudes to law, legal training and anything else that formal law is incapable of explaining. Legal culture is in most cases, when it comes to the comparative study of law, related to the fact that the comparatist tries to understand law more profoundly than by simply looking at the surface level of written law. As noted by Tamanaha, 'Law cannot deliver in and of itself because it swims in the social sea with everything else'.[12]

---

[9] G Samuel, *An Introduction to Comparative Law Theory and Method* (Oxford, Hart Publishing, 2014).
[10] M Van Hoecke, 'Is There Now a Comparative Legal Scholarship?' (2017) 12 *J Comp L* 271, 280.
[11] S Koch and J Øyrehagen Sunde, *Comparing Legal Cultures*, 2nd edn (Bergen, Fagbokforlaget, 2020).
[12] B Tamanaha, 'The Primacy of Society and the Failures of Law and Development' (2011) *Cornell Int'l L J* 209, 247.

III. STRUCTURE OF THE BOOK

In addition to this introduction (chapter one), this book consists of 11 other chapters. In chapter two, the history of comparative law as a discipline is explained in a nutshell. Chapter three contains basic definitions and distinctions concerning the field and the discipline of the comparative study of law (broadly understood). In chapter four, comparative law is placed in the larger field of knowledge ie legal disciplines as a whole. Chapter five tries to offer an answer to the question of why a lawyer should study law comparatively, and what the basic interests of knowledge are in comparative law. Chapter six presents and analyses various basic comparative research strategies and crucial methodological choices which a comparatist must perform. Chapters seven and eight concentrate on comparative methodology by presenting possibilities which can be utilised when explaining differences and similarities and what difficulties comparatists tend to encounter in their research. Chapters nine to eleven deal with macro-comparative law, evolution of legal cultures and how macro-comparatists classify legal systems into different theoretical macro-constructs. All these chapters contain their own conclusions, and for didactic purposes there is also some element of repetition. Key themes, such as legal pluralism and legal transplantation, run throughout the book. Finally, the last chapter provides a conclusion including key points of the book and some ideas about the future of comparative law in the age of globalisation.

2
Comparative Law as a Discipline – A Short History

I. HISTORY OF COMPARATIVE LAW IN A NUTSHELL

THE HISTORY OF comparative law is not an autonomous history of an independent scholarly field of law as a discipline but part of the general history of legal thinking. This is why 'No single history of comparative law has ever been written'.[1] However, there are some fairly good attempts like the article by Hug from 1932 shows.[2] The origins of scholarly comparative study are in the research of societies and people deep in the Western tradition of science. The historic roots of comparative study are connected to public law, although in the twentieth century research on comparative law was mainly concerned with private law. Nevertheless, the intellectual roots of comparative law have never been solely in private law. In this respect comparative law did not even in Continental Europe cover public law but took place exclusively within the *ius commune* tradition and was dominated by private law. However, if examined from modern systematics' point of view, in the modern sense *ius commune* included criminal law and procedural law as well as private law.

During the period of Alexander the Great, the foundations for comparative legal and comparative political study were laid when in the school for philosophers, ie *Lykeion* (Λύκειον) of Aristotle (384–322BC), the constitutions of 158 Greek city states were collected as the material for theoretical and practical comparative study on constitutions. The results of Aristotle's work have been preserved for future generations in the classical work Πολιτικά (*Politics*), where such topics as nationality, form of government, legal status of civil servants, and the issue of the number and nature of laws required are discussed. These issues are still relevant in the reinvigorated comparative study of constitutionalism that has experienced a renaissance in the rise of comparative constitutional law.[3]

---

[1] B Fekete, *Paradigms in Modern European Comparative Law* (Oxford, Hart Publishing, 2021) 1.
[2] W Hug, 'The History of Comparative Law' (1932) 45 *Harvard L R* 1027.
[3] R Hirschl, *Comparative Matters* (Oxford, Oxford University Press, 2014).

A comparative legal work also known by the name *Lex Dei*, the whole name of which is *Lex Dei quam praecepit Dominus ad Moysen*, or 'God's Law (which the Lord Ordered) for Moses', has been known about from Late Antiquity. The work is also known by the name *Collatio legum mosaicarum et romanarum* or 'Comparison of the Law of Moses and the Roman Law'. The exact time when the work was written is not known, but the basic text is assumed to have been compiled in the early fourth century. Only parts of the work have been preserved, but from these it is possible to conclude that it is a work that compares Roman law and Jewish law that has been translated from Hebrew: first Moses' law is inspected, and then the same legal problem is discussed in the light of classical texts written by Roman lawyers. From the point of view of legal history and comparative law, the work is revealing because it contains quotations from Roman lawyers, and simultaneously it describes the author's interest in historical comparative law.[4]

From a more recent period Charles de Secondat, Baron de Montesquieu (1689–1755), and particularly his work (on) *The Spirit of the Laws* (*De l'Esprit des Lois*, 1748), is worth mentioning. Montesquieu was interested in the historical development of law and the comparison of different legal institutions by means of which he hoped to be able to make propositions for the improvement of legislation. The work is a classic of both comparative law and the sociology of law, and some of its ideas are still interesting from the point of view of macro-comparison (more on this later).

From the nineteenth century onwards the field began to settle into its present channels. Sir Henry Maine (1822–88), the first holder of the Chair of comparative law that was founded in Oxford in 1869, published a classic in comparative law and legal history called *Ancient Law*.[5] In this book he drafted his legal-sociological explanation for the difference between Roman law and modern law. According to him, individuals in the ancient world were bound to the traditions of their own social groups, while modern law was characterised by the autonomy of individuals. Maine was a kind of evolutionist who believed – as many legal comparatists still do – in the idea that legal cultures continue to develop from simpler to more complicated.

One of the very few historical presentations on comparative administrative law is *Comparative Administrative Law* in two volumes by Frank J Goodnow (1859–1939).[6] In this he studied France and Germany as well as England and the USA. Goodnow's starting point was his view according to which in modern

---

[4] R Frakes, *Compiling the Collatio legum Mosaicarum et Romanarum in Late Antiquity* (Oxford, Oxford University Press, 2011).

[5] H Maine, *Ancient Law: Its Connection with the Early History of Society, and Its Relation to Modern Ideas* (London, John Murray, 1861).

[6] FJ Goodnow, *Comparative Administrative Law: An Analysis of the Administrative Systems, National and Local, of the United States, England, France and Germany* vols 1–2 (New York, GP Putnam's Sons, 1897).

States questions concerning constitutional law were being neglected, while topics concerning administrative law had risen to the foreground. The prediction has not proved quite accurate as it seems that constitutional law issues have become more visible because of judicial review and constitutional rights.

For both Aristotle and Montesquieu one of the central aims was to create new knowledge from the comparative standpoint in order to improve the political structure of society. In the same way Goodnow intended, by means of administrative comparison, to create knowledge that legislators would be able to use in the development of the administrative system of the future. Maine on the other hand wanted to present a new (more authentic than before, or one that differed distinctly from 'civilised nations') picture of Roman law, because in his opinion Roman law had not been correctly understood. This discussion on the nature of Roman law is still ongoing among Roman law scholars.

The examples demonstrate the unavoidable connection of comparative law to its own period and the prevailing knowledge-interests (why compare?). In the same way, for example, that a doctoral student at a Central European university who is writing a dissertation on the doctrinal study of law resorts to comparative law for different purposes than someone who is writing a dissertation on the same topic but more distinctively from a comparative law perspective. Along similar lines, the senior referendary of the court of appeals who is drafting a practical comparative report on the background to support the knowledge basis of their proposal for a decision makes use of comparative law. Still, the referendary's comparison differs from how the senior legal adviser in the Ministry of Justice drafts the government bill, based on practical comparison of foreign laws, for a new legal institution to be created by means of a legislative measure. Similarly, the critical comparatists who heavily criticise the harmonisation of European civil law or seek to decolonise comparative law scholarship draw their inspiration and methods from totally different directions to those who devotedly work in the interest of legal integration. Briefly: the aims and needs behind comparison determine to a great extent the type of comparison that will be performed. Moreover, legal policy or just plain policy explain more frequently and efficiently than legal theory the need for comparison and the method selected. In this sense, it is safe to characterise comparative law as a diverse field.

A. Birth of Modern Comparative Law

The historical background of comparative law is usually considered to be caused by two motives of a different nature. On the one hand, we talk about *legislative comparative law*, which refers to those connections and cases of comparison when foreign law is studied from the point of view of the development and application problems of national legislation. Modern comparative endeavour that aims at harmonisation continues this tradition. The situation of *scholarly comparative law* was weaker for a long time, and its position lacked recognition.

Some writers have been of the opinion that the first actual work on modern comparative law is the abovementioned *Ancient Law* by Maine.

Both traditions of comparative law are still alive, as will be shown later by the division into practical and theoretical comparison. The starting point of modern comparative law is easier to recognise, because it is invariably dated to the congress on international comparative law (organised by *Société de législation comparée*) held in Paris in 1900. There, the first serious writings that aimed at being systematic and that tried to outline the concept, field and tasks of comparative law were presented.[7]

In the twenty-first century the inheritance of the Paris conference has faced sharp criticism and rejection. The critique has been offered by comparatists with a critical attitude to the legal positivism of the Paris inheritance, which they would like to abandon. But, in reality the Paris inheritance is versatile and in no way monolithic. The idea of the universal nature of law and the optimistic fantasy of the unification of law throughout the world undeniably dates back to Paris: comparatists wanted to look for a common legislative ground for all so-called civilised States (*droit commun législatif*) of that time. Characteristic of the period was that all members of the Paris congress were European and most of them from the colonial powers.

> A general view of the critique and its central ideas is presented in *Comparative Legal Studies* edited by Legrand and Munday.[8] The work is based on the conference that was held in Cambridge in 2000, ie exactly 100 years after Paris. However, in Cambridge the conscious aim was to be detached from the mainstream of comparative law, ie the Paris legacy. The rise of decolonial comparative law has continued to evaluate critically the 1900 Paris legacy.[9]

Apart from being a rough outline the presentation above on the paradigm of comparative law is also very European. In the US, comparative law did not start to thrive until after World War II, and was to a large extent promoted by the flight of a number of prestigious legal scholars. These scholars (so-called emigrant paradigm) were eventually settled in American universities to teach jurisprudence and brought with them their extensive knowledge (their own old law and the new one learned in the US) of comparative law as well as their versatile knowledge of languages. On this existing emigrant base, owing to the possibilities provided by financial and cultural change through globalisation, a foundation was laid for academic American comparative law in the 1990s and that of today. The recent turn to empirical and quantitative methods

---

[7] Reprints of the Paris proceedings are available, see *Actes du congrès de Paris de 1900* (Paris, Société de législation comparée, 2020).
[8] See P Legrand and R Munday (eds), *Comparative Legal Studies: Traditions and Transitions* (Cambridge, Cambridge University Press, 2003).
[9] L Salaymeh and R Michaels, 'Decolonial Comparative Law' (2022) *Rabels Zeitschrift für ausländisches und internationales Privatrecht* 166.

has, however, slightly changed the outlook of comparative law in the US and elsewhere.[10]

Undoubtedly, without European emigrants, there would have been much less comparative law in North America, and it would be intellectually poorer. The flow of learned lawyers from Europe to the US and Canada has not completely died, but this is due to the competiveness of American universities.

II. COMPARATIVE LAW IN THE TWENTY-FIRST CENTURY

Some comparatists have named the twenty-first century as the century of new arrival for comparative law. Their opinion is not unjustified even though their view seems to be a romanticised one. In recent years the profile of comparative law as an approach to law has increased. It has become fashionable in academic circles, and writing on its theory and methodology has increased throughout the whole of the twenty-first century so far. All the same, comparative law is not only the concern of academic research. While comparison is a segment of legal research and teaching, it more and more frequently is an informative tool for the drafting and application of law. Non-comparative legal scholars too have, more daringly than before, started to use the material from other legal systems as part of their own argumentation.

On the other hand, discussion within comparative law has shown that the discipline has lost some of its old methodological and theoretical innocence. It has been challenged by history, sociology, economics and anthropology. This has resulted in disruption of the earlier theoretical consensus while the challenge has turned comparative law into a viable and intellectually challenging activity. At the same time, some of comparative law's bookish outlook has worn off. Comparative law, despite being deemed to be difficult, has appeal in the eyes of aspiring legal scholars. Some of this has to do with the fact that there has been a paradigm shift from narrow to contextual.[11]

In the twentieth century law still seemed simple. The mobility of rules, doctrines and institutions seemed scarce and the borderlines between legal cultures clear. National systems were self-imposedly mesmerised by the fiction of legal conformity and sovereignty. As attitudes changed at the end of the nineteenth century and the beginning of the twenty-first century, it is justifiable to say that comparative law has in many ways undergone a renaissance. There are several reasons for the higher profile. The most important background factors are the development of internationalisation, the European integration in particular and the disruption of legal positivism connected to national law. Globalisation has challenged some of the old assumptions about

---

[10] See H Spamann, 'Empirical Comparative Law' (2015) 11 *Annual R L & Soc Sci* 131.
[11] Fekete (n 1) 161–63.

comparative law.[12] Notwithstanding, the growing impact of comparison has remained at least in part largely at the level of academic discourse.

The growing significance of comparative law is seemingly conceded on Festschrift occasions and when the internationality of legal study is emphasised. Festschrift academic speeches and 'comparisons' mentioned in passing in texts written by researchers who are European law-oriented as well as other external attempts to emphasise comparison only convey a partial truth. There is more talk about than actual practice of comparative law. Europe is no exception in this respect: there is discussion and articles on the importance of comparative law, but so far ambitious comparative studies are exceptions. One cannot help thinking that there is 'much ado about nothing' when it comes to comparative law: it is fashionable to be comparatist but much less fashionable to actually do comparative legal research. Of course, there are exceptions to this rule as the Netherlands and Italy seems to prove: PhD theses with a strong comparative law dimension are held in high esteem.

For instance, in the Nordic countries, compared to Europe in general, the focus on comparative law has remained modest if measured by the volume of research. Nor are there more than a few teaching and research positions in comparative law at universities, and the existing positions have been connected with private international law so that comparative law as a genuinely independent discipline does not really exist. The portion of comparison in the teaching of legal study subjects has also remained modest, and as a study subject it has been overshadowed by international and European law. Further, academic conventions are lagging in development. The structural distortion is balanced by the fact that doctrinal research that makes use of the comparative approach has increased in different fields of law. There are, nevertheless, also new developments like decolonial comparative law and comparative international law that seek to expand the scholarly limits of comparative law.

As a research method, comparative law is still not held in high esteem in the sphere of legal study although there is a broad consensus on its need and usefulness. However, empty vessels make the most noise. In this respect the status of comparative law resembles that of legal history and sociology of law, which likewise are remembered on Festschrift occasions and at various congresses and seminars but hardly ever when faculty structures are planned or resources allocated.

> The first chairs in comparative law were established in France as early as 1832 (*législation comparée*/Collège de France) and in the UK 1869 (*Historical and Comparative Jurisprudence*/Oxford). Along with European integration and globalisation, the position of comparative law has in some countries continued to grow, and it has

---

[12] J Husa, 'Introduction: Globalisation, Comparison, and Legal Scholarship' (2021) 16 *J Comp L* 458 (introductory piece of thematic issue with articles by G Samuel, M Nicolini, M Graziadei, J Raitio, J Hendry and P du Plessis).

remained strong in countries such as Italy where there are a great number of professors within comparative law and where the discipline has a strong status in teaching law at the university level. In Italy comparison was resorted to in the latter part of the nineteenth century when the State constructed its legal identity supported by foreign, particularly German models. Even today there are lots of comparative law professors in Italy. However, in Germany comparative law has a much more modest role in the faculties of law and comparative law is left to a rather small group of dedicated specialists. Then again, comparative study of law has gained momentum in Asia.[13]

It is not only a question of the academic strengthening of comparative law. We can, for example, register the rise of comparative human rights in the twenty-first century which was due to the work of the European Court of Human Rights. Also, the judgments given by the Court of Justice of the European Union have made frequent use of comparative law. Some courts in the former socialist countries of Eastern Europe quite openly seem to make use of comparative approaches as part of their legal decision-making. In the US, on the other hand, the majority of the Supreme Court of the federal State still want to protect its own legal tradition, which in their opinion is without doubt the best in the world. The US is about to be left alone in its stubborn legal nationalism – naturally there is comparative law in the US too, but its role is different from what it is in Europe. Integration has changed the legal mentality climate especially in Europe even though the problems of the EU have slowed down European developments.

Over the past few years one of the major development trends in comparative law has been the breaking away from the limits set by its connection with private international law in the twentieth century. Overall, it can be stated that private law is no longer the boundary for comparative law. In addition, comparison, having got rid of its doctrinal straitjacket, has opened up towards legal anthropology, legal history and legal linguistics.

A. Legal Systematics and Comparison: Private Law v Public Law

Research in comparative law has up till now concentrated on the field of private law. The same applies to the discussion on the original point of view concerning the theory of comparative law. One reason for this has been that the practical needs of comparative law used to arise from the sphere of private international law where issues connected to private law in international relations were studied. Such an issue is, for example, the decision on the choice of law for making agreements. As an academic subject private international law consists of several different sectors, such as the international law of obligations, the international law of family and inheritance as well as the international law of property and international civil procedural law.

---

[13] See 'The State of Comparative Law and its Teaching in Asia', a thematic issue of (2019) 14 *Asian J Comp L*.

The commercial and personal relations between natural and legal persons crossing national borders have traditionally been closer and more developed than the relations between States. Public law, especially administrative law and constitutional law are, as developed sectors of law, also considerably younger than the core of civil law that reaches back to Roman law. On the other hand, several more recent branches of law (eg marketing law, competition law, labour law and social welfare law) are also virtually devoid of contextual links to Roman law. The previous 100 years changed comparative law's focus along a certain route up until the end of the century.

Comparative law was born and grew up in the last two decades of the twentieth century as a by-product of private international law. Almost all comparatists were in one way or another interested in the issues of private international law. Comparative law was a kind of auxiliary method (or little servant) by means of which it was possible to clarify certain issues in private international law. The idea was that private international law was a natural channel that leads to comparative law because foreign law had to be applied.

> Several of the classical researchers of comparative law mastered both fields, with perhaps Ernst Rabel (1874–1955) being the best example. With good reason he can be named as one of the most central figures in academically ambitious comparative study in the twentieth century. Among others, he wrote the classic private international law text *The Conflict of Laws* in the 1940s.[14] Rabel as a person manifested the tight bond between comparative law and private international law. Remnants of this old tradition can be seen all around the globe in law faculties. Internationally, this old connection is still very well known, but is clearly losing ground. One major reason is of a practical nature: it is difficult to be simultaneously an expert in two demanding fields of legal study. And, despite the term 'international', private international law is not really international at all. Moreover, the relation between comparative law and private international law is not unproblematic as these fields have developed in different directions during the last few decades.[15]

The lack of comparison in public law was at that time based on certain legal theoretical beliefs. For public law the most central object of regulation is the operation and structure of the State and its relation to citizens, and therefore it was considered to be heavily bound up with many factors that were external to law, such as political history and ideological factors. The special nature of public law was suspected to form obstacles for the approach used in comparative law. This was earlier seen in the fact that the classic general presentations in comparative law were concentrating exclusively on private law.

> Among the European classics that concentrated on private law there has been *Traité de droit comparé* by Arminjon, Nolde and Wolff, published in three parts in the 1950s,

---

[14] See E Rabel, *The Conflict of Laws: A Comparative Study* (Michigan, University of Michigan Law School, 1945).
[15] J Husa, *Interdisciplinary Comparative Law* (Cheltenham, Edward Elgar Publishing, 2022) 206–13.

Les grands systémes de droit contemporains by René David, first published in the 1960s[16] and *Einführung in die Rechtsvergleichung auf dem Gebiete des Privatrechts* by Zweigert and Kötz, which has been translated into several languages and was first published at the beginning of the 1970s.[17] In the US, *Comparative Law: Cases, Text, Materials* by Schlesinger, which was first published in the 1950s, can be considered an equivalent work. The latest edition of Schlesinger's book, which was published posthumously in 2009, has broken free from the limitations of not only private law but also of non-Western law.[18]

The point of view according to which private law would somehow be less dependent on non-legal factors (such as history, religion and culture) rests on shaky ground. For example, a basic civil institution such as marriage quickly shows a comparatist that legal arrangements and their grounds as well as the factors that influence their acquisition are often found in factors that are outside of law (eg the institution of marriage in Hindu law, Islamic law and Western law). The same applies to legal regulation of family and inheritance; the differences between public law and private law are in this respect mainly superficial. Moreover, the earlier mistaken belief of the straightforward similarity of legal cultures even in the core sectors of private law has proved brittle. We have become more conscious of nuances – a contribution of modern comparative law that is open to diversity and pluralism.

Some recent developmental aspects have put several would-be obstacles for comparative public law in a questionable light. The discussion on the theory and method of comparative law in this millennium proves that public law has caught up with private law, which earlier held the dominant place. The division has been flexible from the start since it has been possible for public corporations to have also a private law relation to a private person or body, as for example when a public corporation buys real or movable property from a citizen. In such a case it is not a question of a public legal relationship that would include the exercise of official authority, and therefore private law regulations are applied.

In recent years the flexibility of the division has become all the more obvious. The nature of the exercise of national public authority has changed, due to, for example, different procurement procedures and the privatisation of public undertakings having eroded the traditional borderline between private and public law. Public undertakings are taken by private actors but on the authorisation given by public power. There are cases, for instance Thailand, where private ordering plays the role of substitute of public law.[19] Hence,

---

[16] The 12th edition was published in 2016; co-authors were C Jauffret-Spinosi and M Goré (Dalloz, Paris).
[17] English translation, T Weir, *An Introduction to Comparative Law*, 3rd edn (Oxford, Oxford University Press, 1998).
[18] Schlesinger's *Comparative Law* was edited and renewed by younger generation comparatists U Mattei, T Ruskola and A Gidi (New York, Foundation Press, 2009).
[19] V Ramraj and T Tengaumnuay, 'Thailand: Privatization of Constitutional Law' in DS Law (ed), *Constitutionalism in Context* (Cambridge, Cambridge University Press, 2022) 517.

it is no longer possible to draw an exact dividing line between these two main sectors of law. The borderlines between fields of law are now subject to constant change. The same applies to the relationship between national, supranational and international law in Europe as well as elsewhere. Drawing dividing lines between fields of law is also made difficult by the fact that, for example, criminal law has slowly started to turn European or even global, and comparative criminal law has gained ground.

The key questions of public law emerged in a completely new way after the political eruption that took place in Eastern Europe in 1989–90. In the wake of the eruption, the adoption (so-called *model shopping*) of renewed constitutional laws and various legal institutions into the legal systems that were purged of their socialist characteristics created completely new ground for practical comparative law. Another major factor in the rise of the significance of comparative public law has been and continues to be European integration, which also includes European human rights. This does not merely concern the European Union, although the EU's contribution to the rise of comparison cannot be denied. Notwithstanding, some of the East European Member States of the EU have proved difficult to fully integrate with the EU's notion of the rule of law (eg Hungary and Poland). Moreover, Brexit has also weakened the momentum behind the EU's legal integration.

In addition, it has to be mentioned that there has been a huge increase in comparative constitutional law since the 1990s to the point where it is now the most vigorous and dynamic area in comparative law in the twentieth century. Jonsson Cornell sums up the development as follows: 'comparative constitutional law has grown in significance and impact from the middle of the 1900s, and in the beginning of the twenty-first century it has become an established discipline and legal method'.[20] In effect, constitutional comparison has been established beside comparative private law and it seems that other fields (administrative law, criminal law) are going to do the same. This change is reflected in comparative law handbooks and encyclopedias that have expanded from their former private law orientation.[21]

On the other hand, talk about the European federation and the death of State sovereignty, which was in vogue as late as during the 1990s and early 2000s, has in the 2020s been less frequent because the European Union has been in great difficulties due to the financial problems of its Member States, Brexit and issues

---

[20] 'har komparativ konstitutionell rätt vuxit i betydelse och inflytande sedan mitten på 1900-talet för att i början på 2000-talet bli ett etablerat rättsvetenskapligt ämne och juridisk metod', A Jonsson Cornell, 'Inledning' in *Komparativ konstitutionell rätt*, 3rd edn (Uppsala, Iustus förlag, 2020) 9–14, 9.

[21] M Reimann and R Zimmermann, *The Oxford Handbook of Comparative Law*, 2nd edn (Oxford, Oxford University Press, 2019); M Siems and PJ Yap, *Cambridge Handbook of Comparative Law* (forthcoming 2023) and J Smits, J Husa, C Valcke and M Narciso (eds), *Elgar Encyclopedia of Comparative Law* (forthcoming 2023).

revolving around the rule of law problems. National *legal cultures*, in spite of their harmonisation, are still in existence. Convergence is a fact, but profound unification is still a utopia: the decrease in differences has not resulted in the similarity of systems and disappearance of all differences. The disputed argument by Legrand (according to which European legal systems are not converging) still holds lots of potential, as Brexit has proved.[22]

There is no doubt that the development in this century has improved the status of public comparative law. The difference between public and private law is in no way significant for the methodology and theory of comparative law. This is due to the fact that *the general questions of comparative law are the same in all subsections of comparative law*. Yet, the majority of the research on comparative law still takes place in the field of private law, but this is no longer so dominant. It is important to emphasise that there is no special 'comparative public law theory' that in some decisive way would differ from the 'comparative private law theory'. The theoretically and methodologically fundamental questions are the same, regardless of the field of law, although different knowledge-interests cause different emphases. It is essential to recognise the research topic and one's own special interest in it and to make the methodological choices based on them. A constitutional comparatist can learn from a civil law comparatist and vice versa. The tendency to develop distinct fields makes no sense from the viewpoint of methodology.

The different characteristics of different fields of law by no means prevent the comparative study of law, but they have to be taken into consideration when attempts are made to explain the differences and similarities detected. It is not, however, easy to study differences and similarities, and the comparatist cannot avoid the irrevocable fact that they should also *understand* foreign legal culture. Comparative legal sociologist Nelken aptly writes:

> All comparative work involves the exploration of similarities and differences: the problem is how to find cross-cultural criteria for isolating and identifying such variables for the purpose of demonstrating similarities or differences in legal culture. This is not merely a technical question.[23]

In comparative methodology a matter is merely a technical problem only very rarely. The intellectual challenge of comparison comes from the difference in legal cultures – diversity and hybridity present their own challenges. It is never easy to understand something that is unknown, and understanding a foreign law can be especially difficult if the challenge of understanding is accompanied with the need to unlearn one's own law. On the other hand, this is precisely where the attraction of comparison lies. Paraphrasing the famous words of

---

[22] P Legrand, 'European Legal Systems Are Not Converging' (1996) 45 *ICLQ* 52.
[23] D Nelken, 'Comparing Legal Cultures' in A Sarat (ed), *The Blackwell Companion to Law and Society* (Malden MA, Blackwell Publishing, 2008) 113–27, 119.

JF Kennedy, lawyers often choose comparative studies 'not because they are easy, but because they are hard'. It is the very challenge of understanding foreign law that ignites the spirit of comparison and invites new generations to venture into the comparative study of law. There is no avoiding the fact that the comparative study of law holds a special kind of appeal for open-minded legal scholars.

3
Comparative Law – Definitions and Distinctions

COMPARISONS ARE MADE in several different branches of law and for many different purposes. Because of this versatility it is impossible to give a definition that would be universal and fit for every purpose. In spite of the versatility, a reasonably general definition can be given. It corresponds sufficiently well with the views of the majority of modern comparatists about what in fact comparative law is. However, such a presentation is inevitably a kind of an average or blueprint, which in a textbook meant for a large audience is unavoidably an all-encompassing approach.

The mainstream of comparative law means here roughly such legal comparison as was born in the early nineteenth century when a compilation of national codifications of civil law was started in Continental Europe. This was by no means the first time comparison took place, but in many ways academic modern comparative law as a discipline owes much to the legal thinking that was born in the nineteenth century as we saw in the previous chapter. Before then the systematic or scholarly aspect of comparative law had not generally been the aim. When academic legal study was transformed, comparative law also changed; we could say that scientification took place, or at least we can talk about the academisation process in which comparative law has distanced itself from a practice-oriented form of legal scholarship and the immediate needs (real or imagined) of the legal profession.

In spite of scientification the basic setting for comparison as a form of research seems relatively uncomplicated. Rudolf Schlesinger (1909–96), summed up comparative law in the mid-1990s as follows: 'To compare means to observe and to explain similarities as well as differences'.[1] In other words it is a question of the similarities and differences found as well as attempts to explain *why* there are differences and similarities in the first place. The basic setting itself is very simple indeed.

---

[1] RB Schlesinger, 'The Past and Future of Comparative Law' (1995) 43 *Am J Comp L* 477, 477.

I. CHALLENGE OF FURTHER DEFINITION

Before attempting to define comparative law in greater detail or to explain the basic elements of comparative research in general, the concepts involved ought to be clarified. In practice this means that a flexible specification has to be given concerning the point of view and topic of this book. What are we talking about and what precisely do we mean when we speak of comparative law? To begin with, it is useful to grasp the starting point which is legal diversity or as Haley puts it: 'Law has no generally accepted or agreed definition'.[2]

> The expressions 'comparative law' (German *Rechtsvergleichung*, French *droit comparé*) and 'comparative legal science' (German *Vergleichende Rechtswissenschaft*, French *science du droit comparé*) are in practice used as synonyms in scholarly literature. If any distinction is to be made, the practice has been that comparative legal science refers especially to comparative law in the academic context. In other words, in a more detailed analysis a difference can be made between practice-oriented and scholarly comparative law, and there has been discussion about this among comparatists. But, from the point of view of an advanced textbook in comparison there is no need to problematise this relative difference between the concepts. In the same way, the question about whether comparative law is 'a research branch' or only 'a method' is irrelevant – it is both of them. It is a question of the purpose of comparison which has the decisive role.

In spite of the above, in the twenty-first century a new division between the expressions 'comparative law' and 'comparative legal studies' was born. The first mentioned group has more proponents than the latter. It continues from the premises on which the abovementioned definition by Schlesinger is based. Researchers who emphasise the critical research approach, and who intentionally want to keep apart from comparative law that has a normative/doctrinal emphasis, in most cases use the latter expression. In this book the expression 'comparative law' is used to cover all legally oriented comparative study. The definition here is inclusive, not exclusive. And by and large, for those who actually compare laws the demarcation question is of a secondary nature. It is more important to use methods that go well with one's comparative study of law than to split hairs about the notion of comparative study of law. In conclusion, the notion of 'comparative law' today is to be conceived broadly.

A. Crossing the Borders

The difference compared to the normative research of the law (doctrinal study of law) is at least to some extent reasonably clear. Comparative law is always an attempt to cross borders that are due to lack of knowledge and in a wider

---

[2] JO Haley, *Law's Political Foundations* (Cheltenham, Edward Elgar, 2016) 2.

sense set by the borders between legal systems: it is a question of an attempt to imagine oneself in the position of a jurist (or a professional who is in charge of a corresponding function) working professionally in the context of foreign law. Albeit, a comparative approach can of course be utilised in doctrinal research or in judicial practice too.

In the comparative law literature this is described by saying that the comparatist should try to think in the same way as the lawyers in the compared system (internal view of law). The idea is plausible, although it is prudent to remember that it is also always largely a fictive idea whose function is to serve as a general methodological guideline for the comparatist. In other words, a Scandinavian lawyer will not turn into a Saudi-Arabian Muslim lawyer regardless of how much they put their soul into it – the same of course works the other way round. Epistemic limits are easier to pinpoint and to theorise over than they are to overcome. The problem is that much of our epistemic constraints are embedded into our legal minds and to become aware of these constraints requires extra effort.

> The lawyer's task demands plenty of knowledge and skills even within one system. An *Internal view* of law is not a thing that can or should be taken lightly. To get to know enough of foreign law in order to understand how it functions (as seen from the inside) is a formidable challenge. Usually we think that the (domestic) lawyer should be able to interpret law, ie they should be able to give a sensible and reasonable meaning to the expressions used in the sources of law when the law is applied. This means that the native lawyer should be aware of the relevant statutory law, case law, legal doctrine and the mutual relationship between different norms. On the other hand, it is obvious that the comparatist does not turn into a lawyer of the systems studied: theoretically she/he is still an outsider although – if comparison succeeds – *a well-informed outsider*. To be a comparatist is to be an outsider, yet, looking from the outside may have benefits too as insiders may be blind to things that are obvious for well-informed outsiders looking from the outside.
>
> There is, however, something that a comparatist should be able to do: according to Bell, the comparatist should be able to *reconstruct* such a picture of the foreign law so that someone who does not know the system could understand the reconstruction.[3] In this way the comparatist's work creates novel reconstructed knowledge of law; a kind of dialogue between the systems studied. This requires that the legal culture be translated so that lawyers in the system under study do not regard the picture given of their law by the comparatist as downright misleading or wrong. All the same, the picture reconstructed by the comparatist is different; a kind of alternative reality of foreign law. This is due to the fact that *the experience horizon of the comparatist* differs from that of the lawyer from within the system.

Above it was argued that definition is not a question of life and death for the comparatist. Be that as it may, perhaps we can say that the basic definition of comparative law has some significance. By means of the definition, comparative

---

[3] J Bell, 'Legal Research and the Distinctiveness of Comparative Law' in M Van Hoecke (ed), *Methodologies of Legal Research* (Oxford, Hart Publishing, 2011) 155, 176.

law stands out from the other legal disciplines and other research on law. Owing to its study subject – law – comparative law differs, for example, from the comparative study of politics or comparative education. However, it is not worthwhile exaggerating the kind of and extent of the differences. Comparative law is a part of social sciences and more extensively part of the study of humankind. To be more exact, comparative law is part of the entity that consists of legal disciplines: a part of the organised attempt to understand human law, a special normative phenomenon that is not limited to a certain State or cultural sphere. In this sense, the endeavour of studying law comparatively is essentially a cosmopolitan attempt. The cosmopolitanism of the comparatist is, by and large, epistemic and does not require the assumption of normative universalism.

In a systematic respect comparative law can be divided into at least two parts. On the one hand, there is the actual *comparative study of law* ('doing it') and, on the other hand, *the theory of comparative law* ('talking about it'). In the former, different legal systems or their parts are studied. In the latter, comparative law itself is under study. Typical for both of these fields is that foreign legal rules and norms and legal decisions or customs as well as their research theory can be studied on several different levels that are not mutually exclusive. Different overlapping approaches complement each other. To a great extent it is a question of the rough and principled division of the comparative law discipline, the use of which is mainly supported by pedagogical factors. Nevertheless, for the self-understanding of the comparatist it can be of benefit as self-identification helps the comparatist to focus research efforts effectively. To that end, it is beneficial to understand one's own scholarly identity as a comparatist.

II. COMPARATIVE STUDY OF LAW

It is possible on the general level to present a blueprint definition and say that comparative research of law aims at lining up different legal systems in order to generate information. Comparative law is aimed at the legal systems of different States (or State-like formations) or their segments that are significant for research problems. But what does the concept of 'legal system' really mean? Every native legal doctrine has its established answers that do not always satisfy the comparatist. The comparatists' dilemma here is clear: they cannot rely on internal definitions even though they must be aware of internal understandings in order to be able to reconstruct foreign law in their own research.

To simplify, *legal system* refers to the entity formed of legal norms, which in addition to statutory law and case law includes customary law, established legal practices, legal concepts and a specified way of handling and classifying legal concepts and norms (ie legal doctrine). In most cases it is a question of a normative system of legal rules that are in force in a State or a State-like formation. 'Legal system' is said to be an entity formed by law in force or valid law. If we use the term 'legal system', we normally mean the more extensive entity that covers the 'legal order' (German *Rechtsordnung*, French *ordre juridique*) and legal thinking as well as including legal-cultural dimensions. For the comparatist, a broad notion of legal system is unavoidable as the legal systems of different countries are not similar.

> It is worth noting that from the point of view of comparative law 'legal system' and 'legal order' cannot very successfully be kept apart. In this book the concept *legal order (Rechtsordnung)* is scarcely used because it is regarded as containing elements also from *legal system (Rechtssystem)*. In comparative law it is impossible to make a clear division between them because in most States these dimensions overlap.[4] Furthermore, there are several systems, for example in States with a Muslim majority that refer to Islamic law, where ingredients of religious norms also seep into the legal system: secular and religious legal norms are intertwined in ways where local religious leaders occupy some of the functions that in Western States are filled by professional lawyers. Amalgamated law and religion may produce surprising outcomes as, for example, Islamic constitutionalism in Iran.[5] In some places in Africa there are chieftains or elders councils which complement the methods used for solving conflicts within the formal national legal system but based on customary law (eg Ghana's Constitution Ch 22 'Institution of Chieftaincy'). These unofficial, but deeply rooted, customary normativities are just as interesting for comparatists who are interested in similarities and differences. It is said that beggars cannot be choosers; we could also say that comparatists cannot be narrow-minded.

A. Universalism?

The prevailing mindset and research ethics of comparison are rather well described by *epistemic universalism* and a conscious attempt to break loose from the limits in legal research set by nation-States. This feature has long been the research-ethical and legal-theoretical mobiliser of many comparatists. For example, Raymond Saleilles (1855–1912), organiser of the World Conference for Comparative Law in Paris in 1900 and a prominent figure of comparative law, saw comparative law as a tool with which it was possible to reveal the universal principles of law. Before him there was the German Anselm von Feuerbach (1775–1833), a legal scholar who thought that comparative law should lead to a kind of universal jurisprudence (German *Universaljurisprudenz*). Nowadays the aims are less ambitious and universalism concerns epistemology and methodology more than substance.

---

[4] In analytical legal theory, however, the attempt to define 'legal system' as a concept may make sense; see eg J Raz, *The Concept of Legal System* (London, Clarendon Press, 1970). But for the comparative law purposes of today these kinds of analytical approaches do not offer a fruitful starting point because they do not embrace the idea of cultural diversity and methodological pluralism.
[5] M Künkler and DS Law, 'Islamic Constitutionalism: Iran' in DS Law (ed), *Constitutionalism in Context* (Cambridge, Cambridge University Press, 2022) 449, 471–73.

And yet, a certain universalism belongs to modern comparative law too. Comparative law is international in nature because it consciously detaches itself from the limits set by the legal system of a nation-State. Comparative analogy dismisses borders from the point of view of information production. Research interests of national legal disciplines focus on their own legal order; therefore, their results remain bound to the nation-State. Importantly, private international law and public international law have normative system-bound aspects and characteristics that separate them from the scholarly comparative law research.[6] However, there are views according to which the fundamental reason for comparative law is in fact to gain a more profound understanding of one's *own* legal system: by studying foreign law it is possible to realise what is typical of one's own law. To put it another way, it can be a case of getting a learning experience of one's own law by means of comparison (as if looking at one's self from the outside).

> The idea of the comparative basic dimension crossing national borders in legal research is not particularly modern or related to globalisation only or to European integration. In fact in the middle of the nineteenth century Rudolph von Jhering (1818–92) complained about it: 'Science has turned provincial, its scientific borders are identical with its political borders: the situation is humiliating and unworthy of science!'[7] The citation in question is probably one of the most popular mantras, which European comparatists have cited with approval through the whole of the twentieth century, and its popularity shows no signs of fading in the twenty-first century. Von Jhering seems to have expressed the basic ethos of the comparative lawyer fittingly and concisely: there is an epistemic urge to cross borders or to gain non-country specific knowledge about law. Even though Jhering's message had a specific nineteenth century German context it still resonates today.

The research approach and academic positioning of comparative law place it among general legal studies. In German legal literature such legal studies are referred to as *Grundlagenfächer*, ie non-doctrinal basic research of law (*Grundlagenforschung*) whose core contents are *Rechtsgeschichte* (legal history), *Rechtstheorie* (legal theory) and *Rechtsvergleichung* (comparative law). These fields are partly committed to the same epistemic premises as the doctrinal study of law; they complete the picture conveyed by doctrinal study and enrich the methodology of legal study, without fully losing the internal legal perspective, unlike the sociology of law. Comparative law as a field of study is undoubtedly one of the *Grundlagenfächer*. However, there are differences too.

Comparative law aims at general legal knowledge that is not as State-specific in nature as in national legal research. Results of comparative law can be utilised

---

[6] J Husa, *Interdisciplinary Comparative Law* (Cheltenham, Edward Elgar Publishing, 2022) 175–213.
[7] 'Die Wissenschaft ist zur Landesjurisprudenz degradiert, die wissenschaftlichen Gränzen fallen in der Jurisprudenz mit den politischen zusammen. Eine demüthigende, unwürdige Form für eine Wissenschaft!', R von Jhering, *Geist des römischen Rechts auf den verschiedenen Stufen seiner Entwicklung*, vol 1 (Leipzig, Breitkopf und Härtel, 1866) 15.

as a part of normative argumentation but its own knowledge-interest is not normative as it is in the doctrinal study of law. It is a question of legal research that crosses national borders and attempts to explain and evaluate the reasons for the similarities and differences of various legal systems and cultures. In fact, the research results concerning national law are valid only within its own legal order. By means of comparison it is possible to understand what kind of legal means have been referred to in other societies in order to reach social aims that are often rather similar. On the other hand, occasionally the aims and measures are different – understanding why this is the case is also among the objectives of comparison. There is an underlying necessity to understand law contextually and its relation to organised human communities.

In the scholarly sense, one of the justifications for comparison has been the idea that, the more there are cases of comparison, the more reliable the conclusions. This eliminates hasty generalisations made on the basis of sporadic or exceptional cases. For these reasons comparative law has been called the school of truth (French *une école de vérité*). In this respect the study of German civil law, for example, would be the sensible choice in many different countries: the famous civil law codification *Bürgerliches Gesetzesbuch* (BGB) that came into force in Germany in 1900 has been the model for several States and it has been copied in many systems. In spite of this, national civil law codifications are not identical to the German ones, which is well exemplified by the Greek case.

> Just as in Germany, the civil codification in Greece (Greek *Αστικός Κώδικας*, 1946) reflects the legal culture and mentality of the country. Its central features are its abstract and systematic nature, reliance on written law and the number of concepts most of which clearly resemble the German legal thinking and to some extent the French one. The book of civil law is very much like the BGB – the autonomy of an individual, private property and freedom of contract are in many places the driving force behind the legal policy, but not in such an obvious and old-fashioned way as in the BGB. The sections or books (*Bücher*) of the BGB are: *Allgemeiner Teil* (general section), *Recht der Schuldverhältnisse* (law of obligations), *Sachenrecht* (law of property), *Familienrecht* (family law) and *Erbrecht* (law of inheritance). The basic structure is exactly the same as in the Greek civil law codification. In spite of this, *Αστικός Κώδικας* is not a slavish copy. It has been built on a variety of material: there are ingredients from Roman and even Byzantine law and German Pandects, a strong influence of the German BGB, something from French civil codification and elements of the Swiss civil law. A clear difference from the BGB is the fact that the Greek codification contains (in the form of written law) such general clauses that were acquired in Germany only through case law after 1900 when the BGB came into force. Reception of foreign law typically requires comparative law-informed tailoring.

B. Research Outcomes and their Use

Results obtained by means of comparison can be used for the formulation of theories, finding new judicial solutions or in legal policy and the drafting of legislation. It depends on the user of the results whether the role given to this information is normative, ornamental, critical or descriptive – when aims are practical, results are part of the normative process. With theoretical aims, a sufficient aim can be knowledge formation without normative aims connected to national or international law. Independent of the use of the results, comparative law is in all cases an extender of the knowledge base. The comparatist could be called the midwife of broad legal knowledge: they are neither the source nor creators of knowledge but persons who help new comparative knowledge to enter into the world and to expand our legal imagination. Importantly, comparative law expands legal minds as it abandons chauvinism and denounces legal-cultural imperialism.

Extending the knowledge base does not mean that comparison would produce, for instance, for the courts a binding norm that is applicable as such. This would be a too straightforward and simplistic picture of a complex matter. Comparison itself does not bring about results that are strictly normative in the same sense as in the doctrinal study of law. This is due to the fact that it is possible by means of comparative law to advance and qualitatively improve legal argumentation. In such a case, additional information is produced by means of comparison, eg whether by the means of legal decision-making a certain interpretation can be entered into when there is a so-called hard case (a decision can be reached only by interpreting laws in a creative manner) at hand. For example, in the European human rights and the Court of the European Union contexts, the comparative dimension often plays some sort of role.[8]

> The European Court of Human Rights often makes use of comparative law in its decision-making. For example, in the case of *Phinikaridou* (2007) the question was about the establishment of paternity and the strict regulation of time concerning the limitation period. The Court referred, as a legal source in its decision, to comparative law (paragraph 58):
>
> A comparative examination of the Contracting States' legislation on the institution of actions for judicial recognition of paternity reveals that there is no uniform approach in this field. Unlike, however, proceedings by fathers for the establishment or denial of paternity ... a significant number of States do not set a limitation period for children to bring an action aiming to have paternity established. Indeed, a tendency can be ascertained towards a greater protection of the right of the child to have its paternal affiliation established.[9]
>
> Several countries took a stand on the child's right to bring an action without a limitation period. In only a few countries has an attempt been made to solve problems caused by the fact that the child was informed of the matters relevant to the parenthood only after the time limit had expired. The comparative argument supported the child's right to know about his/her parent in spite of the limitation period set by the national law.

---

[8] See Husa (n 6) 189–96.
[9] *Phinikaridou v Cyprus* (App 23890/02), 20 December 2007.

C. Restrictions on Use

In spite of the extensive possibilities of using comparative law it has to be remembered that there are limitations concerning the comparative approach. They are caused by the fact that it is never possible to cross cultural borders totally and that law as a contextual phenomenon is so special and multidimensional a study subject that it cannot be totally understood and exhaustively explained – not even by internal lawyers within one system. On the other hand, arguments which represent extreme relativism and according to which understanding anything that is foreign is all but impossible are against the very ethos of comparative law. Everyday experience and common sense do not support such an extreme view: people can understand each other even if their legal-cultural backgrounds are quite different. Understanding has to do with knowledge, and here it does not mean the same as acceptance, which is an attitude. We can understand without accepting and accept without understanding – such is the epistemic constitution of *homo sapiens*.

The dissimilarity of legal-cultural backgrounds does not necessarily result in conflict; instead, different legal traditions can live side by side and even tolerate each other. The same idea of legal diversity fits comparative law very well. It is not a question of the dominance of one legal culture over others but of the perception and recognition of the plurality of legal cultures. Samuel Huntington's (1927–2008) famous theory about the clash of civilisations has never fitted the law: legal cultures learn from each other, and their mutual contacts change cultures. Huntington assumed that people's cultural and religious identities would be the primary source of conflicts after the Cold War.[10] In the legal world this kind of development has not taken place although in the world of politics it may hold some truth. In any case, it is beneficial for the comparatist to become aware of their own strong prejudices and implicit epistemic assumptions.

To recognise prejudice and assumptions is useful and necessary, but a certain sense of reality is also called for. Opportunities for comparative law are always limited to some extent. In particular, if the systems compared are legal-culturally far apart from each other, the capacity of the comparatist to genuinely understand foreign law is inevitably insufficient. This fact easily arises in a situation where the comparatist with a Western background studies religious law or the legal tradition of Indigenous peoples. This does not mean however that culturally unfamiliar law could not be included in comparison. Comparison is a process of meeting the challenge rather than capitulating because of epistemic and methodological difficulties. Mentally, the comparatist is more like *Bob the Builder* (animated character) than the *Great Philosopher*.

> Bob and his group do renovations and other projects. The children's programme underlines conflict resolution and cooperation. In each episode Bob asks, 'Can we fix it?'

---

[10] See S Huntington, 'The Clash of Civilizations?' (1993) 72 *Foreign Affairs* 22 ('The great divisions among humankind and the dominating source of conflict will be cultural').

Other characters always answer, 'Yes we can!' even though their task is very hard to accomplish. Now, the comparatist asks can they study foreign law and compare it, and the answer must be, 'Yes they can!' This mindset may appear as naïve and clearly it belittles difficulties involved in the comparative endeavour. However, this kind of attitude encourages performing comparisons rather than dwelling endlessly on transcendental philosophical problems (which may as such be both relevant and rewarding to a scholar) concerning the epistemology and methodology of comparative law. Much of comparative law is about the courage to step out of the epistemic boundaries of one's own legal system even when knowing the risks involved. Scholarly courage is needed if one seeks to step away from the familiar law and legal culture.

Hence, it is a question regarding the fact that the comparatist ought to *recognise the risk factors involved in the research frame* in order to minimise them. The difficulty of the research frame has an impact on the firmness of the conclusions it is sensible to draw on the basis of comparison. To make it simple we could say that the more demanding the research setting (cultural dimension, linguistic dimension etc), the more cautious the conclusions.

III. THE THEORY OF COMPARATIVE LAW

The theory of comparative law can be further divided into two main parts. Characteristically, in the theory of comparative law an attempt is made to formulate the various legal systems of the world (in a broad sense), classifications and systematisations (typologies, taxonomies) by means of which the typical features of different legal orders are made visible (see in detail chapters nine to eleven). The grouping of legal orders means that the fundamental and permanent ingredients of legal systems are summed up to get informative packages by means of which it is possible, for example, to reach educational goals in comparative law.

A. Macro-comparison

In the theory of comparative law, law groups, legal families, legal cultures and legal traditions are mentioned. Such classifications mainly refer to whole systems/normativities, and they represent macro-comparison whose theory is discussed in more detail later in this book. Typologies with a lower abstraction level are built in different sectors of law, for example in comparative constitutional study where as a result of comparison different typologies of models for controlling the constitutionality of laws can be presented. When constructing legal families, the comparatist tries to illustrate the nature of common legal-cultural phenomena and the reasons for their manifestations. This is how we classify legal orders into Roman-Germanic or common law systems or regard Nordic law as a kind of version of these two that is culturally in a legal sense closer to mainland Europe, ie the legal-cultural sphere of civil law rather than common law.

Roman-Germanic law refers to law that originated in Continental Europe and which is divided into Roman (French part) and Germanic (German part). In the English language literature on comparative law, they are often also called *civil law* countries or the civil law legal family because the legal culture has been greatly influenced by the interpretation of Roman civil law or *ius civile* (originally civil law of the Roman people, distinguished from *ius gentium*, ie the law observed by all nations including Romans) from the Middle Ages. This book uses both expressions side by side when referring to the originally Continental European legal tradition, which has since spread far and wide, in regard to its voluntary or involuntary adoption in the context of colonisation. There is a short epitomised discussion on them in chapter nine, section I, 'Basic Blocks of Macro-comparison' (common law, civil law, mixed law, traditional law).

If general and typical features of foreign legal systems are known, it is easier to understand the place of individual rules, principles and doctrines as part of the entirety of foreign legal systems. The legal significance of regulations or normative customs found is also easier to evaluate correctly. This fact is of importance from the point of view of comparative law as to whether it strives for instant practical aims or has theoretical ambitions. Typically, the most common similar features of different legal systems both facilitate the explanatory function of comparative law and contribute to the study of foreign law, its use in legislation and as part of judicial decision-making.

B. Theory and Methodology

In addition to forming legal families (or patching up other macro-constructions) the theory of comparative law deals with *the methodology of comparative law* and *the problems and solutions related to research* that come up when foreign legal systems are studied. There are, however, several difficulties and hindrances. The main obstacle is easy to pinpoint: there is no single method concerning the theory of comparative law because the method (or each approach) is selected on the basis of the study topic and what the researcher has decided to emphasise. This can be concreticised with an example: what works with the Nordic marital right to property does not necessarily work when looking into the marital right to property in North-African States.

> The methodological issues in comparative law are well described in the extensive *Oxford Handbook* (2019) and the comprehensive *Elgar Encyclopedia* (2012).[11]

---

[11] M Reimann and R Zimmermann (eds), *The Oxford Handbook of Comparative Law*, 2nd edn (Oxford, Oxford University Press, 2019); J Smits (ed), *Elgar Encyclopedia of Comparative Law*, 2nd edn (Cheltenham, Edward Elgar, 2012). *Elgar Encyclopedia* will appear in several volumes and in an extensively expanded format in 2023–2024, J Smits, J Husa, C Valcke, M Narciso (eds).

30 Comparative Law – Definitions and Distinctions

The Cambridge Companion (2012) comes close to the *Elgar Encyclopedia* and *Oxford Handbook*, but it is less voluminous. In a theoretical sense it seems to be also more critical than the Elgar and Oxford books, which assume a more mainstream approach to the discipline.[12] A new *Cambridge Handbook of Comparative Law* will be published in 2023.

In addition to these, a methodological general picture is given in *Methodologies of Legal Research* (2011).[13] *Methods of Comparative Law* (2012) and *Methodology of Comparative Law* (2017) are also useful works for theoretical and methodological issues.[14] Also, the need to bridge the gap between theory and practice in comparative law is today understood better than in the past. The book *Practice and Theory* (2012) offers a collection of texts reflecting on the methodological challenges arising in practical comparative research. *Practice and Theory* also provides useful critical and theoretical reflections over practical methodological challenges.[15] *The Method and Culture* (2014) is a also useful collection in regard to comparative law's epistemology and methodology.[16] *Comparing Law* (2018) offers a systematic account of comparative law as an autonomous academic discipline.[17] *Rethinking Comparative Law* (2021) expands theoretical key issues on theory and methodology of comparative law.[18]

Comparative law methodology attempts to present solutions for the problems that most typically occur within comparative law research. Part of the problem setting and characteristic features apply to all lines of comparative research, while some are more topic-specific. Comparative law has been, and still continues to be, strongly influenced by legal theory, legal history, legal sociology, legal anthropology and legal linguistics. Yet, in practice the legal discipline that is closest to comparative law is the history of law and especially its new research approach that is referred to as the comparative or global history of law, which is practically indistinguishable from comparative law.

The legal historian who studies past law may need comparison in order to understand which rules of law are typical or atypical in the period under study. In the research of the history of the past it is important to understand the need to have a wider perspective, as pointed out by Gordley.[19] Comparatists are severely

---

[12] See M Bussani and U Mattei (eds), *The Cambridge Companion to Comparative Law* (Cambridge, Cambridge University Press, 2012).
[13] Van Hoecke (ed) (n 3).
[14] PG Monateri (ed), *Methods of Comparative Law* (Cheltenham, Edward Elgar, 2012); M Adams, J Husa and M Oderkerk (eds), *Methodology of Comparative Law* (Cheltenham, Edward Elgar, 2017).
[15] See M Adams and J Bomhoff (eds), *Practice and Theory in Comparative Law* (Cambridge, Cambridge University Press, 2012).
[16] M Adams and D Heirbaut (eds), *The Method and Culture of Comparative Law* (Oxford, Hart Publishing, 2014).
[17] C Valcke, *Comparing Law: Comparative Law as Reconstruction of Collective Commitments* (Cambridge, Cambridge University Press, 2018).
[18] S Glanert, A Mercescu and G Samuel, *Rethinking Comparative Law* (Cheltenham, Edward Elgar Publishing, 2021).
[19] J Gordley, 'Comparative Law and Legal History' in Reimann and Zimmermann (n 11) 754.

mistaken if they imagine that present-day legal systems are coherent and logical instead of being organic amalgams that have developed over time. Historians are being ignorant if they assume that the law of a certain period can be studied totally independently of how law has developed elsewhere. Law travels not only from one region to another but also from one period to another. Accordingly, different comparative approaches are firmly interlaced with each other as later in this book (see chapter four, section II and chapter seven, section V) will become obvious. The close connection between legal history and comparative law does not, however, mean that they should be merged.[20]

C. Special Features

In spite of the connections between comparative law and other legal disciplines, comparison can be distinguished from other branches of legal research. In comparative law, and comparative research in general, there are typical methodological problems that do not occur in research methods that are nationally/internally oriented. This fact has produced copious discussion and debate or as Samuel puts it, 'Comparative legal studies, if it has done nothing else, has provoked a number of fundamental questions about methodology'.[21]

When foreign law is studied from outside of the system, the knowledge-interest (why research is being done) differs from the national normatively oriented research. The comparatist is always in some ways *an epistemic outsider* in relation to the unfamiliar systems under study. In this respect the methodology of comparative study on the general level is also an individual specialised field, and this applies to comparative law where the aim is the disciplined comparison of different legal systems.

It is easy to notice that in the twenty-first century there has been very lively discussion on the methods and theoretical assumptions of comparative law. The earlier ideas prevalent in the twentieth century still exist, but they have been complemented by several alternative views of what comparison is all about and how it should be carried out. This development in the theory of comparative law has completely changed its earlier image of being a dust-covered field of study curled up under the arm of private international law: the scenery of methodologies has become more varied, and the attitude to new methods has become more tolerant. Public law comparisons are coming more commonplace. Interdisciplinarity is becoming an increasingly important topic within comparative law circles. The price of development has been the fact that the discipline has become harder to master. This book struggles to pay attention to the

---

[20] Husa (n 6) 25–39.
[21] G Samuel, 'Does One Need an Understanding of Methodology in Law Before One Can Understand Methodology in Comparative Law?' in Van Hoecke (n 3) 177, 178.

relevant recent discussion and the new emphases that spring from it. In a way, we could talk about *new comparative law* – continuing an age-old tradition but in an updated and theoretically renewed manner. To conclude, the key distinctive feature of modern comparative law is pluralism both in methods and in substance. As there are no unavoidable normative goals the comparatist remains open to the global diversity of law.

4

Comparative Law – One of the Legal Disciplines

I. PART OF A LARGER FIELD OF KNOWLEDGE

*L*EGAL SCIENCE (IN its various linguistic versions) or *law as discipline* is often used as an unproblematic general concept; as if there is just one monolithic entity whose object is equally monolithic law. In reality, of course, the attention that different legal research interests put on law is not identical. For instance, legal economics, normative research (doctrinal study of law) and legal linguistics irrevocably perceive law in different ways and from different angles. Yet, they may all be regarded as legal disciplines. Different sub-fields of legal study can be specified depending, for example, on which basic theoretical assumptions they base their work. Legal anthropology, for instance, is bound to be based on different assumptions than analytical legal theory.

We can talk about *the family of legal disciplines* where the oldest member, or core discipline if you prefer, is the doctrinal study of law. Despite a certain amount of overlap, the interests and functions of different branches of legal study differ from each other. The growth of the significance of constitutional and human rights has resulted in a situation where norms and principles in public law have in many ways started to break into/penetrate other fields of law. Interpretation that is favourable for human rights (so-called human-rights-friendly-interpretation) and their direct and indirect dimensions is now reflected in practically all fields of law. In the same way, the European Union's law is part of the Member States' own law and injects non-national elements into domestic systems. The World Trade Organization, in turn, has had a global impact on international trade law.

Comparative law is a distinctive member of the family of legal fields because knowledge-interests, which it tries to satisfy, and methods with which the answer is pursued, differ from the rest of the legal disciplines. This deviation is not a whim (of chance) but is due to a specific reason. It can be argued that comparative law research has a special knowledge base which separates it from the other fields of legal study. Comparison assumes, at least partly, different abilities related to knowledge acquisition than does normative legal research, which concentrates on national or international law. Also the approach of comparatists differs from the perspective of national law: they observe foreign law inevitably from the epistemic viewpoint of an outsider, while a jurist operating inside the system has a viewpoint, which inevitably is theoretically internal (though institutionally external, since it is not a question of a judge or legislator).

As has become clear from the above, in the *comparative study of law* different legal systems (or any organised normativities of large-scale human communities) or their sectors are studied in order to find differences and similarities. In the scholarly oriented research, attempts are made to explain the reasons for these differences and similarities, while in practically oriented research the aim is to draw practical conclusions for legislation, criticism of statutory law or judicial usage.

Approaches used in comparative law can be, for instance, doctrinal (comparison of regulative texts or precedents), socio-legal (including legal practice), legal-historical, legal-linguistic, legal-anthropological or legal-theoretical. If the aims of comparison are practical, the doctrinal approach normally takes a central position, while legal-theoretical aspects rise more strongly to the surface when aims are academically ambitious. As part of the family of legal disciplines, comparative law is in any case suitable for promoting the view according to which modern legal study is a scholarly field, which is *methodologically open* and consists of *various approaches*. Comparative law is among the interpretative (or hermeneutical) sciences and is based on the comprehension of the sources and argumentation although depending on the research topic it can also make use of other materials and methods. Even though the fundamental nature of comparative law is hermeneutical, it does not mean, however, that numerical or quantitative approaches cannot be utilised. Modern understanding of comparative law embraces the idea of a toolbox of methods rather than the one-size-fits-all method. If the research question requires a quantitative approach, then there are no obstacles even though the comparative research process is generally characterised as hermeneutical.

II. A MEMBER OF THE FAMILY OF LEGAL STUDIES

A. Comparative Law and the Normative Approach

Legal doctrine is often called legal dogmatics in Continental Europe (German *Rechtsdogmatik*, French *la doctrine/doctrine juridique*, Greek νομική δογματική, Finnish *oikeusdogmatiikka*), ie the historically oldest branch of legal study attempts to answer the question concerning the normative content and validity of law. It specifies how law must be interpreted by creating concepts and clarity between rules on the sources of law. Doctrine cannot be drawn only from legislation or case law but also from treatises, monographs, articles in law journals, case comments and reviews. Doctrinal knowledge of law consists of rules, principles and concepts and the legal way of reasoning.[1]

---

[1] R Cotterrell, *Sociological Jurisprudence* (Abingdon, Routledge, 2018) 20–24.

Doctrinal study of law is the basic research of normative law that is practised in particular in Continental Europe and in the systems which have been heavily influenced by Continental Europe. For example, Nordic or Latin American countries belong to the legal culture of legal dogmatics in its wide sense, while in common law jurisdictions a similar study approach as a direct counterpart does not exist. Albeit a common law jurist would surely recognise the doctrinal legal study (legal doctrine) of the universities, although an exact counterpart to Continental European legal dogmatics is lacking in their own legal culture. This is why we normally speak of the doctrinal study of law as it works better in terms of translation in many legal cultures than 'legal dogmatics'.

In legal doctrine in most cases it is a question of the study of legal rules (interpretation of legal texts). When legal texts are interpreted, legal doctrine attempts simultaneously to analyse the research object by systematising it. Legal interpretation means that the expression of a provision or some other legal text, such as a precedent, is given a justified conceptual meaning on the basis of sources of law. Systematisation means that the norms under study are organised into a system that would be as coherent as possible. Systematisation and interpretation are closely intertwined because the interpretation of the content of legal sources is also inevitably systematisation: systematisation links legal rules and principles to a specific context of the interpretation. This is, however, not something exclusive to Western legal scholarship. Islamic legal study resembles Western normative legal study, and the doctrinal study of law in particular, which is systematising and interpreting (the authoritative text) as to its theoretical basic nature. Similar features can be found in Jewish *halakha* or Christian canon law.

The doctrinal study of law – unlike comparative law – is normative: it attempts to find an answer to the question about how law *ought* to be interpreted. Yet it is difficult to define legal doctrine methodologically and briefly. In general, it can be said that in legal doctrine interpretative methods (hermeneutical text interpretation) are used on the basis of information available from legal sources when studying the law (formally in force) in a particular community. The majority of European legal research concerns mainly legal doctrine that serves practical goals, although theoretical legal doctrine also exists. The purpose of theoretical legal doctrine is to create systematisations that facilitate the maintenance of the legal system, ie reorganising legal material according to the doctrine of sources of law. The point of view of both theoretical and practical doctrinal study of law is epistemologically *internal*: in a way it is a question of the participant's point of view as once defined by HLA Hart (1907–92) in his famous *Concept of Law*, which in Continental Europe is frequently characterised by a strong commitment to the institutionally and epistemologically internal point of view of the authority applying the law.[2] An internal point of

---

[2] HLA Hart, *The Concept of Law* (Oxford, Oxford University Press, 1961) 89. Basically Hart argued that we cannot truly understand the workings of a legal system from the external point of view. According to Hart understanding of normative meanings requires an internal aspect.

view refers to the perspective of the participant in the system, ie it is paradigmatically the point of view of legal officials like judges. Interestingly, in private international law the institutional commitments are the same as in the doctrinal study of law – internal. The internal point of view basically specifies what kind of motivation (and assumptions) a lawyer implicitly brings to the law.

At first sight it can be difficult to see elemental connections between the national legal doctrine and non-nationally oriented comparative law. The first impression is, however, misleading. One should not overestimate the differences. Practically oriented comparative law can be closely connected not only to private international law but also to the national doctrinal study of law in at least two ways:

1. When there are *problematic situations* in legal decision-making it is possible from among the legal/judicial decisions to look for a clue to how to fill the gaps in the legal system or how to interpret provisions in so-called *hard cases*. Clearly, in obvious routine cases comparative law is only rarely of any use. However, when a decision in an application problem cannot be found from within one's own system, it might prove necessary to 'look over the fence': there is no need to reinvent the wheel each time, not even the legal one.

2. *The systematisation* (of the legal system) of the national doctrinal study of law becomes easier when approaches to the same type of problem applied abroad are studied. It is not a question of direct copying, but of taking something as a model or source of inspiration. Foreign ideas are not necessarily adopted directly from law in force; instead, they are filtered through legal literature and the general doctrines of the national law. Torstein Eckhoff (1916–93) wrote on this by referring to Norwegian law: 'References like this can operate partly as illustrative material and partly as arguments about how questions should be solved by us'.[3]

However, the doctrinal study of law and comparison are not easy to tell apart. The relation between comparative law and legal doctrine can also be decorative in nature. In such cases sections concerning the law of other countries are included in the national legal-doctrinal study; in them the state of positive law in other countries is described. It is crucial to conceive that study originating in the interests of the national legal system mainly describes the points of view of different legal systems concerning the issue under study (*Auslandsrechtskunde*).

From the actual study of foreign law it is also possible to distinguish the kind of modern legal doctrine where foreign legal literature is referred to when

---

[3] 'Slike henvisninger kan deles tjene som illustrasjonsmateriele og dels som argumenter for at spørsmålene bør løses likedan hos oss', T Eckhoff, *Retskildelære*, 5th edn (Oslo, Universitetsforlaget, 2010) 284.

opinions concerning domestic law are presented. In such cases the question is not one of genuine comparative law although there the borderline of practical comparative law is quite fuzzy. On the other hand, comparison that does not serve legal research at all but remains unconnected decoration is futile and meaningless.

> In spite of what is said above, in some countries it has been customary to use comparative law as a hireling of the doctrinal study of law in a way that, from the viewpoint of comparative law, research cannot be regarded as being especially rational. For example, in Denmark the starting point has long been that there has to be a short compulsory comparative survey in a doctoral dissertation on law. Ole Lando (1922–2019) described this attitude as follows: 'A dissertation whose primary aim is something else should have a chapter on foreign law if it seems that information that could benefit the dissertation would be available abroad'.[4] In modern comparative law this idea has been all but abandoned as today it is recognised that there are differences between law as a field of knowledge and law as a field of professional practice.

Clearly, such 'ornamental' or 'decorative' comparative law has only very little to do with genuine comparative law, although descriptions of statutes, principles or institutions that are related to the research topic and are part of the legal systems of foreign countries can have some significance in expanding the knowledge base. Differences compared to comparative study are clear: the starting point for comparative law is that foreign law has to be studied in its context, or that it pays attention to the status of the norms studied in the entire legal system, the attitudes connected to their interpretation and application as well as legal-cultural factors. If comparison is applied to 'spice up' the study of the law in force in one's own country with decorations from foreign law, the whole setting has something that is intellectually untenable: scholarly boasting with ingredients from foreign law does not serve any sensible aim; it is just a ritual relic of the legal thinking from the beginning of the twentieth century. In short, study of foreign law needs to serve a meaningful purpose whether it be academic or practical.

Now, some may wonder if it is worth talking about the difference between the doctrinal study of law and comparative law. The descriptions given of the law of the same country by a comparatist and someone who is legally trained in national law are not identical. This does not, however, mean that one would be 'wrong' and the other 'right'. Descriptions are simply different. They have been made for different purposes. This inevitably causes a certain problem for the comparatist who presents the matter in a slightly different way and with a different emphasis from the national jurist. The comparatist has to understand

---

[4] 'I en afhandling med andet primært sigte bør man kun have et afsnit om fremmed ret, hvis man har set, at der i udlandet kan hentes viden, der befrugter Afhandlingen', O Lando, 'Komparativ ret i juridiske afhandlingar' in *Juridisk forskning* (Copenhagen, Jurist- og Økonomforbundets Forlag, 2002) 83, 83.

that their description and analysis of law is – as far as the foreign law goes – inevitably the description of an outsider. Here is the thing: the comparatist *imitates* or *simulates the internal point of view of the jurist* who operates within the system. Generally it is a question of acquiring a simulated internal point of view, ie methodological construction.

> Adams describes the idea of a simulated internal point of view fittingly: 'The researcher has to understand clearly that they have to reveal the logic of another legal system in a way that it is understood by the participants'.[5] In other words, the context must also be taken into account. Without a context, the study of foreign law may turn into a meaningless exercise considering only black-letter law.

On the other hand, comparative law and the doctrinal study of law share several common features, the most important of which are the hermeneutic perspective on law, reliance on legal sources and the interpretative nature of study. In addition, both are committed to the institutional structures, concepts, and doctrines of the systems under study. This is why the comparatist must also *partially* adapt an internal view on law even though foreign law is seen from the epistemic viewpoint of an outsider.

B. Comparative Law and the Roots of Law

Instead of the law in force, legal history studies the past history of law, legal principles and legal thinking by placing its object of study in a more extensive context of a certain era. In legal history the aim is often to explain how the change taken by law is due to more profound social reasons instead of presenting a chronology of laws. From the point of view of a comparatist, legal-historical knowledge is usually of quintessential significance since in scholarly comparative law in particular it is difficult to explain observations made without knowledge of legal history. For instance, it is also difficult to see how European legal integration could take place at the legal-cultural level without knowledge of European legal culture(s) and the *ius commune* tradition. Profound comparative law that aims to explain matters inevitably assumes past knowledge of the legal systems studied. Altogether, we are not talking about a curiosity or outdated legal information that the comparatist obsessively churns out to be buried in the mass grave of footnotes accompanying their study.

Yet, legal history is also a legal discipline, for it studies legal matters such as legal rules and legal principles. It is interested in legal institutions, legal practices and the legal thinking of the past. In this respect legal history is part of the entity formed by legal disciplines, and practising it assumes an understanding

---

[5] 'De onderzoeker moet goed beseffen dat hij de logica van de andere rechtsorde, zoals die door de participanten daaraan zelf begrepen wordt, moet blootleggen', M Adams, 'Wat de rechtsvergelijking vermag' (2011) 60 *Ars Aequi* 192, 197.

of the internal point of view that law possesses although the research in itself takes place epistemically outside of the legal system (external viewpoint, ie non-doctrinal). On the other hand, methods and other scholarly ideas originate in historical disciplines and partly in social sciences. It is in fact impossible to separate comparative law from the comparative legal history that could perhaps also be called global or stateless legal history.[6]

Often comparative law is seen only to be bound with modern times and existing legal systems. This view is mistaken. Comparative law, unlike the doctrinal study of law, is not tightly bound to law in force and, thus, to an internal contemporary viewpoint. In comparative law research it is also possible to study law that is no longer in force. Comparative law can be legal-historical in the most modest sense when it concentrates on the study of differences and similarities between legal systems which have existed in some period of time in the past. Legal research that emphasises a comparative approach and is concerned with the past (or the relation of the past with the present) can be considered historical comparative law or just plain comparative law. It is difficult to draw a clear line of demarcation between academically ambitious comparative law and non-nationally oriented legal history.

'Match made in heaven' is the expression that has been used to describe the relation between legal history and comparative law. However, the relation between legal history and comparative law is surprisingly complicated and contains various subtle nuances and overlapping elements. Legal-historical comparison has deep European roots. The indisputable classic in the field, *On the Laws of War and Peace* (*De jure belli et pacis*, 1625), the work of Hugo Grotius (1583–1645), who is called the father of modern international law, is worth mentioning. In this classic, legal solutions that were in accordance with natural law were sought. Of more recent scholars Alan Watson (1933–2018) in particular emphasised the close relation between legal history and comparative law.[7] Watson thought that the study of legal transplants and interaction of historical connections between legal systems and legal rules (especially Roman law) is in fact what comparative law ought to be all about.

In legal-historical research, the research object can be studied with a comparative approach without the comparative method being particularly explicitly in the foreground. For example, in the study by Antero Jyränki (1933–2020), variations of models for legal ideas from the beginning of the eighteenth century to the twentieth century were studied. They were related to the 'stateless' validity of constitutional law and were adopted in various States. The comparative approach of the work by Jyränki is seen in the fact that similarities and differences of solutions (controlling of constitutionality) adopted in different systems

---

[6] T Duve, 'What is Global Legal History?' (2020) 8 *Comp L History* 73.
[7] See A Watson, *Legal Transplants: An Approach to Comparative Law*, 2nd edn (Athens GA, University Georgia Press, 1993).

are discussed and the reasons for these differences are also explained by means of the history of ideas and political history.[8]

The cumbersome nature of the legal-historical research method(s) is connected to its demanding nature, since mastering the history of any one legal system is very difficult. When the number of legal systems increases, the problems of mastering them increase accordingly. They do not, however, make legal-historical comparison impossible. Certainly, the research frame is demanding, but frequently it is also fruitful and insightful.

> The legal-historical researcher must in all cases engage in some sort of comparative law because their own conceptual context is bound to the contemporary period. Aware or unaware, the historian makes comparisons between the present period and the period they are studying. The close connection between comparative law and legal history is clearly seen in the fact that almost all researchers who are regarded as pioneers in modern comparative law were in contact with the nineteenth-century German Historical School of Law (German *Historische Rechtsschule*), which was represented by great scholars like Friedrich Carl von Savigny (1779–1861) who underlined the historical study of positive law. Savigny was not only influential as a legal historian but also for comparative law as a discipline as is explained in *The American Journal of Comparative Law* (1989).[9] Against this background, it certainly comes as no surprise that as a branch of research and study, modern comparative law is closer to comparative legal history than it is to (normative and internal) private international law or legal doctrine.

From the point of view of legal disciplines it can be stated that almost everyone who is seriously engaged in comparative law acknowledges explicitly the historical dimension of law and its significance in the attempt to understand and explain law. In comparative legal history, under study are factors that have influenced the history of legal systems and by means of which it is possible to explain why legal systems are the way they are now. The emphasis is on the macro-level of comparative law because comparative legal history attempts to understand the interdependency between legal systems and cultures.

In practice the comparative legal historian often analyses how and why legal ideas spread from the legal systems of some regions to other States and other continents. The transformation (or diffusion, migration) of ideas as part of the diffusion process can also be the subject of study. Comparative legal history has in the past few years become increasingly popular among both legal historians and comparatists.

A good example of the vitality of the field is the journal Comparative Legal History, which was started at the beginning of 2013 and is published by Hart Publishing. It is also the official journal of the European Society for Comparative Legal History. In practice, comparative legal history has become popular and

---

[8] See A Jyränki, *Lakien laki* (Helsinki, Lakimiesliiton kustannus, 1989).
[9] (1989) 37 *American J Comp L* 1.

there have been calls from that camp to merge legal history and comparative law.[10] Yet, to actually combine legal history and comparative law is not a walk in the park.[11]

C. Comparative Law and Sociological Dimensions of Law

The sociology of law studies the effect of legal rules on the behaviour of people and the connection between law and social reality. The sociology of law is part of the study of society (ie social science), but the object of its interest means that it is also part of the legal disciplines. It is for the field of the sociology of law (or even more broadly socio-legal studies) to find out how legal rules are observed and how the working of the society is affected by legal norms, principles or institutions. When the sociology of law is practised as part of the entity formed by legal disciplines, we are talking about a multi-disciplinary field of study, ie socio-legal studies. As a multi-disciplinary field it can be placed somewhere between the doctrinal study of law and social sciences. As Siems points out 'socio-legal comparative law not only considers the positive law but also other data related to society'.[12]

Basically, the sociology of law perceives law in the social context. At its best it reveals the interdependency and reciprocity between the law, economy, politics and culture. As part of legal disciplines it widens the legal horizon when observing law not only as an autonomous normative order but also as a social factor that covers legal doctrines, legal practices and legal institutions (external view).

The relation of comparative law to the *sociology of law* ought to be quite close, and it can be said that these two branches of legal research ought to share certain common ideas of law and its study. Among the many approaches of the sociology of law there is the view that human behaviour is influenced not only by legal rules but also by many other factors, while in legal study in general – and in the legal-doctrinal study of law in particular – there is a tendency in the civil law legal family to underline the importance of legislated rules and in the common law tradition the precedents established in higher courts. Simply, comparative law cannot be committed to an approach that puts too much emphasis on written rules: customs and practices are sometimes more important than codified legal rules or leading cases. In Indigenous and religious legal cultures normativities may be distinct from official law but they are still regarded as genuine normativities by those who belong to those cultures. Consequently, modern legal comparison as a field of research cannot help but resemble the sociology of law or, in a more general sense, socio-legal studies: the internal normative viewpoint of legal doctrine is lacking.

---

[10] H Pihlajamäki, 'Merging Comparative Law and Legal History' (2018) 66 *Am J Comp L* 733.
[11] J Husa, 'Seeking a Disciplinary Identity' (2020) 8 *Comp L Hist* 173.
[12] M Siems, *Comparative Law* (Cambridge, Cambridge University Press, 2014) 144.

However, comparative law does not identify with the sociology of law as only the former tries to find a type of synthesis between the reality (external) and normativity (internal) of law. In practice, comparative law settles for finding comprehensible hermeneutical explanations and reasons for why law is what it is in the systems compared. Most comparatists are, despite their sympathy, amateurs as sociologists of law. This does not, however, prevent them using socio-legal materials, quantitative approaches and explanations when the comparatist tries to explain differences and similarities. Besides, differences between disciplines have in the twenty-first century been diminishing since comparatists have in the past few years started to discover empirical materials and their (at least partial) statistical use. Partly, but not completely, this has been connected to the theory of *legal origins* (more about which later).

> Owing to the empirical or legal realistic views on legal sources, it is not easy in the sociology of law or comparative law to fall into an attitude (positivism) that emphasises statutory law and formal sources of law at the expense of legal reality. For example, in the field of constitutional law this is demonstrated by the effect that the factual political constitution has on the interpretation of the legal constitution and on the position of established constitutional practice as the de facto source of law. As an example of the other extremity we could mention, for example, a study of customary law practised by Indigenous people where there are not necessarily any written sources of law, and therefore the only study method left is an empirical (anthropological or ethnological) field study that is based on observation and can include interviews or participant observation. In other words, it would not only be ethnocentric but also positivistic to define law in a narrow manner that excludes customs and other forms of organised normativities of large-scale human communities.

Both in the sociology of law and comparative law the aim is to explain observations made – the sociology of law tries to offer generalising answers concerning the relation between the society and law, while an ambitious comparatist tries to find hermeneutical/historical reasons for the differences and similarities found between legal systems. Both can also operate to extend the knowledge base in the drafting of legislation or judging cases in courts. One informs of normative regulation models and the other of the empirical reality of *living law*.

> The idea of living law (German *lebenden Recht*) was originally formulated by Eugen Ehrlich (1862–1922) and he referred it to normative law (as a social fact) which dominated social life even though it has not been posited in written legal propositions. Ehrlich formulated his ideas on living law as a critique of the formal and conceptual German legal doctrine of *Begriffsjurisprudenz*.[13] For comparative law, Ehrlich's ideas were and are important because he emphasised the role of societal norms which comparatists cannot leave aside. This importance comes from the fact that Ehrlich was not a legal-anthropologist or a comparatist (studying culturally different law) but was talking specifically about Western law.

---

[13] See E Ehrlich, *Grundlegung der Soziologie des Rechts* (Munich, Duncker, 1913).

For Ehrlich the study of normative social facts was a genuine legal science, not the study of empty concepts. An independent legal science would not study words but rather facts, and this science would not serve a practical purpose but pure knowledge.[14] Even though the legal-cultural context of today is very different from the times of Ehrlich his ideas still remind comparatists of the importance of looking beyond positive law.

In principle, legal sociology ought to be capable of shedding light on questions that are connected to the efficiency or functionality of a legal rule. By means of comparative law, alternative or completely new approaches can be found for legislation or legislative amendments. In the widest possible meaning both try to explain how legal order affects human behaviour and what position the legal system (or other types of organised normativity) has in the social order. On the other hand, sociology often aims at generalised explanations (nomothetic research) while in comparative law and legal history the explanations in most cases concern individual cases (idiographic research), and comparison has not generally aimed at extensive theory formation with the exception of the theory of legal origins.

Statistical Comparative Law has been slowly in the making for the whole of the twenty-first century. Some comparatists have felt confident in saying that no statistical methods from economics should be accepted while those who think more sensibly see the situation like Michaels: 'The newly reemerged interest of economists in law is something we comparative lawyers should cherish and support, not dismiss'.[15] On the other hand, the problem in the use of these materials is making them commensurable because in different countries information is collected and recorded in different ways and on different grounds. In spite of this the comparatist should be reasonably sure of the commensurability and compatibility of the quantitative materials. In this, comparatists may learn from sociologists and those who are accustomed to using quantitative methods. Yet, there seems to be no convincing arguments against usage of numerical/quantified data in the comparative study of law. Accordingly, we can safely agree with Siems when he concludes that 'numerical comparative law can contribute to many core topics of comparative law, such as judicial comparative law, legal transplants, legal families, and comparisons as a basis for making policy recommendations'.[16]

It is crucial to underline that the comparatist is not interested only in normative rules or principles (written or unwritten). They have to observe the nature of the law as a specific cultural tradition. Socio-legal study and the study of comparative law do not identify with each other, but socio-legal elements are included in comparative law as an equally natural element alongside

---

[14] Original quotations from the very beginning of the book underline studying 'nicht Worten handelt, sondern Tatsachen' and serving the pure knowledge: 'nicht praktischen Zwecken dienen will, sondern reiner Erkenntnis', ibid 1.
[15] R Michaels, 'Comparative Law by Numbers?' (2009) 57 *Am J Comp L* 765, 792.
[16] Siems (n 12) 186.

normative material. From the point of view of comparative law, the empirical reality and normativity of law are intertwined; the significance of positive law only opens up in legal reality. This also has serious consequences for the self-understanding of comparative lawyers. Namely, comparatists are only very rarely legal formalists (positivists) who emphasise the form of law – those who are formalist are not held in high esteem in the field.

Particularly close to comparative law is the *comparative sociology of law*. There the aim is to make comparisons between societies in order to be able to understand the differences and similarities in socio-legal phenomena in the societies compared. The comparative sociology of law has as its basis similar ideas to those of comparative law because it too is interested in intercultural dialogue, innovations and legal loans, ie the diffusion of law and legal ideas. The aim is to produce knowledge on how legal systems of different States or other organised societies really operate and to explain what causes the differences and similarities. *De l'esprit des lois* (1748), the classic study of Montesquieu, was ahead of its time and is the pioneering work of both the comparative sociology of law and comparative law.

The definition of comparative study by Nelken points out how close comparative law and the comparative sociology of law are to one another: 'All comparative research involves the search for social, cultural and other similarities and differences'.[17]

> Among the most central topics in research and theoretical discussion in the sphere of the comparative sociology of law in the twenty-first century have been the definition of legal culture and how it should be studied. An introduction to the thematics is offered by the work *Adapting Legal Cultures*, which also presents how the comparative sociology of law, comparative law and comparative legal history are very closely connected with each other.[18]

> Publications by Friedman have played a major role in the development of the field; they are closely connected with his sociological criticism of comparative law. The main target of his criticism was the methodology of traditional comparative law. According to Friedman, it did not have a logical method, but instead two rough ways of approach: comparative doctrinal/normative interpretative analysis and system level taxonomy, or macro-comparison.[19] As a result of this criticism, among other concurring critical views, the concept of legal culture has subsequently risen to the centre of both the sociology of law and comparative law.

> Lately, a new amalgam of socio-legal (ie law and society) studies and comparative law has emerged: *comparative law and society*. This field is but another addition

---

[17] D Nelken, 'Comparative Sociology of Law' in R Banakar and M Travers, *Law and Social Theory*, 2nd edn (London, Bloomsbury, 2014) 344.
[18] See D Nelken and J Feest (eds), *Adapting Legal Cultures* (Oxford, Hart Publishing, 2001).
[19] For a concise view of Friedman and comparative law, see eg T Ginsburg, 'Lawrence M. Friedman's Comparative Law' in RW Gordon and MJ Horwitz (eds), *Law, Society and History: Themes in the Legal Sociology and Legal History of Lawrence M. Friedman* (Cambridge, Cambridge University Press, 2011) 52.

to the common fields of comparative law and the sociology of law. It is defined by Clark as 'the common and overlapping area of two -constituent disciplines: comparative law and society'.[20] Moreover, in this new field researchers grasp the legal system as comprising more than merely the formal legal rules. Clark continues to say that 'a system involves regular interactions among elements that together make up an entity with boundaries'. Basically, comparative law and society marries the societal and legal elements under a comparative framework so that more than just one system is studied simultaneously. As a result, some form of interdisciplinarity is virtually impossible to avoid.

Traditionally, it has been typical to separate normative legal research from the non-normative study of law on the basis of epistemological differences. Earlier it was typical to keep the internal and external approaches to law clearly apart. In this division, the sociology of law or socio-legal studies has been placed (epistemologically, institutionally and methodologically) in connection with the point of view of an outsider and comparative law in between the internal and external ground. In the discussion of the field in recent years it has become clearer than ever that the basic legal-theoretical distinction between internal and external had been too rough. Riles sums up the scholarly landscape as follows: 'Comparative lawyers and socio-legal scholars increasingly understand that they are both insiders and outsiders, both participants and critics, at once'.[21] Without a shadow of a doubt, Riles hits the nail right on the head: comparatists are *both* outsiders and insiders. This fact places the comparatist and legal historian epistemically in a rather similar type of position: external and internal dimensions are inherently part of the comparative endeavour that takes place in an epistemic no-man's land.

In fact, the rise of legal culture to become the epicentre of research in both comparative law and the sociology of law has done the trick and broken the earlier way of perceiving the relation of these disciplines to legal doctrine. Differences between disciplines seem less important now since we have again recognised and admitted the significance of the legal context also for the normative study of law and especially for the comparative study of law. However, taking the socio-legal or law-in-context dimension into account does not miraculously transform the comparatist sociologist, but it does require taking into account 'the embeddedness of the legal problems as they present themselves in the different countries studied' as Bell says.[22] What is more, marrying social science and comparative law in an interdisciplinary manner is a tall order indeed.[23]

---

[20] DS Clark, 'Preface' in DS Clark (ed), *Comparative Law and Society* (Cheltenham, Edward Elgar, 2012) xiv–xvi, xiv.
[21] A Riles, 'Comparative Law and Socio-Legal Studies' in M Reimann and R Zimmermann (eds), *The Oxford Handbook of Comparative Law*, 2nd edn (Oxford, Oxford University Press, 2019) 773, 795.
[22] J Bell, 'Legal Research and Comparative Law' in M Van Hoecke (ed), *Methodologies of Legal Research* (Oxford, Hart Publishing, 2011) 155, 170.
[23] J Husa, *Interdisciplinary Comparative Law* (Cheltenham, Edward Elgar Publishing, 2022) 170–71.

D. Theoretical and Philosophical Dimensions of Comparative Law

The legal theory or jurisprudence (German *Allgemeine Rechtslehre*) is connected to the theoretical study of legal rules, principles and institutions as well as legal phenomena in general. The theoretical study of law and legal phenomena is characteristic of legal theory. At first sight, legal theory and comparative law appear quite close and further away from normative legal doctrine. They observe the language of law and legal concepts from an angle that is not tied to any particular system.

> Sartor describes the freedom of comparative law and theory of law from any system by saying that because of this they have to distinguish the characterisation of a concept and the assumption that the concept applies to a certain domain.[24] The doctrinal study of law need not (in fact must not) keep apart the characterisation of a concept and the assumption of its belonging to a certain domain. From this point of view legal theory is dependent on comparison because philosophical analysis does not solve the problems related to legal concepts. von der Pfordten makes a fitting conclusion: 'full understanding of the status of concepts in law would have to inquire into how the formation and interpretation of legal concepts work in different legal systems and different parts of the law'.[25] For a comparatist this looks like a longer way of saying that a comparative approach is needed.

So, legal theory is in many ways connected to comparative law. If the theory of law and its birth or nature is examined, it is possible by means of the knowledge gained by comparative law to prove that there is no one 'correct' concept of law: common law, civil law, the laws of Indigenous peoples and various religious legal systems perceive even the basic matters in different ways. Similarly, when legal practices are studied, it is epistemologically emancipatory to break away from ethnocentrism as described earlier in this book. In particular, in cases when the legal order is intimately connected with religion, the knowledge horizon must be widened a long way from Western positive law towards contexts of law. Part of the epistemic challenge is to minimise the effects of Eurocentrism and the previous colonial mindset.

Therefore, one should be aware that colonial research attitudes are not implicitly upheld. What modern comparative law does not need is epistemological neo-colonialism, which can be seen in the field of *law and development*. It becomes elemental to grasp that as comparatists we are not dealing with curiosities when we study the legal systems of African tribal law, Northern Aboriginal peoples, Asian legal culture(s) of the Confucian type or Islamic law. From the point of view of legal theory, such studies help us to see the theoretical basic assumptions of our own law as well as what law is and what its nature is in

---

[24] G Sartor, 'Understanding and Applying Legal Concepts' in J Hage and D von der Pfordten (eds), *Concepts in Law* (Dordrecht, Springer Verlag, 2009) 35, 53.
[25] D von der Pfordten, 'About Concepts in Law' in Hage and von der Pfordten (ibid) 17, 33.

comparison with other systems. The point is to try to avoid ethnocentrism which constantly seems to plague the comparative study of law.

It would be a mistake to assume that ethnocentrism would be a problem only for comparative law. In anthropology too we have numerous examples of such thinking as Lucien Lévy-Bruhl (1857–1939) clearly shows. He was interested in what he called 'the primitive mind' (*la mentalité primitive*), which he placed as a counter mindset to the Western mind. Lévy-Bruhl thought that the primitive mind would evolve towards the Western mind, ie from primitive to *civilisée*.[26] In comparative law these ideas can be found in Saleilles' ideas about common law of humanity (*droit commun de l'humanité civilisée*).[27] Today's comparative law is more open to conceiving the diversity and pluralism of law.

When we deal with the philosophy of legal doctrine, comparative law has an expansive influence on the methods of knowledge acquisition. Far too often legal-theoretical constructions seem to be built entirely from the point of view of either the civil law legal family or the common law legal family although the legal theories on the structure, nature and sources of law are meant to be global. For instance, by means of comparative law research it is possible to realise how extensive the concept of the legal source actually is. The relation between comparative law and legal theory has caused well-deserved attention, but at the same time it has also revealed an extremely wide variety of questions and answers.

A classical Nordic example of comparative law that serves legal theory is the study of marriage and divorce law in the late-1950s by Otto Brusiin (1906–73).[28] Brusiin focused on how regulations concerning marriage depend on social, historical and ideological factors. It is a legal-theoretical study that Brusiin was engaged in that made use of comparative law material and the comparative approach.

Legal theory in connection with comparative law has usually been connected with a certain field of law, as for example Gordley' s work on the theoretical origins of contract law shows.[29] In his book Gordley combined the legal-historical and comparative law approach with the study of systemic structures of contract law in the light of the philosophy of Greek Antiquity. He subsequently extended his comparative law and legal-historical study of legal philosophy widely over the whole field of private law in his later seminal work concerning the foundations of private law.[30]

Another example that is widely known and quoted in the theory of comparative law is comparative jurisprudence as sketched by Ewald. Ewald has stressed the significance of nineteenth-century constitutional theory in understanding the German civil codification *Bürgerliches Gesetzesbuch* (BGB) as a civil law where the way of

---

[26] See L Lévy-Bruhl, *La mentalité primitive* (Paris, Alcan, 1922).
[27] B Fekete, *Paradigms in Modern European Comparative Law* (Oxford, Hart Publishing, 2021) 74–75.
[28] O Brusiin, *Zum Ehescheidungsproblem* (Helsinki, Akademische Buchhandlung, 1959).
[29] J Gordley, *Philosophical Origins of Modern Contract Method* (Oxford, Clarendon Press, 1993).
[30] J Gordley, *Foundations of Private Law: Property, Tort, Contract, Unjust Enrichment* (Oxford, Oxford University Press, 2007).

thinking clearly differs from classical Roman law. Ewald's central theoretical idea was that comparative law would move from studying rules to the study of the underlying philosophy of foreign law. On the other hand, Ewald emphasised the academic freedom of general comparative law in relation to actual legal theory and philosophy. The development of Ewald's theory is best found in a massive article about comparative jurisprudence from the mid-1990s.[31]

The influence of comparative law, legal cultures and legal pluralism that is currently widely known and approved has also been recognised in legal theory, as is seen in *Objectivity in Law and Legal Reasoning*.[32] Nor can the variety of cultural ideas that are related to various contexts be ignored any longer in legal theories. Yet, of these two fields comparative law is well ahead of legal theory when it comes to conceiving the legal-cultural contingency of law.

It has become increasingly obvious that legal-cultural context has a great significance for legal theory as is pointed out by Dessau in his book about national aspects of non-national legal theory.[33] Dessau highlights the cultural foundations on the basis of similarities and differences between the Central European (German) and the Nordic (Finnish and Swedish) views. The conclusion is that the doctrines on sources of law are different in different legal cultures and that there is no 'correct' or global way to define the doctrine on sources of law.

Philosophies of comparative law are still a relevant area of discussion in comparative law scholarship in general.[34]

How about other disciplines then? At present it is no longer a question of legal philosophy, socio-legal studies and legal history. The connections have changed since comparative law itself has become a more open and polyphonic field of study. And yet, comparative law is currently linked to legal theory in many ways because transnational law, legal pluralism and the study of legal cultures questions and criticises the Western theory of law and legal positivism in particular. In particular, Twining has tried to construct a new global but legal-culturally sensitive legal theory.[35]

Another good example of comparative law which focuses on the twenty-first century is that of Menski whose massive work *Comparative Law in a Global Context* criticises various theories in legal positivism (especially those of Kelsen and Hart) and develops the theory of legal pluralism.[36] Menski's theory is

---

[31] W Ewald, 'Comparative Jurisprudence (I): What Was it Like to Try a Rat?' (1995) 143 *Uni Pennsylvania L R* 1889.

[32] See J Husa and M Van Hoecke (eds), *Objectivity in Law and Legal Reasoning* (Oxford, Hart Publishing, 2013).

[33] See C Dessau, *Nationale Aspekte einer transnationalen Disziplin* (Berlin, Duncker & Humblot, 2008).

[34] *Critical Analysis of Law* (2021) 8 Special Issue: The Philosophies of Comparative Law, eds l Siliquini-Cinelli and J Husa (cal.library.utoronto.ca/index.php/cal/issue/view/2549).

[35] See eg W Twining, *General Jurisprudence: Understanding Law from a Global Perspective* (Cambridge, Cambridge University Press, 2009).

[36] W Menski, *Comparative Law in a Global Context: The Legal Systems of Asia and Africa* (Cambridge, Cambridge University Press, 2006).

closely connected to and influenced by legal anthropology, from the research tradition of which Menski reinterprets both legal theory and comparative law. When Menski views the classics of Western legal theory critically, he also himself creates – just like Twining – a novel global legal theory that is not based on the fundamental ideas of Western law. The basic observation of Menski's legal theory of comparative legal anthropology is clear: he brings out the connection that exists between the culture-specific nature of legal theory, where the implicit focus is on the West, and the Western concept of law.

> Pluralistic legal theory was originally introduced to the field of comparative law through legal anthropology. It was filtered by the global legal theory that had been influenced by comparative law and developed by the abovementioned Twining as well as Tamanaha.[37] An example of classical legal pluralism (in the same State/region rules can be applied that are overlapping or parallel) is the Marriage Law in West Sumatra. Marriage is institutionalised simultaneously in three different systems, which are, as well as the formal system of the State, the *adat* law (an ethnically and locally differentiated Indonesian customary law) and the Islamic law. All of these admit different views on contracting a marriage, its conditions, legal effects and dissolution. In practice, however, they are difficult to tell apart. The large size of Indonesia and its lack of unity enable the existence of several variations. To be able to compare them with each other, it is necessary to build a conceptual framework (legal-pluralistic theory) that can be applied simultaneously in all these different forms of marriage: they are not mutually exclusive. The point here is that these kinds of pluralist situations have become more commonplace in Western legal culture as well. Thus, it would be too narrow and simplistic to regard legal pluralism as a condition which concerns 'other' law only.

Comparative law can also be connected to the legal theory of natural law where an attempt is made to perceive the content of common concepts, such as 'right' or 'justice'. According to natural law thinking, there is a system of legal rules that is based on the natural state of human beings. It has been considered that such regulations of natural law (Latin *ius naturalis*) are in force despite States' systems of statutory law. According to the rational natural law theory, it is possible to discover what is 'naturally right', ie in accordance with natural law, when the actual life of a human being is combined with sensible behaviour. From this we have to detach the view presented in private international law, according to which the court should select from among the applicable laws the law whose application results in the best *material* end-result.

From the point of view of natural law, comparative law might be considered to have offered a medium for finding the content of natural law that is independent of positive legal systems by studying different legal solutions that have been adopted into different legal systems. However, in practice natural law theories have not relied on comparative points, but rather they have relied on

---

[37] See eg BZ Tamanaha, 'Understanding Legal Pluralism: Past to Present, Local to Global' (2007) 30 *Sydney L R* 375.

philosophical arguments and points. Notwithstanding, by means of comparison it can be observed which legal solutions in the laws of different nations are uniform and long-lived and which, on the other hand, are liable to change and are variable from nation to nation. Only in the first-mentioned case can the legal solution in question be in the sphere of natural law. The idea is somewhat similar to one that was mentioned above in connection with finding customary international law.

The position of the theory of natural law has for a long time been rather weak, but lately it has again aroused interest, for example in connection with international human rights. In the Western view human rights apply to all people equally despite cultural differences. In some contexts the nature of international human rights is described as a positivised natural law. Several Asian and African States have opposed (in some respects) the vehemently individualistic features of Western human rights thinking. Opposite views are often condensed into a reluctant theoretical setting where freedom and well-being are contrasted. These difficulties cannot be denied but at the same time one has to conceive that in essence they are of a political nature and not of a legal nature. For example, Russia ceased to be a contracting Party to the European Convention on Human Rights in March 2022 as it had become openly reluctant to respect the ECHR rights. And one has to bear in mind that there are of course various basic types of natural law: Jewish, Christian, Islamic, and Hindu law each have their own versions of natural law. All in all, the comparatist needs to be ready to look beyond a narrow notion of law so that the global diversity of law becomes visible.

E. Linguistic and Economic Dimensions – Comparative Law Reloaded

The methodological and disciplinary openness of comparative law as well as its flexibility is best demonstrated by the fact that in comparison several different fields of law, depending on the research goals and also different approaches used, are combined. Yet this is not necessarily an undesirable eclecticism but methodological pluralism. Comparative law can be practised with many different emphases from legal to theoretical and from theoretical to legal-economic or from historical to sociological. The fact that there is no single method or single objective is 'a salutary phenomenon, since the comparison of laws has been constantly present, in varying forms, as an affirmation of the willingness of lawyers to learn from the experience of others' as Glenn says.[38] Good examples of the readiness to connect to other disciplines, which is in-built in comparative law, are relatively recent fields of study such as *comparative legal linguistics* and *comparative law and economics* (or *comparative law and finance*).

---

[38] HP Glenn, 'Against Method?' in M Adams and D Heirbaut (eds), *The Method and Culture of Comparative Law* (Oxford, Hart Publishing, 2014) 177, 188.

The legal-linguistic dimensions are based on the legal-theoretical observation concerning the special relation between language and law. As pointed out by Glanert, the challenge is unavoidable because legal texts are structured and written in a manner that reflects a particular legal culture.[39] There is no avoiding the challenge set by foreign legal language(s).

In Western culture, as distinct from many Aboriginal or African traditional cultures, written language is an inherent constituent of law. In short, the relation between language and law is of a fundamental character. Law is power dressed in words and generally used by a State. When legal languages are studied comparatively the comparison takes place somewhere between comparative law and the linguistic study of legal language. In comparative legal linguistics, one of the great pioneers is Mattila, who studied legal language as a language for special professional purposes. His approach (legal linguistics or *jurilinguistique* in French) is combined with comparative law and comparative legal history. The study of foreign legal languages becomes possible owing to the fact that legal languages are not studied only from the linguistic point of view but also as part of their legal and legal-historical contexts.[40] This is often essential because, for example, in legal Chinese the terminology is partially based on Germanic models and lately also on Anglo-American models: the influence is visible as well in the concepts and terms of the legal language. Now, to understand what is essentially a hybrid legal language one needs skills not only in modern Chinese (*Pǔtōnghuà*), but also in legal German and legal English.

The comparative legal linguist can compare the development, structure or vocabulary of different legal languages. Mattila's interesting and challenging book has awakened great interest among both comparatists and scholars of legal language. The innovative idea of Mattila was to place legal language against its legal-historical and comparative law background because the concepts of legal language hold on to earlier legal-historical layers and interaction with other systems and legal languages.

> For example, in present-day Spanish administrative and legal language, the influence of the Arabic concept *alcalde*, which corresponds to mayor, is seen. The concept was introduced into Spanish by the expression *qâdi*, which refers to a Muslim judge and the definite form of which is *al-qâdi*. During the Muslim period (711–1492) Christian inhabitants who spoke different varieties of local Spanish started to refer to the administrative judge with a Spanish word *alcalde* (or *alcaide* in Portuguese). It is of historical interest that owing to its colonial history, in the Southern States of the USA the expression *alcalde* was used to refer to the mayor up to the nineteenth century. The same word, as an empty legal-linguistic vessel, has had different meanings in its travels through the legal history and legal cultures.

---

[39] S Glanert, 'Law-in-Translation' (2014) 20 *Translator* 255.
[40] See HES Mattila, *Comparative Legal Linguistics: Language of Law, Latin and Modern Lingua Francas*, 2nd edn (Farnham, Ashgate, 2013).

Economic dimensions too have been included in comparison from as early as the 1990s. Comparative legal economics has from the late-1990s been one of the fields of research that has caused most discussion and has been most frequently referred to. It has combined economics and comparative law in an interesting but also somewhat problematic way. Among the best-known topics in the twenty-first century has been the *legal origin theory* by means of which a clear connection was created between economic development and macro-comparative law. The theme is still topical and debates on it continue even though the original formulations have been softened throughout the years.

The legal origin theory was actually born around the middle of the 1990s, and especially at the end of the decade from the articles published by La Porta and Schleifer among some others. In these studies it was claimed on the basis of empirical material that in States which belong in the sphere of common law that is of English origin, markets and business are regulated in a different way from that of Continental European and Nordic law, ie civil law.[41] Legal and institutional differences seem to be reflected in the economic productivity and activity of these countries. Flexible capital and credit markets are arguably typical in common law countries, and they developed more quickly than in the countries belonging to the Continental European legal culture.

These differences appeared to be a reflection of the fact that legal systems differed from each other in their attitude to property and contract law and to the role of the government in the regulation of the economy. One of the basic ideas was that the common law approach produced (so ran the argument) a more flexible labour market because within its sphere labour market relations were subject to less, more flexible regulation than was the case in civil law systems.

> For classical (ie carried out by jurists) comparative law, the observations of the big differences in economic efficiency came as an unpleasant surprise because in comparative law the opinion has long been that, while common law and Continental European law differ from each other in respect of legal technicality, they were considered to operate functionally alike. In comparative law, the legal origins theory has not been approved because it is seen to be blind to legal factors that are superficially different but in reality perform the same functions. The analyses of the origin of law theory have with justification been blamed for being short-sighted with regard to factors that are outside formal law and to legal-cultural factors. A general picture of the theory and the criticism surrounding it is given by the extensive compilation *Legal Origin Theory*; the work consists of key articles that support and criticise the theory.[42] Altogether, bringing in economics to the comparative study of law implies that comparative legal research can be done with the help of economic models.

---

[41] See EL Glaeser and A Schleifer, 'Legal Origins' (2002) 117 *Q J Economics* 1193; and R La Porta, F Lopez-de-Silanes and A Schleifer, 'The Economic Consequences of Legal Origins' (2008) 46 *J Econ Literature* 285.
[42] See S Deakin and K Pistor (eds), *Legal Origin Theory* (Cheltenham, Edward Elgar, 2012).

III. COMPARISON AND FIELDS OF LAW

Above, comparative law has been described by dividing it up by means of the methodological approach taken. Legal studies can also be sorted out more traditionally by applying divisions according to the field of law, which means that we can talk about, say, comparative public law or comparative civil law. In a more specific division we can, for example, divide public law further into administrative law and constitutional law. Moreover, constitutional law as a field of study can be further divided into the study of institutions (eg division of powers between legislature and government), the study of public finances (eg budgetary power and watchdog power) and the study of fundamental rights. Along similar lines we can talk about comparative civil law whose special fields are, for example, comparative family law, comparative property law or comparative tort law.

Yet, when the place of comparative law as part of legal study is outlined, the division according to fields of law does not have a decisive significance because one can study comparatively private as well as public law, statutory law, case law or customary law. On the other hand, the field of law to which the practically oriented comparative law is attached has in some cases a clear significance for comparison and methods applied. Here, international law as well as private international law and public international law are discussed.

A. Private International Law

Private law refers to the part of the national legal system that mainly regulates the cross-border interrelations of individuals. When private law connects with *private international law* it is typically a question of a situation where the decision is made on which court is competent to examine a border-crossing legal relationship. Another possible issue is to decide which State's internal law should be applied in the case at hand. The traditional field of private international law is concerned with legal rules such as this. Such typical rules are, for example, *lex fori*, which refers to the law of the country in which the action is brought, whereas *lex causae* refers to the law governing the substance of the case at hand. Now, if the connecting factor results in a situation where the law of a foreign country is applied, the court has to find out the actual content of the foreign law to make a decision on the case.

The object of finding the materially best possible solution presupposes comparison between alternatives offered by different legislations. Rabel, a classic scholar of comparative law and private international law, stated in his famous work *The Conflict of Laws* that the knowledge-process in the application of private international law is necessarily of a comparative nature.[43] In other

---

[43] See E Rabel, *The Conflict of Laws: A Comparative Study*, vol 1 (Michigan, University of Michigan Law School, 1945) ch 1.

words, private international law appears to have close contact with comparative law. Notwithstanding, the field of private international law is more restricted: actual comparative law can at its widest cover all the States of the world, seldom deals with a concrete case and the researcher does not have the burden of having to solve the case.

> From the point of view of comparative law, it is important to observe that private international law does not mean the same thing everywhere, not even within Europe. For example, in the Nordic Countries it means broadly a field of law and also a specific approach to law. However, for example in Germany, it means more narrowly only those legal rules which connect different legal systems in a situation of norm-collision. These kinds of rules are needed when the legal relationship between private persons is international, as it is, for example, in cases where the parties live in different countries. The basic pluralist challenge is that the law of more States than one is applicable in the situation at hand. In English-language literature this is often referred to by the expression *conflict of laws*, which appears to be a more restricted expression than *private international law*. Which law is applied in a case is usually solved by means of the models for decision that are included in the connecting rules (eg *lex causae* and *lex fori*). On the other hand, there are other States where private international law has a more extensive interpretation, so that it also covers the international jurisdiction of courts as well as the recognition and enforcement of foreign judgments.

> Private international law is – as explained above – owing to its very starting points contrary to legal pluralism, which at present is among the main ideas of comparative law. Whereas the legal pluralist approves of the overlapping plurality of the legal rules that are in use in the same area, private international law attempts to make a justified choice among laws of different countries and in this way to delete the overlapping plurality. It comes as no surprise then, that the expression *choice of law* that in the English language is often used for private international law sums up the idea: a certain law has to be chosen. In comparative law such an overarching normative goal as this simply does not exist, ie comparative law is not only aware of legal pluralism, but in many cases it also seeks to embrace legal diversity.[44]

By means of private international law it is possible to solve legal problems concerning the applicable law, international jurisdiction of the courts and the recognition and application of foreign court decisions. Problems are caused by the fact that the case has legal connections with several legal systems and practices. Typically the case can involve, for example, spouses with different nationalities requesting divorce. In such cases it has to be decided which court has the jurisdiction to grant the divorce and which country's law the court must apply in the case. If the legal system involved in the case differs radically from one's own legal culture, getting reliable legal information might prove to be very challenging. As a result, comparative law information has relevance as a means to an end.

> Although comparative law and private international law are different, both fields are demanding. The amount of information that has to be gathered on the foreign law

---

[44] Husa (n 23) 206–13.

can sometimes be considerable, as, for example, in a case decided by the Finnish Supreme Court in 2011.[45] In the case, which related to the alimony to be paid after divorce, a great amount of information on Swiss law was gathered. The case concerned the secondary claim for alimony that was presented by the spouse, who remained in Switzerland, to the spouse, who had moved to Finland. The entitlement of a spouse to have alimony was in this case solved according to the Swiss law. Knowledge of the foreign law was in the first place gathered by the district court, which had requested executive assistance on Swiss law and legal literature. In addition, both parties presented to the district court statements by Swiss lawyers about Swiss law and legal practice concerning the issue.

On closer inspection, the relationship between private international law and comparative law is somewhat uneasy. From the point of view of private international law, comparative law is needed as a help-tool, for example in finding out if any norm of a foreign law or its application is against the *ordre public* (application would clearly be against the principles of the legal system of the foreign country in question), in which case auxiliary comparison is getting close to actual comparative law. Differences are not necessarily drastic and yet they do exist.

In other words, private international law clearly intersects with comparative law, but as fields of study and research they do not merge much at all. There is one crucial difference. The rules of private international law are based on each country's *own* law, legal practice and doctrinal study of law. There is a certain false notion here that is caused by the word international because the law in question is the national law (internal and normative viewpoint): it may not be the law of the country in which the case is decided, but it is a law of a country (ie domestic law in one sense or another). It is noteworthy, though, that national rules have been harmonised by means of multilateral agreements and shared regulations. The aim is to avoid problematic situations where the legal organs of two different States argue over competence, with each country considering themselves to have competent jurisdiction and giving in the same case – in the worst case – decisions that are different. The idealistic aim is that a domestic court should know foreign law as well as the foreign system's own legal organs do (so-called loyal or authentic application). This would, however, require a far-reaching study on foreign law rarely possible in time-pressured judicial working conditions.

Now, private international law is not by nature binding on States like public international law. It is the State's internal law that is applied in such private law circumstances which have international contact points. Private international law is a practically oriented field of law that, however, has something in common with actual comparative law owing to the non-national legal sources that are characteristic of it and its interest in cross-border problem-solving. The constructive significance of comparison has in recent years been seen in

---

[45] The Finnish Supreme Court decided (KKO: 2011:97) to apply Swiss law by vote (3–2).

contexts where different States, by concluding agreements, have standardised their private international law regulation. It is somewhat unfortunate that in the curricula of law at universities, private international law is often taught in the same contexts as comparative law: even though they partially overlap the knowledge-interests differ. Even those private international law scholars who underline the potential importance of comparative law admit that in practice there clearly is a lack of interest in comparative law analyses.[46]

As has become clear above, contemporary methodologically pluralist comparative law ought to be separated from private international law: it is practised not only in different fields of law but also in several different ways, which in many cases have nothing to do with private international law. The old academic umbilical cord between private international law and comparative law has got thinner but is not completely cut. Be that as it may, the most recent legal-cultural and legal-pluralistic emphases continue to erode the connection between private international law and comparative law: for the comparative law of the twenty-first century the very theoretical basis of comparison is something (combining internal and external, pluralist) that private international law regards as a problem that needs to be solved: the modern comparatist embraces pluralism and hybridity whereas the private international law scholar – although recognising the plurality of law – hopes to make them disappear. However, one sometimes sees genuine comparison done by courts of law; this is rare in civil law whereas it seems more typical in the common law.

> There is an example from England: *The National Blood Case*.[47] It is a kind of model case of versatile comparison and of the use of non-national legal literature in particular. In the solution reference is made to writers from several systems: Clark, Dahl (Denmark); Griffith, Henderson (USA); Hodges, Howells, von Marschall (Germany); Newdick, Rolland (Germany); Stapleton, Stoppa (Italy); Taschner, von Westphalen (Germany) and Whittaker (UK). The comparative survey covers Austria, Belgium, Denmark, France, Germany, the Netherlands, Portugal, Sweden and the US, in such a way that there is reference not only to legal literature but also to legal practice. In addition, the court (Queen's Bench, a department of the High Court of Justice) is not content with studying only one legal language, ie English, but to support the interpretation of the directive applied, investigates also versions in other languages and justifies this by saying that 'some guidance can be obtained from other languages in which the directive was published, all of which are of equal weight'.

B. Public International Law

In legal systematics, public international law, or in other words the legal rules that determine the legal relationships of international legal entities

---

[46] G Rühl, 'Who's Afraid of Comparative Law?' (2017) 25 *Eur R Private L* 485 (holds that Europeanisation of private law has resulted in devaluation of comparative law).
[47] *A and others v National Blood Authority* [2001] 3 All ER 289.

(States and international organisations in particular), is separated from private international law. Typical instruments of private international law are conventions (international treaties and agreements) and uniform laws prepared jointly by several States or international organisations. When comparative law is related to public international law, the question is, for example, about Article 38(1) of the Statute of the International Court of Justice (see chapter five, section V.D) operating within the framework of the United Nations and the provisions of its Charter, which regulates which legal sources the Court shall refer to when it solves disputes presented to the court. Sometimes it is a question of general international legal principles existing in all legal systems and acknowledged by States in their domestic law; however, they can also be applied on occasions where conventions or customary law do not offer enough guidance on which the judgment of the International Court could be based.

The International Court of Justice has since the end of World War II considered that international courts can impose obligations not only on States and international organisations but also on individuals. Human rights in particular have later on been given a central position as well as a significant role in international law. In this connection the system of the Council of Europe, including a surveillance system that is more efficient than the UN system, has assumed a significant role. Differing from the judgments of the Human Rights Commission of the UN, the resolutions made within the framework of the European Convention on Human Rights are also legally binding on the contracting States (obligation to amend legislation).

Enforcing the European Human Rights Convention is mainly based on the operations of the European Human Rights Court. However, the Court does not alter the original domestic decision; it is not a Court of Appeal as such. Its judgment concerns the State, which according to the Court has not carried out in its own legal system the obligations set by the Convention. The Court's case law can in certain cases have great significance that exceeds the wording of the Convention itself.

The human rights of the European Convention on Human Rights can be considered to form (among the Member States of the EU, all of whom have joined the Convention) a harmonised human and basic rights standard whose impact is within narrow bounds based on the surveillance organisation connected to it. Human rights included in the Convention have been altered in the interpretation practice because the Court interprets the Convention dynamically and regards the Convention as a dynamic instrument – it changes and lives in accordance with the interpretation practice of the Court. Crucially, interpretation is therefore not confined by the wording of the Convention. This in particular offers certain possibilities for comparative law viewpoints. Some go further and argue that the comparative law approach is an important and, as such, even an essential part of the ECHR system.[48]

---

[48] P Mahoney and R Kondak, 'Common Ground' in M Andenas and D Fairgrieve (eds), *Courts and Comparative Law* (Oxford, Oxford University Press, 2015) 119.

Ultimately the contracting State can be obliged to change its legislation and also possibly to pay compensation to the injured party for the damage caused by the violation of the Convention obligation. Yet, the challenge faced by the system is the immense backlog of cases, which has made the system extremely slow. Another problem is that some contracting Parties (eg Turkey), which have ratified the Convention but whose legal cultures are not capable of properly fulfilling or even promoting the obligations set for them by the Convention, do not appear to be taking the judgments of the Human Rights Court seriously.

The Human Rights Court has for a considerable time made use of integrative comparative law as a method for making comparisons. Together with the EU Court, both courts have introduced elements from other legal systems into their non-national systems. Albeit, this has not meant significant growth of the actual comparative legal approach, but instead has increased exploitation of different comparative points of view (so called *human rights comparativism*).[49] In short: the significance of practice-oriented comparative law has increased because of European human rights.

> Skills in comparative law can be useful in domestic administrative courts too when procedural demands that might be required by the EU Court are evaluated upon the application of EU law. Comparative law makes it possible to understand foreign/unknown concepts and different legal institutions as part of their original legal system, and this increases the knowledge base of international administrative law and decreases the potential for false interpretations. In essence, comparative law makes it possible to understand EU law and to define its fundamental characteristics.[50] At present the most advanced sector of international administrative law is European administrative law although it fits rather poorly into the framework defined by actual international law: EU law differs in many ways from traditional international law and this applies to the field of administrative law as well. What is clear though, is that comparative arguments are also made use of there, but that operations are supranational rather than international.

Finally, when it comes to international law it is possible that today's pluralism also causes fragmentation. There are so many bodies of law and various international actors from governments to various non-governmental organisations. Comparative law research can, however, help in building new common ground not only by showing whether or not there is a common approach among States but also by providing a common methodology for international adjudication. These qualities are discussed in the new emerging field of comparative international law which is interested in analysing differences and similarities in how legal systems understand, interpret and apply international law.[51] Developing

---

[49] See eg E Örücü (ed), *Judicial Comparativism in Human Rights Cases* (London, British Institute of International and Comparative Law, 2003).
[50] J Raitio, 'To Compare is to Understand' (2021) 16 *J Comp L* 539.
[51] A Roberts, PB Stephen, P-H Verdier and M Versteeg, 'Conceptualizing Comparative International Law' in A Roberts and al (eds), *Comparative International Law* (Oxford, Oxford University Press, 2018) 3–4.

international law closer to modern comparative law may also mean a narrowing of the gap between international law, comparative law and social sciences.[52]

IV. DIFFICULTY OF DEMARCATION

It is worth noting that the differences between branches of legal research are not clear-cut. In most cases we have to operate around the borders of different orientations. Especially when it comes to the comparative study of law, there is the evident phenomenon of overlapping approaches and the difficulty of drawing distinct demarcation lines. Harold C Cutteridge (1876–1953) has formulated it well: 'The comparative method lends itself to the study of any branch of legal learning'.[53] This is, undoubtedly, one of the key factors for why the comparative approach has become more and more popular in the twenty-first century. The flexibility of comparative methodology may be an asset in today's transnational legal world where boundaries and borders have become more porous than before.

For example, a typical legal problem concerning the wording in a statutory law, which is a paradigmatic task of the doctrinal approach, can also contain some comparative aspects if it concerns a factor that is familiar (a roughly similar type of question) not only within the domestic legal system but also in other legal systems. This would not, however, be a question of actual comparative law research but – at best – of the auxiliary usage of comparative elements in research that is as to its nature doctrinal and deals with positive law. In a similar fashion, often, the comparatist *exploits* sociological, economic, linguistic and historical elements as part of the study. This does not transform the comparatist into a quasi-sociologist, quasi-anthropologist or quasi-linguist – it is a question of learning and benefitting and drawing inspiration from other disciplines. The key words, in an up-to-date common sense meaning, are methodological openness and the inquisitive state of mind of the comparatist. Broadly speaking, modern comparative law is a field open to interdisciplinarity.

A crucial observation is that comparative law cannot be limited to formal law; one must often look beyond the statutory law or leading cases. Earlier in this chapter Ehrlich's concept of *living law* was referred to, and it seems to encapsulate much of the need to know also about the various contexts of law. Also the reality of law has to be investigated, ie what really happens in actual practice. For example, a comparatist studying British constitutional law will rather quickly notice that sources of law are not limited to *statute law* or rules and

---

[52] E Justyna Powell, 'Comparative International Law and the Social Science Approach' (2021) 22 *Chicago J Int'l L* 147.
[53] H Gutteridge, 'The Value of Comparative Law' (1931) *J Society of Public Teachers of Law* 27, 28.

principles created by leading cases, but that legal sources are to be found also from the established *constitutional conventions*. Just as quickly the researcher of public international law would notice that it is impossible for them to limit their legal sources to international treaty texts only, since customary international law also has to be included because it too has a formally acknowledged position. And when acquaintance is being made with customary international law, it is essential to know what kind of provisions or precedents States have recognised as binding law (*opinio iuris*). Moreover, in EU law national, international and supranational elements are interlocked with each other, and comparative aspects function as a kind of glue in between the various legal ingredients.

It is not only a question of aiming at the empirical level of law but also of the fact that positive law in itself has changed. The structure of law has been altered through border-crossing developments, and the traditional hierarchical relationships between fields of law, and legal systems that have been pruned to fit into their different national compartments are now more flexible than before. The functions of different legal systems can be described as *legal tapestries*. Law is seen as containing threads that have different contact points and surfaces in a kaleidoscopic manner. The knots formed in the net are connected with each other through it and are interdependent via several threads. Comparative law is in such cases one of the important tools by means of which one can orientate oneself in the legal tapestry that crosses national borders. In other words, comparative law is often a meta-discipline in the doctrinal study of law or simply a practical instrument in a legally diverse world.

> In spite of the change in legal cultures and pluralism, something permanent can be detected at least within legal disciplines. According to Hannu Tolonen (1945–2005), 'Law is a kaleidoscope that can be outlined in almost countless ways'.[54] Legal disciplines also outline law from different points of view. In Western legal culture, the doctrinal study of law has for centuries dominated jurisprudence and the way that professionals study and approach law and legal questions. However, the doctrinal approach has never been the only way to conceive law legally.
>
> Completely different perspectives are available today, and there is even methodological, not only legal, pluralism. From the point of view of comparative law, it is worth referring once again to the idea of *Grundlagenfächer* that is used in German jurisprudence. With this expression reference is made to the essential companions of the doctrinal study of law, the kind of meta-disciplines of legal study, ie legal history, comparative law and the general theory of law. Dutch jurists refer to meta-disciplines as *grondslagen van de rechtwetenschap* or *metajuridica* – they refer to the non-normative study of law carried out by jurists. Comparative law finds its academic home in this metajuridica but also within the fields of law, which may benefit from comparative points of view or from which inspiration on the basis of comparisons may be drawn. It seems justified to draw a distinction according to which comparative

---

[54] H Tolonen, 'Oikeus ja sen tulkinnat' in J Häyhä (ed), *Minun metodini* (Helsinki, WSOY, 1997) 279, 279.

law is part of *metajuridica* as Gorlé points out, even though comparative law is less abstract than more theoretical disciplines of legal theory and the philosophy of law.[55] Even though comparative law has developed toward a more scholarly field it cannot totally lose its connection to law as goal-oriented professional practice without risking the loss of its identity as a field of legal knowledge.

It is important to understand that meta-disciplines have a close connection with the normative study of law because it is their task to open up the legal contexts or to place law in time and space not only in the narrowly understood internal normative sphere of a particular legal system. In this respect comparative law has an important legal-cultural basic role that is related to the identity of the jurists, which Modéer formulates as follows: 'The identity of lawyers is, namely, bound with the presentations, which lawyers create in time and space with the help of their legal knowledge structures'.[56]

Basically, all meta-disciplines of law, naturally including comparative law, are legal knowledge structures referred to by Modéer – this is where their real contribution to today's legal study lies. Comparative law is part of the twenty-first-century legal understanding, not simply an eccentric academic field of study that is only meant for a tiny elite, a little armour-bearer in the judge's quest for choice of law (in case of private international law) in the application of foreign law or the inexhaustible store of ideas for a law drafter. Of course, it can be all of these things, too, but it is crucial to underline that the genuine and lasting value of comparative law lies elsewhere: it opens up new legal horizons and, thus, expands one's vision of law, one's own law included. In a more philosophical language, the horizon of one's own law and that of the foreign law are fused together creating new insights into law in general.

Even in the world of globalising law, comparative law has a place in highlighting the significance of differences and local nuances which embody the very idea of global legal diversity. To that end, comparative law functions as a form of critical legal scholarship as it opposes oversimplified visions of normative universalism and the accompanying ideology of homogenisation.

---

[55] F Gorlé et al, *Handboek rechtsvergelijking* (Mechelen, Wolters Kluwer, 2007) ('Rechtsvergelijking is veeleer een deel van de metajuridica' and it is 'veel minder abstract') 76.
[56] 'Juristernas identiteter är nämligen förbunda med de föreställningar som juristerna skapar om tid och rum med hjälp av sina rättsliga kunskapsstrukturer', K Å Modéer, 'Östersjöområdets rättsliga kartor' in J Kekkonen (ed), *Norden, rätten, historia* (Helsinki, Suomalainen lakimiesyhdistys, 2004) 193.

5
Why Compare?

THE COMPARISON OF laws is a discipline where *methodological and theoretical pluralism* prevails. There are different competing views of what comparative law is and what it is not. In spite of the differences all views are connected by one common feature. Comparative law, like any form of legal research, is normally regarded as an activity that always has an aim. Comparison is not a hobby that the jurist elite can busy themselves with along with (more serious) doctrinal study of law. Undoubtedly, comparative law is time-consuming and in many respects is a rather challenging way to engage in legal research. But, from the history of comparative law we know that comparison has always had an aim and purpose. This is still the case today. There is no point comparing if it does not serve a meaningful purpose.

For example, the learned men in the Greek Πόλις of Antiquity were interested in the laws of other city States. For ancient Greeks, the human-made law (νόμος) of the city State differed from the law of nature (φύσις). Greeks also applied the norms of other city States to their own cities if they considered them applicable. The ancient Romans were profoundly aware of the fact that their law, the Roman law, was their own (*ius civile*), but they understood that law that concerned all people (*ius gentium*) applied also to them. Later this Roman heritage transformed and developed into the medieval *ius commune*.

> The term *ius commune* ('common law' in Latin, German *Gemeines Recht*), which is frequently used in comparative law and legal history, refers to the entity that was born in the Middle Ages as a synthetic combination of reinterpreted Roman law (in particular *corpus iuris civilis*), Catholic canon law and the legal study practised in universities. Hence, in German it is also called *römisch-kanonische Recht*, ie Roman-Canonical Law. The Middle Ages is not an accurate expression, but here it refers to the period between 400–1400 AD. The Middle Ages were named at the end of the fifteenth century and the beginning of the sixteenth century by humanists for whom this period represented a period of intellectual regression. In legal history the period is not as 'dark' as its reputation. Roman law was born in Antiquity to begin with, ie in ancient history, which refers roughly to the period between 2500 BC and 600 AD. From the point of view of legal history, the periods cannot be distinctly separated from one another because regional differences were vast. In any case, *ius commune* used by comparatists refers to this later Roman law tradition that

declined only when natural law scholarship and codification movement grew stronger.[1] More importantly, *ius commune* and the practice of comparing laws within the Continental European legal sphere are intertwined.

I. STARTING POINTS – CREATING ADDED VALUE

Comparative law attempts, in accordance with what has been said earlier, to disengage from the limits of national legal systems (as well as international law, if needs be) that restrict the acquisition of the knowledge of law. Often only when legal systems are examined from the outside, is it possible to see the distinctive historical features, for instance, of the division between the fields of law, the relativity of legal concepts and the embedded political and social nature of different legal institutions. Law is part and parcel of the society's cultural entirety – law is the law of human communities. Or, as the Latin phrase has it, *ubi societas, ibi ius*: where there is a society there is law. And, this leads inevitably to an unsurprising revelation: human communities are not similar all over the world, thus the law applied to human beings and their social constructions (eg marriage, contract, tort etc) cannot be the same everywhere.

Solutions in one's own legal system that seem natural and self-evident can appear in a new light when compared to solutions in other systems; then it is easier to assume a critical view of their self-evident truth and to conceive their weaknesses and strengths more accurately. Also the foreign influence on one's own legal system becomes visible and can therefore be faced by conscious and critical evaluation. Comparison often works as a legal cultural eye-opener, ie it demonstrates to the comparatist something crucial about law in an unexpected way.

The non-national nature of comparative law is considered to facilitate the understanding of foreign cultures and consequently to both promote and facilitate cross-border cooperation. On the other hand, when foreign law is studied, it is very difficult to avoid making unconscious comparisons if for no other reason than that explaining in your own language the content of a foreign law in an understandable form requires implicit comparison. Simply, the translation of foreign concepts and terms requires comparative knowledge about law.

Above all it is a question of how *consciously* the comparative element is included in the study of foreign law. It is fundamental to comparative law that the comparative element is consciously included in the research design and that the comparatist openly tells the readers what they have done in the study and how they have done it. Covering up research approaches and emphases or upholding a hidden agenda is not a decent research practice in comparative law as it becomes impossible for an outsider to evaluate what has been done and how it has been done. Open argumentation belongs to good research practice

---

[1] P Stein, 'The Ius Commune and its demise' (2004) 25 *J Legal Hist* 161.

because it increases the justifiability of the comparatist's reasoning and conclusions. Correspondingly, clandestineness and hiding one's own research decisions and emphases is bound to decrease their credibility and significance. There are also ethical dimensions of research connected with credibility and significance (more on this in chapter six, section XIII).

Among the legal disciplines, it is expressly comparative law that entertains the comparative element (Latin *comparatio* = comparison), and merely getting acquainted with foreign law or international law is not equal to being genuinely engaged in comparative law. Essentially, if there is no actual comparison involved, then, it is not comparative. Yet, learning of foreign legal systems and legal cultures is an essential preliminary phase for comparative study of law. As a preliminary phase it is a natural part of the comparative process that always consists of several steps. On the other hand, the differences between describing foreign law and actually comparing it with other law are not overtly dramatic as foreign and comparative law are bound to overlap.

In general, the comparatists assume that comparative law is expressly comparing and that descriptive knowledge of foreign law (German *Auslandsrechtskunde*) is a constitutive part of the actual comparative process. So, comparison should produce knowledge with value-added, not only valid, descriptions. Adams compresses it into an essential question: 'What actually is the added value of such comparative exercise?'[2] That is: comparative law should produce some value-added, and by means of comparison it should be possible to surpass the trap of the mere organised description of foreign law. Ideally, the process advances from valid description to understanding and from decent understanding to relevant explaining. Moving from description to understanding and explanation is a crucially necessary step in the comparative study of law if it wishes to be something more than the mere study of foreign law.

II. COMPARISON AS A CROSS-BORDER FORM OF KNOWLEDGE ACQUISITION

Basically, comparative study is a challenge of identifying differences and similarities as observed above. The fundamental object of comparative law is to acquire knowledge on what separates the legal systems or cultures studied and what connects them and to explain or assess what has caused the differences and/or similarities. The method of knowledge acquisition is comparison, which is a natural cognitive model of human ability. When we talk about comparative law or comparative study in general, we often forget to mention this natural connection with everyday thinking and intuitive knowledge acquisition. Someone who

---

[2] 'Wat is eigenlijk de vergelijkende meerwaarde van dergelijke exercities?', M Adams, 'Wat de rechtsvergelijking vermag. Over onderzoeksdesign' (2011) 60 *Ars Aequi* 198.

practises the doctrinal study of law might consider comparison as an 'academic peculiarity', although at the basic level of making sense of the world, this is not the case. To be sure, doctrinal study is epistemically much more distant from common sense thinking than making comparisons.

When we in a scholarly context see the term 'comparative law', a rather abstract scientific method might easily come to mind. As stated above, in reality comparison is (almost) the most natural method to acquire and increase information about the world that is beyond our own immediate native understanding. Comparison is our inborn constitution for acquiring experimental knowledge and a way of thinking that enables us to acquire practical knowledge. According to the basic definition of Jansen, 'Comparison is the construction of relations of similarity or dissimilarity between different matters of fact'.[3] This is clearly something we do every day by way of asking questions: is this bag heavier than the other one; is today colder or warmer than yesterday; which of these products lasts longer; which of these cars is more expensive; is it more expensive to travel by aeroplane than by train etc.

It is a question of investigating the relations between different matters from a particular point of view: observations concerning difference and similarity are implicitly constructed. Moreover, comparison is also a basic method of scientific knowledge acquisition.

Terminology can be confusing. It seems natural to separate different fields of science and to include legal studies in the entity of all sciences. On the other hand, it is clear that the normative doctrinal study of law, legal theory, comparative law and the history of law are not science (Latin *scientia*) as such. The old Latin name for legal study (and its derivatives in other languages), on the other hand, are derived from the word *prudentia* (Latin *iurisprudentia*), which emphasises *learnedness* and *skill*. Palmer fittingly states: 'Omniscience is an excellent end but it is not invariably appropriate and cannot be the everyday standard of comparative law'.[4]

In this respect comparative law preferably belongs to *humanities* studying human culture rather than to the same category as medicine and astronomy. In this book the way of conceiving comparative law familiar to the usage found in many languages is not used; instead, comparative law is regarded as a form of *prudence*, ie jurisprudence understood in a broad manner. This refers to *prudentia*, which is practical wisdom, not to *scientia* (Greek φρόνησις) Yet, we can observe that jurisprudence has several features that are also found in *scientia*: principles in the use of references, obligation to give justification, following of research-ethical principles, methods based on arguments, collective control of the community of researchers and so on. There is plenty of likeness to science,

---

[3] N Jansen, 'Comparative Law and Comparative Knowledge' in M Reimann and R Zimmermann (eds), *The Oxford Handbook of Comparative Law* (Oxford, Oxford University Press, 2006) 305, 310.
[4] VV Palmer, 'From Lerotholi to Lando' (2005) 53 *Am J Comp L* 261, 287.

but it is not a question of exact science. In German terminology it is, however, seen as a form of operation that can be described as a member of the family of sciences (*Wissenschaften*). The change from *Rechtsgelehrsamkeit* ('learnedness in law') to *Rechtswissenschaft* (legal science) can be traced back to German legal scholarship of early nineteenth century (eg for Friedrich Carl von Savigny law was a scientific matter).

Some schools of thinking formed by comparatists have also tried to define comparative law as science in a more exacting sense, as was demonstrated in 1987 by the original programme declaration of the Trento circle that was formed around Rodolfo Sacco (1923–2022): the five principles describing comparative law are all permeated by an aspiration for scientification.[5] Later in the Trento sphere of influence have been included, in addition to the original members (eg Sacco, Gambaro, Monateri Bussani), other researchers who do not attempt to commit themselves to the original programme declaration that was renewed in 2004 by Gambaro and others.

So, the basic cognitive setting in comparison is relatively clear. How do we actually know that something is, for example, cold? How can we maintain that one matter is big while another is small? Before we created a modern absolute thermometer scale, our only way to define cold was to compare it to warm and then conclude what the difference in temperatures meant in concrete terms. In order to know what can be labelled as small, we have to be able to say what is big. Understanding these differences and similarities is not purely a natural and inborn capacity but also a skill learned by experience and enabled by the innate capacity for comparison of the human mind. It is a question of the perception of the relative position between matters, the basic operation of human observation. The human mind figures out various sorts of proportions very well, ie one grasps relationships that exist between the size, colour or amount of two things. Modern comparative law studies normativities beyond narrowly defined law but its scholarly power is still based on the act of comparison; it is for the comparatist to decide what kind of units they want to include in the comparison.[6]

A. About Proportions

A matter is something in particular because it is something in proportion to something else: the argument that there is 'inefficient and insufficient protection provided by law' in the People's Republic of China has a sensible meaning only if we know what 'efficient and sufficient' protection provided by law means. Mere suggestions are not sufficient. Suggestions have to be proportioned, ie we

---

[5] The original programme is from 1987 (The Trento Manifesto containing five core theses) and it was signed by eight Italian comparatists; see R Sacco, 'Legal Formants: A Dynamic Approach to Comparative Law (I)' (1991) 39 *Am J Comp L* 1.

[6] M Siems, 'The Power of Comparative Law' (2019) 67 *Am J Comp L* 861.

should say 'inefficient' in proportion to something and 'insufficient' compared to 'sufficient'. The comparatist has to explain the arguments of their comparative study for readers to assess. The reader can in this way evaluate if they would reach similar conclusions on the basis of the same study and similar data.

There is almost a tautology here: comparison (to compare) is the cognitive foundation pillar of comparison. Through comparison and the establishment of concepts, such elementary conceptual categories (in a social sense) as being small and big or slow and quick have been formed. We understand what is republic because we know its conceptual counterpart monarchy. In the law of compensation (or tort law), the concept of intangible damage becomes comprehensible when it is compared to material damage, in property law the concept of immovable property is understandable when it is compared to the concept of movable property, a petty crime is understandable when it is compared to a felony and so on.

The conclusion is obvious: the basis of comparative study is not detached from common sense; it is instead the intuitive starting point of *human knowledge formation*. The everyday thinking in itself and the practical knowledge needed in daily pursuits often depend on the intuitive use of the comparative method although we do not consciously think that we are using any special comparative method. Moreover, there is a deeper philosophical kind of proof of a person's existence based on the sheer fact that someone capable of any form of comparison necessarily exists. Paraphrasing (French *je pense donc je suis* or Latin *cogito, ergo sum*) René Descartes (1596–1650) stated: 'I compare, therefore I exist' ('*Confero, ergo sum*'). This is no more no less than the premier principle of all comparative study (Descartes' *le premier principe*). In short, comparative law is simply an advanced application of comparative knowledge formation. The intellectual engine of comparison is built into the human mind, legal or otherwise.

Now, in comparative law the comparatist seeks to find another system to which their own legal system could be compared and it would be possible to look for certain commonalities or differences. When it is a question of a conscious quest for differences and similarities between legal systems as well as for their explanation, we can call it proper comparative law. If in the research, for example, several foreign legal systems are merely introduced and described consecutively or parallel to each other (system A, system B, system C etc), then it is not comparative law because there is no act of comparison involved. Still, a great deal of the legal research carried out under the banner of comparative legal research or comparative law is mainly parallel description of foreign legal systems where comparison is lacking. Often it is the question of mere *Auslandsrechtskunde*, which in fact could in itself be useful information in the drafting of legislation or the application of the law. Also the language of publications has here its own role: a genuinely international study is linguistically comprehensible even for those who are outside the system. Unfortunately, this puts less common languages in a disadvantageous position because it favours more common languages.

So, making comparisons and drawing conclusions on their basis is a built-in capacity in human beings who aim at knowledge. In the same way, everyone who studies foreign law is engaged in first-stage intuitive and the spontaneous comparison of law because the context of their own understanding is based on the epistemology of their own legal system ('pre-understanding', German *Vorverständnis*). This is why comparative law helps them paradoxically to comprehend their own legal system better and improves the possibilities to develop it by enlarging the knowledge basis – comparative law enables us to grasp our own legal system in a different light or reflected in a different mirror. The epistemological idea here is simple: if comprehension of foreign law requires in terms of knowledge more than the doctrinal study of law in one's own system, it means that law contains culturally bound implicit elements. Law is, in fact, always *law in context*. If culturally bound elements define how law is understood, interpreted and applied, why would the comparatist's own system be some sort of capricious exception in this respect? For the comparatist, knowledge of law is unavoidably relational as to its nature.

> Many comparatists of the twentieth century have underlined comparative law as a study method that offered new stimuli in the comprehension of one's own law. Some have gone even further since the concept of shock therapy has been used in this context. The expression 'the laboratory of truth' has been used to describe this dimension of comparative law. Bogdan takes this way of thinking even further: 'a lawyer who has studied only their own legal system, cannot have a full understanding of that system'.[7] Bogdan's point is an important one; by studying only one's own law one cannot gain full understanding of that system. In other words, to perceive something that is one's own is possible when one's own is viewed with the eyes of an outsider (epistemic alienation). Metaphorically it is a question of a kind of out-of-body experience and observing the 'legal body' from the outside: *out-of-body-experience* relates to an epistemic feeling of separation from one's own law and being able to view, to an extent, one's own law from an external perspective. To that end, comparative law may be conceived as an ordinary form of legal scholarship even though it assumes an external viewpoint to law.[8]

Also in the study of general jurisprudence the comparative approach has plenty of possibilities when study no longer is so bound to the systems of nation-States as it previously was. By means of teaching comparative law and foreign law it is possible to transfer the focus of legal study away from learning detailed rules and instead to concentrate on the general principles and features of the legal system. More significance is also given to the international dimension of law as part of instruction and research within all branches of law. Through comparison it becomes possible to proportion the familiar to the unfamiliar – this generates new knowledge and novel insights about law.

---

[7] 'den jurist som endast har studerat sin egen rättsordning, inte kan ha fått en full förståelse av denna rättsordning', M Bogdan, *Komparativ rättskunsp* (Stockholm, Norstedts juridik, 2003) 28.
[8] See SA Smith, 'Comparative Legal Scholarship as Ordinary Legal Scholarship' (2010) 5 *J Comp L* 331.

Along with the European Union law, European human rights and the globalisation of law, comparative law is more clearly and indisputably constructed on law as a normative phenomenon in itself: different systems contain elements that oblige us to compare. When, for example, the realisation of the harmonisation obligation set by an EU directive in one's own country is interpreted, the realisation of the directive in other Member States has to be studied as well. Implementation norms in other languages can also be inspected to give grounds for making the interpretation. Legal texts that can be studied side by side are simultaneously available in several languages: in essence this is comparing laws and legal languages.

B. Different Needs

Despite their common sense origin, scholarly comparison and practical goal-oriented comparison have parted from one another. Above all it is a question of conceptual systematicness, clarity and discipline but also of controllability and reliability. Comparison is reasonably easy in physical and chemical sciences because the laboratory conditions can be controlled to a considerable degree. In research concerning the cultural characteristics of people it is impossible to attain full scientific reliability with methods that would be ethically acceptable. Be that as it may, this has not prevented the use of the comparative method in the research of politics and law in the past. In different periods and different legal disciplines there have been different knowledge-interests, which have been and still are possible to satisfy.

> According to the oral tradition of ancient Rome – for such an early period it is difficult to find facts – in the 460s BC, the Romans sent a delegation to Hellas to get acquainted with the legislation of Greek city States in order to gain a knowledge base for the creation of a compilation of laws. The idea was to enact a comprehensive body of laws that would provide not simply for individual cases. This has been reported to be the comparative history of the Twelve Tables (Latin *Leges duodecim tabularum*). These laws have had great significance for the development of Roman and subsequently European law.
>
> In Iceland around 930 AD a man called Úlfljótr was sent to Norway to learn about law. When he returned after about three years Iceland would go on to have a law and administration system of its own prepared on the basis of what he had experienced and learnt. Úlfljótr is known in legal history as a kind of *lagman*, ie 'a speaker of law' (*lögsögumaðr*).
>
> The need for information and the world have changed. For example, the operation of lawyers working in the area of the European Union for the harmonisation of European private law differs from the ancient models because nowadays integration of several different systems is consciously the aim. In other words, the aims and contexts of comparison are different, and they have an effect on what is done and how it is done, ie methods and aims of comparative law have been and still are contingent, not definite.

Some fields of knowledge seem to be more relevant for comparative law than others. Legal history teaches the comparatist. History is useful for the perception and explanation of the legal context, but one must beware of slipping into the world of myths and romanticising law. A good example of this is the case of the classic white statues of Antiquity that have since been proved to have been originally painted in glaring colours: it has been difficult for those who had internalised the classic image to accept the crumbling of their own romantic and mythical ideal. The same has applied to many ideas that we have had of Roman law into which illusions and ideals of each period have been loaded while the legal-historic accuracy has been given a minor role.

Tuori has argued that Roman law has always been purposefully interpreted from the viewpoint of present needs.[9] In short, accuracy is good but not always plausible as an aim. Occasionally it is difficult to perceive where we are and where we will go, as Otto Kahn-Freund (1900–79) pointed out: 'Perhaps we should not overestimate the problems of today which may not have been those of yesterday and in a kaleidoscopic world are not likely to be those of tomorrow'.[10] Despite being conservative as to its nature, law is in constantly and slowly transforming.

III. COMPARISON AS THINKING OUTSIDE THE BOX

Apart from the fact that comparative law deals with the acquisition of knowledge for different purposes, it is characterised in a way described above by genuine internationalisation and the attempt to become detached from the epistemic limitations set by one's own legal system. Often, though not always, it is also a question of the *Universalist* attitude to law and legal research that is well described by Hessel E Yntema (1891–1966) in the late 1950s, who stated that 'legal science does not admit chauvinist isolation'.[11] This means that quite frequently comparatists consider that only such study, which is not limited to the law of only one system, may be considered as the scientific study of law. Notwithstanding, perhaps we should not have as orthodox a view as this on comparison because comparison can be used in many different ways, and they do not necessarily exclude one another. Also, it is not a question of competition because national legal study (legal doctrine) has its own natural position and function as well as legitimisation for existence.

It seems justifiable to argue that comparative law is fittingly described by its desire to detach itself from the mental straitjackets set by any given legal system.

---

[9] K Tuori, *Ancient Roman Lawyers and Modern Legal Ideals: Studies on the Impact of Contemporary Concerns in the Interpretation of Ancient Roman Legal History* (Frankfurt am Main, Vittorio Klostermann, 2007). Tuori highlights various implicit assumptions that have actually guided the so-called 'romanistic legal science'.

[10] O Kahn-Freund, *General Problems of Private International Law* (Leiden, Sijthoff & Noordhoff, 1980) 193.

[11] HE Yntema, 'Comparative Law and Humanism' (1958) 7 *Am J Comp L* 493, 498.

According to Yntema, aiming for high scholarly quality in itself was an action in opposition to legal chauvinism: he was well ahead of his time because only now in many traditional faculties of law has the genuine internationality of legal study been understood. But there is more to it. Some romantics who have been inspired by legal history have even longed for a return to the Continental European *ius commune* tradition.

Regardless of the fruits of the comparative approach, a practising national lawyer may be left wondering about the detachment from the knowledge of their national law. Here we find the heart of the matter. The attempt to break away is important if for no other reason than the fact that national legal systems were not born or have not grown in isolation. Legal institutions and schools of thought and doctrines as well as institutions have affected each other and continue to do so. The legal purity of the national law in connection with regulations, institutions and doctrines is, as it has often been, more a normative fiction than a fact. We have adopted from others a lot more than we can comprehend: many legal institutions are in constant circulation. We are simply not distinctly aware of the layers of loans, borrowings and copying that still exist. Systems are a patchwork of diffusion and interaction as well as of national ideas, ie most national systems are, as are States themselves, *cosmopolitan* as H Patrick Glenn (1940–2014) argued.[12] For Glenn, the idea of the 'Nation-State' was a failure and we are in need of a cosmopolitan theory of State.

> Legal history can present examples of such borrowing on a massive scale. In 1926, for example, Turkey borrowed quite consciously from a foreign legal culture, ie Switzerland, whose Civil Code (*Zivilgesetzbuch*, 1907) it copied and put into force (*Türk Kanunu Medenisi*, revised edition 2002). On the one hand, it was a question of the authority that Swiss law, as a law of a technically high standard, had at that time in Turkey. On the other hand, it was also a question of need because Turkey was being modernised and needed to import such legal provisions as it did not have the professional capacity to create those that would fit the State, which had just broken away from the traditions of the Ottoman Empire and was aiming at drastic and large-scale modernisation. The Swiss codification was suitable for reception because it contained fewer provisions and the contents of provisions were scantier than in many other codifications. We may also mention other examples such as Bolivia (1830), the Republic of Haiti (1852) and the Dominican Republic (1854), all of which adopted the 1804 *code civil* of France either in full or almost in full.
>
> Adoption of foreign law usually takes place on a smaller scale, as for example the adoption of American institutions and legal-cultural practices. Examples that can be mentioned are class actions or plaintiffs' claims for compensation that have risen sky-high, and which reflect American legal ideas rather than Continental European ones. At present, the plea bargain method is about to start spreading. The EU has brought about a lot of legal borrowing and diffusion of legal ideas. And conformity and points of contact have also been increased by the European Convention on

---

[12] See HP Glenn, *Cosmopolitan State* (Oxford, Oxford University Press, 2013).

Human Rights and the practice of the European Court of Human Rights. As a result, for example, in European law there are more and more such elements whose thorough understanding requires getting acquainted with their non-national origins and basic ideas.

Why is the crossing of borders the lifeline of comparative law? What is so special about it? This doubt is uttered by legions of national doctrinal scholars. And yes, it deserves to be answered. Let us take an example of an imaginary State that had been surrounded by impervious walls for several centuries. How could any 'jurist' or 'legal scholar' try to talk about their society or even describe it to any outsider? What could they compare their society to, or how could they know what they should say about their society? Would they be capable of explaining what is considered law in their society, what the legal system or form of government of the isolated State consists of or what law is like in their society etc?

The description that the abovementioned person would offer of their own society and legal system would be incomprehensible for other people, because owing to the isolation it would be impossible to describe even simple things; is it possibly a democracy or perhaps a monarchy, is the court system divided into general courts and administrative courts, is penal law severe or lenient etc? (The portrayal could naturally be treated as a detailed description, but it would be essentially slower and also difficult to understand since there would be no comparison standards.) To make it concrete: Islamic law does differ from Western law, but a Muslim jurist is able to describe their law to an American jurist, and vice versa. To think otherwise would mean underestimating the basic human ability to think and learn. Certain commensurability is usually a fact: research interest is focused on an abstractive normative set of rules that is based on certain sources. Of course the content of the rules may differ, the style of normativity may differ, the sources may be different, but we are still dealing with human societies and organised large-scale normativities we normally label as a 'legal system'. That is to say, comparative law is a refined form of human ability and the desire to make sense of things by comparing them.

A. Away from Ethnocentrism

In greatly simplified terms, the realisation and comprehension of human matters, even the simple ones, presumes the existence of general concepts that are based on comparison. The fact that we describe, say, German law by saying that it is trying to be systematic and logical and call English common law casuistic and unsystematic presumes the existence of certain comparative background criteria. For example, the difficulty of describing the English *trust* (as a property arrangement where there is double-ownership between the owner and the beneficiary) is mainly due to the fact that there is no similar legal institution in Continental Europe. The functions that are taken care of by trust in England are on the Continent dealt with by other legal measures. Yet, there is comparability and epistemic and even practical commensurability as shown by the fact that the Japanese system (essentially a civil law system) received trust successfully already in the early twentieth century.[13]

If a researcher is deprived of the opportunity to extend their study beyond the boundaries of their own community, they are in danger of staying cognitively blind: a Scandinavian jurist who does not perceive their own law as a sibling of other Nordic systems will not understand the legal-cultural position of their own law and a New Zealand lawyer not perceiving their own law as a form of common law is virtually one-eyed. Comparative law attempts to avoid such blindness and therefore consciously aims at relying on a framework that is comparative.

We can see here more profound dimensions, too. To summarise what was said earlier in the chapter: comparison is a natural activity of the human mind. Understanding an individual fact presumes an understanding of the facts that are related to the matter. Because it is easier for us to grasp our research topics in a context, a research approach that crosses the borders of national legal systems is needed if we want to maintain that we really know something about law. Comparison is the engine of knowledge without which we cannot obtain knowledge that actually surpasses that of our limited cultural sphere.

In the end, the attempt to compare law is also a question of the *rejection of ethnocentrism*, or the pushing away of the implicit thought pattern that national solutions are always superior or at least 'normal'. This does not necessarily mean deep commitment to universalism but rather commitment to the fact that in the world of law we can learn from others. On a very general level we can talk about the broadening of consciousness and the cultivation of the ability for legal thinking. Needless to say, these premises are not obvious everywhere in Western culture. For example, the isolationism that is again gaining ground in the US serves the rest of the world very poorly (which of course is the case with the US too). Brexit has caused similar isolationist effects and has complicated the European legal scene as the mixing of common law and civil law seems to have taken a big step backwards.

Comparative law is probably the most efficient way to get rid of the national mental straitjacket that restricts the acquisition of legal knowledge in a broad sense. This does not mean, however, the rejection of the national law's normative point of view. The internal legal point of view has, of course, immense practical legal value. Nevertheless, knowledge gathered as a result of comparison can also be of assistance when one's own legal system is being developed. Von Jhering, a famous German legal historian of the nineteenth century as well as an expert on universal jurisprudence, noted that 'only a fool will reject the bark of the cinchona because it did not grow up in his vegetable garden'.[14]

---

[13] See M Tamaruya, 'The Transformation of Japanese Trust Law and Practice' in YK Lieuw and M Harding (eds), *Asia-Pacific Trusts Law* (Oxford, Hart Publishing, 2021) 215.
[14] R von Jhering, *Geist des römischen Rechts*, vol 1 (Darmstadt, WBG, 1955) 8–9 [originally published in 1852].

However, it is clearly not advisable to borrow and use just anything. Comparison presumes certain basic caution because models copied from foreign legal systems can include endogenous problems that are not known in the receiving country, ie the fruit von Jhering was referring to can also contain harmful 'remnants of pesticides'. Ultimately this does not differ from enjoying the fruit of somebody else's garden: one has to taste and evaluate the edibility of different fruit, to savour the taste and to decide on how best to use them. One should also beware of mistaking ornamental plants for edible ones (see chapter 6, section III.A).

> Legal-cultural ways of thinking as well as the legal mentality have their impact. For instance, while the Supreme Court (ie court of cassation) in the Netherlands (Hoge Raad) often has the Supreme Court of Germany (Bundesgerichtshof) as the source of inspiration for its decisions, in the neighbouring country, Belgium, the court of cassation (Hof van Cassatie/Cour de cassation de Belgique) looks for its inspiration from the court of cassation in France (Cour de cassation). Hondius fittingly speaks about applicational development of law by means of 'looking over the border'.[15] Often it is a question of selective borrowings, which could also be called 'learning from and with the neighbour'. Furthermore, it should go without saying that all borrowings need to be tailored.

IV. BASIC KNOWLEDGE-INTERESTS

The starting point for comparison is quite clear: it is an attempt to acquire knowledge (independent of any specific legal systems) of law by means of comparing laws. Such an aim is very extensive and covers several different fundamental elements. The key point is easy to discern: it is important *to recognise the knowledge-interests* (German *Erkenntnisinteresse*, ie knowing-interests or epistemic interests) of the study, or the motivation for why comparison is carried out, as well as what kind of knowledge is looked for and what is the purpose of comparison. When the approach of the comparative study is chosen, orthodoxy in carrying out the ideas of a particular school of comparatists is not advisable. However, commitment to the purpose is crucial so as to not blindly follow a path advocated by any particular school of thought.

It is essential that the comparison carried out or just the study of foreign law genuinely serves the purpose of the study instead of just remaining self-sufficient decoration or a presentation of unconnected matters, ie ornamenting one's study with trivial foreign law accessories. If comparison does not contribute to carrying out the actual research assignment, it is worth considering whether comparison/study of the foreign law is at all worthwhile. Here, however, we must separate the fact that, for example, in the doctrinal study of law it is perfectly

---

[15] E Hondius, 'Rechtsvorming' (2006) 55 *Ars Aequi* 327. The subtitle of this article is 'een blijk over de grenzen', ie look over the border.

normal to refer to foreign law or non-national legal literature and to use it as a part of the argumentation in accordance with the ways allowed in the doctrine of the sources of law. However, in such cases it is a question of interpretation and systematisation or critique of one's own law, not of comparative legal study. The same difference applies also to private international law, the aims of which differ from comparative law which seeks to understand *and* explain.

We can apply a game metaphor: it is not sensible to referee a basketball match with the rules of football, even though they are both ball games. *Mutatis mutandis*: it is not necessary for jurists to commit themselves to the theories of comparative law, just as comparatists need not yield to the ideas that the national doctrinal study of law has about the way legal research should be carried out. On the other hand, it is not advisable for the doctrinal study of law and comparative law to drift so far apart that the fruitful interaction between them dies out. Both are established members of the family of legal disciplines. And, possibly, there is a certain special connection still to be seen between private international law and comparative law although their knowledge-interests clearly differ from one another: practical application versus understanding and explaining. Regardless, some overlap is bound to exist.

So, comparative law can be used for many different purposes; therefore it is not justified to define different interests in too limited or exhaustive a way. Albeit, it is possible to distinguish several basic types of comparative knowledge-interests. On the one hand, the comparatist's interest in knowledge acquisition can be integrative or contradictive. On the other hand, the comparatist's interest can be related to a special method that serves the comparatist's purpose and is used to carry out comparison. Comparative law (or merely the study of foreign law) can also have a significant role in legal education. In the following, five basic interests are listed:

Basic knowledge-interests

1. Integrative
2. Contradictive
3. Practical
4. Theoretical
5. Pedagogical

V. INTEGRATIVITY AND CONTRADICTIVITY

In *integrative interest* the comparatist concentrates on similarities between the subjects compared. This comparison interest can also be called the harmonisation interest of law or the unification interest of law. *Harmonisation* in its modern sense means the general attempt in legal policy to bring about as complete a harmonisation of legal systems or their parts as possible in such a way that the biggest deviations are eliminated and a minimum standard with which all parties must comply is created.

States carry out harmonisation by means of different international legal approaches, but extensive harmonisation of law has been practised within the European Union. It is a question of coordination of many branches of law and of bringing them closer so that major differences are eliminated from the systems (result: *identical* applicable rules). This can be done when minimum requirements or standards are first created by the help of comparative constructions.

Unification goes a step further; here, the target is not merely minimum standards that concern certain fields or the similarity of certain parts of the legal systems. Here, a more profound legal unification is aimed for (*same* applicable rules). In unification an attempt is made to replace two or more legal systems with a new system that would take the place of the previous ones. Integrative comparison can be used for both purposes. It is also important to realise that neither unification nor harmonisation is a legal choice (how to apply a rule or precedent) or a comparative choice of method but is dictated by political targets set. Comparatists whose background is in private international law tend to be in favour of unification for practical reasons, while modern comparatists are considerably more reserved on the topic and feel more sensitive towards legal-cultural differences. Especially critical and postmodern comparatists have underlined contradictive comparison and the existence of legal-cultural differences.

Contradictive research interest pays special attention to differences and emphasises the fundamental difference between systems. In research practices it is a far more rarely used comparative method than the integrative research interest. In general it comes into question when the systems compared are very different in their legal cultures, such as criminal law that is based on Shari'a and Western criminal law. Also, it is fair to say, the basic ideas of critical comparative law have a strong contradictive undertone. This undertone has been, by and large, an epistemic countermove against the earlier harmonisation-oriented practical comparative approaches. A key scholar in contradictive comparative law has been Legrand. He has consistently underlined the significance of differences in the comparative study of law, thus opposing adamantly the spirit of sameness and uniformisation.[16]

A. The Historical Dimension

Harmonisation is not historically merely a modern legal phenomenon, but instead it is known in legal history. It certainly did not begin as late as the European integration of the late twentieth century. The chain of events with legal-historic significance started in the thirteenth century with the importance

---

[16] See *Am J Comp L* (2017) 65 Special Issue (articles by P Legrand, J Gordley, JQ Whitman, RA Miller, S Munshi, and P Zumbansen).

of research and teaching in Roman law and the Romano-Germanic 'common law' (German *Gemeines Recht*, French *droit commun*, Spanish *derecho común*) that was born from it. In European legal history it is possible to differentiate the birth history of the integrative comparative interest from within the *ius commune* tradition – from the Middle Ages to the nineteenth century – that was born out of Roman and canon law.

It was as late as at the beginning of the nineteenth century when the era of massive national codifications finally brought an end to the soft Central European integration and started to stress the boundaries of national law. The birth of comparative law in the modern sense was accelerated as a countermove to the underlining of borders and national emphases. In the nineteenth century, private international law as a field of law was born out of the situation where national boundaries had become a problem in contracts and marriages that crossed borders between States and legal systems.

> In the Middle Ages it was typical in legal decision-making to cross national borders when the rule that would probably solve the case was looked for. It is important to notice that at that time jurists studied the legal source material and authorities in order to find from the common *ius commune* tradition a legal rule the same as in their own legal system, not in order to obtain from foreign law inspiration for their own decision-making. Needless to say, the modern choice of law questions and application of foreign law (ie conflict of laws) is far from the medieval inclusive tradition.
>
> The core of the *ius commune* tradition was reinterpreted in Roman civil law, which meant that comparison of laws that was applied to find *ius commune* was only governed by public law to a small extent. Although Roman civil law has had a great impact on the development and formulation of legal thinking, from the point of view of public law almost as central a position was filled by the French Revolution and the legislative development that has resulted in the birth of modern constitutional law and administrative law. The historical roots of private law go deeper than the roots of public law, but the growth of the significance of fundamental rights and human rights has evened out the differences between fields of law and added connections between them.[17]

When codifications multiplied and the trend for national legal thinking strengthened in the nineteenth century, the significance of integrative comparative law decreased considerably. *Contradictive* comparative study started to assume a more significant position. With the rise of legal positivism State sovereignty became the basis for legal thinking and international law. Comparative law began to turn into a specialised field whose knowledge-interest became more conscious of nationality. Legal borders were constructed and the study of law started to become increasingly national; instead of an inclusive approach the exclusive approach became the paradigm. Legal and epistemic obstacles were

---

[17] For the main features of *ius commune* and how it evolved into legal doctrine in thinking and writing, see F Wieacker, *A History of Private Law in Europe*, trans T Weir (Oxford, Oxford University Press, 1996). The original German version, *Privatrecht der Neuzeit*, was published in 1967.

erected alongside the birth of nation-States. Nation-States proliferated across the world from the beginning of the 1800s by replacing old empires and kingdoms and thus wiping away the relatively shared legal-cultural world of *ius commune*. State-entities understood the nation as a sovereign territorial unit with its own ethnic, cultural and legal contents. The so-called Westphalian order based on international law relies on the idea of State sovereignty.[18] This idea did not, however, apply to colonised areas that received *ius commune* as it was forced upon the colonies by the colonising powers.

So, legislative national needs in particular started to dominate in comparative study; foreign laws and legal institutions were investigated in order to find good examples of legal solutions and legal innovations acquired. The fundamental motif was very instrumental: there was a desire to copy (presumably) the best parts of foreign law in order to assimilate them into one's own law. This kind of engineering-type of comparative law is very clearly aware of the differences between systems and carries out instrumental comparison by bearing in mind the development of one's *own* law.

At the same time the colonised regions outside Europe were in many ways force-fed with the so-called civilised, or Western law. Law was sold, bought, exchanged and sometimes stolen: legal inventions have never known of copyright. Humans' sphere of law is permeated by stolen ideas and illicit loans – social innovations travel when people travel. However, they do not spread the same way epidemics do, because the needs and objectives of groups of people have an impact on the acquiring and borrowing of social innovations. Law travels but it does not seem to travel simply at its leisure as it is animated by some need.

Legal historians have described the nineteenth century as a period of great national codifications during which jurists turned their attention to the (internal) interpretation, systematisation and analysis of the codifications produced. At the level of legal practice, persons who had assimilated comparative legal knowledge started to turn into experts who were expected to have an answer to one question in particular, ie how to apply foreign law in cases that crossed the borders of national legal systems. In this kind of instrumentalist comparative law the emphasis was typically on finding differences instead of finding similarities.

It is easy to realise that this kind of comparison seems to fall quite naturally on private international law: basically there is no desire to compare and explain as such, but to determine the country whose legislation is applied to international legal relationships (what is the right legal forum, which State's law ought to be applied, what is the influence of the court decision of one State on another State, and so on). Relations between States were elementary and few in number

---

[18] D Croxton, 'The Peace of Westphalia and the Origins of Sovereignty' (1999) 21 *Int'l History R* 569.

compared to the world today although individuals were not much bothered by borders in those days either: business or love does not much care for distinctions between legal systems. Also, private international law, unlike comparative law, is *a field of law*. In the European Union Member States, private international law is essentially based on national law, which in fact is complemented by EU law (which is partly enforced without special national efforts to bring them into force). In short, private international law (or conflict of laws if you prefer) and comparative law should no longer be regarded as natural allies. Their fundamental interests of knowledge are different, and it goes without saying that comparative law is not a field of law but a legal discipline.[19]

B. Integration in Europe

The integration development in Europe has meant that the focus on European comparison is again moving towards integrative comparison, which means that it in a certain sense recalls a kind of new European *ius commune* system. Within the European Union the integrative comparative law interest is manifested in several ways. At its purest it appears in the introduction of the EU Charter of Fundamental Rights according to which the rights are protected in accordance with the competence, functions and the subsidiarity principle of the Union. These rights are said to be based explicitly on the *common constitutional traditions* of Member States and their international commitments, the European Convention for the Protection of Human Rights and Fundamental Freedoms, the Social Charters adopted by the Council of Europe and the case law of the Court of Justice of the European Union and the European Court of Human Rights. Here, the starting points are by no means confined to any one national system: constitutional traditions are conceived as commonly European.

In Europe the main question has long been legal harmonisation, which has been less demanding than unification. This is apparent in many central fields of law, such as contract law where the national contractual systems of the Member States are different in many ways. At the Union level some common regulations have been given for certain problematic cases. In practice, such harmonised regulations cover limited fields of contract law, the emphasis being on contracts in consumer law in particular. Brexit has brought complications to the idea of common European legal tradition as the UK is taking steps in other directions.

It is essential to notice that even in cases where harmonised regulations are applied, as a rule they offer the Member States an opportunity to apply other bodies of law, if they so wish. That is why the EU internal market does not have a standardised and comprehensive set of contract law norms that firms and consumers could apply in business that crosses the borders of Member States.

---

[19] J Husa, *Interdisciplinary Comparative Law* (Cheltenham, Edward Elgar, 2022) 196–203.

80 Why Compare?

This is a big challenge for the internal market in the Union since the market economy of the Union, which is based on the free movement of goods, capital, services and people seems to require deep legal coherence. At present the European system is more like a *legal kaleidoscope* than a coherent system: there are significant similarities but also discrepancies as Brexit clearly demonstrates.

> Harmonisation based on legal cooperation has been carried out in the Nordic Countries, too. In fact the Nordic Countries have cooperated in legal matters for over 100 years. An important informative background factor has been the Nordic Lawyers' Meeting (organised for the first time in 1870, and at present organised every third year). One example of the influence of Nordic legislative initiatives is that at the beginning of the previous century laws that were very much alike were enacted in the fields of commercial law and contract law (the pieces of legislation are still partly in force). Harmonisation projects were carried out for most of the twentieth century. According to the Helsinki Treaty signed in 1962, Nordic cooperation would be continued in order to attain uniformity of regulation in the field of private law. In addition attempts have been made to establish uniform rules relating to criminal offences. Harmonisation has been aimed at in all fields of legislation where it has been considered appropriate. In practice the membership of three Nordic countries in the European Union has complicated the traditional Nordic cooperation in the field of legislation. In fact, the legal integration of Nordic countries has largely been replaced by European integration.

For all actors in Europe, loose harmonisation has not been a sufficient aim in legal policy. Apart from the supporters of deeper integration, in legal disciplines there have been fascinating and far-reaching schools of thought related to the topic. Paul Koschaker (1879–1951) suggested nostalgically that the development of European legal systems should be built on the foundation formed by classical Roman and later Germanic legal features.[20] In the background of the unified European law there are two trends of legal thinking that are influenced by both legal history and comparative law. Brexit and the EU's internal rule of law problems with some of its Member States have created doubts about the extent of deep-level legal harmonisation in Europe. To paraphrase Horace: you can drive legal cultural differences out with a pitchfork, but they will keep coming back.

C. New or Old *Ius Commune*?

European integration has stirred much interest in the ranks of legal historians as well. On the basis of legal-historical discussion it seems that we can talk about not only the *ius commune* tradition but also about the more recent 'common legal tradition'. It allows for considerable free choice concerning interpretation and for a kind of flexible pluralism in legal practice. More far-reaching is the

---

[20] Koschaker considered Roman law essential in the attempt to try to rebuild a common European legal culture; see P Koschaker, *Europa und das römische Recht* (Munich, Verlag Biederstein, 1947).

idea of a new *(novum) ius commune* law, which is to a large extent based on a novel legal-culturally common late-modern European law that is the result of the work of courts and different European institutions and legislative instruments (eg the EU Charter of Fundamental Rights). The Union's Constitution project that was rejected in the referendum in 2005 represented a line of strong general harmonisation and even federalism. In the 2020s, the approach has been more cautious; the financial crisis, Brexit, rule of law problems, the COVID-19 pandemic and the war in Ukraine have at least temporarily slowed down the legal-cultural impetus of integration. We have heard voices of protest and discontent from countries which used to be very active and open in their integration policies.

In practice, the big financial and institutional crises of the past few years have brought up many obstacles for schools of thought that promote profound legal-cultural unification. Although *ius commune* is an educational historical analogy, its real weight as a common legal-cultural basis for the modern Union is unavoidably vague. On the other hand, if *ius commune* is the source of legal-cultural inspiration, mainly in connection with legal methods and legal mentality, the situation is different. In the context of the contents of substantive law there is hardly any sense in going back to the old. Hesselink has asked: 'Why should the future resemble the past ... study of legal history is unlikely to provide current lawmakers with clear-cut answers'.[21] There may be a lesson for comparative law here. The usefulness of legal history cannot and should not be denied, but neither can it be regarded as the storage room of legal ideas where future decisions are stocked and from where whatever is needed can be fetched at will. Legal history should not be pruned down into empty concepts into which present-day jurists referring to the legal-cultural nostalgia inject a content that seems best suited for their legal taste.

In any case, in European legal harmonisation it has been essential to observe the active role of the courts. Integrated law is created by means of not only treaties and statutory law but also by interpretations made by the high courts. Particularly the Court of Justice of the European Union has in this respect had an important role in the application and creation of law.

In accordance with Article F(2) of the Maastricht Treaty of 1992 in regard to the European Union, the Union valued as general principles of Community law the fundamental rights in the form in which they were guaranteed in the European Convention on Human Rights and in the form in which they appeared in the shared constitutional traditions of Member States. The Court of Justice of the European Union created this principle in the *Stauder* case by talking about human and fundamental rights specifically as a part of common general

---

[21] M Hesselink, 'Non-Mandatory Rules in European Contract Law' (2005) 1 *Eur Rev Contract L* 43, 62 (he continues: 'And from which historical periods should we borrow our rules for the future?').

legal principles.[22] It was not only a question of substantive law, but the Court expressly brought up the need for comparative examination in the belief that it was

> impossible to consider one version of the text in isolation but requires that it be interpreted on the basis of both the real intention of its author and the aim he seeks to achieve, in the light in particular of the versions in all four languages.

In other words, versions in different languages had to be compared so that a kind of shared European core could be constructed comparatively.

According to an interpretation practice established in the EU Court, fundamental rights have for quite some time been considered to be a central part of such general supranational principles of law as to be guaranteed by the EU Court. The Union Charter that came into force later institutionalised the settled case law that the Court had already earlier assumed. Already, at a quite early stage, the EU Court had based its interpretation on stimuli that has been offered by international human rights and the common constitutional traditions of Member States. A classic example would be the case of *Internationale Handelsgesellschaft* in connection with which the EU Court ruled that fundamental basic rights are such principles of law that their observation had to be secured in the legal system of the EU.[23]

The court stated in the *Hauer* case that being aware of the fundamental rights of the Member States presumed that the viewpoints of the constitutions in States were studied.[24] The Court aimed at resorting to the comparative approach when interpretation was needed or gaps in law were found. National systems indicated, on the one hand, what kinds of interpretations are possible and, on the other hand, what kinds of problems could be related to different interpretations. For example, in the administrative process, in connection with principles related to administrative law, the praxis of the EU Court includes a landmark case, *Transocean Marine Paint Association* concerning the hearing procedure.[25] The other party to the case considered that its procedural right to be heard had been violated. The problem was that EU law did not contain a regulation on hearings: for the proposed decision the Advocate-General of the Court ran through the systems of Member States and constructed the proposal on the hearing principle prevailing in Member States (six out of the nine States that at that time were in the EU). Importantly, the proposed decision was produced by means of comparative deduction.

In the *Transocean* case EU law had detected a gap, but the situation had to be solved in a uniform way. Even though the Court in its decision did not

---

[22] 29/69 *Stauder v City of Ulm* [1969] ECR 419.
[23] Case 11/70 *Internationale Handelsgesellschaft mbH v Einfuhr und Vorratsstelle für Getreide und Futtermittel* [1970] ECR 1125.
[24] Case 44/79 *Hauer v Land Rheinland-Pfalz* [1979] ECR 3727.
[25] Case 17/74 *Transocean Marine Paint Association v Commission* [1974] ECR 1063.

refer to argumentation that was built on comparison performed by the Advocate-General, it can be considered that the judicial core of the case was partly built on the comparative study of the legal systems of Member States. The foundation of this comparative law-finding is basically the same today.

> The Court's interpretation ideology of legal policy presumes comparative law has not changed although there are already 24 official languages in the Union. For example, in the case *Commission v Finland* in 2007 the Court stated:
>
> Although the Finnish version of that provision contains no reference to the requirement that overheads be allocated 'pro rata' to the operation in question, that fact is of no consequence, since it follows from settled case-law that Community provisions must be interpreted and applied uniformly in the light of the versions existing in all the Community languages and since, in this case, the language versions other than the Finnish expressly refer to the requirement that overheads be allocated pro rata or proportionally to the operation in question.[26]
>
> In its preliminary ruling in *Nowaco* the Court stated that precedents for 'all the other language versions' are already established legal practice (*settled case law*).[27]
>
> All these judgments uphold the basic idea that brings up the need for comparing laws: 'impossible to consider one version of the text in isolation'.[28] In practice, this means that the national lawyer of a Member State must master other legal languages as well in order to be able to really grasp EU law. In this case comparative law, or comparing different text versions (practical comparative legal linguistics), is an auxiliary tool in the interpretation needed in finding a solution.

The legal dimensions of the European Union differ from public international law in many ways. From the point of view of comparative law, it probably is sensible to perceive that the Union law is a legal system of its own kind (Latin *sui generis*) and ultimately serves integrating Europe. To reach the aims of integration, Member States have voluntarily restricted the sovereign rights that they have according to the traditional international law. The treaties are laws that are directly applicable in Member States as are the legal rules (regulations) of the Union: they are not separately enforced in the Member States. This is where the secondary law of the Union differs from the norms of international law: regulations are immediately enforceable whereas directives leave certain national leeway as to how to achieve the aims set by the directive.

The special features of EU law are clearly demonstrated by, for example, the fact that the EU Court applies methods of interpretation that differ from national methods and approaches of legal interpretation. The fact that European judicial argumentation about law is teleological (ie goal-oriented) is demonstrated in particular in cases in which the Continental European civil law

---

[26] Case C-54/05 *Commission v Finland* [2007] ECR I-2473.
[27] Case C-353/04 *Nowaco Germany GmbH v Hauptzollamt Hamburg-Jonas* [2006] ECR I7357.
[28] See also eg Case 55/87 *Moksel Import und Export* (1988) ECR 3845 at [15]; Case 268/99 *Jany and Others* (2001) ECR I-8615 at [47] and Case 188/03 *Junk* (2005) ECR I-885 at [33].

and common law characteristics of both the source of law and the tradition of legal interpretation are often reflected. In addition to these, in recent years the use of argumentation that is based on human and fundamental rights has increased, although it has not altered the basic picture of legal culture in EU law: from the point of view of legal culture EU law is a kind of a 'megamix'. Accordingly, there has been a tendency in comparative law to perceive EU law as a mixed legal-cultural form, a hybrid between the legal cultures of the Member States and EU law and the European Convention on Human Rights. The role of goal-oriented comparative law has been even described as 'an essential tool' for the European Court of Justice.[29]

In addition, it is important to note that it is not simply a question of how courts or legislators operate. In the context of the European Union a kind of semi-official doctrinal harmonisation has been performed; the best example of this might be the Common Frame of Reference (CFR) that was formulated for contract law. It was formulated by the order of the Commission and by means of a European research community. It was preceded by a project called Principles of European Contract Law (PECL), which, however, remained less comprehensive in coverage. Preliminary projects were undertaken in the early-1980s under the leadership Lando (the so-called Lando Commission).[30] These ventures have brought the European researcher community to the forefront of non-national legal development, simultaneously increasing the importance of comparative law as a tool of integration.

> If and when CFR is not actually statutory law, then what is it? Roughly, it is a 'toolbox' whose aim is to help in the development of pan-European law. CFR is not legally binding, but national legislators can apply it when they implement directives nationally. According to the initiative of the Commission (2001), CFR had to contain clear definitions and common terminology for the fundamental concepts of contract law. The intention was to increase convergence between the contract law systems of different countries.
>
> In 2009, the international academic network of researchers revised and published the *Draft Common Frame of Reference*, which contained principles, definitions and model regulations for European private law. Definitions contain important legal terms, such as 'contract' and 'damage'. The Commission applies CFR as a tool: the intention was to create more coherence in European private law.[31]
>
> The proposition for a *Common European Sales Law* (CESL) proved the value of CFR as a construction method even after the proposal was withdrawn in December 2014.

---

[29] K Lenaerts and K Gutman, 'Comparative Law Method and the European Court of Justice' (2016) 64 *Am J Comp* L 841, 864.

[30] Underlying ideas on the basis of PECL, see O Lando, 'Principles of European Contract Law: An Alternative or a Precursor of European Legislation' (1992) 56 *Rabels Zeitschrift für ausländisches und internationales Privatrecht* 261.

[31] *Draft Common Frame of Reference* (DCFR). Full Edition. Principles, Definitions and Model Rules of European Private Law. This massive (6,563 pages) collection was edited by the Study Group on a European Civil Code, and Research Group on EC Private Law (Munich, Sellier, 2009).

The Common European Sales Law was meant to become an optional contractual system alongside the national systems of the Member States – it could have been applied if the parties agreed on it. In any case, CESL is a tool for legal harmonisation, which tries to diminish the difficulties caused by national legal systems, and which seeks to govern the buying and selling of goods in the European Union. A crucial idea of CESL was that businesses ought to identify the provisions of another Member State's applicable law and negotiate this law. This, in turn, would have remedied the problem of consumers facing fewer choices at higher prices in their domestic market. The CESL proposal offered traders the choice to sell their products to citizens in other Member States on the legal basis of a unified 'set of contract law rules, which stand as an alternative alongside the national contract law' (alternative legal regime). The proposal did not gain uniform support and it was withdrawn and a new modified proposal is to be expected. For example, the UK did not support it because it regarded it as too incomplete, unworkable in parts, uncertain as well as unclear.[32] Brexit seems to have undermined further the potential significance of the CESL project (and of course similar possible future projects).

In any case, the CFR is interesting but from the point of view of legal linguistics also quite prone to criticism: it was prepared and produced in English, but in fact its contents have in many places been reasoned in legal German and French, not in common law English. Furthermore, the result was not what was expected because the extensive publication only contained the general part of the project. This did not necessarily serve the objective, which was to simplify legislation that concerns contract law. Nevertheless, as a comparative law project CFR is somewhat unique; it succeeds in indicating what possibilities an integrative approach that crosses national borders could have. This is a kind of a proof of the boon and bane of comparative law.

D. The International Dimension and Knowledge-interest of Comparison

Sometimes legal scholars have difficulties telling international and comparative law apart even though there are obvious differences between them. Comparative law differs from public international law to a certain extent, in the same way as it differs from private international law. In spite of the differences, comparative law can be a kind of medium or help-tool for the international fields of law that are normatively oriented. For example, comparative law can assist international law institutions, such as the United Nations, by analysing obligations under international law in the systems of different States. Comparative law is also often in instrumental use, when international treaties are being drafted. By means of this, common standards and practices can be located. Also other points of contact between comparative law and international law that are even clearer exist.

---

[32] See eg G Dannemann and S Vogenauer (eds), *The Common European Sales Law in Context: Interactions with English and German Law* (Oxford, Oxford University Press, 2013).

Within public international law, the integrative interest is familiar from the Statute of the Court which governs the operation of the International Court of Justice, which is an organ of the United Nations. According to Article 9, the members of the Court have to represent 'the principle legal systems of the world'. In Article 38(1) the fundamental rule specifies the legal sources, which the Court must apply when deciding disputes submitted to it. The first source mentioned is international conventions (subarticle (a)) and international custom, as evidence of a general practice accepted as law (subarticle (b)). Besides international conventions and custom, in Article 38(1) subarticle (c) 'the general principles of law recognized by civilised nations' are mentioned as sources of law.

International Court of Justice: Statute of the Court Article 38(1)

1. The court, whose function is to decide in accordance with international law such disputes, as are submitted to it, shall apply:

    (a) International conventions, whether general or particular;
    (b) International custom, as evidence of a general practice accepted as law;
    (c) The general principles of law recognized by civilized nations.

In addition to conventions, the article distinguishes customary law and principles of law. The concept 'civilised nation' that reflects the aura of the so-called new imperialism (1870–1914) has undoubtedly lost its earlier significance. Nevertheless, when no solution to international legal dilemmas is found from the texts of agreements or customary international law, it is possible to look for the solution in the national principles of law, which nations generally acknowledge in their own legal systems. Nowadays the expression 'international law, as recognised by the principal legal systems of the world' is used instead of referring to the English expression 'civilised nations' or the corresponding French expression '*nations civilisées*', which are not only legal but also value statements.

The international principles of law to which the article refers are part of national legal systems, and therefore finding such principles presumes comparative examination of the existing legal systems. Up till now the judges and jurists have been said to be mostly guessing what these principles might be. Integrative comparative law would be needed in examining the content of the principles to which the article is referring. Often the case has been that an international judge or arbitrator has settled for the principle of law taken from their own legal system without checking if the same principle is recognised in other legal systems. The principles provided by the article have so far remained open to interpretation and the use of comparison has remained unsystematic.

General principles of law complete the entirety of international law formed by contracts and customary law. They offer a possibility to deal with such subject areas of international importance that have not yet been thoroughly regulated by the norms of customary law or international agreements. Principles that are included in the national legislation of all or most States can be considered generally recognised legal principles; in other words, knowledge acquisition of some sort by comparison of laws is inevitably needed. On what other grounds could any legal principle be claimed to be common to all if not on grounds of some kind of comparison? It is, therefore, possible to conceive instrumentalist comparative law as an attempt to find general international law principles.[33]

In public international law, general legal principles referred to in the article have been of importance when problems with the relation of international organisations with regard to their own employees have arisen. For example, good faith (Latin *bona fides*) and hearing both of the parties (Latin *audiatur altera pars*), which was the issue in the abovementioned *Transocean* case, have been among the principles applied.

To genuinely understand customary international law, one has to get acquainted with practices applied by States; then it is possible to give an answer to the question: when can a custom be considered binding international law or when is a custom 'a constant and uniform usage'? Only when States act in a particular case recurrently in a particular way, which is considered binding also in international law, is it a question of customary international law with clear normative significance. On the other hand, it has to be noted that when a particular practice is considered part of customary law, every State is not invariably required to follow the practice. Albeit, general acceptance of a practice is sufficient if behaviour deviating from the practice is considered to be against usual practice (Latin *opinio iuris*).

> It has to be also noted that if departing from the practice is frequent and on a large scale, the case might well be that a new practice is being formed. The new practice can then gradually replace the old practice as part of customary international law. An example of a practice that is so far debatable but which may still become accepted is so-called *peace enforcement*. In practice, the UN has given its forces more extensive authorisation than is used in peacekeeping in a situation where peace has not yet been restored. Grounds for extended application of military force have been found from the provisions of the Charter of the United Nations.

Perhaps the best-known example of customary international law is humanitarian law. International humanitarian law (or laws of war) refers to law with which an attempt is made to ease the effect of armed conflicts. The purpose is to regulate the methods and means of warfare. In defining these norms, court judgments and writings of leading experts are used as subsidiary sources of law.

In the last few centuries there have also been successful attempts to codify customary international law into international agreements. In this way disputes on the contents of customary law are alleviated and States perhaps become more willing to involve provisions that they have themselves been explicitly approving. Distinctions are difficult to draw when it comes to customary international law.

---

[33] J Ellis, 'General Principles and Comparative Law' (2011) 22 *Eur J Int'l L* 949.

88 *Why Compare?*

Sometimes the issues of the tradition and principles of international law can become intertwined.

> In the by now classic ICJ case on *Fisheries*, Norway tried by means of a law to draw its limit of territorial waters in a way that the UK considered to be a violation of international law; it exceeded the limit of three nautical miles, which the UK considered to be the limit in international law.[34] However, there was no certainty about the validity of the three nautical mile norm, and Norway argued for special protection of the coastal fjord region. The ICJ found that the Norwegian law on the matter was not contrary to international law, although it violated the practice of international law (the ICJ was sceptical about the source of law value of the custom), because there were in the Norwegian solution – in any event – special grounds that were considered reasonable (principle of equity).

In other words, comparison of laws is a useful method if we want to find out generally what the concepts and institutions of customary international law are made of. In both cases mentioned, comparison starts with the assumption according to which there are included in the written law or legal practice of different countries more general supranational principles of law, which it is possible to utilise when looking for the contents of international law. For example, analogies from the national system to the international can be used in interpretation. However, when principles found from national legal systems are applied in international law, the filling of gaps in law has to be performed with a certain caution, and the aim must be that the national solution fulfils the requirements of international law. So-called comparative international law is a new scholarly movement that seeks to tackle these issues by fusing 'international law substance with comparative law methodologies'.[35]

> In this connection we can mention also the WTO, the World Trade Organisation, whose objectives include solving disputes in the field of international trade. The WTO attempts to solve disputes in international trade relations on the basis of a special conciliation procedure. The WTO has developed a common legal basis for solving disputes because the solutions made by the WTO leave considerable scope for interpretation. It is a question of a novel *lex mercatoria* or customary commercial law that crosses borders and includes, for example, international arbitration agreements and the practices of liability distribution that are in fact observed in international contractual situations. It should, however, be kept in mind that *lex mercatoria* is a contested notion and it has faced a lot of criticism.[36] When judging questions concerning proportionality, necessity and balancing comparative law may be a helpful tool because these legal terms, which are crucial in the WTO system, may have

---

[34] *Fisheries Jurisdiction (United Kingdom v Norway)*, Judgment (18 December 1951) ICJ Reports 1951, 116.
[35] A Roberts, 'Comparative International Law' (2011) 60 *ICLQ* 57, 73.
[36] G Cuniberti, 'Three Theories of Lex Mercatoria' (2014) 52 *Columbia J Trans L* 369.

different meanings in different systems even though they are apparently (linguistically) identical. Comparisons are helpful for structuring and rationalising the process of interpretation of WTO rules. Moreover, sometimes the rules and principles have been borrowed and distilled from national legal systems.[37]

The basis of the acceptance theory, ie *opinio iuris* (the sense of legal obligation, Latin *opinio juris sive necessitates*, ie 'an opinion of law/necessity'), on the *iuris* that the practice that is generally accepted can become a binding international law is probably not so weak a criterion as it might at first seem. It simply requires sufficiently wide acceptance among States, in which case it can turn into customary international law. Hence, it also binds the States which themselves have not accepted the custom. The most important function of *opinio iuris* could be that it prevents practices that are generally unacceptable from turning into customary international law. From the point of comparison, essential here is the fact that the behaviour of different States in the matter in question has to be comparatively studied before it is possible to claim that a particular custom is generally accepted.

The argument that a practice is sufficiently widespread and strong is, unavoidably in the end, based on comparative study. And even then it is not an evident thing that *opinio iuris* exists: for example in the *North Sea Continental Shelf Cases*, the ICJ held that States' 'frequent or habitual performance of certain actions does not, by itself, establish opinio iuris'.[38]

We can detect similar dimensions in the sphere of Islamic law where comparative law also has practical legal effects and functions. The significance of comparative law is due to the supranational nature of Islamic legal culture and the fact that enactment and application of modern law has to be coordinated with Islamic law. It is essential to compare modern law and Shari'a law (in Arabic 'the path to water') in order to be sure of their compatibility. It is a question of making interpretative constructions in which practices of not only the schools of Islamic law but also different States that belong to the sphere of Islamic culture are viewed. In practice, the importance of comparison is also underlined by the fact that fields regulated by modern law are considerably more extensive than those of Islamic law, where the scope of regulation that Islamic law covers directly is mainly limited to questions of family law and certain parts of criminal law. It is rather a question of harmonisation related to the way of thinking and basic ideas of Shari'a. As Islamic law has become the subject of comparative law research, methods of comparative law have been discussed, as Islamic law is both non-State law and religious law.[39]

---

[37] See eg D Palmeter, 'The WTO as a Legal System' (2000) 24 *Fordham Int'l L J* 444.
[38] *Germany v Denmark and the Netherlands*, Judgment (20 February 1969) ICJ Reports 1969, 3.
[39] H Harasani, 'Islamic Law as a Comparable Model in Comparative Legal Research' (2014) 3 *Global J Comp L* 186.

E. Other Dimensions

Above, particular attention has been paid to European law and public international law. For a long time there have been actors other than the European ones, such as, for example, the abovementioned WTO. In this connection we can mention the International Institute for Unification of Private Law (Unidroit), which is important from the point of view of comparative law and is an independent intergovernmental organisation. Its aim is to investigate the needs and methods with which it is possible to modernise, standardise and coordinate private law, especially international commercial law. Unidroit was founded in 1926 and initially operated as an auxiliary organ of the League of Nations. In 1940, it restarted its operation. The membership was limited to States, the number of which is at present 63.[40] Unidroit publishes *Uniform Law Review*, which is its bilingual (English, French) flagship publication.

The Member States of Unidroit are from five continents and represent different legal, economic and political systems as well as different cultural backgrounds. Unidroit has developed international commercial contracts principles which are model rules concerning the sale of goods and the offer of services. With these instruments standards have been created which legislators in different parts of the world have used as models for their own regulations. In addition, model rules have been made available for parties to different types of commercial contract, when they have not been able to name the model rules as the law that is directly applicable to a particular clause of their contract. In such cases reference to Unidroit standards has been included in the contracts; it is a question of a kind of complementing regulation. Unidroit represents soft international legal harmonisation, a kind of new *lex mercatoria*.

VI. PRACTICAL v THEORETICAL APPROACH

In many academic disciplines the practical and theoretical are rather sharply distinguished from one another. In comparative law, however, sharp demarcation does not seem to stand on firm ground. Occasionally, the outcomes of academic comparative law can as such be used to serve practical purposes. In turn, sometimes academic research can benefit from information produced for practical purposes. This means that these two basic comparative interests cannot be completely separated from one another. Yet, we can say that the purpose in the practical study approach is comparison that directly serves legal policy and the drafting of statutory law or judicial decision-making. In it, an attempt is made by means of comparing legislation or case law to create a sufficient knowledge

---

[40] www.unidroit.org/about-unidroit/overview/.

base for a new government bill, legislative amendment or inspiration for solving a problematic legal issue.

A. Practicality

Practicality refers to something which is governed by practice rather than theory. This feature has normally been a part of the comparative law approach: comparing has been concerned with something deemed as practically useful. Comparison may be part of legal problem-solving 'as a tool of construction' by means of which it is possible to attempt to fill gaps in the law/legal system. This kind of problem-based comparison is not necessarily limited only to a certain legal culture, although the best-known example is from common law.

> The example to which modern day comparative law literature often refers is the famous decision in *White v Jones* by the House of Lords. In that case arguments formed by means of comparative law were used in the construction of the decision. Lord Goff remarked on the matter as follows: 'the question is one which has been much discussed, not only in this country and other common law countries, but also in some civil law countries, notably in Germany'.[41]
>
> In the UK, reference to foreign law is not often direct; instead, foreign law is utilised by means of the literature on comparative law, as for example in *McFarlane v Tayside Health Board*, where the House of Lords referred to Continental European precedents, the *ius commune casebook* (*Casebook on Tort Law*) and other comparative literature.[42] So, common law seems to be capable – independent of the way of reference – of making use of the experiences in other legal systems. The basic idea appears in *R v Kingston* where Lord Mustill stated: 'In the absence of guidance from English authorities it is useful to inquire how other common law jurisdictions have addressed the same problem'.[43] This way of thinking recognises the legal-cultural similarity of common law systems, although of course there are differences between different countries.

However, attitudes in the common law world vary. In the judicial culture of the US the attitude to the use of comparative arguments has generally been quite negative, because the mentality in their legal culture is extremely nationalist. In the words of Antonin Scalia (1936–2016), who was a prestigious conservative judge in the Supreme Court of the United States:

> We judges of the American democracies are servants of our peoples, sworn to apply (…) the laws that those peoples deem appropriate. We are not some international priesthood empowered to impose upon our free and independent citizens supra-national values that contradict their own.[44]

---

[41] [1995] 2 AC 207.
[42] [2000] 2 AC 59.
[43] [1995] 2 AC 355.
[44] A Scalia, 'Commentary' (1995–96) 40 *St Louis Uni L J* 1119, 1122 (speaking extra-judicially).

For a comparatist, it is curious how Scalia automatically assumes the special nature of American legal culture because 'the values of others' are not like 'their own values'. (Drawing a conclusion like that would require comparison, which Scalia is lacking – in other words, he simply assumes that there are differences.)

Scalia undoubtedly supported a nationalistic legal idea, according to which judges shall be faithfully and strictly bound to the law that is in force in their State – ultimately the Federal Constitution. According to him, this means that courts in their decision-making are not allowed to refer to nor even to look for support or inspiration in arguments of comparative law. But, it is not only about Scalia. It is more extensively a question of the idea of dissimilarity of American culture and of emphasising the thesis of individuality in the field of legal culture. It is fair to note that this thesis is controversial even in American legal culture: not all American jurists agree even though during the past decade there have been growing tendencies to become more isolationist.

> On the other hand, it can be stated that attitudes in the US have not always been this reluctant. In the renowned *Miranda* decision by the US Supreme Court on the rights of the arrested person, the famous Chief Justice Warren stated: 'The law of the foreign countries described by the Court also reflects a more moderate conception of the rights of the accused as against those of society when other data are considered'. The law of foreign countries constituted a comparative supporting argument in the forming of the preliminary ruling. By means of comparison (looking at foreign systems) the underlining principles of the US' own law were specified and supported, ie the Court did not use foreign law as a source of law but rather as a source of judicial inspiration.[45]

In practical comparison the aim is to instrumentally benefit from foreign rules, legal principles or established legal practices either as such or when applicable as in the abovementioned cases of the International Court of Justice and the EU Court. Also the European Court of Human Rights has to be mentioned in this connection because it has often used comparative arguments in its decision-making even though its manner to utilise comparative law leaves room for scholarly critique.[46] The fundamental starting point is obvious: the reason for the practice of practical comparative law is, first, in obtaining practical aims, ie in problem-solving. The need for practical comparative law is easy to justify by the division of labour and the role that has been given to the doctrinal study of law in this division, in the case of courts through the assumption of justified legal reasoning, and in legislation by the attempt to create better regulation. Furthermore, private international law is a good example of practically oriented comparison that has a practical legal interest in problem-solving.

Now, practical comparative law settles for a lower methodological and theoretical standard than the more demanding comparative law research, which

---

[45] *Miranda v Arizona* 384 U.S. 436 (1966).
[46] See eg J Husa, 'Judicial Impartiality, Decorative Comparative Law, and the Human Rights Court' (2020) 27 *Maastricht J Eur & Comp L* 387.

seeks not only to understand but also to explain. In practical comparative law the aim is not to study foreign law at the level of legal culture, but to get acquainted with the legal texts of foreign countries and the surface of their legal system. And the idea of private international law about 'authentic interpretation' of foreign law remains a dream in most cases. On the other hand, practical comparative law can also have a connection with the doctrinal study of law, in which case the aim is to solve common problems with interpretation related to the application of domestic law on the basis of foreign examples. In such cases, however, direct argumentation concerning the content of domestic law cannot in most cases be done; instead, the comparative observations are more like additional or persuasive argumentation.

Practical comparative interest is often characterised by a close connection with immediate political objectives behind legislation. In legal history one of the best-known examples is the Napoleonic *Code civil*. In the nineteenth century, it became a kind of superbly popular legal export item. The *Code civil* was adopted in several countries, not only in Europe but also in South America. It is worth noting, however, that this codification was by no means a purely French innovation. It is partially based on the older European legal tradition, ie *ius commune* whose roots again are found in the Roman law of late-Antiquity and the French regionally differentiated customary law (French *pays de coutume*) from the end of the eighteenth century.

> From the history of constitutional law we can present as an example of practical comparison the Japanese *Meiji* Constitution of 1889, which was directly copied from the Constitution of Prussia. Another example is the Constitution of Russia of 1993 into which the Constitutional Court system was adopted as an institution – with some modifications – from the German 1949 Constitution (*Grundgesetz*). The Swedish *Ombudsman* institution has been borrowed by dozens of systems in different modified versions of the original.

For example, in the guide for drafting government bills in Finland (HELO, 2019) which is widely used in Finnish law drafting, the starting point is that there should be sufficient information on 'foreign legislation related to the matter' in the proposal.[47] In the practical survey, foreign law should also be clarified so that corresponding projects, either already in force or in preparation, particularly in the Nordic countries and the Member States of the European Union, are presented. Comparison has to be followed up if the government proposal contains solutions that have been influenced by foreign models.

According to the HELO Instructions:

> the Bill should contain information on foreign legislation to the same point, as well as pending legislative projects in other countries ... the purpose of this information

---

[47] Older version available also in English: *Bill Drafting Instructions* (Helsinki, Ministry of Justice, 2006).

is to provide the reader with an outlook to various legislative solutions to the same problem, a mention should be made of whether the foreign examples have had an effect on the solution reached in Finland.[48]

At its best this kind of comparison is competent *Auslandsrechtskunde*, at its worst it is a superficial description on the basis of the scarce English language material that is easily found on the Internet and which is sometimes of dubious quality. Often the fault is not with law-drafting personnel performing the background study but is due to political urgency and scanty resources. Political need dictates the schedule and resources, hence comparison tends to remain superficial or decorative.

The connection between comparative law and practical aims and goals is explained by comparative law's capacity to offer for solution possibilities that exceed the horizon of experience that there is in a single legal system. For example, in the case of courts, at its simplest the whole system of jurisdiction is based on the principle that courts know the law (Latin *iura novit curia*). So, by means of comparative law it is possible to enrich and extend the storage of legal ideas and innovations that is available for those who develop and maintain the legal system. In this respect comparison, that is a result of a practical comparison, also enables an efficient search of 'better' or at least different solutions. Another common reason is the need to fill the gaps. In essence, there are two ways to use comparative law by the courts: it may provide support (rule or outcome) or it may provide a normative model.[49]

B. Theoreticalness

Usually, *theoretical* refers to things which relate to general principles or ideas rather than the practical use of those principles or ideas. However, in comparative law theoretical does not mean the same as hypothetical, ie something which exists only in theory. Yet, the actual state and role of scholarly comparative law in the development, assistance and criticism of legislation, normative customs or supranational court decisions has remained rather modest. This, however, is not necessarily due to the fact that there would not be the desire or ability to engage in comparative research. Mostly it is a question of the timetables being too tight and the personnel resources available in law-drafting too small. The same problems of course apply to drafting the legislation in general, not only to comparison. As to courts, urgency and the piling up of cases are the problems preventing time-consuming comparative research, which aims for deep-level understanding and explanations.

---

[48] ibid 14.
[49] M Andenas and D Fairgrieve, 'Courts and Comparative Law' in M Andenas and D Fairgrieve (eds), *Courts and Comparative Law* (Oxford, Oxford University Press, 2014) 3.

The theoretical research implies that research serves theoretical interests and that the amount of legal knowledge is increased. The theoretical approach attempts not only to search and locate differences and similarities in the positive law, cases or doctrines studied, but also to explain their reasons. In addition to how, also *why* is a question that needs an answer. Here a big step is beyond the knowledge-interest of the private international law: to solve a problem by applying law is different from understanding and explaining why there is a problem in the first place.

> It is a question of the researcher studying foreign legal order to examine questions that are basically theoretical or to systemise law structurally, its concepts and models in the background. An example of the latter is the work by Suksi on the forms and practices of the referendum.[50] There a referendum typology was constructed, which meant that this constitutional institution was theoretically typified into idealised types. By means of the typology that was created, the study material was analysed for a more profound further study. In the voluminous book about the Europeanisation of Nordic property law written by Sandstedt, two different legal-cultural approaches to ownership were studied: the substantial way to emphasise ownership as a whole and the functionalist way to break ownership into different functional relations.[51] Sandstedt looks at and compares the Nordic approach with the Continental approach. The conclusions made by Sandstedt challenge the traditional Nordic understanding of property law in a way that is based on the settings and ideas of comparative law.

However, there are some genuine differences between interests. In short, theoretical comparative law cannot be immediately justified by practical reasons. The desire to understand and explain differs inevitably from the desire to solve legal problems. On the other hand, it is difficult to think of such a comparative law study that would not have some relevance from the point of view of legal practicalities. Perhaps some utterly postmodern legal-theoretical comparison can produce outcomes that are difficult to utilise in practice.

Although the theoretical approach clearly aims at increasing the amount of knowledge, it can also offer material for the improvement of the knowledge basis for comparison that is carried out for legislative or judicial interest. The theoretical approach is based on the idea according to which not even the national legal system is (as far as knowledge is concerned) an autonomous entity that is separate from other legal systems. Legal systems of other States may also be using legal approaches/socio-legal solutions, which are built around a bundle of legal thoughts that may be of the same type. In theoretical comparison, legal problem-solving of this kind can be theoretically examined, and hence, therefore, the content of the basic solutions in one's own legal system can be more clearly perceived. The foreign law acts in such cases as an intellectual mirror for one's own law or, as the German saying has it: 'im Fremden Spiegel sehen wir

---

[50] M Suksi, *Bringing in the People* (Dordrecht, Martinus Nijhoff, 1993).
[51] See J Sandstedt, *Sakrätten, Norden och europeiseringen – Nordisk funktionalism möter kontinental substantialism* (Stockholm, Jure Förlag, 2013).

das eigene Bild' (ie in a foreign mirror we see our own image). Globalisation of law has, nonetheless, changed the overall picture to an extent. Graziadei points out that comparative law may still have a role in the globalised world of law in clarifying how various legal regimes (local, national, regional, global) interact at different levels.[52]

As demonstrated above, it is obvious that it is not possible to fully succeed in keeping the practical and theoretical comparison interest apart. Theoretical comparative law can also use a normative approach, which is typical of a practical approach (eg a provision of public international law). In the same way integrative and contradictive comparison interests are inevitably approximate basic classifications that are partially overlapping. It is a question of the *basic orientation* in the research interest, ie what is the aim of comparison (why comparison is carried out at all). It is useful for the researcher to recognise their own basic orientation because it has an impact on the type of methodological choices that are sensible and justifiable to make.

VII. PEDAGOGICAL – COMPARISON IN TEACHING AND LEARNING LAW

Comparative law pedagogy refers to the art of teaching, ie it concerns the principles of teaching comparative law and foreign law. However, comparative law as such is also a method used in legal teaching. The pedagogical interest at the base of comparative law is related to acquiring a better understanding of one's own legal system and to the development of a critical approach to one's own law. Both these dimensions naturally reduce often implicit ethnocentric attitudes and facilitate border-crossing research. In a world that is more and more vehemently internationalising, such knowledge that contributes to the understanding of the views and legal concepts of others is required.

Basically, it is a question of an ability to understand foreign law and legal culture in the form it takes in the basic assumptions and understanding of others. It is a question of an ability to make conclusions that are at least reasonably correct in the sphere of foreign law, as well as legal thinking in general and in the legal language that is typical of a particular foreign legal culture. There is a distinct difference from private international law, where the aspiration for authentic interpretation does not assume a committed attempt to understand and explain the cultural social interaction between law (as a normative creature) and the human being.

The further apart the legal systems in question are in a legal-cultural sense, the more significant a position the knowledge of comparative law (or foreign law in general) assumes. This is illustrated, for example, by the collision of

---

[52] M Graziadei, 'What does Globalisation Mean for the Comparative Study of Law?' (2021) 16 *J Comp L* 511, 535.

Islamic and Western concepts of justice: discussion on mere principles is difficult enough because there are such significant differences in basic concepts and approaches to law. In such cases knowledge of the concepts and origins of Islamic law is cognitively and often also strategically vital for a Western lawyer. Discussion and making one's own points of view comprehensible become easier with contextual knowledge. Islamic legal culture is one of the major legal traditions of the world, and general knowledge about it cannot be anything but useful for a Western lawyer: merely the existence of already relatively numerous Muslim populations in the non-Muslim countries causes a need for knowledge. When the cultures of the people meet, then their legal cultures also meet. This meeting is not necessarily conflictual as to its nature. Islamic banking is only one example showing that reconciliation between legal cultures is not impossible.

> Islamic and Western law seem to be legal-culturally conflicting although in the reality of the world's law overlapping and hybridity is more likely. Sometimes hybridity can be seen in the positive law. For example, in the Ghanaian Constitution, Acts, decrees and corresponding norms that are on a lower level than Acts, the common law that was in force until 1992 and the customary law of Ghana are recognised as sources of law. Just as in the common law culture, the judgments passed in superior courts have a great significance as precedents. Customary law on the other hand refers to traditional law and Shari'a law, which are followed by ethnic groups in different regions. The judicial organisation of a Western style is complemented by institutions that are applying law and are considered to belong to the sphere of the customary law of Muslim judges and chieftains' councils. The whole entity represents clear intra-State legal pluralism based on statutory law, too. Moreover, it is not only about internal pluralism in Muslim countries but also about the migration of people and their ideas about law.

It is, for example, considerably easier for civil servants who become involved in European administrative law to operate successfully as part of a multicultural legal environment if their legal knowledge is not limited to their own legal system. The judge who is applying the marital right to property to a Muslim family benefits from knowledge of Islamic law: they understand argumentation that is based on Islamic law better and are at least to some degree capable of appreciating the significance of such arguments from the point of view of the person who presents them (this does not mean accepting those arguments or granting them a role as sources of law). Foreign legal cultures can be taken into consideration as evidence concerning the beliefs held by parties, even if they would not be given legal significance as a source of law.

In addition, the study of comparative law material (foreign rules, doctrines, cases, ideas etc) has a significant role in the modern jurist's ability to think. Getting acquainted with the law and different legal cultures of other countries improves the ability for nuanced legal thinking, and argumentation becomes more versatile when different points of view are taken into consideration. If students are offered the models of one country only, their knowledge capacity for versatile argumentation weakens. Comparative law opens up legal thinking but it certainly does not mean that foreign law would gain the position of source of law as such.

From the point of view of law, teaching comparative law may have a key role for the legal mind. An effective modern law curriculum suited for globalisation is one which can stimulate students to learn legal thinking, not just the legal rules of a country. Comparative law and/or foreign law and even an approximate knowledge of different foreign approaches to similar types of questions may be regarded as a valuable tool for the construction of *a pluralistic legal mind*, which is prepared to look over the borders of legal systems. Non-national laws, customs and legal doctrine are good material for learning for anyone who seeks to cultivate a pluralistic legal mind for the twenty-first century.[53]

Comparative law material and foreign language studies are of pedagogical importance. And it is noteworthy that a particularly profound study of foreign law is not needed here: if a student gets acquainted with the history as well as general grounds and typical features of, say, the common law by means of comparative law literature, it becomes easier to approach the law of England and Wales, Canada, New Zealand and the US as well as the law of all these countries that have been influenced by the common law for one reason or another. The significance of non-national legal general knowledge should not be belittled in the present-day world. The obvious fact that law and legal ideas travel when people travel should also be taken into account: the global world of law is also a world of migrating law. In this new world comparative law is 'central to understanding legal phenomena and ideas' as Twining says.[54]

> The objectives of pedagogical comparative interest are better realised if comparative law is not given a minor role or labelled as a curiosity in legal academia, but if it is instead included from the very beginning in the study of national and supranational law. This applies both to public and private law. There are strong grounds for this in the very nature of law, which has never stopped at national borders, or as Pihlajamäki argues: 'Of its basic nature, law is an international phenomenon, not national; and by political decisions it can be confined only to a certain extent'.[55] Legal norms and doctrines travel with the salesman just like technical inventions; it is almost impossible to stop them because a human being is instinctively interested in new things, and our capacity to adapt is considerable. Sceptics undoubtedly have a point when they doubt things like legal transplants' simplified assumptions of similarity or legal convergence of European law, and yet, the reality of human capability ought not to be denied: the legal-historical evidence is overwhelming. In short, law travels.

---

[53] J Smits, *The Mind and Method of the Legal Academic* (Cheltenham, Edward Elgar Publishing, 2012) 144.
[54] 'An Interview with William Twining' (2021) 16 *J Comp L* 445, 457.
[55] 'Oikeus on perusluonteeltaan kansainvälinen, ei kansallinen ilmiö, ja sitä voidaan kahlita poliittisin päätöksin vain tiettyyn rajaan asti', H Pihlajamäki, 'Vertaileva oikeushistoria muuttuvassa maailmassa' (2009) 38 *Oikeus* 420, 423.

It is, for example, considerably easier to understand basic institutional decisions of constitutional law if one is acquainted with a number of other basic models (British parliamentarianism, US presidentialism with its separation of powers, French semi-presidentialism etc). In the same way, several of the most central principles (eg the principle of constitutionalism and the idea of public administration laid down by law derived from that principle) are supranational by nature. Principles adopted in different countries can be used to facilitate interpretation of law and the theory of administrative law in other countries although the principles in question would not be exactly the same. And this does not concern only one field of law, but, for example, the Norwegian application of the principle of rule of law can be perceived with more insight if it is related to, for example, the German, Chinese or English version of the same legal basic idea: there are similarities *and* differences.

In the same way, for example, for the comprehension of contract law it is of great benefit if one recognises the difference in the concept of a contract between civil law and common law. There are differences in attitudes to the basic legal-cultural factors: why is bona fides important in Continental Europe but not so important on the other side of the Channel? Why is a literal interpretation of contracts in favour in the UK? Why are commercial practices of such a big significance for the British? And so on.

What is said above does not, however, mean that it would be possible to lump together, say, all the Member States of the European Union and to talk about a reasonably uniform European contract law on the level of legal maxims, for example. This is verified by a huge body of work that is based on comparative law and earlier operations of the Lando Commission and which has been published in three massive volumes, namely *The Commission on European Contract Law* and *Principles of European Contract Law I & II and III*.[56] Later developments led the CFR to prove that comparative law has the ability as a supranational constructive method to promote harmonisation. To what extent convergent legal texts can create coherent legal culture is quite another question; a question of politics rather than law. In any case, it is useful to grasp that projects like this are bound to contribute to learning new forms of legal thinking that are not otherwise available to the internal gaze of the national legal doctrine.

Importantly, the endeavour of studying law comparatively is an intellectual journey that is always about learning and choosing to be exposed to legal ideas that are essentially foreign. In this sense, comparative law as a form of legal research is a process of learning by doing.

---

[56] O Lando and H Beale (eds), *The Principles of European Contract Law, Parts I and II* (The Hague, Kluwer, 2000); and O Lando, A Prüm, E Clive and R Zimmerman (eds), *The Principles of European Contract Law, Part III* (The Hague, Kluwer, 2003).

6

Basic Strategies in Comparison

I. INTRODUCTION

COMPARATIVE LAW RESEARCH contains several phases, ie the comparative approach has to be conceived as a *process*. Comparative research is a chain of steps where the overall comprehension of the study topic is a gradual (hermeneutical) process. The comparative process can be conceived of as a series of operations, which are carried out by the comparatist and which in the end have a final outcome, ie a publication or a thesis. Understanding of the whole is based on understanding individual parts and how individual parts refer to the whole.

Usually, the scientific study process has a specific predetermined course where getting acquainted with the study subject proceeds via intermediate phases (data collection, description, analysis, conclusions etc) to reporting on the study in the form of a publication. In comparative law, however, study is hardly ever a one-way process that runs like a train. Occasionally there will be setbacks and the scholar has to backtrack and either reinterpret or dismiss the view they earlier assumed. In contrast, the application of foreign law in court is inevitably a more one-way process due to the internal normative viewpoint and timetables: courts are obliged to produce answers to legal problems put to them. Comparative law as a form of border-crossing legal research rests on different assumptions. Accordingly, engaging in comparative law teaches methodological humbleness – becoming disheartened is not an option and the energy caused by annoyance is not approved of and should instead be channelled into new attempts. The process of comparison tends to be circular as understanding foreign law takes place as a gradually evolving process where individual parts and the whole interact.

> By and large, comparative law research follows philosopher and great educational thinker John Dewey's (1859–1952) pedagogical basic idea, ie 'learning by doing'. This kind of pedagogy refers to an *experiential* way of learning. Learning involves learning through experience and reflection on comparison in which the learning process of the comparatist as an active individual is at the forefront. Experiential learning does not mean that the theory and methodology would be useless, but it does point out that the process of comparing laws is always also about learning-by-doing. A positive side-effect here is the demystification of the research process – comparative research is not a mysteriously cumbersome challenge which is necessarily confusing and intimidating. One of the underrated features of comparative approach is its

ability to promote not only quality of research but also to encourage positive attitudes towards research and experiential learning.[1]

It should also be observed that the phases in the research process are interactive. This means that the next phase of the process can have a specifying effect on the previous one or it can change it altogether. Comparative study is by nature continually moving. By reading and interpreting source material, acquiring additional information and comparing material from different sources we can make advances in charting the differences and similarities of the systems compared and in the attempt to give them rational explanations. This process also includes personal reflection of the comparative research steps taken by the comparatist themselves. Different phases alternate, and occasionally returning to the basic assumptions is needed. In this sense the work of the comparatist is rather similar to that of the doctrinal scholar even though the epistemic viewpoints on law are different. The philosopher would talk about a *hermeneutical circle* of comprehension and the pedagogue of a learning process, ie experiential comparative law learning.[2]

All study processes contain phases where selections, limitations and clarifications are needed for the process to go forward. The comparatist too has to make choices that determine how the research proceeds. One has to decide which legal systems (or other large-scale organised normativities) to compare and which elements are selected for comparison. What is the data like (extent/depth) and which factors influence its acquisition process? How is the material acquired? How good are the scholar's own language skills? Is field study needed or is it possible to manage the project by using only documented material that already exists? The choices made depend on the aims of comparison as well as on the comparatist's own knowledge-interests, ie there is no one-size-fits-all method. If one wants to study the customary law of an Indigenous people, the Internet naturally is not a sufficient source of knowledge. Or if one seeks to have knowledge about preparatory phases of statutory law in a ministry, then one does not interview Indigenous tribe elders. A more practical point is that the availability of sources – not only their comprehension – is also of significance in this respect as some materials may be inaccessible.

A. Method – Methodology

Learning is an important part of doing comparative law, but even learning has to start from somewhere. A lawyer, and not even a comparative lawyer, is

---

[1] Dewey's ideas on education are best presented in his book *Experience and Education* (New York, Macmillan, 1938) in which he explains his educational philosophy.
[2] For a more detailed discussion about how hermeneutical theory may provide useful principles for educational thinking, see S Gallagher, *Hermeneutics and Education* (New York, State University of New York Press, 1992).

never genuinely in a *tabula rasa* situation. Comparative law as an activity that is goal-oriented and that pursues new knowledge cannot start from a completely haphazard starting point but, depending on the study approach, methodological choices concerning the acquisition and use of material have to be made both before and during the study. There is a distinct difference here with regard to private international law in which the court is in a different situation, because procedural rules are domestic and are applied without choice as they are the legally binding valid legal rules of a country. Comparative law as a field of study is not bound by judicial chains.

In research, one of the fundamental characteristics is the systematic nature of approaches and the desirability for as high a degree of their justifiability as possible. It is essential that approaches that have been chosen can be rationally justified and explained to others. Also the comparatist needs a basic research strategy, which has been drafted in advance by taking into account the goals of comparison and the feasibility of the research results that are possible to obtain. Accordingly, the notion of method needs to be conceived in a flexible manner.

> Method can refer to a very specifically defined scientific study approach in which case *methodology* refers to a theory on such scientific methods. A method is in this respect a particular way in which a chain of study steps are taken in a predetermined way (Latin *modus operandi*). In natural sciences the exactness, the numerical accuracy and predictability of the phenomena are emphasised. In economics, modelling and statistical methods are heavily referred to. But, in legal study the concept of a method and methodology are essentially more extensive and far less exact as to their nature. Here, legal research does not differ from other cultural studies or humanities. Regardless, there are no principal obstacles to use empirical or quantitative methods as comparative law is open to many sorts of methodologies. To that end, it has been argued that comparative law could transform into a more quantitative field of study in general.[3]
>
> Grounds for this kind of broad conception of method and methodology are found in the word method itself because the word is actually formed from the Greek words *metá* (μετά) and *odós* (οδός), which mean following a path or a certain route. Combined these words form μέθοδος, ie a method. In comparative law a method denotes all practices and operations by means of which pieces of information describing phenomena are collected and the justifiable rules on the basis of which interpretations concerning the study topics are formed and argumentatively expressed. Owing to the pluralisticity of law, it is also a question of a plural matter, ie of method*s*. Plurality makes sense: many laws, many legal cultures and many legal languages must also mean many methods.

It is owing to legal culture, the ultimate study object of comparative law, that the method cannot be seen in a way that emphasises scientific exactness, which is the case in natural sciences and other disciplines that extensively use quantified

---

[3] H Spamann, 'Large-Sample Quantitative Research Designs for Comparative Law' (2009) 57 *Am J Comp L* 797.

methods. In comparative law, method really is a path to be followed. From there it follows that the methodological hints and guidelines presented in this very book should be taken as tips on how to walk the path. In the general methodology of comparative law it is not possible to present a clear-cut methodology with accurate demarcations for the simple reason that the study subjects and knowledge-interests of scholars differ from each other. Global diversity leads to diverse methodology.

> Örücü has fittingly stated on the methodology of comparative law: 'how this comparison is to be carried out has no standard answer'. Furthermore, according to her it is not even possible to speak in exact terms about the methodology of comparative law but of 'methods employed in comparative law research'.[4] Notwithstanding, in spite of the restrictions it is possible to present some sort of methodological guidelines. The possibilities, however, vary according to the different themes studied. According to Bradley, comparative family law would pass for social science: 'Comparative legal studies in this area involve applied political analysis: as such comparative family law qualifies as a social science'.[5] Moreover, fields like comparative sociology of law are virtually impossible to tell apart from sociology of law that draws from social sciences.[6]

Notwithstanding, in comparative law the usual starting point is clear. Comparative law can in principle use any method as long as it is possible to get answers to the questions that interest the comparatist. In general, the research process in comparative law is *hermeneutic*, ie understanding in nature, and it looks at different legal systems both from the outside and from the inside. The hermeneutic approach aims at understanding and interpreting the legally relevant behaviour of people, legal culture or legal text and explaining the meanings involved in legal language. This kind of approach is typical also in qualitative social science and the humanities. Notwithstanding, it is possible to use both empirical and quantitative approaches in comparative law research.

The fact that in comparative law the aim is to explain differences and similarities that have been found does not make it any less hermeneutic: it is a question of what kind of study process is used to explain legal culture and what factors are taken into account. Hermeneutic explanation becomes possible through comprehension since statistics do not replace the creative study process of the interpreter and the hermeneutical viewpoint of the comparatist. Statistical data are useful and in most cases underused in comparative law, but the comparatist must also remember that no statistics explain why the judge feels tied to the doctrine of the sources of law of their country or why certain legal institutions are so peculiar if looked at from the outside (eg common law trusts and equity).

---

[4] E Örücü, 'Methodology of Comparative Law' in J Smits (ed), *Elgar Encyclopedia of Comparative Law* (Cheltenham, Edward Elgar, 2006) 442, 446.
[5] D Bradley, 'Family Law' in *Elgar Encyclopedia*, 2nd edn (2012) (n 4), 314, 333.
[6] R Cotterrell, *Sociological Jurisprudence* (Abingdon, Routledge, 2018) 3.

104 Basic Strategies in Comparison

The basic strategies of comparative study can be divided by qualitative criteria into two parts. Strategy here simply means a plan by means of which aims set for comparison are sought. On the one hand, methodological choices of a technical nature have to be made while, on the other hand, strategic basic choices of a theoretical nature must be made. They do not follow each other in strict chronological order but more likely take turns during the study process. However, making this difference is not always unproblematic because the theoretical and technical aspects are often interrelated as has been made clear above. Moustaira puts this well:

> The methods used or those that ought to be used are complicated because they are activated in a variety of different levels (of research) and the higher the level, the harder it is to distinguish methodology from epistemology and theory.[7]

B. Methodological Choices of a Technical Nature

The technical nature of the methodological choices made in comparative law refers to their close connection with the study material (collected data). The study material can consist of official material (statutory law, precedents etc) only, of knowledge about the application practices and customary law or knowledge of the attitudes and beliefs of the professionals in law. In connection with strategic choices of a technical nature, the scholar has to decide on matters that to a great extent determine what the nature, coverage and method of acquisition of the material are like. And these are questions that should be pondered before the actual acquisition of material.

In this connection, at least five different technical basic choices can be told apart. During the study process these phases can alternate, and the comparatist can end up changing the basic research-design they had originally made. Naturally the list is not exhaustive, but it probably covers the most common basic methodological choices that sooner or later come up when comparing laws.

Technical-Methodological Alternatives

1. Micro/macro
2. Longitudinal/traverse
3. Multilateral/bilateral
4. Vertical/horizontal
5. Monocultural/multicultural

---

[7] 'Οι μέθοδοι που χρησιμοποιούνται ή που πρέπει να χρησιμοποιούνται να είναι περίπλοκες διότι ενεργοποιούνται σε μια ποικιλία διαφόρων επιπέδων και όσο υψηλότερο είναι το επίπεδο, τόσο πιο δύσκολο είναι το να διαχωρισθεί η μεθοδολογία από την επιστημολογία και τη θεωρία', E Moustaira, *Δικαιικές επιρροές στο πλαίσιο του Συγκριτικού Δικαίου* [*Legal Influences in the Framework of Comparative Law*] (Athens, Sakkoula, 2013) 27.

Importantly, the above alternatives are not methods per se but more like methodological choices that help the comparatist to grasp what kind of comparative research it is that they are doing.

II. SCOPE – FROM MACRO TO MICRO

A. Comparison – Macro and Micro

In comparative law study a basic division between the micro-level and macro-level is possible just like in economics. In economics, micro-economics studies small economic units (individuals, enterprises, individual lines of business) and the economic decisions made by them. Macro-economics investigates extensive economic phenomena that take place on the national or international level (business cycles, economic growth, unemployment, international trade etc). On the macro-level the point of view is more general than it is in micro-economics. A similar basic distinction based on the level of study also applies to comparative law. The micro/macro-dimension is related to the extent to which different legal systems are compared, ie owing to its fundamental nature it is a question of scale and focusing.

The distinction is defined, for example, by Cuniberti: 'On the micro level it is possible first of all to compare certain institutions or special issues .... On the macro level comparison focuses on the function of legal systems and their fundamental features'.[8]

In *micro-comparison* the object of study is either individual *legal rules* (or a legal rule) or individual legal *institutions* (or an institution). Legal institution can in this context refer to two things. On the one hand, a legal institution can refer to a positive law institution, such as a court, administrative organ or a legal person such as a limited liability company/corporation or a foundation. For instance, the notary institution that operates in Continental Europe and is lacking in Nordic countries is an example of a significant legal-cultural institution. On the other hand, several different normative and operational legal institutions, such as marriage, trusteeship, bankruptcy or transfer of guardianship are mostly micro-level legal institutions.

In micro-comparison, research can be aimed at legal rules (also individual legal concepts), which regulate broadly the same thing and are compared with each other. For example, comparative family law studies the differences and similarities in the way in which different systems deal with, for example, adoption,

---

[8] 'À un niveau micro-juridique, il est tout d'abord possible de comparer des institutions particuliéres, ou des questions particuliéres ... À ce niveau macro-juridique la comparaison a alors pour objet le fonctionnement des systémes juridiques, et leurs caractéristiques fondamentales', G Cuniberti, *Grands systèmes de droit contemporains*, 4th edn (Paris, LGDJ, 2019) 21.

marriage and civil union/partnership, same-sex marriage, marriage settlement and marital right to property, property of the spouses, potential divorce, care and visiting rights of children and paternity etc. Legal rules have to represent at least two different legal systems, but the upper limit in the number of regulations or legal decisions compared depends on the personal interests and skill set of the scholar and on the resources available (opportunity to travel, timetable, availability of research assistance etc). In most cases the comparatist should probably not gather too many study objects because one can become lost in the depth of the analysis. In fact, as a rule of thumb, it is often worth saying a lot about a little, not a little about a lot, as overly extensive descriptions of foreign law may omit the actual comparison.

> In micro-comparison, provisions or judgments are legal solutions of a concrete nature to legal problems. It can, for example, be a question of comparing norms that regulate the position of a party in an administrative appeal. What do they have in common and how do they differ? What is the reason for similarities and differences? Do the systems under study have a separate organisation for administrative jurisdiction or are the issues on legal rights in public administration solved in general courts? Traditional micro-comparative study of legal institutions has been practised in private law for quite a while. As an example we can mention the massive work concerning marriage and divorce by Burge.[9] The extensive comparative study of gifts by Hyland is a more recent example of an extensive and in-depth study of a single legal institution.[10] The majority of micro study has up until now concentrated on different sectors of private law; however, public law comparisons are far more frequent these days than they used to be. For instance, comparative study of constitutional law has experienced a kind of a renaissance during the last decade.[11]

In *macro-comparison* comparison takes place between *legal systems* or even between legal families/cultures. Macro-comparison does not concentrate on individual legal rules, institutions or concrete problems and the ways by which to solve them; instead, the abstraction level of the topics compared is higher. Comparison could for example be aimed at issues that concern, for example, legislative methods, the style of writing provisions, the branches of law and the doctrine of legal sources or even the style of entire legal systems, ie legal cultural-features characteristic of them (see chapter nine).

B. New or Old – Micro or Macro

In macro-comparison several different theoretical frames have been used (more on this later). To begin with, comparatists debated about legal families, but later

---

[9] W Burge, *The Comparative Law of Marriage and Divorce* (London, Sweet & Maxwell, 1910, originally 1838, pt 3 in the Series Commentaries on Colonial and Foreign Law).
[10] R Hyland, *Gifts – A Study in Comparative Law* (New York, Oxford University Press, 2009).
[11] R Hirschl, *Comparative Matters: The Renaissance of Comparative Constitutional Law* (Oxford, Oxford University Press, 2014).

several other macro-constructions appeared alongside them; the best-known of them being legal cultures and the latest legal traditions. All of them basically concern the same thing: the typification of legal systems into bigger groups according to their overall characteristics. Macro-comparison has for a long time been at a standstill, but in 100 years at least some progress has been made. In fact, one of the large legal families of the twentieth century, ie socialist law, has almost disappeared.

> At the beginning of the twentieth century, race, nationality and culture were still significant concepts and played a key role in the classification and typification of different legal systems. For example, according to the influential classification made by the prominent Georges Sauser-Hall (1884–1966) in 1913, the legal systems of the world could be classified into the laws of the following: (1) Aryan peoples (Indo-European peoples); (2) Semitic peoples; (3) Mongolian peoples (main groups being Japan and China); and (4) uncivilised (barbarous) peoples, including for example the law of Negroes (sic!) and the law of Melanesians.[12]
>
> Racist classifications like the one above have absolutely *no* place in modern comparative law: racism is of its nature against the basic assumptions of comparative law and the deep ethical commitments of comparative legal studies in general. A modern comparatist must not practise intellectual colonialism or implicitly prefer the paradigms of their own Western law to the solutions made in radically different legal cultures – fallacy of superiority has no place in modern comparative law, no more than the feeling of inferiority. Instead, one should aim towards a balanced research, which tries to study, compare, explain and learn from different legal cultures. One of the most important developments in recent comparative law scholarship has been the attempt to decolonise the comparative study of law so that global legal diversity could be taken into account.[13]

It seems obvious that in the twenty-first century in particular, the nature of macro-comparison has changed. The differences between legal cultures are no longer emphasised; instead, more attention is paid to their similarities, and models are constructed on how different legal traditions can live side by side in a peaceful relationship. Dreams about a uniform global law that would follow Western legal culture have been buried; pluralism is flourishing. The demarcation between micro- and macro-comparison is all but clear as it is quite flexible. It is often possible to use both points of view in a study so that they complement one another in such a way that one of the approaches is chosen for the starting point for comparison. The micro-comparatist might have to get acquainted with

---

[12] See G Sauser-Hall, *Fonction et méthode de droit comparé* (Geneva, Kundig, 1913) (droits aryens et indo-européens, droits sémitiques, droits mongols, droits barbares). Sauser-Hall based his classification on race; each race had its own legal evolution which could be found inside each race ('qu'à l'intérieur de chaque race', 63).

[13] L Salameyh, R Michaels, 'Decolonial Comparative Law' (2022) 86 *Rabels Zeitschrift für ausländisches und internationales Privatrecht* 166.

the history and general doctrines of foreign legal systems in order to understand better how the individual rules and institutions under study work as a part of the entity of the legal system and legal culture. On the other hand, the macro-comparatist might have to study individual norms or single cases to understand what significance the general characteristics of the legal system being studied has on the level of legal practice.

> A good example of a classic work that has already been forgotten is the study by Ernest Glasson (1839–1907) that was published in the late-1800s and is called 'The Civil Marriage in the Antiquity and in the Principal Modern European Legislation'.[14] In his study, Glasson divided marital right to property into categories according to macro-principles by separating systems that had been influenced by Roman law, systems that were immune to Roman law, ie common law, and systems that combined ideas from Roman law and national laws. Glasson's approach would still today be a plausible method for connecting micro- and macro-comparisons: the micro-approach is analysed on the basis of the division at the macro-level.

In light of the above, one might be tempted to ask why should the study of micro- and macro-levels be kept apart? Indeed, there are no reasons for rigid distinctions in a discipline so pluralistic as to its nature. It is a question of the basic point of view or of a kind of angle of incidence to comparative study where the question is of the recognition of the comparatist's own knowledge-interest. A micro-comparatist can never completely exclude the macro-level from their study, nor the macro-comparatist the micro-level. For example, the basic nature of an Islamic marriage as an agreement between families can easily remain an oddity if the comparatist does not know Islamic legal culture in general. In the same way the rule of law in Western legal culture remains insignificant if attention is not paid to what it means in different applications and what kind of ideologies and legal-historical developments there are in the background. Most creatures in the sea of law are like icebergs: only the top is easy to see, and most of the mass is below the surface. This is also the reason why the comparatist must look beyond formal law and take the context(s) of law into account. In other words, the comparatist is obliged to try to look under the surface.

III. IN TIME AND SPACE – THE TIME DIMENSION

The comparative aspect concerning the longitudinal and immediate (present time) dimensions is related to the issue of historical comparative law that was discussed in the previous chapter. This is a question of the time dimension *before/past – now/present* that is connected to the acquisition of the basic

---

[14] E Glasson, *Le mariage civil et divorce dans l'antiquité et dans les principales législations modernes de l'Europe* (Paris, Durand et Pedone-Lauriel, 1880). Reprinted by Nabu Press in 2011.

material for the study; in other words, if the law being compared is in force (so-called valid law) or if there is included in the comparison legal material that is no longer in force.

German comparatists and legal historians have already, for a while, been talking about the fact that law exists simultaneously in two different dimensions, which are impossible to keep apart. Law is simultaneously in time and space (German *Zeit und Raum*). While a micro-comparatist, in particular, is often interested in how a rule or legal institution works at the present time, another comparatist with a more theoretical orientation can also be interested in how the provision or institution in question has earlier worked in other legal cultures. We can possibly talk about the descent of law, genealogy of law or even the genetics of law (see chapter ten). As has already been stated in this book, the relation between comparative law and legal history is intimately close as these fields are closely related. Moreover, it has been recently argued that legal history is important for all legal research as there is a need to understand how law and legal institutions are constructed.[15]

In the ordinary setting of comparative law it is a question of comparison that is related to the present time and where the interest is not first and foremost in the law of the past. When comparative law is practical in nature, it is often also *horizontal comparison* because the court or legislator which is aiming at socio-legal solutions is generally not *ex officio* interested in provisions or the legal history of the past. *Longitudinal comparison*, on the other hand, takes *points of comparison also from legal history* and therefore its character is often more theoretical and its nature is to focus on general knowledge. In the longitudinal comparison (or comparative legal history if you prefer) one or more legal systems in different periods of time are studied comparatively.

According to most theorists of comparative law, the historical aspect in comparison is particularly important, because in order to understand the content of rules, principles and doctrines in a foreign legal system, one also has to know their historical development. Yet, knowledge of the historical development is not necessarily related to theoretical comparative law only because efficient use of legal innovations made in another legal system may require knowledge of the historical development of the norms and institutions under study. In the same way, Raitio has emphasised the need for a more profound understanding of EU law, so that when decisions of the EU Court are evaluated, the circumstances and situation at the time of the decision-making are taken into account.[16] By means of the contextualisation of recent history that Raitio is referring to, it is according to him possible to better understand also the substance of practical legal issues of EU law. In other words, it is not a question of a matter of curiosity or academic dandyism: temporal contextualisation may also be crucial for

---

[15] R Sandberg, *Subversive Legal History* (London, Routledge, 2022).
[16] See J Raitio, *The Principle of Legal Certainty in EC Law* (Dordrecht, Kluwer, 2003) ch 1.

a normative and internal standpoint. A clear indication of the close relationship between comparative law and legal history is the rise of the new scholarly field of comparative legal history that seeks to combine legal history and comparative law.

How about legal loans and borrowings? It is in fact easy to transfer legal institutions and ways of thinking from one country to another by means of statutory law but, and here lies the problem, it is impossible to transplant the legal-political-social milieu. Legal culture that has been formulated in the legal-historical process cannot be turned into an export product. So, in practice *legal transplants* can result in a certain rejection (unpredictable complications, disturbances and unexpected consequences) in the legal system at the receiving end. This is the case even if the adopted loan were modified and tailored to fit. The issue of legal transplants has been touched upon on several occasions in this book, but the following section seeks to present an all-encompassing discussion by building on what has already been said.

A. Transplants and Loans

The study of legal transplants (or loans, transfers, transpositions, translations) and legal loans as well as the copying of ideas or legal neo-colonisation is a research field where the connection between legal history and comparative law is most clearly demonstrated. The follow-up of a legal idea presumes understanding of its legal content (to some extent) in both the legal system and the receiving court. In a certain way, it is a question of a kind of detective work where the detective follows in the footsteps of a suspect by means of indirect proof and the power of deduction. The challenge is to hold the strings together and build out of them a comprehensible narrative with a plot.

> Watson, in his classic work *Legal Transplants*, which was published in 1974, introduced the concept of a legal transplant.[17] In Watson's theory it is important for a legal transplant to have a historical connection between the systems or more precisely between the regulations of the systems. In other words, it is not a question of a reception where it could be specifically indicated what has been adopted from the foreign law, when the adoption took place and how the movement actually happened. What is essential is only the 'relationship of one legal system and its rules with another'. By the process of moving Watson simply meant the moving of a rule or a system of law (mainly Roman) from one country to another.

It is useful to keep in mind that in the theory of legal transplants the question was expressly of adoption of the *central idea*, not necessarily of word-for-word

---

[17] A Watson, *Legal Transplants: An Approach to Comparative Law*, 2nd edn (Athens GA, University Georgia Press, 1993).

copying. When on the basis of a foreign model a corresponding construction of one's own law is moulded, it is possible to say that foreign law has been borrowed and thereby the legal culture of the receiving country has been affected. In this way the law of the US has had a significant impact on European systems in the legal fields related to commercial activity from the mid-twentieth century (eg leasing, factoring and franchising). The theme is of particular interest for comparative law. Study on borrowings and legal transplants breaks the idea of the nationality of law and its bonds to a system by pointing out the reciprocal relations that cross these national restrictions. Here we can quote the idea of Pihlajamäki:

> global law consists of both national and international ingredients, both of which are in a continuous and accelerating movement. To perceive this whirlwind of continuum and interruption, a kind of legal supernova lawyers need tools.[18]

The longitudinal study of comparative law is, basically, just the sort of theoretical approach that in the quotation is referred to as perceiving the legal supernova. However, engaging in a study like that is not a particularly easy task for lawyers. For example, the criticism of the transplant theory was severe from the very beginning. Kahn-Freund presented the best-known early criticism, which turned out to be quite influential.[19] He justified his criticism with the significance of the social context of law. According to him, the whole concept of transplant was out of place in the world of law, although it was possible to refer it meaningfully to a surgical operation in which a kidney of one individual was transplanted to another. According to the core of Kahn-Freund's argument 'we cannot take for granted that rules or institutions are transplantable'.[20]

If one now looks at the idea of transplantation, something seems to be rather evident. It would be essential to observe the societal context of law, or the result could be transplant rejection in the new system. In the case of a legal loan it is influence that takes place in a *mutated form*. Here is the thing: a mutated loan is still a loan although in some respect it is a loan gone wrong. The success of a loan is not the same thing as making a loan as such because one can certainly copy a rule or an institution from another country, but whether it really works in the receiving system is quite another question. Today's majority view on transplants seems to hold that transplants are possible and take place but, notwithstanding, they are far from simple and there are lots of subtleties and nuances involved.

Later the transplant criticism swelled over its limits in the comparative law discussion: in the 1990s critical comparatist Legrand presented his relativistic

---

[18] H Pihlajamäki, 'Vertaileva oikeushistoria muuttuvassa maailmassa' (2009) 38 *Oikeus* 420, 423.
[19] See O Kahn-Freund, 'On Use and Misuse of Comparative Law' (1974) 37 *Modern Law Review* 1 ('its use requires a knowledge not only of the foreign law, but also of its social, and above all its political, context', 27).
[20] ibid.

view of the sheer absurdity of (mainly private law) legal transplants.[21] Currently concepts like *legal translation, legal transfer* and *legal transposition* are used. The great majority of comparatists continue to use legal transplant either solely or in parallel to other conceptualisations. Notwithstanding, it would seem that Watson's original concept has become rooted to the theory and terminology of comparative law – in spite of its problematic nature. Altogether, it would seem, the most fruitful criticism against Watson's transplant metaphor has been the idea of replacing it with the concept of *legal irritant*.

> Discussion has continued, and for the concept of legal transplant various replacements have been proposed, with one of the best known among them being the proposal in 1998 by Teubner who represents the theoretical sociology of law. Teubner emphasised the fact that the result of transplantation can be anything. Therefore, we should not speak of a legal transplant but of *a legal irritant*.[22]
>
> Teubner's most important idea in this respect is related to the nature of the transplant, because in Watson's thinking the transplant appeared to be something that can be controlled and somehow predicted. Teubner denied this and stressed that when something is transferred from one foreign legal culture to another, something unintended happens, but not what is expected: it is not transplanted into another organism, rather it works as a fundamental irritation which triggers a whole series of new and unexpected events. In other words, what follows the transplantation is certain evolutionary legal dynamics whose consequences it is extremely difficult, if not impossible, to predict.
>
> Recently scholarship on legal transplants has expanded, for example, geographically to East Asia and Oceania, substantially to constitutional borrowings, and theoretically to cultural study of law.

Independent of the type of conceptualisation that is selected, legal borrowing has continued to increase with internationalisation, globalisation and European integration. To be sure, legal diffusion, borrowing, copying or transplanting *does* take place – it is, however, quite a different question with regard to how well it actually works and whether it leads to the desired results or not. So, it may as well be that Michaels has a fair point when he says that 'we may grudgingly have to admit that Alan Watson is not, in the end, as uninteresting as we make him out to be'.[23] Whatever criticisms we may pose, it remains a fact that the migration of law is taking place everywhere or, as Tohidipur puts it: 'Legal rules are extracted from one context, transferred and implanted in another context, or migrate across sometimes fluid borders and so on'.[24]

---

[21] See P Legrand, 'The Impossibility of Legal Transplants' (1997) 4 *Maastricht J Eur & Comp L* 111.

[22] See G Teubner, 'Legal Irritants: Good Faith in British Law or How Unifying Law Ends Up in New Divergencies' (1998) 61 *Modern Law Review* 11 ('it works as a fundamental irritation which triggers a whole series of new and unexpected events', 11).

[23] R Michaels, 'One Size Can Fit All' in G Frankenberg (ed), *Order from Transfer – Studies in Comparative Constitutional Law* (Cheltenham, Edward Elgar, 2013) 56, 78.

[24] T Tohidipur, 'Comparative Constitutional Studies and the Discourse of Legal Transfer' in Frankenberg (n 23) 29, 33.

Discussion on legal transplants is still ongoing among the comparatists and new layers of scholarship are being added to the earlier literature. New dimensions are being taken into account, for instance, there is more focus on places beyond the Global North and there are new openings that address transplants against the backdrop of literature studies.[25]

IV. QUANTITY

In comparative research the strategic basic solution of a technical nature can in addition to the depth or time dimension be related to the number of sources, ie legal systems from which the material is gathered. In *bilateral* comparative law, comparison takes place between two (at the most) different legal systems. The advantage of bilateral comparison is the concentration on strictly limited material (from two systems only), which means that only a few cases are studied, but they are studied thoroughly. Bilateral comparison (or comparison among a very small number of legal systems) can also be called *case-oriented*. The aim is to get as deep as possible into the legal systems compared by getting acquainted with their general doctrines, legal culture and historical development in detail.

Case-oriented study can be seen as qualitative or *idiographic* (ie concerned with unique facts like in history) in its nature. The results achieved by it are not considered to represent knowledge that is empirically generalisable; instead, it is a question of profound comprehension and explanation of individual cases. This does not, however, mean that knowledge created by means of case-oriented study approach could not be applicable in other cases, too, as the grouping of legal families by Siems indicates.[26] In comparative law there are both idiographic case studies, where only a few legal systems are under study and a certain aspect in them is thoroughly observed, and a *nomothetic* (ie inductively reasoning) study approach as appears in the research on the *legal origin theory*.

> The comparative study on judicial reasoning and legitimacy by de S-O-l'E Lasser is an example of a valuable study that concentrates in depth on a small number of cases.[27] Lasser studies comparatively the French Court of Cassation, the Federal Supreme Court of the United States and the EU Court. In this study the differences in the argumentation used in the application of law are shown in how judges argue and explain when they decide cases and how the judgments are justified. Here is the thing: the conclusions made by Lasser are not capable of generalisation; instead they expressly only concern the systems studied when presenting the ways in which superior courts

---

[25] V Breda (ed), *Legal Transplants in East Asia and Oceania* (Cambridge, Cambridge University Press, 2019) and J Husa, *Interdisciplinary Comparative Law* (Cheltenham, Edward Elgar, 2022) 89–97.

[26] M Siems, 'Varities of Legal Systems' (2016) 12 *J Inst Econ* 579.

[27] See M de S-O-l'E Lasser, *Judicial Deliberations – A Comparative Analysis of Judicial Transparency and Legitimacy* (Oxford, Oxford University Press, 2004).

in these systems justify their judgments: it is a question of understanding the legal cultures in the systems studied and the positioning of the supreme judicial decision-making in the overall context of the legal culture.

In *multilateral* comparative law, more than two legal systems are compared. This kind of approach can be characterised as *variable-oriented* study, the most significant advantage of which is the great number of cases studied. This means that the degree of the generalisability of knowledge increases, but the weakness of the reach (how deep into the legal culture or context of law the study reaches) is a problem. In variable-oriented study it is not easy to get beneath the surface, and the study remains simply as an organised description of mere written provisions or other formalities.

> Examples using a refined quantitative analysis are in particular to be found in the sphere of the *legal origins* theory where statistical data and methods of statistics are regularly used. A more recent example, and possibly more relevant from the point of view of comparative law is an article by Gelter and Siems about citing foreign law in courts. This article provides interesting quantitative evidence, from the European supreme courts, in order to assess the usage of cross-citations over borders.[28] A second example is Law's study of constitutional archetypes that focuses on constitutional narratives boiling down to three archetypes.[29] More generally, arguably, there are signs of study of law taking a turn towards computational legal studies that mean more data-driven research. For example, the call for empirical research has been heard in comparative constitutional law where quantitative analyses have become more commonplace in the study of constitutional design and rights.[30]

In light of the previous discussion, from the point of view of the comparative law methodology, two useful basic considerations can be made. The first point is that the number of objects in comparison is subordinate to the scholar's own knowledge-interest. If the purpose is to review quickly different alternative normative models (rules, principles, doctrines, precedents etc), one can cast the net as widely as one would desire without a worry. Put simply, the purpose is to find out what possibilities there are 'on the map of solutions' for the legal question that interests the scholar. It is a question of charting basic alternatives descriptively. Secondly, it has to be noted that the number of solutions correlates with the depth of the study. A useful rule of thumb could be the following: the more objects of study there are, the more limited is the study in its depth; and the fewer objects of study there are, the deeper it is possible to dig into the foreign law and legal culture.

> Yet, in some cases, an idiographic anthropological method is virtually the only possibility as, for example, when studying oral Inuit law, which uses gossip and

---

[28] M Gelter and M Siems, 'Citations to Foreign Courts – Illegitimate and Superfluous, or Unavoidable? Evidence from Europe' (2014) 62 *Am J Comp L* 35.
[29] DS Law, 'Constitutional Archetypes' (2016) 95 *Texas L R* 153.
[30] N Petersen and K Chatziathanasiou, 'Empirical Research in Comparative Constitutional Law' (2021) 19 *Int'l J Const L* 1810.

banishment as forms of normative social control. Even though Inuit law does not work in similar ways to Western State-centred law it is clearly an organised form of normativity within a human community. So, such essential Inuit expressions as *maligait*, *piqujait* and *tirigusuusiit* refer to something that has to be followed, done or not done (normativity). Today, these expressions are often used as equivalents for modern Western concepts of law, and for comparative law this seems to work relatively well although the legal-cultural contexts are very different. Today, Canadian law is a generally accepted form of law among Inuits who still perceive Canadian laws as a *qallunaat* (ie not Inuit, but white people as a group) institution.[31]

The above can be explained in plain English: if the research of a strictly limited question in, for example, three systems is one's main job and the time spent on the project is three to four years (ie the typical time spent in completing a PhD-thesis), then without a doubt one gets deeper into these three legal cultures than the person who spends the same four years studying the same question in 12 systems. However, this is just a rule of thumb and does not recognise the differences in the skills of the scholars and researchers or other resources available to the comparatist.

V. THE DIVERSITY OF LEGAL SYSTEMS – TRANSNATIONALITY

The verticality and the horizontal aspect are related to the question of *the different theoretical character of legal systems*. National legal systems are not the only legal systems, as they can be of different types. For instance, in this book the expression of large-scale organised normativity has been used. Legal systems can be classified on the national–international axis although this division is rough and also otherwise losing some of its significance. A continuously growing share of national norms either originate in international law or are otherwise caused by international legal obligations.

Supranational law also has to be added to the axis. The EU law that forms its own legal system, which is partially independent of national law and international law, represents supranational law, while the jurisdiction of international organisations is in general limited by the sovereignty of States. Somewhere there are also the practices that are applied in cultural sub-groups, such as Inuit, Hindu, Islamic, Sámi, Maori, and Jewish family law, and the customary norms of the Indigenous peoples, which have not been recognised by the official system/official systems in spite of their empirical local or more global efficiency. However, in some cases the State-system officially recognises all different normative bodies as sources of law, for example in Ghana. Owing to the diversity of legal systems, the decision on the level of the legal systems to be compared is among the decisions of a more technical nature.

---

[31] See eg N Loukacheva, 'Indigenous Inuit Law, "Western" Law and Northern Issues' (2012) 3 *Arctic R L & Pol* 200.

Horizontal comparison concerns comparison between legal systems from among different legal systems (eg on the national level of the USA–Finland–France) which, however, are qualitatively on the same level, ie there is some formal equivalence. *Vertical comparison* on the other hand is carried out among legal systems that are qualitatively of a different level, which means that comparison can concern the fair judicial procedure within, for example, international law, EU law or the legal systems of States. Vertical comparison has as its starting point the following: (1) the very existence of different legal systems, and (2) the parallelism of different legal systems. The more there is pluralism, the more *polycentric levels* of various normative systems exist, the interdependence of which is not to be organised by means of a simple hierarchy. And it has to also be noticed that different norms adjust to each other and somewhat change in their interaction. For example, common law courts can (with their decisions) convert customary law or business practices into precedents more easily than in the civil law systems. Civil law, in turn, tends to convert other generally accepted normativities in the form of positive law.

> Different influences become intermingled, which the so-called *angrezi sharia* proves. This is a question of the fact that in the UK the official law is the dominant system, but Muslim law has become a kind of parallel unofficial law that is observed alongside the official system. Muslims feel that they are being bound by the Shari'a law and the modern English law. In practice devoted Muslims adjust their own interpretations of Shari'a but do not abandon it. In the words of Pearl and Menski: 'South Asian Muslims in Britain appear to have built the requirements of English Law into their own traditional legal structures'.[32] Obviously, this kind of mixing takes place all over the world as legal cultures and various bodies of norms interact more than before.

A. Transnational Law

Over the last few years in comparative law research and discussion, several themes and fields of study have emerged that deviate from the earlier prevalent horizontal, ie traditional, comparison between States. The globalisation of law and partly the legal integration in Europe have had an impact on this. Yet, this new kind of comparative law approach has several features that are typical of the earlier comparative law: the core desire to cross national borders in knowledge acquisition, the pluralistic view of the sources of law, as well as multiculturalism and the methodological openness compared to the national doctrinal study of law. The most interesting and challenging of these new dimensions is the so-called *transnational law*. It is not just a question of a new field of law but also a new method to perceive law in a way that is independent of vertical levels and old national 'container-boxes' of law.

---

[32] D Pearl and W Menski, *Muslim Family Law*, 3rd edn (London, Sweet & Maxwell, 1998) 75.

Transnationality is not only related to law, but it refers in a more general way to the legal processes and relations which cross the borders of nation-States and in which central actors are no longer the traditional States, as in international law. The concept of transnationality is not new – as early as in 1956 Jessup challenged, in anticipation of the future, the conceptual and disciplinary limits that both public and private international law set for the supranational dimensions of law. According to Jessup's definition, transnational law included: 'all law, which regulates actions or events that transcend national frontiers. Both public and private international law are included, as are other rules, which do not wholly fit into such standard categories'.[33] As late as the twenty-first century the development has turned Jessup's pioneering concept into a promising new point(s) of view. By means of it, it is possible to assess the challenges of the present and future law that are less bound by the paradigms of earlier legal thinking.

The rise of transnational law requires changing the traditional Western ways of thinking about law and methods with which it is studied: it is also a question of recognising the global relations of dependence and influence. Transnational law is evolving into a field that is in tension between the local and global. It also breaks the traditional demarcation between public law and private law and between official and unofficial law.

> Transnational law obscures the traditional distinction between the horizontal and vertical viewpoints and at the same time challenges the earlier way of thinking of law as being a phenomenon that originates from and within a State. Around the world the discourse about transnational law has become almost a fashion. Having said that, actual transnational legal research does not in fact yet exist. One of the most interesting sketches of this new borderless – kind of universal – legal discipline is by Smits who has spoken for normative but international/non-national legal disciplines without any yearning for the old *ius commune*. Even though not clearly underlined by Smits, his approach seems very much like a modern version of the earlier German idea of *Universaljurisprudenz*.[34]

So far the colossal problem in the transnational point of view is its lurking cultural bias: it seems to be distinctly the result of Western legal thinking. Jurists speaking about it are either from the West or have assumed the Western way of legal thinking. As a theoretical model and discourse, transnational law could, however, also include epistemological dimensions that are non-Western. In many respects Islamic law and Hindu law, for example, can be seen as a kind of transnational law. Once again, it is a question of the point of view taken. For the Western comparatist, Islamic legal culture poses a challenge because in the West law is associated mainly with the nation-State whereas in Islamic legal

---

[33] P Jessup, *Transnational Law* (New Haven, Yale University Press, 1956) 1–2.
[34] J Smits, *The Mind and Method of the Legal Academic* (Cheltenham, Edward Elgar, 2012).

culture, law is governed mostly by the personal dimension which is defined on the grounds of religion or possibly even a sect within religion.

> The Islamic world of Muslims forms in principle one big community (*ummah*) where the central uniting factor is the religion. Within that community Islamic law has great significance although regional and disciplinary differences are clear. While the central source is the Koran and *Sunna*, the transnational dimension is seen in the legal consensus (*ijma*) of the community. *Ijma* refers to the legal consensus regarding basically any matter related to sharia. Importantly this consensus on judgements crosses the borders of States and is, thus, basically transnational as to its character.
>
> In the literature the expressions *Sunna* and *hadith* (speech, statement) mean the same in practice, ie the tradition of Prophet Muhammed. In a more detailed sense *Sunna* refers to all acts of the Prophet that create norms, while *hadith* refers in a more limited way only to what the Prophet has uttered. The term *Sira* that is used in literature covers both dimensions. Basically the *hadiths* uttered by Muhammed as the Prophet are normative, while those uttered in other roles (eg as a husband) are not normative.
>
> Islamic law is certainly a significant legal culture, but it is not a monolith. Islamic jurisprudence is divided into schools of which the best-known five main schools are equal, at least in principle. The schools are *Hanafi*, *Maliki*, *Shafi'i* and *Hanbali* and the Shia school *Ja'fari*. Among these schools there are slight differences in individual issues and emphases, for example in connection with the marriage law.[35]

The comparative law approach also has a special role in Islamic law because it is, as described by Mallat, 'an essential component of the contemporary Muslim world, because the enactment and interpretation of all "modern" legislation in every Muslim country is subjected to scrutiny for its compatibility with Islamic law'.[36] An example is provided by the Constitution of Pakistan, Article 227 of which deals with provisions relating to the Koran and *Sunna*. According to this article, 'All existing laws shall be brought into conformity with the Injunctions of Islam as laid down in the Holy Quran and Sunnah … no law shall be enacted which is repugnant to such injunctions'. Pakistan, however, is not an exception as Sharia clauses conferring preferential status upon Islamic law is actually a popular way of Islamising not the constitution but also the overall legal order.[37] In a general sense, Islamic law is a similar type of overall legal yardstick as human rights are for most Western countries: legal systems are evaluated by using a common yardstick, which is used when compatibility is being monitored. Furthermore, in a certain sense Islamic law is like a religiously tuned early

---

[35] A Black, H Esmaeili and N Hosen, *Modern Perspectives on Islamic Law* (Cheltenham, Edward Elgar, 2013) 111–27.

[36] C Mallat, 'Comparative Law and the Islamic (Middle Eastern) Legal Culture' in M Reimann and R Zimmermann (eds), *The Oxford Handbook of Comparative Law* (Oxford, Oxford University Press, 2006) 609, 611.

[37] DI Ahmed and T Ginsburg, 'Constitutional Islamization and Human Rights' (2014) 54 *Virginia J Int'l L* 615, 635.

version of transnational law. Yet, regarding Islamic law as a form of transnational law requires the comparatist to decolonise their epistemic point of view as seeing religious law as transnational is by no means a conventional way of looking at things.

VI. CULTURAL DIMENSIONS AND OVERLAPPING

The focus of this book, and simultaneously of modern comparative law, is legal culture that extends beyond the boundaries of the formal legal system. Together with thinking that emphasises legal pluralism, legal culture is elemental enough to widen the gap between private international law and comparative law. Culture can also have a different role to play as a part of the study process of comparative law. One of the methodological basic choices in comparison can concern the cultural grounds on which the legal systems for the comparison are selected. For example, when Western and non-Western legal systems are compared, it is a question of *cross-cultural* comparison. The fact of whether or not the countries in other respects belong to the same more general cultural sphere does not have a decisive influence because the decisive factor is the nature of the legal system (or more restrictedly of some limited field of law).

> It has been underlined throughout this book that the legal-cultural dimension (in the context of law) is of the utmost importance to the comparative study of law. Surprisingly perhaps, the embeddedness of law in culture has proved to be a difficult thing to conceive for Western lawyers. Rosen puts this well: 'It is no mystery that law is part of culture, but it is not uncommon for those who, by profession or context, are deeply involved in a given legal system to act as if "The Law" is quite separable from other elements of cultural life.'[38] For the comparatist, aiming to understand and explain the connection between culture and law, the context of law cannot be sneered at. Modern comparative law research seems to require us to look beyond positive law as the context lies at the heart of the endeavour to study law comparatively.

Comparison is *intracultural* when it takes place between two or more legal systems that are part of the same legal culture. For example, it would be easy to see that comparison between the systems of appeal in Sweden and the People's Republic of China is cross-cultural. If a corresponding comparison took place between Denmark and Norway, it would clearly be comparison within the same cultural sphere. The choice between these two basic approaches depends – just as with the earlier choices – on the aims of comparison and the knowledge-interest and preferences of the comparatist. Language skills (the ability to benefit from legal information in foreign languages) are also of importance.

---

[38] L Rosen, *Law as Culture: An Invitation* (New Jersey, Princeton University Press, 2006) 6 ('law is so deeply embedded in the particularities of each culture that carving it out as a separate domain and only later making note of its cultural connections distorts the nature of both law and culture', xii).

The availability and intelligibility of the material can also influence the choice. Accordingly, if the aim is to make a profound scholarly study of Islamic law, this could be difficult unless the scholar reads Arabic. In this way, if a Nordic comparatist is interested in Finnish law, they can go astray if they settle for non-Finnish source material: formally the picture can be right but the legal-cultural reach of such a half-hearted attempt remains low. The 'Nordic problem' with Finland may be that in spite of the official status of Swedish (as a minority language), it is difficult for an outsider to get a *full* legal-cultural picture of Finland unless they are also able to benefit from material in Finnish. Translations are indeed useful but if one seeks to dig deeper into a legal culture, then relying on translations becomes problematic.

In connection with the basic strategic solutions of a technical nature it has to be pointed out that different elements can indeed be mixed together in comparison, or they can be part of the same study while simultaneously forming successive or alternating phases. It would be easy to assume that longitudinal study is always case-oriented (idiographic) in nature because it attempts to give demanding historical explanations. However, this idea that at first sight seems obvious is not true as, for example, historical comparison carried out by means of time series proves.

A. Too Many Sources?

The increased number of different legal databases and their increasingly easy availability via the Internet has opened up lots of opportunities for quantitative technical-strategic basic solutions in comparative law study. Old-timers in the twentieth century could only have dreamt of the possibilities of today. In the same way, through the Internet it is at present considerably easier to get material on foreign law than was the case in the past: legislation, case law and legal literature are readily available. In fact, paradoxically, the past lack of sources has been replaced by a huge oversupply.

Be that as it may, the abundance of sources does not change the basic epistemic challenge of comparative law: how can a Western comparatist understand, say, the tradition of Hindu law? Or vice versa, the foundation and the quintessential ideas of Hindu law differ to a great extent from Western paradigms, but still Hindu law has its own place for example in India, whose system mainly seems to follow the common law. To comprehend Hindu law one has to combine different historical layers by means of which it becomes possible to understand at least English sources (let alone the Sanskrit ones).

> Hindu law (*dharma*, ie a kind of natural order) is old but it too has changed. A significant change in the historical development of Hindu law occurred in the sixteenth century when India fell under Islamic rule, and the jurisdiction and administration fell under the influence of Islamic law. The formal position of Hindu law improved in the British period of the nineteenth century when it was given an official status.

The British period also meant restrictions in the sphere of Hindu law because its application was limited to certain fields of law while at the same time the British general law with regard to India was correspondingly expanded. The British power, on the one hand, advanced the position of Hindu law but, on the other hand, prevented its spread to new fields of law that had been born because of social development. As a practical result of the Anglo-Hindu law the classical Hindu law and jurisprudence started to weaken or petrify.

The applications of classical *dharma* were altered in the British period and, for example, the legal fields concerning private property and the law of obligations were formulated solely as a result of the common law. The attempts of British judges and administrators to follow Hindu law in their decisions were due to an insufficient knowledge base that was often distorted and detrimental to the development of Hindu law. As a result, a combination, which was not quite Hindu law nor British case law (there was a general development of a similar type in British Africa), was created. In general, courts were expected to apply the common law in their decisions, but it was possible that Islamic or Hindu law was applied if it was a case of family law or law of inheritance. The basic situation is still the same although India, of course, is an independent State. Yet, Hindu law is stateless law and not confined to India.

Today modern Hindu law carries and develops the tradition of Anglo-Hindu law in India. Modern Hindu law is a similar type of personal legal system along with equivalent systems for Muslims and Sikhs. So, even though there is change and mutation, there is also continuation and evolution of the Hindu legal tradition. Menski points out that: 'there will always remain an element of dharmic foundation in the legal system applying to, and being applied by, Hindu people'.[39]

A new problem has taken the place of the earlier lack of sources; now they are in abundance. The comparatist has to *screen* the information given by the sources and to carefully assess their up-to-datedness and reliability. All this requires a combination of several approaches (ie toolbox of methods) and connecting different ways of knowledge acquisition and analyses. All the same, it is essential that the comparatist is able to reconstruct the contents of foreign law/legal culture in the light of the (reliable) sources that they have had access to. The ease of finding sources has not changed the necessity of legal-cultural literacy (knowledge that specifically relates to law): on the contrary, it has gained more significance. To be sure, there is an overload of comparative law information which requires knowledge gained through studying foreign law. Alongside the growing number of sources and information, computational studies have opened up new research avenues. Computational data creation, collection and analysis techniques are gradually gaining a foothold.[40]

To conclude, today it is not enough merely to find sources but also to be able to decide which sources are to be trusted and which are to be treated with due

---

[39] W Menski, *Hindu Law* (Delhi, Oxford University Press, 2008) 65.
[40] W Alschner, 'Sense and Similarity' in R Whalen (ed), *Computational Legal Studies* (Cheltenham, Edward Elgar, 2020) 9.

suspicion. To that end, the classical skills of the comparative legal scholar are still needed.

VII. METHODOLOGICAL CHOICES OF A THEORETICAL NATURE

In most cases, theoretical choices of methodology come up at the stage when the preliminary research material has been gathered, and some sort of overall picture of it has been formed. The comparatist has in their material acquired some sort of legal-cultural 'biopsies' or 'snapshots' of the legal systems that they study. It is of course impossible to grasp the whole legal system or entire legal systems to be studied simultaneously, which means that the material acquired (provisions, court judgments, knowledge of legal practices, legal history etc) is a *reconstruction* of the actual study subject/object. Such a fictive biopsy is also a specimen of the legal culture and language of which the comparatist has to form an understanding and from whose sources they have to be able to operate when research operations are carried out. Legal-cultural literacy gained through scholarly work is of importance if the comparatist hopes to go beyond mere description of foreign law.

During the orientation that is part of the first stage, the comparatist has to construct a preliminary idea of how they will proceed in the study: what will be studied, ie what is compared on the basis of which comparison is executed (so-called *tertium comparationis*, see chapter seven) and what the basic strategy is by means of which the comparison proceeds. Here the question is of the second-stage contact with the data. Basic theoretical methodological choices have to be made and a more general theoretical frame of reference has to be planned. It is important to see that more specific choices cannot be made without a reasonable amount of preliminary knowledge. Various methodological choices do not form a particularly logical continuum. However there are, although the list is certainly not exhaustive, at least four such basic choices:

Basic Theoretical-Methodological Alternatives

1. Functional
2. Structural
3. Systemic
4. Critical

VIII. FUNCTIONALITY – FUNCTIONAL COMPARATIVE LAW

In traditional mainstream comparative law the aim has been to solve the methodological problem of comparability by trying to reach below the surface level of law. Instead of comparing only legal texts (legislation, cases) attempts have been made to find out how the basically *same socio-legal problem* (in the form the comparatist recognises it or thinks to have recognised it) has been solved in these different systems. Ultimately the aim of this kind of comparative law is (on the basis of the source material) to conceive what in each legal system is typical and what its relation is to the surrounding society, political and economic systems and culture. In practice this ought to happen by analysing differences and similarities in relation to the same socio-legal problem, for example, such as dissolution of a marriage, control of the constitutionality of laws or entering into a valid contract or a common method in judicial decision-making (why this procedure, why not the other procedure etc).

Study that represents mainstream research has been built on the recognition of *similar* legal problematising for decades. It is a question of a comparative study approach that belongs to the sphere of comparative mainstream research and mainstream theory and which is customarily called *functional comparative law*. This approach has not developed in a vacuum but was first influenced by such scholars who were engaged in private international law. This approach is still at the epicentre of the mainstream study although critical comparatists have increasingly criticised it from the end of the twentieth century.[41] The problem with the criticism is that the critics have not been able to offer a similar rule of thumb – a method or approach that would be at least reasonably explicit. Indeed, it is easy to dish out destructive criticism while constructive criticism is more demanding.

On the other hand, insights offered by critical comparative law also concern the law itself and the fact that traditional comparative law has not been able to, for example, reveal the questionable social hierarchies, colonialist heritage or inequalities. It has been argued that by means of critical comparison it is possible to pinpoint more clearly the mechanisms of social power and control which have been hidden by the legal language and the quasi-objective legal structures and in most cases remain unobserved by the normative doctrinal study of law. According to the critique, functional comparatists have generally accepted the approaches and outcomes of each system they have studied.[42] This approach, where law is accepted without critical questions, is said to prove that functionalists have up until the last few years implicitly shared the doctrinal internal view of law held by national jurists.

The situation is however changing, and there are visible cracks everywhere in mainstream comparative academia. This development has coincided with the weakening of the traditional scholarly umbilical cord between private international law and comparative law. Comparative law has gradually distanced itself

---

[41] There is a rich literature on functionalism in comparative law. See eg M Graziadei, 'Functionalist Heritage' in P Legrand and R Munday (eds), *Comparative Legal Studies* (Cambridge, Cambridge University, 2003) 100; J Husa, 'Functional Method of Comparative Law' (2013) 2 *Eur Property L J* 4; R Michaels, 'The Functional Method of Comparative Law' in M Reimann and R Zimmermann (eds), *Oxford Handbook of Comparative Law*, 2nd edn (Oxford, Oxford University Press, 2019) 345.

[42] Husa (n 25) 158–66.

from the normatively oriented conception of law in order to become a more independent field of legal scholarship. Against that background, the centrality of functionalism has faded.

A. The Same Idea as a Starting Point

In *functional comparison* the problem setting typically takes the form in which legal institutions and practices in the legal systems studied have a similar problem-solving function. In functional comparison the aim is to localise how the same (or almost the same) socio-legal problem X is solved in different legal systems. The provisions and practices to be compared are selected because the aim is that by means of them the same socio-legal problem could be solved, and therefore the aim is to find *functional equivalences*. In other words, in functional comparative law the research frame is built on the factual (in the opinion of the comparatist) – not conceptual or terminological – analogy of the institutions and provisions compared.

Functional comparative law was for a long time in the position of being the basic methodology in the academic literature concerning the field while others have mainly complemented it. The fundamental idea of functional comparison is based on the fact that different provisions, institutions or normative practices can in different legal systems have similar functions. In turn, provision and legal practices which are similar at face value (eg terminological similarities) can in different legal systems have different functions in spite of their superficial similarity, ie linguistic similarities (so-called 'false friends' syndrome) are not the same thing as legal similarities. False friends refers to a situation in which the comparatist finds pairs of terms, institutions or legal words in two (or more) legal languages that appear linguistically similar (ie they have the same or almost the same form) but differ significantly in content.[43]

> For example, if the comparatist would like to study the methods for controlling the constitutionality of Acts in the Finnish, US and German systems, they would find hardly anything of significance unless they were to search for functional equivalences. When the scholar asks the basic functional question of which institutions control constitutionality in these legal systems, for Finland they would end up with the Constitutional Committee of the Parliament, for the USA with the Supreme Court of the United States and for Germany the Federal Constitutional Court. This example reveals that different organs carry out the same function. On the other hand, organs with exactly the same name (*cf* false friends) can functionally have considerable differences, as comparison between the President of Germany and the President of the USA proves. The former is mainly a representative organ while the latter is an

---

[43] See CJW Baaij, *Legal Integration and Language* (Oxford, Oxford University Press, 2018) 206–207.

organ with a considerable constitutional prerogative. *Homonymy* (which is a special type of false friends situation) is a problem caused by words that in spite of their identical spelling, and possibly even pronunciation, have different meanings and is something that functionalism seeks to overcome.

Comparison between Western and Islamic inheritance law can also be taken as an example: in both, the issue in the functional sense is the distribution (the same legal problem) of the inheritance of a deceased close relative. In Western thinking, this is permeated by human and basic rights, the difference in the inheritance case between a man and woman per se is not (any more) recognised, whereas in Islamic inheritance law the share of the female heir is half of the share of the male heir. In Western law, estate distribution is regulated in the formal legal system but in Islamic law the source is the Koran, the way of life ie *Sunna* prescribed as normative by the Prophet Muhammad and Islamic legal literature (*fiqh*).[44] The Koran determines two-thirds of the estate distribution and so one-third of the estate is distributed on the basis of other sources of law. So, the shares of the inheritance are defined on the basis of family kinship in accordance with the ratios defined in the Koran.

In the West family connections are defined more narrowly, and the direct heir (independent of the sex) is entitled to a certain lawful inheritance portion, which cannot be denied, not even by a will. In short, functional models for the solution of certain socio-legal problems (eg distribution of inheritance) are, in spite of their distinct differences, operationally parallel because they regulate property that becomes available when a relative dies either as inherited in accordance with the law or – at least partly – bequeathed by a will. According to functional comparative law those different arrangements administer – in spite of legal-cultural differences – the same socio-legal function. Crucially, that kind of functional equivalence is why different arrangements are comparable in the sense of the functional comparative approach. Functionality is about comparability, not about similarity.

Functions cannot be seen with a naked eye, which is why a conceptual framework that is applicable to all systems studied has to be built in order to reveal (or to construct) them. The system's own view of the function is just one opinion because the comparatist's view (epistemically) is the view of an outsider. In most cases the comparatist has to build the conceptual-analytic framework themselves, by means of which comparison can be carried out in a balanced way.

If one sees the world through the methodological point of view of functional comparative law, legal language and its relation to the legal reality becomes a problem. As Hannu T Klami (1945–2002) stressed it is crucial to understand that the conceptual counterpart is not necessarily the real counterpart when it

---

[44] *Fiqh* does not directly correspond to the Western view of jurisprudence or the doctrinal study of law, but it is very close to them. It is a question of scholarly activity carried out by jurist-theologians, a result of which legal literature that is based on analogies has been created. It refers to Islamic rulings on the basis of sources of Islamic law (collective sources of Muslim jurisprudence or general principles of Muslim jurisprudence *usul al-fiqh*). A classic introduction to Islamic law is Noel Coulson's (1928–86) book *A History of Islamic Law* (Edinburgh, Edinburgh University Press, 1964).

comes to legal norms and concepts.[45] At its simplest it is a question of scholars themselves building a conceptual framework through which they can examine all the systems in their comparison from the viewpoint of an outsider. The basic idea is to avoid putting systems in different positions but, then again, there ought to be a desire to treat all systems in the same way – including one's own law – which must not be given a legal-cultural or legal-theoretical preference (attempting to avoid bias).

The fundamental purpose in functional comparison is comprehensible and easy to perceive: the purpose is to construct a description of foreign (and often simultaneously with one's own, too) law from the viewpoint of an outsider. The picture is partially objective in the sense that it has been expressly informed, and the study approach is the same (or it should be the same) in connection with every system. It is a question of a different objectivity from that of natural sciences; more fittingly we can talk about the candour of study and the obligation of the scholar to present the facts that have influenced the study as honestly, openly and precisely as possible. We can talk about a special research technique called *epoche*.

> Instead of the objectivity of the natural sciences we can aim at something that in social sciences is called epoche (or bracketing). In connection to the research process, epoche refers to the action of the comparatist where they consciously bring up (and explain in detail) their study-related beliefs, hypotheses/expectations and theories concerning the legal systems studied. When this has been done, they should attempt to bracket ideas. In an ideal case this would mean excluding one's own notions for the duration of the research.[46]

> However, in fact it is a question of certain methodological *fiction* because even in this way comparison will not in a scientific sense be completely objective (total freedom from legal-cultural suppositions). Notwithstanding, the comparatist can act like this – and being conscious of their own biases – at least attempt to approach foreign law as being as devoid of prejudice as possible. Identification of personal bias is especially an exercise for the comparatist in order to minimise pre-research bias or at least to become aware of the existence of bias.

For example, for a Western comparatist studying Islamic law or the customary law of Indigenous peoples, such an operation in awareness is definitely a useful part of a study process that aims at being sincere. It is not a question of the comparatist having to dismiss their own embedded ideas but that the comparatist would become *aware* of their potential effect on the research project and particularly on the conceptual frame built for comparison. To simplify a great deal, the comparatist ought first to identify what they expect to discover and then deliberately put aside these expectations about foreign law. Unfortunately

---

[45] HT Klami, 'Comparative Law and Legal Concepts' in *Oikeustiede-Jurisprudentia* (Helsinki, Suomalainen Lakimiesyhdistys, 1981) 1.
[46] T Groenewald, 'A Phenomenological Research Design' (2004) 3 *Int'l J Qualitative Methods* 42.

for comparatists, this is much easier said than done. Regardless, it should be attempted.

> Rheinstein used to give advice on this matter which although immensely difficult to apply is apparently simple in nature: 'Try to forget that you have ever studied law. Never approach a problem in the way in which you would approach it at home'.[47] Rheinstein gave this piece of bracketing-methodology advice to young European jurists who had arrived in the US – knowing only too well that the advice was anything but easy to follow: forget (for a while) who you are and what you have learned, that should suffice! Although Rheinstein did not use ethnographic vocabulary, his point was that of an epoche-approach: only when the comparatist puts aside their own ideas about the foreign law, does it become viable to grasp the legal-cultural experience through the (imagined) eyes of the domestic lawyer who actually 'lives' the foreign law (internal view). Yet, the comparatist merely reconstructs foreign law from the basis of sources and their own understanding. That is the inevitable price of being an observer, not an actor.

B. Getting Rid of System-specific Labels

Beyond dispute, from the point of view of the comparatist, is that the advantage of the functional approach is to get rid of misleading labels. Functional comparison is not meaningless even if in the legal systems compared the societal conditions (which form a more extensive context to law) are different to a considerable extent, as far as the comparatist manages to find (ie to construct) functional equivalents. In general, suitability for comparison is the crucial and simultaneously most difficult issue in any comparative study – one has to be able to justifiably specify in what particular manner the objects compared are comparable, ie what qualities (things as such are not compared, but the qualities of things) can be compared sensibly. When the comparatist has managed to construct the research frame to the extent that it is possible to carry out comparison, they still have to sort out the differences and similarities in how the study topic has been legally (in its wide sense, ie normatively) organised in the systems under study.

Occasionally, labels can be not only misleading but also downright incomprehensible unless they are set in the context of their own legal culture. Areios Pagos, the Supreme Court of Greece, is a good example of terminology that is difficult to interpret.

> The court is also known internationally by the name Areios Pagos (the spelling differs a bit from language to language). As the term describing an institution of a foreign law Areios Pagos as such is meaningless – its direct translation does not convey any

---

[47] M Rheinstein, 'Comparative Law – Its Function, Methods and Usages' (1968) 22 *Arkansas L R* 415, 421.

legal information. The name refers to one of the hills in Athens: Areios Pagos or the hill of Ares (Άρειος Πάγος). Ares was the God of War (the Romans' Mars), one among the Olympian Gods in Greek Antiquity. In Greek Antiquity, murder charges and other serious crimes were judged in a place that was called the Hill of Ares. The name of the court has its background in the myths but it is not in respect of the ancient God of War but of trials of ancient Athens. The name could be characterised as a tradition-conscious bow towards the developed civilisation of Greek Antiquity.

Among the several courts of Athens in the classical period, Areios Pagos of Antiquity was the one which was most respected. As a modern judicial organ Areios Pagos is an appellate court or the Court of Cassation: it only handles legal problems, not issues of evidence. In this, Greece follows the example of France where the Supreme court (Cour de cassation) supervises the way in which lower courts observe legal rules and principles in their case law (in criminal and civil matters). So, this takes place in a situation in which a certain combination of facts is regularly repeated in a case where there is no written provision that could be directly applied or where it is subject to interpretation. The French term *cassation* can be derived from the verb *casser*, ie the court cancels the decision of the lower court if, and only if, it considers that the lower court: (1) did not follow the right juridical process, or (2) misinterpreted the law. So, in Areios Pagos ancient Hellas and latter day France meet and fuse together.

It is also necessary to emphasise that the functional framework enables the study of both differences and similarities. Critique has maintained that functionalism seeks only similarities, but this should not be the case, ie the functional approach does not include any assumptions of similarity even though some influential scholars (eg Zweigert and Kötz) have thought so. Yet, occasionally, functional comparatists have concentrated on emphasising solely the similarities of the systems compared. In such cases the question is mostly of the knowledge-interest that serves harmonisation or unification. The functional approach, as such, is equally applicable to the study of both similarities and differences. The functional approach in itself does not assume aiming at harmonisation or unification although in unification projects it has been the frequent approach.

Here is the thing: the comparatist cannot decide in advance what their study will reveal. Occasionally differences come up, while at other times similarities will appear. If the scholar decides in advance that either one of the dimensions will be emphasised, it is a question of a choice in research policy. Örücü sums it up fittingly: 'What is wrong is to look only for similarities and overlook differences or look only for differences and overlook similarities'.[48] This is a very good methodological rule of thumb for the contemporary comparatist.

C. Problems and Transformation of the Functional Approach

In the epistemological sense the functional comparatist is simultaneously inside and outside of law: when the comparatist studies individual national systems

---

[48] E Örücü, *The Enigma of Comparative Law* (Leiden, Martinus Nijhoff, 2004) 213.

they are bound to the valid law and the existing internal ideas (ie legal doctrine) about sources of law. This seems inevitably to lead to some sort of legal conservatism. However, as an outsider the comparatist examines different systems in a parallel setting in a study frame that is independent of the systems themselves. This type of functionalism can be described as legal *problem functionalism* that concentrates on the micro-level of law and ignores the sizeable social structures – which are essential for the different functional trends of sociology – to a great extent. As such, problem functionalism is a heuristic rule of thumb that is characterised by a downright lack of theoreticalness. As a counterbalance for the lack of theoreticalness, functionalism is also a reasonably flexible methodical rule of thumb that allows the scholar plenty of creativity. Importantly, it is more of a rule of thumb that an exact method.

Finding functional counterparts is possibly the most efficient approach when the legal systems under study differ from each other significantly. For example, in a comparison between Finland and Sweden there would probably hardly ever be any need to get started by finding functional counterparts because the legal systems of the two countries are so similar that decisions assumed in them and their positioning in the entity of the legal system are likely to be very much alike. The troubled nature of the functional approach is related to its difficulty, because it can sometimes be very difficult to estimate which institutions carry out the same function in different legal systems. Problems can go far deeper. How do we in the first place know that all legal systems would have a number of specific universal legal functions that must be performed?[49] Indeed, is this kind of an assumption simply too bold to hold water? When understood properly, the functional approach does not assume such a stretched universalism. During the research process, different assumptions can take turns and the comparatist can end up changing the basic methodological assumptions first made.

Carrying out functional comparative law is made difficult by the far-reaching specialisation of the different branches of legal fields, in which cases the opportunities to look for functional counterparts are poor because the scholar of administrative law knows administrative law and the scholar of civil law knows civil law. In addition, one should have a readiness to acquire knowledge from other branches of legal disciplines such as legal history, legal sociology, legal anthropology and legal economics. This need not mean the requirement for mastering all fields of law. Having said that, it means a readiness to cross the borders between legal fields in knowledge acquisition. At present it is also important to perceive the fact that a functional approach does not exclude other approaches. Functionalism is certainly *not* the only method in comparison.

> The extensive work by Hyland on gifts[50] shows that it is possible for the old functionalistic school that is interested in legal rules and the more recent comparative law

---

[49] G Dannemann, 'Comparative Law: Study of Similarities or Differences?' in M Reimann and R Zimmermann (eds), *The Oxford Handbook of Comparative Law*, 2nd edn (Oxford, Oxford University Press, 2019) 390.

[50] R Hyland, *Gifts – A Study in Comparative Law* (Oxford, Oxford University Press, 2009).

that is influenced by anthropology to live side by side. Although Hyland himself has a critical view of the functionalistic way of performing comparative law, his massive work represents in fact such (modified) functionalism that it can be considered functionalistic comparative law of the twenty-first century. Yet, Hyland's approach might also be described as a structural comparison (see section IX of this chapter).

The starting point for Hyland's monograph is that for the past 2000 years Western legal systems have been obliged to change the basic principles that regulate the gift. By the gift Hyland means the transfer of property to someone else for free so that the disposal is based on voluntariness, which means that the property of the donor decreases while the property of the donee increases. The work examines how the legal concepts of the gift have been changed to correspond to the different social practices in England, France, Germany, Italy and Spain. The work also contains extensive sections where the concept of gift in anthropology, history, economics, philosophy and sociology is clarified. The approach is versatile, simultaneously anthropological, doctrinal and partly legal-historical.

It has been argued above that comparison which is labelled functional is a rough methodological perception model for a study setting and nothing else. Slavish and straightforward implementation of functionalism involves serious risks. If the assumption of the functions of legal rules and legal institutions becomes mechanical, law is in danger of being reduced into utilitaristically defined functions, which are assumed to be identical in all societies. That means that the cultural and symbolic dimensions of law are left aside although it is well known that law often has significant symbolic functions: a mere look at the architecture of the buildings housing the Supreme Courts of States speaks for itself. The deeper layers of each legal culture remain completely closed when mere facts are resorted to; explanations can remain superficial if only a comparison of solution models for problems that are recognised to be formally legal is stressed. In sum, the functional approach must not make one blind to the use of alternative approaches like ethnographic or other sorts of qualitative or quantitative methodologies. Attempting to study law interdisciplinarily has become one of the defining features of modern comparative study of law.

D. Translating Legal Language and Functional Comparison

Legal translation is one of the most significant questions in comparative law. In fact, during recent years some comparative law scholars have started to highlight the important role of translation in comparative law. For instance, Glanert has underlined that the problem of translatability ought to be the focus of the comparative study of law.[51] In legal translations the aim is that the legal content of a document in legal language (source-language) is correctly conveyed to the

---

[51] S Glanert, 'On the Untranslatability of Laws' in S Glanert, A Mercescu and G Samuel, *Rethinking Comparative Law* (Cheltenham, Edward Elgar, 2021) 161 et seq.

reader whose native language (target-language) is not the language of the translation. In practice, this presumes that the terms that represent legal concepts are correct in the legal sense. Legal-linguistically the basic situation in translation is the same as in functional comparative law: to establish the equivalence. In such a case the translator tries to find from the foreign system the legal institution which to as great an extent as possible has exactly the same role in a similar situational context.

On a general level functional comparative law and legal translation can be considered to be virtually the same thing. The differences are created by the difference in the knowledge-interest. The comparatist compares the solutions (functions) adopted in different systems for the same (or approximately similar) socio-legal problem and looks for differences and similarities. Ultimately, they try to find an answer to why there are similarities and differences by searching for answers in history, economy, politics, culture and, for example, geography. The translator tries to translate foreign law legally correctly. In both, the question is ultimately the same thing, ie a serious attempt to understand *foreign* law by edging with subtlety under the surface of legal language, which is a language for special purposes (ie a language which is a formalised and codified variety of everyday language and is used for legal purposes).[52]

While for the translator the foreign legal system and culture are the context for good-quality translation, knowledge of the language of the foreign legal system is the prerequisite for the good-quality study of foreign law. Apart from legal history, the linguistic dimensions have a very special significance for a comparatist who tries to cross not only the borders between States and cultures but also the borders between legal languages. The significance of the language causes problems for the comparatist, but also within systems, the changes in the language used are of great legal cultural significance.

> When the language of the legal culture changes in its surroundings, also the system's own legal language is under pressure. For example, in the USA in Louisiana the language of law and legal study that originally was French has got into difficulties because with the weakening of the position of the French language the ability of Louisiana lawyers to even understand and make use of Roman (civil) law has deteriorated dramatically. Another example is Cyprus where the common law that dates back to the British period has to be transformed into the legal language of Greece.

> At present the system in Cyprus is based on the written Constitution but since the UK governed Cyprus up until 1960, the common law is also in force. English does not have an official status as a legal language, but up to the present day it has had a strong unofficial legal cultural status.

> There are numerous examples: legal Italian is in the sense of the scholarly study of law a sort of 'Italian legal German', which still today reflects the impact of the German doctrine that originated at the end of the nineteenth century. By means

---

[52] H Mattila, 'Legal Language' in J Humbley G Budin and C Laurén (eds), *Languages for Special Purposes* (Berlin, de Gruyter, 2018) 113.

of standard Italian, legal Italian is hard to understand: the influence of German *Pandektenrecht* transformed into Italian *Pandettistic*, which can still be seen in the Italian legal process and legal education. This is no wonder, since key scholars who founded Italian private law in the 1800s were very influential Romanistic scholars (eg Filippo Serafini 1831–97), and had been trained in Germany by Pandectists.[53]

There may be differences between legal linguistics and comparative law. In legal translation the principle of functionality is not treated with critical postmodern opposition as easily as in comparative law for the simple reason that when translating there is no need to make such far-reaching decisions about the similarity of legal systems as older mainstream functional comparative law is accused of making. In general, the translator need not start to explain in detail at the general (legal) level what the reason is for their choice of particular functional equivalents in the translation: the focus is solely on the translation of the text.

On the other hand, if it is a question of a comparative legal linguist, the translator hardly succeeds unless they know the legal and historical contexts of legal languages. Legal linguistics and comparative law are inevitably allies in cases where a serious attempt is made to understand the legal messages contained in a foreign legal language in a competent way.

IX. STRUCTURAL DIMENSION

A. Structural Elements

In structural comparison *similar structural elements* are searched for (or occasionally attempts are made to explain why there are none). When structurally similar elements are found, they are examined in order to be able to explain what socio-legal functions they have in the legal systems studied or how they were born and acquired their present form. It is a question of examining *legal architecture*, which is outlined by Stolte as follows: 'the modern codes of private law have been built with the same bricks, although, of course, under different architecture'.[54] Stolte speaks of Continental codifications and how the end-results of the codifications differed from each other in spite of the same Roman structural components (norms, principles, institutions, doctrines etc). Within the context of a different architectural view and legal culture, different codifications were created. Everyone who has played with Lego bricks realises what this is all about: the same law-parts can fit together in a myriad of ways resulting in various legal-cultural kaleidoscopic views.

Structural comparison can be seen as a specialised application of functional comparison. In structural comparison it is possible to investigate, for example,

---

[53] NE Hatzimihail, 'Cyprus as a Mixed System' (2013) 6 *Civil L St* 38.
[54] B Stolte, 'Is Byzantine Law Roman Law?' (2003) 2 *Acta Byzantina Fennica* 111, 122.

how legal systems are divided into different fields of law whose similarity or difference is being studied. On the micro-level, the comparatist can try to explain why and how in England a *trust* or a case where one person (a settlor) gives assets to another person (a trustee) to keep safe or to manage on behalf of another person that enables a kind of double ownership differs from the Continental European law, where similar functions are handled in a different way. English law regards a trust as an arrangement where one or more trustees are made responsible for holding assets. The assets which can be, for example, buildings, land, money or shares or even antiques, are placed in a trust for the benefit of one or more 'beneficiaries'. According to Maitland (1850–1906), the trust was 'the greatest and most distinctive achievement performed by Englishmen in the field of jurisprudence'. It was a legal institution of 'great elasticity and generality'.[55] However, there are no actual civil law equivalents and such institutions as the Roman *fideicommissum* or the German *Treuhand* cannot be genuinely equated with common law's trust.

> Relatively few comparative law studies, however, identify themselves as concentrating in particular on the structures of the legal systems. One exception is the work of Häcker titled as *Consequences of Impaired Consent Transfers*, which in particular aims at being a structural study where English and German law are compared.[56] Häcker examines the competence to transfer movable property on the basis of consent and situations where it is declined. She reflects on contractual principles and regulations, laws of property and restoration of unfounded advantage. Comparison covers the rules and principles governing impaired consent transfers of movable property.

In structural comparative law it is possible to operate for example with such concepts as the basic model of regulation where criminal law systems may be described as punitive or restorative. The classifications of constitutions that have been created by means of comparison are an example of basic models that have been found by comparison. The purpose of such classifications is to offer knowledge of the structure and field of constitutions. As a result of comparison among others the following classifications of constitution have been recognised: written/unwritten; coherent/dispersed; rigid/flexible; monarchic/republican; and federal/unitary. In reality, it is a question of basic alternatives that concern the constitutional governance model and which only seldom materialise as such in the living legal systems. The basic models mentioned, however, offer a conceptual framework by means of which it is easier for the comparatist to approach the constitutions and constitutional laws that are part of foreign legal structures. In this respect, the results of structural comparison have to a great extent the same function as the legal families that have been constructed as a result of theoretical comparative law, ie creation of general information and offering of a framework to facilitate understanding to start with.

---

[55] W Maitland, *Selected Historical Essays* in HD Hazeltine, G Lapsley and PH Winfield (eds) (Cambridge, Cambridge University Press, 1936) 129.
[56] B Häcker, *Consequences of Impaired Consent Transfers* (Oxford, Hart Publishing, 2013).

Owing to its theoretical knowledge-interest, structural comparative law often has close contacts with general jurisprudence and the intellectual history of ideas in the sphere of which the methods to organise the legal material in a specific structural way adopted in different legal systems are studied. A classic example is the distinction between private law and public law, which does not exist as such in the common law. However, the questions and disputes on the theory of comparative law have occurred in the context of the mutual comparability of systems that belong to different social systems rather than within the disciplinary boundaries of general jurisprudence.

Sometimes it is difficult to tell structural comparison apart from other types of comparative approaches. For instance, Cappelletti's study on strict liability focuses on comparative analyses of legal reasoning. Study has structural dimensions although the focus is on finding out what are the most typical arguments used to justify the imposition of strict liability in four systems (England, the US, France and Italy). The study reveals and discusses a variety of patterns concerning legal reasoning on strict liability.[57]

B. Structural Comparability

The dispute over the comparability of socialist and Western legal systems formed a source of disagreement that lasted for decades and could not be solved before the socialist systems that had rested on a planned economy, centralised planning and single-party-system broke down. Socialist law was, however, modified civil law spiced up with Marxist-Leninist ideology and a Soviet type of public law. Discussion has subsided but by no means ended; focus has shifted towards the East. The commensurability of Asian and Western ideas of law (eg the rule of law and constitutionalism) has caused discussion in relation to its political base and human rights as well as the protection of private property and also the (alleged) unfitness for comparison of Islamic and Western law.

According to one view that has been acclaimed, the historical revolutionarity of the Eastern-European legal development in the 1990s turned the ex-socialist legal sphere into a laboratory for comparative law. The study of it was seen as vitally important – there was an opportunity to see how institutions and legal borrowings adopted from foreign systems adjusted to the receiving countries that in parts differed a great deal from the Western system. The extension of the sphere of the EU Member States has added a new layer to the change in the Eastern-European legal culture by further increasing uniform features (of the written law).

When Eastern Europe was transformed from socialist law closer to Western law, use was made of several transplants and Western models. This, however, did not mean a

---

[57] M Cappelletti, *Justifying Strict Liability* (Oxford, Oxford University Press, 2022).

quick turning point in the earlier legal culture because in Eastern Europe the doctrinal study of law is still national and tinged by legal positivism. The status of comparative law in the former socialist countries is not to be applauded, although for the EU Member States the situation has changed in the respect that by means of comparative law, it has become possible to make EU law easier to understand. As the cases of Poland and Hungary indicate, the transformation from socialist legal culture to West European style of governance and law has not been a walk in the park.[58]

Moreover, Bulgaria is an example of a State where there have been problems with corruption and organised crime more clearly than in other EU countries, and Bulgaria has not progressed in its development towards the rule of law as well as had been expected. Partly it is a question of the difficulty of removing the bad practices that over the past decades have been formed in the legal culture: they will not disappear just by renewing legislation and adopting legal borrowings and EU law from other countries and from the EU. The problem is the role of informal practices (unofficial normativities) inherited from the pre-EU membership legal and political culture.[59]

Generally speaking, it is a question of legal reality and legal culture, not only black-letter rules. Similar discussion is taking place, for example, in connection with Chinese legal culture and Western legal loans and transfers. In this sense the old comparability discussion has not died a death but it has, instead, transformed into its present reborn form. Today, discussion circles around the notion of the rule of law and illiberal constitutionalism.

Structural comparative law also includes studies where there are special contexts that are legal-culturally important and remain outside of the actual fields of law, such as, for example, the position of precedents among sources of law in different legal systems. In such cases comparative study comes very close to legal theory as for example in the seminal work *Interpreting Precedents* from the late-1990s.[60] In the book it is proved by means of comparative study that it is not a question of a black and white dichotomy – precedents are binding versus precedents are not binding. It is a question of a continuum where validity is given different weight in different legal cultures. By means of study, precedents can be placed in their own legal-cultural contexts.

The structural dimensions of legal systems can sometimes have a great significance on comparative study. The same legal institutions can in their own systems be attached to particular socio-legal contexts in which the comparatist coming from another legal culture finds it difficult to fully perceive. This includes also the changes in positive law over time, as a result of which legal institutions can change contexts in their own legal cultures. For the comparatist legal cultural variation is always a challenge, for it can result in a misconception about the fundamental difference of the foreign law although it might simply

---

[58] T Drinóczi and A Bién-Kacata (eds), *Rule of Law, Common Values, and Illiberal Constitutionalism* (Abingdon, Routledge, 2022).
[59] M Kurkchiyan and DJ Galligan (eds), *Law and Informal Practices: The Post-Communist Experience* (New York, Oxford University Press, 2003).
[60] N MacCormick and RS Summers (eds), *Interpreting Precedents* (Dartmouth, Ashgate, 1997).

be just differences of degree or a lack of syncretisation in the legal-historical progress (roughly the same phenomenon in different times).

As an example we can mention such a basic private law institution as *marriage*. For most of the history of Europe, marriage has been an economic contract between two families or extended families (ie including kin) by means of which it was possible to arrange the marriage between these families: love or devotion or any other affectionate opinion of those about to be married was not taken into consideration in the contract. Through the influence of the Christian church, marriage became in modern times the kind of sacrament we have today: it is based on affection and in the theological sense reflecting the relation of the human being to Christian God. At present, the starting point in Islamic law is that marriage is not a sacrament and is not related to attachment: it is a question of a contract (between the families of the bride and groom) that includes such basic elements of contract law as proposal and acceptance.

The Islamic contract marriage of this kind can also include conditions, one of which is the condition of the temporary nature of the marriage. One of the factual functions of the *mut'a* (contract) marriage that is recognised by Shia Muslims can be evasion of the banning of a sexual relationship outside marriage, in other words it can denote prostitution. (The purpose of the *mut'a* marriage seems to be making temporary sexual intercourse possible in accordance with Islamic rules.) From the point of comparative law, it is important to see that in such cases the institution called marriage is connected to different sections of the legal systems of the Western and Islamic systems. To make it functionally simple: if a normal permanent marriage (*nikah*) is of its legal nature a deal based on a contract (as social *and* legal institution), *mut'a* is hire based on a contract.[61] In the Western legal culture, however, marriage, deal and hire are connected by the fact that they in their own systems are legal acts having significant economic repercussions. Yet, as noted by Smits, the Christian type of lifelong marriage is not actually self-evident if it is placed in the context of Islamic notions of marriage.[62]

All this may sound rather exotic to the Western comparatist but as a matter-of-fact situation it is much more nuanced than it appears on the surface.[63] There are internal hybridities. Otto describes the hybridity of Islamic law fittingly: 'Throughout history and throughout the Muslim world, sharia has been shaped and reshaped, influenced by local customs, reconstructed by colonial law, and more recently by national legislatures, administrators, courts and international treaties'.[64] Crucially, comparative law researchers need to take this into account.

---

[61] For a more detailed discussion, see S Haeri, *Law of Desire: Temporary Marriage in Shi'i Iran* (Syracuse, Syracuse University Press, 1989).
[62] J Smits, 'On Lifelong and Fixed Term Marriage' in SP Donlan and J Mair (eds), *Comparative Law* (London, Routledge, 2019) 87.
[63] See AA An-Náim (ed), *Islamic Family Law in A Changing World* (London, ZedBooks, 2002) providing a view of different interpretations, customary practices and State policies concerning Islamic family law.
[64] JM Otto, *Sharia and National Law in Muslim Countries* (Leiden, Leiden University Press, 2008) 6.

C. Dynamic Approach

The best-known study approach that is placed somewhere in between functional and structural comparison was born in Italy where, owing to tradition, the practice of comparative law in its different forms at universities is considerably more extensive than in many other civil law countries. There is a so-called *dynamic approach*, which is related to the functional-structural comparative law. The main developer of the approach, Rodolfo Sacco (1923–2022), paid attention to the fact that when the similarity or divergence of the law in different systems is studied, in some issues several sources of various types should be consulted.

It is a question of legal-cultural rules that define how law is created, used and studied in that particular system. It is a question of the legal-cultural reasons and theoretical constructions that concern the creation and use of law. Sacco and his followers described this entity with the term 'legal formations', or in Italian *formanti giuridici*. In the English literature on the field it has been translated as *legal formant*. It is a question of a more extensive and contextualised interpretation of a legal-culturally extended source of law or institution. Legal formants are basically legal propositions (eg doctrine on sources of law) that have an effect on the solutions of legal problems: they are not rules but more like definitions stating principles which are used while constructing judicial/legal decisions. So, formant is not a singular thing but instead refers to the plurality of legal elements combined.

> According to Sacco (and Gambaro), the central function of comparative law is to discover the legal-cultural formations that prevail in each system and that are not confined to formal law because different implicit principles, practices and methods that are not expressed in writing should be taken into consideration in comparison. The situation is like this because in spite of quite similar legal texts, in some cases the interpretation of law is different in different systems. In addition, it is worth noting that even within the same legal family it is possible that a different view has been taken in the same case in different countries. Also in the same country, disharmony might prevail about some matter between the different legal formants, which is demonstrated by the differentiated source of law doctrines in different fields of law.
>
> Sacco has classified three basic types of the legal formant, which are the legislative formant (*formante legislativo*), jurisprudential formant (*formante giurisprudenziale*) and doctrinal formant (*formante dottrinale*). Sacco's theory is acclaimed worldwide, in particular owing to his article on legal formants.[65]

It should be made clear that the study of legal structures is not connected to the social science structuralism that is known in anthropology and sociology. In the background of that kind of structuralism there is a common idea according to which society consists of different symbolic systems. Among the ideas of actual

---

[65] R Sacco, 'Legal Formants: A Dynamic Approach to Comparative Law' (1991) 39 *Am J Comp L* 1.

social scientific structuralism is the studying of the effects of structures on the behaviour of people as part of their communities. That type of structural analysis is also based on the observation of relations formed by symbols. It is possible to practice comparative law, too, with such structuralist emphases, but in most cases a slightly less 'saturated' study of legal structures is used. The study of legal formants is apparently the kind of structuralist comparative law that has been developed the furthest in the scholarly sense. However, the 'legal formants' approach has not gained such great popularity among comparatists who have various versions of functionalism. Moreover, the dynamic approach and functionalism seem to partially overlap. This, as such, is not a weakness but a proof of the fact that methodological issues in comparative law tend to be interrelated despite school of thought differences.

X. SYSTEMIC APPROACH

In *systemic comparison* a specific legal institution or structural part that belongs to a legal system is 'separated' from its national context and placed side by side with solutions on the similar type of socio-legal problem by the other legal systems compared. The objects for the comparison are picked from different legal systems and set in the theoretical context (comparative framework) constructed by the comparatist. An example of this approach is provided by de Visser, who concentrates on the institution of constitutional review in Europe: de Visser studies how constitutional review is *organised* in the systems of 11 EU Member States.[66] If the object selected for comparison is included in the scholar's own legal system, it becomes possible by means of system comparison to observe one's own national solution as if from the outside: how do the arrangements in one's own law relate to the corresponding laws of other systems?

In systemic comparison – as in comparison in general – the comparatist is the one who has to construct the conceptual framework or the theoretical model by means of which comparison is carried out. The criteria for the comparison do not emerge from the study objects on their own. The scholar's own knowledge-interest is in a significant position, which is why the nature of systemic comparison in most cases is theoretical comparison where the aim is to increase the amount of knowledge.

The Achilles' heel of systemic comparison is its conscious attempt to remain methodologically detached (external point of view) from those legal systems from where the legal solutions that are compared come. On the one hand, this approach enables knowledge formation that is detached from national legal systems and thus serves the theoretical aims of comparative law. On the other hand, when we withdraw from concrete legal systems and socio-legal solutions

---

[66] M de Visser, *Constitutional Review in Europe* (Oxford, Hart Publishing, 2014).

adopted in them for our study, several epistemic problems appear. The most central of these problems concerns the fact that the comparatist can misinterpret a foreign model if they do not consider foreign law in its entirety, ie the total amount of things considered legal from the point of view of a national lawyer. The problem can to some extent be avoided if functional equivalents are searched for when selecting objects for comparison. Having said that, it is sometimes very difficult to tell apart systemic comparison from structural comparison, a part of which it can also be. A system can be seen as operational (dynamic) while structures are not operational (static) in the first place.

An example of systemic macro-comparison is comparative criminal law where it is possible to distinguish three different Western criminal procedure regimes (or control regimes), which are the common law regime, Romano-Germanic (civil law) regime and Nordic regime. These are of course comparative generalisations by means of which generalisations in reasonably analytical form can be presented:

1. Common law is based on legal principles, which were born in legal practice at the turn of the eighteenth and nineteenth centuries and with which the opportunities of the prosecutor and defence counsel to act in a criminal case were limited. Compared to other regimes, the common law judges are rather passive up to the point when judgment is pronounced. The common law regime has been built on the notion that from the beginning of the process there would be laymen (jury) involved, and due to this, different complicated rules were introduced to compensate for the laymen's lack of legal knowledge. The punishment is specifically a punishment for a crime.

2. In the Roman-Germanic (civil law) model the legal practices have their roots in academic doctrine and law is approached scholarly, which means that judges are regarded as highly educated jurists. The considerably extensive authorities of the academically educated professionals diminish the freedom of action of the laymen and defence. The end-result is the rather bureaucratic machinery of legal practice, which operates on the terms of the legally educated and remains barely comprehensible for the laymen. One key function of punishment is to separate offenders from a society.

3. The Nordic model is a kind of hybrid between common law and the Romano-Germanic law, but it is not so much a case of Nordic countries having been directly influenced by them but because it is based on the Nordic legal culture. The Nordic legal culture is characterised by its communal nature and social-political basic emphasis. One of the basic principles of the system is to level off social inequality by means of intervention by public authorities. While in particular both the Anglo-American common law and Romano-Germanic model attempt to detach the offender from a society, the basic aim of the Nordic model is to socialise the perpetrator from imprisonment back to a society. (Yet, the model for this probably comes from Germany where the Reformation and the jurisprudence of the nineteenth

century were influential.) In addition, judges are more layman-like than the Continental European ones. From the point of view of the comparatist these differences at the systemic level have concrete effects on comparison: for example, the assessment of the action of judges is not based on exactly the same criteria in, say, France, the US and Sweden. The legal-cultural contexts differ significantly at the system level although each of these three regimes belongs to the cultural sphere of Western law. In connection with details it is functionally difficult to draw a parallel[67] between the regimes although in general and on the macro-level comparability seems relevant especially if compared with non-Western models.

XI. CRITICAL STUDY APPROACHES – TWO EXAMPLES

The critical approach is even more multifaceted than the previous ones, and it is not possible to define it with the specificity that would be equal to the definition of the previous three basic dimensions of comparative study. Usually there are two types of criticalness: (1) attitude to earlier comparative law is critical and it is considered to concentrate too much on Western private law similarities and practical goals; and (2) the aim is to include dimensions that are not descriptive to as great an extent as the case has been in traditional comparative law. This can also be described as method criticalness and content criticalness. This manner by which to divide critical approaches is clearly not the only one; for instance Siems uses a distinction between 'law as discourse' and 'law as politics'. The difference between Siems' distinction and the one used here is not significant because these critical forms of comparative law are both postmodern and they 'illustrate that there is considerable diversity in the way comparative law can be approached'.[68] Critical approaches do not form any coherent methodology, rather, they are an expression of the methodological and theoretical diversity of modern comparative law.

A. Deep Level Comparison and Mentality

Among the best-known adherents of critical comparative law is Legrand who is one of the most interesting and controversial theorists of recent years. Some comparatists adore his approach and theories, while others are of the opinion that Legrand exaggerates. From the 1990s Legrand has become mainly known in European legal scholarship for the fact that he sharply opposes the idea of

---

[67] For more extensive comparative discussion, see RJ Terrill, *World Criminal Justice Systems*, 8th edn (New York, Routledge, 2014).
[68] M Siems, *Comparative Law*, 3rd edn (Cambridge, Cambridge University Press, 2022) 161–67.

the cultural unification of European law.[69] Another central characteristic is the emphasis on dissimilarity – Legrand's core idea is to emphasise differences in comparative study while traditionally the trend has been to emphasise similarities. According to Legrand, comparative law is the study of the fundamental differences of different systems where the methodological guideline is precisely the *difference*.

Unlike for Continental European legal scholars in general, for Legrand regulations and concepts are manifestations of the legal-cultural surface level, which is something of less importance. They form a small part of the mental programme that a certain legal culture or a legal system that belongs to a specific legal culture forms. He emphasises the significance of the subsurface cultural structures of law of which the rules of law and legal concepts reveal very little, although they reflect the deep structure of the law. This does not mean that the rules of law would not be valuable or that they should not be given significance. It is rather a question of what epistemic significance the rules of law and legal concepts are considered to have in the comparative law study. This means going well beyond descriptive reporting on foreign law.[70]

According to Legrand, the significance of a legal rule is never revealed by just examining the rule itself, ie the rule does not ever explain itself. The significance of a rule is the function of epistemic assumptions. Epistemic assumptions again are culturally and historically defined factors. The comparatist has to assume such an attitude to study the cultural, political, anthropological, linguistic, psychological and economic background factors instead of the significance of the surface level of the rule or concept. Thus every single manifestation of law (eg legal rule, court decision, statute enacted by a legislator) has to be seen as a complete social fact. Therefore, the most central feature of a legal rule is not its nature as a normative directive but its nature as a reflection of something that is more important and more essential for the law itself.

Due to the emphasis on the significance of the deep level of law, Legrand has suggested that comparatists should investigate the cognitive structure of a particular legal system and especially the epistemic grounds of that cognitive structure, which he refers to by the name *legal mentality*. The examples with which he concretises the matter deal with the differences between English common law and Continental European (Roman law), which according to Legrand are so significant that the representatives of these systems can never completely understand one another. Therefore, the comparatist should settle for imagining with empathy and insight how it would feel to jump into the shoes of a jurist in another system and to approach the same problem based on the same legal-cultural way of thinking of the other (jurist).

Mentality usually refers to the mental disposition of an entire society or to a kind of total attitude. From the point of view of comparative law it can often be a very

---

[69] P Legrand, 'European Legal Systems Are Not Converging' (1996) 45 *ICLQ* 45.
[70] S Munshi, 'Comparative Law and Decolonising Critique' (2017) 65 *Iss Supl 1 Am J Comp L* 207.

significant factor, as for example when the legal culture of Japan is assessed. The system of the written law of Japan is Western, and on the basis of written sources it is impossible to tell it apart from Western systems. On the other hand, it seems that the role of formal law is less significant in Japan than elsewhere because many disputes are not taken to court but solved by negotiation and arbitration before they become lawsuits.

One example of Japanese legal mentality is that although courts have a formal right to control the constitutionality of laws enacted by the organ of Parliament, ie *Kokkai* (Japanese 国会), they avoid declaring laws unconstitutional. This is due to the fact that according to the Japanese legal mentality, the court shall manifest moderation and respect to *Kokkai*. In short, on the basis of positive law the system appears American in style, but not in practice.[71] The explanation is connected to the legal culture and legal mentality: borrowed rules and institutions work differently in culturally different situations.

The ontology of law, ie the respect in which it can be suitable for the basis for comparative study, is, according to critical comparative law, a symbolic medium by means of which communities try to understand themselves better. According to Legrand, comparative study increases the understanding other legal cultures have of themselves by illuminating that specific cultural way in which they understand their own law. The core task of law would be to function as one important method in the social psychological identification of a community. Otherwise comparative law in his opinion turns into a rather senseless undertaking with no noteworthy scholarly significance or rationale.

In the European debate Legrand with his opinions was in the opposition. This is arguably due to the fact that he is so grimly opposed to, and continues to oppose, common codified European civil law. In this resistance he has, it would seem, overreached. However, for comparative law epistemology the core message of his critical comparative law is significant and important – comparative law cannot settle for studying law as it is defined by the national doctrinal study of law; instead, law has to be also seen in a different cultural and philosophical context – where the subsurface assumptions of law (eg understanding of time, space, legal reasoning and validity) are more important than the surface level of regulation. Bell commented on Legrand and noted that the comparatist must 'learn about the society and not just the legal system', but it does not make it (JH comparison) impossible because 'otherness does not result in incommensurability'.[72]

If this approach to comparison is evaluated in the light of how the same legal problem is understood, the rule orientation of the traditional comparative law is turned upside down, no more no less; we should not examine rules, concepts, principles or even legal theories, but the implicit (cultural) commitments that are at the background of these theories should be studied instead. However,

---

[71] N Kawagishi, 'The Birth of Judicial Review in Japan' (2007) 5 *Int'l J Const L* 308.
[72] J Bell, 'Legal Research and Comparative Law' in M Van Hoecke (ed), *Methodologies of Legal Research* (Oxford, Hart Publishing, 2011) 169.

such critical comparative law does not offer a clear methodological guiding principle, so in this respect it is in a weaker position than the mainstream study. In recent years, Legrand's scholarship has gained ground and his pioneering work in underlining the significance of differences and diversity is acknowledged more broadly than before.[73] The important message of Legrand is that comparative study of law should be conceived as a way to approach legal foreignness through interpretation and representation.[74]

However, as noted by Siems, Legrand's openly confrontational style has undoubtedly made it difficult for his views to gain more popularity among comparatists.[75]

B. Postcolonial Methodology – Orientalism

Another example of a critical study approach that is important from the point of view of comparative law methodology is the critical and emancipatory study that has crystallised around *legal orientalism*. Legal orientalism refers to the generalising study of Asian law which embodies an implicit colonialist attitude. For example, because the study of Chinese law and the global significance of China in general are growing, the study of Chinese law has become an increasingly popular sector in comparative law and the study of foreign law. Legal orientalism and the discussion related to it give a clear picture of the type of methodological problems that may lie ahead. The concept of orientalism and the postcolonial discussion connected to it was introduced in the theoretical and methodological discussion of comparative law at a surprisingly late stage. In this regard comparative law was not at the forefront, but lagged behind legal anthropology, ethnology and history. Generally, legal orientalism is connected to a broader intellectual movement that seeks to dismantle normative universalism in international legal studies as the decolonisation has revealed hidden biases of Western legal scholarship.[76]

In a seminal article, Ruskola introduced orientalism into the comparative law discussion and combined it in an interesting way with the postcolonial theory.[77] The theoretical framework of Ruskola's article was connected to the school of thought that we are accustomed to calling postcolonial.

The postcolonial theory is a way to perceive a more extensive research tradition. Generally, it refers to the process of decolonisation and the period

---

[73] JQ Whitman, 'The Hunt for Truth in Comparative Law' (2017) 65 *Am J Comp L Issue Supl 1* 181.
[74] P Legrand, 'The Guile and The Guise' (2021) 16 *Asian J Comp L* 155.
[75] See also Siems (n 68) 167–68.
[76] S Pahuja, *Decolonising International Law* (Cambridge, Cambridge University Press, 2011).
[77] T Ruskola, 'Legal Orientalism' (2002) 101 *Michigan L R* 179. For a more refined version, see T Ruskola, *Legal Orientalism* (Cambridge MA, Harvard University Press, 2013).

after that. In fact it is used in reference to several matters although they do have clear uniting factors. Of course, time periods are the most obvious factor: it is a question of the tradition of the critical emancipatory theory that followed the dismantling of the structures of colonialism. Postcolonialism is quite closely related to the study of ethnicity and racism as well as to the study of feminism and literature. The crux from the point of view of comparative law is that Western legal concepts are no longer automatically accepted as the self-evident yardstick for different legal culture(s). Attempts are made to give the legal Other (written with a capital O because of radical difference from Self) a voice of its own.

> The target of Ruskola's argumentation was the culture-bound view that was based on cultural history and according to which there has never been real law in China. This is the basic epistemic theoretical starting point of Western legal sociologists, legal historians and comparatists, which only crumbled surprisingly late. With the real law Western comparatists meant either as directly defined or implicitly the kind of law that in Weber's (1864–1920) classical sociology of law is referred to as legal rationalism. Often Western comparatists connect the concept of real law with the liberal legal system in general and with such an idea of constitutional State where the State delimits not only the competence of other actors but also its own competence – it is a question of voluntary submission to the normative power of law.
>
> From the point of view of comparative law, the traditional description has the epistemic structural fault that it in fact does not so much describe Chinese law but produces a Western representation of the legal culture of China, which tells more of the comparatist than of the law in China. This is due to the fact the conceptual instruments offered by the traditional sociology of law are not really applicable to the study of Chinese legal culture because the traditional Chinese legal culture is not and has not been 'rational' in the Western sense. Crucially, this does not mean that Chinese legal culture would be necessarily 'irrational' – much depends upon how rationality is conceived and defined.

Ruskola criticises the various opinions that Western scholars have had of law in China and its significance in different historical periods. Western analyses are characterised by stability, which seems to be inconsistent with the history of China. The ideas of several Western scholars on Chinese legal culture have been surprisingly similar although the social system has changed drastically. Many of these stereotypes that epistemologically disturb comparatists have not only been stable as to their content but also their functions have remained unexpectedly constant: they have reinforced the idea of the qualitative superiority of the European-American civilisation in relation to the Chinese one.

At present, Western ideas are used to justify the attempts to transform China into a State that would fit into the global neoliberal economic system. The opinions according to which there has never really been endogenously proper law in China serve Western scholars well in the construction of their own identity instead of contributing to understanding the otherness that Chinese legal culture represents. According to the core of criticism, in a way Western legal scholars educate and teach China what it means to be a State where there is 'proper' law. According to the critical analysis of Ruskola, it is the implicit legal-cultural premises of the Western comparatist's own that cause implicit bias; on the other hand, these premises depend unavoidably on how the scholar in question understands or defines law. The problems introduced by Ruskola also emerge when Western legal scholars want to teach the Chinese (or other Asians) what proper law is like.

Undoubtedly, China is difficult to perceive because at present it is as a legal culture a kind of hybrid between the Western regulation models, the traditional Chinese legal culture and the socialist system.[78] Explaining it as a legal culture that is based on Confucianism simply ignores the tremendous development in legislation that has taken place in China over the past 30 years. On the other hand, if China is evaluated solely on the basis of (transplanted) positive Western-style law, it is not possible to obtain a profound grasp of the country's legal culture; instead, one ends up describing written positive law. And yet, it is not quite socialist either.

> An example that well reflects the hybrid nature of law in China is the court system, which is organised in the Western way but is not, however, politically independent. For example, the Supreme People's Court of China, Zuìgāo Rénmín Fǎyuàn (Chinese 最高人民法院) is responsible for its operation to the Congress and its Permanent Committee. Judges are nominated for a term, which may increase the dependence of judges on political decision-makers. However, law in Hong Kong, which belongs to China, is to a large extent based on the English common law while in the law of Macao, which also belongs to China, there is still a very strong Portuguese influence on law and legal culture. For almost 500 years Portuguese law has been the main reference which means that Macao is actually a bilingual (Portuguese and Chinese) civil law system. According to the Chinese principle of 'One country, Two Systems' the Macao Special Administrative Region of the People's Republic of China (Portuguese *Região Administrativa Especial de Macau da República Popular da China*) still maintains Portuguese civil law as the legal-cultural foundation of its law.[79] Hong Kong has come closer to mainland China during the governance of Xi Jinping as the principle of One Country, Two Systems has lost much of its earlier potency.[80]

Ruskola's legal orientalism is the epitome of more general movement that seeks to decolonise comparative law. One of the underlying features of decolonial comparative law is to genuinely recognise global diversity of law. A key step in the intellectual process is the realisation of a simple fact: 'The discipline of comparative law, as it exists today, is structured and dominated by the Global North'.[81]

---

[78] See A Chen, *An Introduction to the Chinese Legal System* (Hong Kong, LexisNexis, 2021).
[79] See I Castellucci, 'Legal Hybridity in Hong Kong and Macau' (2012) 57 *McGill L J* 665.
[80] A Chen, *The Changing Legal Orders in Hong Kong and Mainland China* (Hong Kong, City University Press, 2021).
[81] L Salameyh and R Michaels, 'Decolonial Comparative Law' (2022) *Rabels Zeitschrift für ausländisches und internationales Privatrecht* 166, 167.

XII. DEPTH OF THE STUDY – DECISIVENESS OF THE KNOWLEDGE-INTEREST

To complement what is said above, it is possible to perceive the methodological and theoretical dimensions of comparative law by starting from what the scholar is interested in, ie what is the specific purpose of the comparative study (why one compares). Such an eclectic approach results in a kind of perception that complements earlier analyses and partly overlaps with them. In this way a pluralistic view can be presented of modern comparative law that has broken loose from the grip of private international law and legal doctrine.

It is now possible to identify several legitimate *stages of comparative law research*, as not one of them is right or wrong as such. It is significant that the scholars themselves recognise their own knowledge-interest and apportion their study not only to it but also to the resources available and their (or each individual's own) ability. In short: if the scholar does not know Chinese, naturally a profound study of Chinese law or legal culture cannot be the aim. On the other hand, nothing prevents the use of, for example, English translations if the scholar wants to make use of Chinese law for some less demanding purpose. However, one should *not* draw such an erroneous conclusion that an excellent knowledge of the language would automatically result in an excellent comparative study: command of language/s is just one of the skills that is related to carrying out comparative research. Legal-cultural literacy is more important than the technical mastery of a language, ie methodological sensibility and sensitivity towards foreign legal material is needed.

Activities that are carried out in connection with the drafting of legislation, when models for the development or criticism of one's own law are searched for, can be considered *first stage* comparison. This is not systematic comparison but action dictated by practical purpose and need. At that stage it is only seldom possible to ponder the theoretical background conditions of the study of foreign law to any great extent. An example of the *second stage* comparison could be the harmonising study interest that has over the past few decades gained great popularity in Europe; with it the best or most economically efficient solution for a socio-legal problem that occurs in several systems is looked for. The modern practical human rights comparison often has such features in the operation of the European Court for Human Rights. In the EU Court comparison is in the same way interested in solving problems and filling in gaps in law, just like in a national court when foreign law is applied in a case that belongs to the sphere of private international law. The EU Court uses goal-oriented comparison when interpreting EU law to ensure it is applied in the same way in all Member States. The second stage comparison is more demanding than the first stage one because there has to be an outside yardstick (eg economic efficiency etc) that gives comparison a certain scale or common comparative framework.[82]

---

[82] Husa (n 25) 189–96.

The *third stage* comparison can be regarded as comparison within a certain field of law where differences or similarities are looked for in a more systematic way so that there is a conceptual reference frame that is not from within the systems being studied. It is also characteristic of the third stage comparison that there the knowledge-interest is often also normative and virtually identical with the study interest of the doctrinal study of law. It is fair to say that in practice it is difficult to tell apart the comparison of the second stage and third stage, and often these interests are intermingled. It is, in the end, a question of what the comparatist emphasises.

The *fourth stage* comparison is already completely inside the knowledge-interest of comparative legal study, and there the scholar looks for explanations for differences and similarities so that the study in parts comes close to the sociology of law, legal history and legal anthropology. As comparative legal study, the fourth stage is described by the fact that the scholar no longer has a normative knowledge-interest nor are they any more epistemically committed to any specific national or international knowledge-interest. The *fifth stage* comparative law is difficult to tell apart from the fourth stage because often the fourth stage comparative law irrevocably results in fifth stage problematisation, including the development of the theory and methodology of comparative law. Also macro-comparison, ie classification of legal cultures or legal families, typically belongs to the fifth stage comparison although other comparative settings also benefit from these findings both in teaching and research (chapter nine, section IV).

The abovementioned stages are simplified methodological blueprints, and the list is by no means complete. Naturally it is possible that, for example, a court applying foreign law would end up drafting a research-level account of that law. On the other hand, a judgment is not a research report. The above illustrative listing aims at demonstrating that there are several different fields in comparison as well as many legitimate ways to compare. What is at stake here? Ultimately it is a question of the fact that the pluralism of modern law is also accepted in the methodology of comparative law. Moreover, decolonising the epistemology of comparative law is also important as it opens a path towards embracing the global diversity of law. What is provided here is not a ready-made choose-and-use or one-size-fits-all methodology; instead, the scholar has the final responsibility: no methodology or method saves the study if comparison is not used to serve the comparatist's own starting goals. In short: superficial ritualistic comparison could not be more useless. If the comparison serves no rationale, then why compare at all?

What is said above contains a useful common sense methodological idea. It is quite likely that for every comparative study project an individual way to approach has to be built from the tools provided by comparative law's toolbox of methods. Accordingly, what is essential in comparative law is that instead of hollow imitation of a specific method or approach, foreign law is given fair treatment and the study is carried out as honestly and accurately as possible.

Yet, what the comparatist produces is a reconstruction which is not identical to the viewpoint entertained by internal lawyers.

If and when this kind of *common sense* attitude to the methodology of comparative study is assumed, simultaneously the methodological-theoretical straight-laced attitude is given up and it is accepted that no general all-inclusive theory of comparison exists. Owing to a lack of a one-size-fits-all method, the comparatist is personally accountable for the method(s) used. Reporting of research results should be comprehensible and open: the reader ought to be able to grasp what is said and on what grounds. Another point of view that in this connection ought to be abandoned is the disciplinary independence of comparative study as a field of legal study, which esteemed theorists in the twentieth century emphasised; in the conditions of the present-day disruption of the nation-State, it is no more the relevant intrinsic value that it earlier was considered to be. Modern comparative law is necessarily open to insights and methods of other fields of knowledge.

This would mean that the attitude to the comparative study method ought not to be seen as a separate theory or approach but as a *principle* related to all legal/law related study. If we think in this way, then the most important and possibly the only actual tool for study is an open and inquisitive mind. What is significant is the degree of seriousness and compassion with which comparison is performed and how thoroughly the conclusions are argued: foreign legal documents and practices have no way of speaking for themselves for those who look from the outsider's epistemic point of view. It is the comparatist's task to make foreign material 'speak': first to the comparatist themselves and then to those who read the published outcome of the research. Finally, it also remains a task for the comparatist to speak on behalf of all the compared systems within the framework of the research performed. In this sense the comparatist is, ultimately, a kind of a mediator between different legal cultures.

XIII. RESEARCH ETHICS

It is not possible to define research ethics conclusively but it refers to the practices that belong to the research process and which are approved of in the scholarly community. It is a question of the internal control within the scholarly community that includes research-ethical principles. Those principles are also the guidelines for comparative study and they have one main purpose: they are to prevent in advance so-called bad scholarly behaviour and enhance good research practices.

Several ethical points of view are included in the stages of the research process in comparative law. As it presumably is not possible to perform such a study under laboratory conditions, occasions involving ethical problems are not downright clear. In its most common form, research ethics means using the methods and practices accepted by the epistemic community of legal scholars for planning and performing the comparative study and reporting on it at a later stage. In the investigation of foreign law carried out in the context of private international law, these practices are not truly required because an internal view and normativity bound to judicial function (what law should be applied to the case at hand?) are not comparable to scholarly work that has no immediate normative goals serving legal professions.

If the comparatist investigates factors that are culturally sensitive, as can be the case in the study of the law in other cultural spheres, they must also consider the ethical decisions more thoroughly. For example, when interviewing individuals or hearing informants, attention has to be paid to whether hearing them has an impact on their position as part of their own communities. In the same way it can often be well grounded in individual cases to use other neutral expressions (eg the accused, plaintiff, person A, person B etc) instead of personal names.

If in the study of foreign law material containing personal data is collected or if a topic is politically, culturally or religiously sensitive, the comparatist should be on the alert. The same applies to potential practical assignments in connection with which it is advisable to think what kind of knowledge needs one wants to fulfil and what kind of aims one wants to promote with one's comparative knowledge. A classic example is a well-paid expert assignment abroad offered by a government with a notorious reputation: from the point of view of the research ethics of comparative law, which emphasises universalism, accepting an assignment like this in an expert's role seems (when observed from outside) to be terrible scholarly behaviour indeed.

Another issue concerns so-called scholactivism, ie a combination of scholarship and activism. It is, of course, for the comparatists themselves to decide how they conceive their role as comparative law experts. Albeit, if the comparatist seeks to stress certain material outcomes it may jeopardise their position as mediators between legal cultures. Whatever the role the comparatist assumes it is beneficial to be self-aware of possible ethical dilemmas involved.[83]

A. Honesty in Research

From the viewpoint of research ethics there are at least two central issues in comparative law: the control of the tension that is due to cultural differences and the honesty in carrying out research. In the first case it is a question of the tension that is created between (unknowingly) defending one's own legal-cultural *Anschauung* and the respect for the foreign legal cultures. The comparatist ought to try to find a balance between their own legal values (eg respect for human rights, democracy, the rule of law) and the cultural respect they have

---

[83] See T Khaitan, 'On Scholactivism in Constitutional Studies' (2022) 20 *Int'l J Const L* 547.

towards the foreign legal culture. To be sure, there is no need to reject one's own values but it is worthwhile to make them known to oneself and to the readers (*cf* epoche approach). Importantly, as the comparatist is not doing doctrinal study there is no pressing need to take normative stands (what the law ought to say).

Secondly, in the tension mentioned the question is regarding the fact that the comparatist bases their arguments on the research made and on the sources that have been available (and are specifically referred to). The purpose is to avoid a situation where the aim of the comparatist's work is only to strengthen the opinion that they already held before comparison. Ideally, the comparatist should be open to acquiring new knowledge and have a relaxed attitude towards the crumbling of their own advance hypotheses. Therefore, it is not acceptable to cook up a story of one's own and to patch it with sources that support it if other sources do not support it. Overall balance is probably not fully attainable but as a goal it certainly has a legitimate place in comparative methodology. The aim is to understand, compare and explain – not to say how things should be according to law.

A certain epistemic and cultural veneration for foreign law is among the fundamental ethical starting points of modern comparative law. It is a question of the attitude to research of foreign legal cultures. The purpose is not to praise foreign law blindly or to denounce it as deranged. The aim is to become aware of one's own innate epistemic and cultural prejudices. This does not so much influence the conclusions of the comparatist; it is acceptable to call something bad if it is bad or good if it is good, on the condition that there are grounds and criteria for doing so. If the socio-legal solution studied in foreign legal culture is contrary to human rights, it can of course be brought up, there is no place for affectation (legal xenophilia, ie an affection for foreign law/legal culture) if justified criticism is called for. On the other hand, comparison does not necessarily include making value-judgements on law.

Ultimately, it is a question of *methodological sensitivity* in the study of foreign law and legal culture without upholding the belief of the automatic superiority or inferiority of one's own law. Of essence, here, is which measuring tool is used: does it favour a certain system? In short, the comparatist should not take sides before actual research has taken place. Comparative study may weaken or strengthen the beliefs or stereotypes that the comparatist has; however, what happens ought to happen on the basis of actual comparison and not on the basis of prior beliefs or stereotypes. Keeping an open mind is important; it is the bread and butter of being a comparatist.

Among the typical ethical problems in comparative study there is an unbearable phenomenon that occasionally appears and which could be called *intentional cover-up*. Here the theory is that the comparatist should openly report to the readers the sources that are in a foreign language and to other domestic scholars the sources that are difficult to understand/or obtain. If thoughts and ideas that the comparatist presents as their own are in fact those of foreign scholars, the comparatist clearly breaks the study ethics.

The achievements of the legal scholars from foreign legal cultures must be taken into consideration in a proper way and referred to properly and with sufficient exactness even though one's own readers would not be able to understand them owing to the language used. This is, perhaps, the most attractive form of plagiarism when the scholar has an opportunity to make use of material in rare languages. Knowledge of rare languages is a strength for an honest comparatist, not something that tempts the comparatist to turn into a scholarly pickpocket hiding under a linguistic garment. In other words, honesty is an important part of studying law comparatively.

XIV. COMPARATIVE METHODOLOGY – HEURISTICS?

In this chapter a variety of methodological basic choices that have to be made before and during the comparative study were introduced. At the same time it has become obvious that the methodological toolbox for comparison does not form an exact methodology but contains a number of useful rules of thumb. Owing to the multitude of legal cultures and the interests of the comparative scholars, the theory and methodology of comparative law is for the most part heuristic in nature.

Heuristics is related to the study process because it is an approximate method by means of which it is usually possible to get sufficiently close to a good end-result. Owing to its basic nature, a heuristic method is not exact. Among typical heuristics are rules of thumb or educated academic guesses, both of which are based on limited but sufficiently large amounts of knowledge. Applied to the study process, it is a question of the comparatist not having to think with one's own method about everything from the start. Heuristics does not offer ready-made or one-size-fits-all solution models of how comparative study can be constructed. It is a question of a kind of art of discovery, which is based on the Greek word for 'I found' or 'I exposed', ie *hevrísko (εὑρίσκω)*.

> The methodology of comparative law can owing to its nature be defined as a heuristic compilation of rules of thumb on exposure and discovery in comparative law. Here it is fitting to quote the words of Brusiin:
>
> 'The methodological general lines that the comparatist outlines when beginning the process are just clarifying work hypotheses that they over the process frequently have to check. But in case they have no conscious guidelines to start with, comparative law easily becomes a confused collection of separate details.'[84]
>
> In other words, the comparatist has to have some guidelines with regard to what they are doing and why. A general idea of the comparative process helps to carry the study through, and here comparative heuristic methodology has a natural place and role. Essentially, it is about learning by doing.

---

[84] O Brusiin, 'Oikeusvertailusta' (1954) 52 *Lakimies* 434, 439.

Although the choices discussed above are rather concrete in nature, what is lacking is the fact that hardly anything concrete in the interrelation between the choices and process of comparison has been mentioned. The same shortage applies to almost all literature on comparative law: demands pile up but concrete instructions of how to actually go about comparison do not. It is rare to see practical and organised descriptions that are presented in an explicit form on the different phases of the comparative law study process and the issues related to the different phases. The comparatist however is not completely lost, not even at the early stages of their scholarly path. It is possible to use studies completed earlier for model learning, ie *experiential learning*, which benefits from models but is not the same as the pure imitation of other studies.

Many writers give some sort of advice and hints but they are not coherently connected to the actual study process. Partly this is due to the heuristic nature of the comparative law methodology, which means that getting acquainted with studies and experiential learning from them is of great significance. Pluralism and diversity in modern comparative law does not make this any easier. This does not perhaps differ from the nature of law itself as Oliver Wendell Holmes (1841–1935) said as early as in 1881: 'The life of law has not been logic: it has been experience'.[85] This idea can be interpreted in many ways, but it fits extremely well the methodological experiences of comparatists. Much of learning to compare is to learn by doing – moving from details to an overall view and back in a hermeneutical process of research. One is obliged to accept a certain amount of insecurity but still be willing to undertake the endeavour of studying law comparatively.

---

[85] OW Holmes, *The Common Law*, first published 1881 (New York, Barnes & Noble, 2004) 1.

7
Comparing – Differences and Similarities

WHAT HAS BEEN written in previous chapters has made it obvious that getting acquainted with the contents of foreign legal systems or the parallel description of different legal systems is not really comparative law as such. To be sure, parallel description of foreign legal systems inevitably requires steps and measures that are part of the comparative process (such as translation and organising of the source material). Such activity can fittingly be described by the German concept *Auslandsrechtskunde*, which means informed description of a foreign law to the legal community of one's own country. On the other hand, there is the knowledge of one's own law, ie *Inlandsrechtskunde*. The comparatist cannot acquiesce in the mere description of systems on the basis of parallelism only; instead, they should aim further towards understanding and explaining. In fact, the urge to understand and explain is what separates modern comparative research from mere description.

Committed and systematic comparison between more than one legal system or between their specific parts is the core of comparative law. The aim of comparison is not to produce general presentations of law, such as legal system A, legal system B, legal system C, but to create knowledge about differences and similarities by means of comparing. Nor is it sufficient simply to describe the application of a foreign law by introducing correct facts and findings. In research-focused comparative law it is crucial to proceed further than to *Auslandsrechtskunde* and to try to find explanations for the differences and similarities that are found by comparing. The methodological core questions central to comparative law are as follows: what is compared and how is it done? One of the key questions concerns the yardsticks (standards used in comparison) by means of which the comparison is carried out. Comparison is methodologically crystallised into the yardstick although the final aim is a well-argued explanation of differences and similarities.

One of the main problems, that cannot be answered in this chapter, concerns which legal systems one should choose to be compared. As there is no standard answer available it is up to the comparatists themselves to make these decisions when they choose which systems they want to compare and why.[1]

---

[1] See L-C Wolff, 'Comparing Chinese Law … But with Which Legal Systems?' (2018) 6 *Chinese J Comp L* 151.

I. NEED FOR A YARDSTICK FOR COMPARISON – *TERTIUM COMPARATIONIS*

For the comparison to make sense, the objects compared must have at least some common characteristics or features, which form the common denominator for comparison. This is no small feat. Here care has to be taken; it is not a question of the similarity of the objects compared but of the fact that the *certain qualities* are compared from chosen points of view. Fundamentally, it is a question of epistemic commensurability: of a common feature in a matter that interests the comparatist. However, commensurability does not imply stressing similarities and putting aside the differences. In short, commensurability does not presume similarity – anyway, what would be the point in comparing things that are similar? To put it another way, a common feature (a quality shared by two or more) enabling comparison is not the same as a similar feature. Wallace puts it well:

> Rather than choosing to prioritise similarity or difference, ways can be found of translating human experience across (legal) cultural difference, and treating that difference as something other than fascinating strangeness.[2]

In the mainstream theory of comparative law this common feature is referred to with the reconstituted (ie not actually a classical expression) Latin expression *tertium comparationis*. It is necessary not only in comparative law but in all comparative research in general. *Tertium* is not equal to some comparative common denominator, but is instead a methodological term of a higher abstraction level that is not actually concretely connected with the object compared and is used as the common denominator that makes comparison possible. It refers to *a common quality* that two things, which are being compared, share. Importantly, without it, comparison in a disciplined sense is not possible and comparison is easily reduced to a general description of fascinating strangeness.

The common denominator can be a shared feature or function by means of which comparison becomes sensible. As such, this methodological principle is simple and follows common sense. For example, it would be quite absurd to compare the tastes of pasta and washing-up liquid. However, if we wanted to compare their colour, chemical composition or weight, comparison would not be impossible although the sense of it would probably still be highly questionable. The point of the characteristics compared is a factor for which each comparatist is personally responsible (because of the comparative framework constructed by the comparatist themselves), but the possibility for comparison is an absolute prerequisite. Without at least some epistemic commensurability the comparison turns into an idle exercise or remains as mere description of foreign law.

---

[2] CJ Wallace, 'Law, culture and Euro-Crime' (2014) 48 *The Law Teacher* 154, 158 (Wallace refers to Roger Cotterell).

Need for a Yardstick for Comparison – Tertium Comparationis

In light of the above, one of the most important tasks of the comparatist is to choose a yardstick by means of which the comparison is carried out. Unfortunately, the choice of the yardstick for comparison is at the same time also one of the most difficult methodological tasks of the comparatist. In any case, the answer to the problem with the comparability of cases always depends on the context in which one wants to compare the objects selected. It is a question of the epistemic point of view taken to the objects chosen for study; from the framework of approach to the theme.

> *Tertium* is Latin and means third, ie in this case *tertium comparationis* is the third part of the comparison. It is a question of a yardstick that enables comparison. So, if we want to know what is regarded as cold or warm weather, we need a scale. The scale can be, for example, the Celsius scale by means of which temperature can be measured. In such a case the Celsius scale is a yardstick that allows comparisons and defines temperatures that are above (+) or below (−) zero. Without such a yardstick it would not be possible for people to evaluate commensurately the temperature of, for example, the popular holiday destinations. Naturally one has to define also what is defined as hot, and on which grounds, when using the Celsius scale. In the same way we can say that apples and oranges are comparable although according to a well-known figure of speech, apples and oranges cannot be compared: if acidity, nutritional value, taste or colour is used as the yardstick, sensible comparison is possible.
>
> That is: a comparatist in the field of criminal law could consider, for example, the system of criminal sanction in system A as severe, in system B as lenient and in system C as something between the two when the case in question concerns judging crime X committed in circumstances Y by actor Z (in circumstances where the evidence is not disputed). In order to be able to draw these conclusions, they must investigate a similar crime that has been committed by a similar actor in circumstances with corresponding facts. To that end, the comparatist needs a yardstick, in this case a cause on the basis of which they consider the system severe or lenient (eg the duration of imprisonment, harshness of prison conditions etc). The yardsticks applied enable the inspection of the same case in different systems so that systems are evaluated on the basis of similar criteria. Yardsticks are by no means objective and are not particularly scientific, but because of them, balanced comparison becomes viable. In short, the *same* yardstick but a *different* system. This is, crucially, about the chosen comparative point of view that does not elevate the comparatist above their cultural preconceptions but enables certain *epistemic distance* from their own law.

As above, in a functional comparative setting the rules, institutions or legal practices have to serve roughly the same problem-solving task as part of a legal system in order for it to be sensible to compare them. Structurally similar elements or legal institutions found in structural comparative law are studied in order to be able to explain what kind of tasks – deviant or convergent – the structures have in the legal systems studied. In such cases the functions of the institutions compared are different in different legal systems, but the institutions are, however, the same (functionally).

For example, functionally it would be justified to compare, for example, the Constitutional Committee of the Finnish Parliament and the Constitutional

Court of Italy if the study object were to be the control of constitutionality, while in structural comparison the corresponding organs would be the Supreme Court of Finland and the Supreme Court (or Constitutional Court) of Italy, which as judicial institutions are similar at least in the sense that they operate as the highest courts of their country. But what does this mean from the point of view of *tertium comparationis*? Now, it is possible to compare the supervisory organs of constitutionality in many respects: nature of norm control (concrete/abstract); controlling organ (court/other organ); organisational control (centralised/decentralised); effect of control (regulation annulled/regulation stays in force) etc. It is also possible to speak of different legal-cultural features in the supervision of the constitutionality of laws. For instance, Kessel perceives a special Scandinavian norm control model which differs from the German model.[3]

> The scholar's own interest is again vitally important: *tertium* does not emanate by itself from preparatory work on legislation, positive law, court cases, normative customs or legal literature, and it is not a question of *tertium* meant by the legislator or any individual actor. On the basis of what the comparatist has read and learnt, they themselves have to construct a yardstick or several yardsticks (*tertia comparationis*) out of which they investigate the systems chosen; the comparative framework is of the essence here.
>
> It would be essential that the yardstick is not built implicitly on the basis of the comparatist's own legal culture, but that the yardstick would methodologically treat the objects of study somewhat impartially – in spite of their differences. In jurisdiction the yardstick is in most cases a legal-conceptual framework, which should not directly reflect any of the systems studied. As Franz von Benda-Beckmann (1941–2013) stated: 'For intercultural and historical comparison one needs analytical concepts'.[4] The comparative yardstick is just the sort of analytical concept that he meant.

In systemic comparison the socio-legal solutions to various problems are detached from their national context and set parallel to the solutions adopted by the other legal systems compared. The systemic comparison does not presume that the legal solutions compared are necessarily each other's functional counterparts. *Tertium comparationis* is in this case too a conceptual framework that the scholar has constructed, and its existence is based on the assumption that the system-specific solutions are commensurable to the extent that it makes sense to compare them. Also in the systemic comparison the comparatists themselves build the conceptual context or the theoretical framework (eg constitutional classification or referendum typology) by means of which it is sensible to compare them. For example, a political ideology can also be in question, such as, for example, liberalism in the US versus the welfare state ideology of Sweden, according to which the societal order (and accompanying legal basic solutions)

---

[3] See R Kessel, *Die Kontrolldichte Der Normenkontrolle in Skandinavien Aus Deutscher Sicht* (Frankfurt am Main, Peter Lang, 2011).
[4] F von Benda-Beckmann, 'Who's Afraid of Legal Pluralism?' (2002) 47 *J Legal Pluralism* 37, 42.

has been formed. Such legal-ideological differences can explain many characteristics in the field of social welfare and labour law as well as in economic, social and educational rights.

In comparative law the interest is focused in most cases on the comparison of different rules or more specifically on how different legal systems have solved a similar (in a broad sense) socio-legal problem. The basic requirement of this kind of comparison is that the legal rules to be compared concern at least roughly the same thing. What is problematic is the fact that the equivalence between legal rules or institutions is in fact solved only after comparison. This presumes that the comparatist even before the start of study has working hypotheses by means of which the material for the study is gathered in the first stage (methodological choices of a technical nature are specified on the basis of this starting hypothesis – one needs something to build on the initial comparative framework). This is where scholarship on comparative law theory and methodology becomes useful as it may provide inspiration and guidance.

A. *Tertium* and the Preference for Functional Comparison?

From among the basic comparative strategies, the functional approach seems to offer the clearest and seemingly least problematic answer to the problem of comparability. In the twentieth century this approach gained the position of a paradigm, as explained earlier in this book. This, as such, is no wonder because it offers simple common sense rules according to which comparison can be carried out. It might make sense to note that comparative law's functionalism bears hardly any resemblance to the functional approaches of social sciences. Functionalism in comparative law is mainly a construction of practical-minded jurist scholars who have moved over from private international law, the first fumbling attempts of which were sketched as early as in 1900 at a conference in Paris. Its starting point is clear: the aim is to detach the comparatist from the misleading labels and legal-cultural assumptions of their own law. The core of the ideological inheritance still makes sense in the twenty-first century even though its position as a leading methodological paradigm has been challenged by many.[5]

The approach gained its paradigmatic position internationally when the classic work (now more or less outdated) of Zweigert and Kötz was translated into many languages. In the last few decades functionalism has been heavily criticised by different condemning comparatists but, notwithstanding, in practice the dominating position of functionalism seems not to be threatened. But nowadays the approach is not the dominant force and there is no reason to regard it as the only correct method – because it is not. All the same, it belongs to the

---

[5] J Husa, 'Functional Method in Comparative Law?' (2013) 4 *Eur Property L J* 4.

methodological toolbox of a comparatist, and perhaps there is still room for it in the toolbox of private international law and legal harmonisers, too.

> Criticism of classical functional comparative law, as it is still frequently referred to, was presented by Frankenberg as early as the mid-1980s in his seminal article 'Critical Comparisons'.[6] Frankenberg's article started critical discussion on functional comparative law. The discussion has not yet abated. A good overview of the discussion is presented by Michaels in his extensive article about the functional method.[7] While Frankenberg with juicy exaggeration and witty sneers made fun of functionalists, Michaels' starting point is that the fault with functionalism is that it has not been developed far enough as a scientific comparison method. This author has been developing a view that mediates between these extreme interpretations.[8]

To be sure, much of the criticism of functionalism has been justified. On the other hand, the basic ideas of functional comparatists are still useful, particularly for comparative lawyers, at least in the heuristic sense. Accordingly, if the comparatist really wants to study the contents of different legal systems, it makes absolutely no sense to rely on similar labels (so-called *homonymy)* of legal rules, institutions or concepts as the starting point. In this respect the fundamental methodological principle of functionalism has not been fully abandoned even though its popularity has undoubtedly fallen as pluralism has gained ground.

It seems that it is possible to avoid some problems burdening the comparative framework if functional commensurability is taken as the starting point for comparison. In such cases the shared function is the common denominator, which simultaneously is the *tertium comparationis* of comparison. However, it is essential to notice that *tertium* is not an objective point of observation; constructing it does not make the study scientific in the sense of natural sciences. Frankly, the newly created Latin term *tertium comparationis* has a great ring to it, but it is a mere rule of thumb. On the other hand, it is possible by means of *tertium* to carry out analytical and systematic comparison where the aim is to treat different objects of comparison in relatively the same way despite their dissimilarity. Tertium is, in essence, a means to an end.

If the yardstick for comparison is chosen on a functional basis, it however has to be realised that the actual function of legal rules is what counts, and not, for example, convergent aims (legislator's *inventionie ratio legis*) that are pursued by positive law or by the courts. Surprisingly perhaps, even functionalism presumes a context for legal rules. Rabel formulated this already in the

---

[6] G Frankenberg, 'Critical Comparisons: Re-thinking Comparative Law' (1985) 26 *Harvard Int'l L J* 411.
[7] R Michaels, 'The Functional Method of Comparative Law' in M Reimann and R Zimmermann (eds), *The Oxford Handbook of Comparative Law*, 2nd edn (Oxford, Oxford University Press, 2019) 345.
[8] See J Husa, 'Farewell to Functionalism or Methodological Tolerance?' (2003) 67 *Rabels Zeitschrift für ausländisches und internationales Privatrecht* 419.

1920s: 'Law void of the legal practice related to it is like a skeleton without muscles. The nervous system is formed by the prevailing doctrine'.[9]

Such methodological requirements presume acquaintance with legal practice, which means that written law, precedents and official preparatory material (*travaux préparatoires*) form only a part of the relevant sources. On the other hand, these requirements are factors that undoubtedly complicate functional comparison and make quite considerable methodological demands on comparison. And, it must be borne in mind, functionalism is not always applicable even in all practical purposes.

> An example of a special case is the fact that in the field of international law the intentional interpretation is emphasised in the Law of Treaties, which means that *travaux* and the circumstances prevailing at the time of the treaty's preparation have great significance in interpretation. Article 31 of the Vienna Convention on the Law of Treaties 1969 contains a general interpretation rule, according to which treaties between States shall be interpreted in good faith in accordance with the ordinary meaning to be given to the terms of the treaty in their context and in the light of its object and purpose. In this respect the comparatist has to observe in the international Law of Treaties the intention of the treaty regulations as the primary factor in functional comparison.

Although functional comparative law has been moderately emphasised above, it has to be observed that when *tertium comparationis* is searched for, the interests, aims or principles at the basis of legislation can also be the aim of comparative law. The comparatist can also try to reconstruct intentional explanations in which case the targets of study are the intentions (eg *ratio legis*), scholarly theories or political ideologies that are behind a certain legal decision. For example, attempts have often been made to explain EU case law with the integration ideology. And law and economics researchers are interested in the economic efficiency of law and other such things instead of purely legal functions.

However, to study legal intentions is clearly more difficult than to construct a comparative framework on the basis of rough functional comparability. It is difficult by means of research to genuinely pinpoint intentions, interests and aims, and often an approach with a strong touch of intellectual history is needed alongside legal material.

> An example of demanding historical and legal-theoretical comparison is the early study by Tolonen of the development of legal regulation related to limited liability companies.[10] Tolonen studied company law theoretically and comparatively in the

---

[9] 'Ein Gesetz ist ohne die zugehörige Rechtsprechung nur wie ein Skelett ohne Muskel. Und die Nerven sind die herrschenden Lehrmeinungen', E Rabel, 'Aufgabe und Nodwendigkeit der Rechtsvergleichung' (1924) 13 *Rheinische Zeitschrift für Zivil- und Proceßrecht* 279, reprinted in HG Leser (ed), *Ernst Rabel Gesammelte Aufsätze*, III (Tübingen, JBC Mohr, 1967) 4.
[10] See J Tolonen, *Der allgemeinen Erklärungshintergrund und der wirtschaftlichen Ordnung und seine Anwendung auf das Aktiengesellschaftrecht* (Helsinki, Suomalainen tiedeakatemia, 1974).

1970s and shows how various economic and institutional theories have been developed in the context of a market economy. The central (micro-economic) explanatory model for the legislative changes is constructed on the divergence of the economic theory from the so-called classical theory towards the so-called dynamic theory. Subsequently, steps have been taken in the same direction within the framework of the *legal origins* theory but with considerably more economic emphasis.

II. DIFFERENCES AND SIMILARITIES

To explain foreign law means to make it plain and render it intelligible so it becomes understandable for an outsider. One of the central aims of comparative law, a rather bold one, is to explain the law of mankind in different contexts. Understanding the law of the compared systems is vital in order for the comparatist to be able to explain the reasons for the similarities and differences they have found: why in system A is the prerequisite for liability for damages a clear causal connection between the act and the damage caused, but in system B an assumption of a causal relationship in connection with the intent or negligence of the originator. Circular reasoning here is not sensible: in system A the matter is caused by provision X, and in system B the matter is caused by provision Z. Such an explanation lifts itself up by the bootstraps because it does not explain *why* in systems A and B different approaches have been adopted to solve the same legal problem (defining the party liable for compensation). A wider perspective is needed if and when comparison steps away from mere description and ventures into explanation.

It is especially arduous for the comparatist to break loose from the influence of their own legal culture and to look at their own and foreign law fairly, without unintentional ulterior motives (bias). In this respect the comparatist's work approaches anthropology and ethnography: for lack of hard scientific proof, statistical conclusions and conclusive evidence, material has to be interpreted, and different hints and clues have to be looked for. In practice, power of deduction, imaginative thinking and legal literature are more essential than statistics, formal legal texts or the national doctrinal study of law.

The comparatist's work gets all the more challenging when they begin to look for clues needed for explanation. The task is comparable with detective work where the perpetrator is uncovered by means of small details, or clues that do not reveal anything for someone who is uninformed on the matter. In the same way, the hunter in the past was by means of seemingly unimportant traces (footprints, broken branches, scent etc) capable of formulating a sort of hunting reality, which was not concrete as such. It is a question of observations forming a narrative continuum where it is possible to understand the plot and its development: things just seem to fall into their natural places forming a narrative. The plot method (or method of clues) has been sketched by art historian Carlo Ginzburg (b 1939) in particular.[11] This method suggests that informal, almost intuitive, knowledge allows us to conceive much more easily than what can be seen. In other words, on the basis of the material that the comparatist has gone through and analysed, it is possible to proceed towards explanations up to the point where the interpreted and organised pieces of evidence fit together and a narrative emerges. In the same way, the comparative research report narrative should have a plot and be a comprehensible entity for its readers, not a descriptive list of facts like a telephone catalogue that moves from country to country – in the age of the Internet these kinds of catalogues are simply outdated.

Methodologically looking for clues – particularly in the explanatory phase in the case of comparative law – is compatible with ethnographer Clifford Geertz's (1926–2006) methodological concept of *thick description*.[12] In this case it means a thick description of the legal cultures under study. Legal cultures here are normative systems that are constructed of established legal structures of meaning: they are the context of legal culture (written, unwritten) where various actors (legislator, judge, researcher, laypeople) are in interaction with legal rules and institutions. While the comparatist attempts to explain differences and similarities, they simultaneously conceptualise and theorise their research objects: it is a question of reconstruction of law where the comparatist from the viewpoint of an epistemic outsider kind of simulates the action of jurists in different systems. Thickness offers some kind of methodological backing: the thicker the description, the more credible the conclusions. Or vice versa: the thinner the description, the more unconvincing the credibility. Importantly, this does not work with quantitative approaches as they work differently to the qualitative approaches discussed here.

Comparative law research does not seem to fulfil the requirements for a study setting as in the exact sciences (eg physics, chemistry, astronomy), but it still attempts to avoid bias and prejudice. The comparatist tries by means of its own research setting to get rid of ethnocentrism and legal-cultural bias, but it is probably virtually impossible to completely break loose from the influence of one's own cultural sphere. Neither can the comparatist become fully detached from their own conception of the world and the deeply rooted basic ideas on, for example, what is right and what is wrong or if human rights are universal or not. And yet, it is still possible to attempt to reduce adverse effects, ie identifying and avoiding bias is important for sustainable comparative research practice

---

[11] See eg C Ginzburg, 'Morelli, Freud and Sherlock Holmes: Clues and Scientific Method' (1980) 9 *History Workshop* 5 ('Reality is opaque; but there are certain points – clues, signs – which allow us to decipher it', 27).
[12] In specific see C Geertz, *The Interpretation of Cultures* (New York, Basic Books, 1973) ch 1 ('culture is not a power, something to which social events, behaviors, institutions, or processes can be causally attributed; it is a context, something within which they can be intelligibly – that is, thickly – described', 14).

(*cf* epoche approach). Unfortunately, avoiding bias is difficult to achieve if and when the Western scholar studies non-Western laws and legal cultures (eg orientalism discussed in the previous chapter).

Owing to these factors the comparatist mostly looks for such explanatory factors as they find possible and sensible on the basis of their experience of the world of law. Therefore, they also unconsciously refrain from many such potential explanations and insights that another comparatist might perhaps find significant. That is why academic literature on the history of law and sociology of law, as well as other multi-disciplinary legal literature, is important because by means of it the comparatist can expand the horizon of their understanding and come up with new ideas and insights. In the explanatory phase this takes on a crucial role when description ends and the scholar attempts to proceed to understand and explain.

Although different comparatists emphasise different explanations, they frequently pay attention, however, to groups of matters of a similar type to explanatory factors. It is specifically a question of a number of explanatory factors because there is hardly a single case where the special features of a legal system can be explained (with any reliability) by means of a single factor. This kind of pluralism was recognised by the thinkers of the Enlightenment. For example, the philosopher Voltaire (actually François-Marie Arouet 1694–1778) wrote that, 'Three things ceaselessly influence the human mind: the climate, the government, and the religion'.[13] Indeed, it is possible to distinguish a number of different overlapping factors, which form the core of the explanations in comparative law. These explanatory factors are not presented here as they would form a kind of a compulsory list, which every comparatist would be obliged to check in comparison in a particular order. It is a question of a cluster of clues and hints that may be helpful. It indicates from where it is possible to look for explanatory factors and what the emphatic types of explanation (standing out in a striking manner) that comparatists use are generally like.

Explanatory Factors in Comparative Law

1. *Cultural factors* – religion, culture, ideology and mentality
2. *Economic factors* – economic system and economic resources
3. *Historical factors* – political history and sources of legal influence
4. *Geographical factors* – land, neighbouring countries and climate
5. *Other factors* – unexpected factors and surprises

III. CULTURE AND EXPLANATION

As became clear at the beginning of the book, it is difficult to define culture. Legal culture is a part of the larger culture of a country/system, and yet it is

---

[13] 'Trois choses influent sans cesse sur l'esprit des hommes, le climat, le gouvernement, la religion', Voltaire, 'Essai sur les mœurs et l'esprit des nations' (originally 1756) in *Œuvres completes de Voltaire*, vol 19 (Paris, Société littéraire-typographique, 1784) 352.

difficult to define in an exact manner. This causes troubles for the comparatist. In fact, all serious comparative law study is simultaneously the study of foreign legal culture. In the same way, most explanatory factors with which the comparatist attempts to explain the differences and similarities found are somehow of a legal cultural nature. In such cases culture refers to something quite general. We can for example make generalisations and speak about Western culture, which is an umbrella term for the form of culture that has its origin in Western Europe but that later on spread to other continents; to North America and Australia in particular and also to a great extent to South America. Yet, there are reasons to be cautious when speaking of the spread of Western legal thought as the case of public international law in Asia shows. For instance, the liberal and constitutionalist value-oriented views on the international legal order have not been unanimously accepted in Asia.[14]

A central factor by which cultural regions are defined is *religion* (broadly understood). This is the case although religion was not in general given much of a role in traditional comparative law which in the twentieth century was dominated by European civil jurists – although it lurked in the background implicitly.

> When the mainstream comparative law of the twentieth century is looked at, it becomes clear that the study of the relation between religion and law was not held in very high esteem. Even in extensive works the practice was usually to simply dismiss the significance of religion by referring to it in only a very small number of pages. This was not necessarily caused by the fact that comparatists would have been blind to the obvious connection between religion and law; more likely the reason was that the emphasis of comparative legal studies was elsewhere (ie doctrinally conceived private law).
>
> In practice, a great amount of academic endeavour was aimed at studies where the emphasis was on the similarities and differences between common law and civil law. This meant, nonetheless, that comparatists made an unconscious background assumption according to which it was not particularly important to pay attention to religion: the religious context of both common law and civil law was roughly the same Christian European culture. In this kind of intellectual climate it was not considered necessary to devote time to the study of Hindu law, Islamic law, Jewish law or Indigenous law because they all formed an exception to the common Christian American-European main rule. However, now it seems that religion has made a sort of comeback in comparative law, and there is a growing number of comparatists who are prepared to take into consideration the impact of norms and doctrines with a religious background. This does not mean that the significance of religion has grown as such, but it is a question of recognising the significance of religion for legal cultures. This recognition has inevitable methodological consequences for it expands the scope of comparative study of law by recognising religions as contexts of law. Notwithstanding, comparative study of religions has not been commonplace in comparative law.[15]

---

[14] J d'Aspremont, 'International Law in Asia' (2007) 13 *Asian YB Int'l L* 27.
[15] N Doe, *Comparative Religious Law* (Cambridge, Cambridge University Press, 2018) which focuses on the regulatory instruments of Jewish, Christian, and Muslim religious organisations in the UK.

Factors related to religion generally have the most obvious impact in the field of family law (marriage, inheritance etc) and in criminal law in the determination of punishment. Religious factors can also reflect on other fields of law in which cases their impact is particularly vehemently seen in attitudes to human and constitutional rights. For example, in Islamic countries the view of constitutional rights and their restriction seems to deviate from Western attitudes. Or the attitude to abortion in Greece and Ireland is different from that in Norway and Sweden. The way to perceive human and constitutional rights individualistically and with an emphasis on personal freedoms (ie stressing the rights of an individual) is not as such generally accepted in Asia. In connection with Asia it has been customary to refer to general legal cultural effects of Confucian legal mentality.

> In Confucian thinking the rules that dominate the life of an individual have been considered to be norms of a moral or ceremonial (*lǐ*, 理) nature, rather than that rules of law (*fǎ*, 法) especially set by the State. Resorting to legal order presumes a conflict between the plaintiff and the defendant or between the prosecutor and the accused while Confucianism aims allegedly at compromises. A formal rule of law that actors must follow is considered to cause more inconvenience than benefit to the community. The reason for this is that the rigidity of formal rules is thought to prevent the correct consideration of ethically relevant circumstances. A person who refuses conciliation and wants to resort to legal rules is in Confucian thinking a bad person from the point of view of the community: the results of a formal legal system and the formal legal process presumed by it are considered somewhat disgraceful in nature. Traditional Chinese social ethics is said to have avoided the specific definition and maintenance of rights because of its mentality. Yet, from Chinese legal history we are familiar with the opposing school of legalism (Chinese *fǎjiā*, ie 'legalists') during the sixth century to the third century BC. However, Confucianism is rooted deeply in the Chinese legal mentality. As Qin says: 'Nowadays, the rule of law has been written in Chinese Constitution, but Chinese still think in Confucianism way subconsciously, law still is not a favourable way to solve disputes'.[16] Regardless, it would be a step too far to consider the law of the People's Republic of China Confucian as the reality is more complicated and different cultural layers are mixing with each other.

Religious factors can also explain differences between the legal systems of countries, which are within the same religious cultural sphere. For example, the attitude to marital divorce can vary in Christian countries according to whether the countries are Catholic or Protestant (Ireland v UK), Orthodox or Calvinist (Cyprus v Netherlands). When such differences are explained, religious factors are of great significance. On the other hand, religious explanations should be sufficiently specific in order to benefit comparative law. In some cases a difference has to be made, for instance, when Shiite Islamic law is compared to Sunni law: these differences should not be ignored by saying in a general way that it is

---

[16] G Qin, 'The Thinking Way of Confucianism and the Rule of Law' (2008) 1 *J Politics & L* 68, 74.

a question of Islamic law. There are differences in emphasis between different schools of Islamic law as well as between the applications in different States. For example, polygamy, which is widely accepted in Islamic law, is formally forbidden in countries such as Tunisia and Turkey.

> According to the codification relating to the law concerning persons (*Code du Statut Personnel*), which came into force in Tunisia in 1956, polygamy is forbidden (art 18.1: 'La polygamie est interdite'). A Tunisian statesman and independence activist, the first President of the country and legislative reformer Habib Bourguiba (1930–2000) argued for the ban on polygamy using argumentation based on Islam. Turkey had already earlier (in conflict with traditional Muslim law) as a part of an extensive reform programme forbidden polygamy in its civil codification which was copied from Switzerland in 1926. At present, the criminal codification of Turkey defines polygamy as a crime (art 230). On the other hand, in Ghana, where the common law is followed, polygamy is allowed for Muslims to whom Shari'a is applied in this respect.

Religion is related to comparative law also in the respect that law (in the form of rules) in itself has a close connection with religion. This may come as a surprise to the modern Western comparatist because it seems quite a paradox. Nevertheless, in the opinion of several comparatists and anthropologists the law today has a role in the modern world that is similar to the role that religion played earlier. Berman outlines this as follows: 'Though not universal among transcendental religions, faith in law is common to all civil religions'.[17] This is true in particular in the Western cultural sphere although for example in the Nordic countries the status of law as a kind of religion does not seem as credible as for example in the US or Germany. On the other hand, Islamic and Jewish law – or at least some parts of law – embrace openly the idea of the religious foundation of law. In short, it would be a mistake for the comparatist to rule out religion when they attempt to explain differences and similarities.

In many cases, law seems to offer means for peaceful coexistence and methods for solving disputes between nations and cultures. In addition, in comparison that takes into consideration the different systems in the world it is impossible not to notice how significant a role religion or other strong philosophical theories have had and still continue to have in relation to law. A particularly clear example is offered by Islamic law (especially if one seeks to explain differences and similarities) where the law is a minor part of the more extensive Islamic culture, which challenges Western views in many ways. On the other hand, Islamic law is in its scope of application rather narrow, and it covers modern law to a rather limited extent. The systems of Iran, Pakistan and even Saudi Arabia are actually a combination of Western models, domestic customary law and

---

[17] HJ Berman, 'Faith and Law in a Multicultural World' in M Juergensmeyer (ed), *Religion in Global Civil Society* (New York, Oxford University Press, 2005) 69, 84.

Islamic law: different legal elements are mixed into legal-cultural pluralism so that the significance of the different elements varies according to the situation and people. (Islamic law has been normally applied mainly to Muslims.)

The significance of religious law as an object of study and more generally religion as a factor that helps to explain differences and similarities needs to be recognised. For a long time it has been implicitly assumed that religion has no role in civil law and common law. However, for the modern comparatist with a Western background it is useful to remember that 'Western law is full of values that come from the Christian religion'.[18]

A. Mentality

Explaining the differences between legal systems can also be more generally based on cultural differences in which case the explanatory factors used are the cultural special features of the countries/communities in question. In comparative law such explanatory ethnological factors as the character or mentality of the nation have been used. This type of explanatory factor is mostly encountered when Western legal systems are compared to, say, Asian or African systems (this may tell us something about epistemic bias). This is based on a point of view according to which, for example, in the Far East the attitude to law has arguably been different from the attitude in the Western countries, where law is considered to have a central role in the governance and direction of the society. For example, in Japan the attitude to law has long been dualistic because there the functionality of the Western legal system is considered to be based on its affinity for conflict although maintenance of the social order would, according to the traditional Japanese view, require mainly conciliation and persuasion. These legal-cultural special features, however, keep weakening as the Japanese legal culture becomes more and more Westernised. In any case, mentalities seem to matter. Yet, while making these sorts of generalisations there is a risk of falling into legal orientalism and, thus, exocitize foreign law according to one's own imagination.

> At present, Japanese law is classified as Asian mainly on geographical grounds. Many lawyers today argue that Japanese law is practically a Western system that mainly follows the Continental European model: there are, however, places where US law has a strong influence and certain places that can still be described as being in accordance with the so-called Asian legal culture. According to Koichiro in Japan 'the law is important mainly in symbolic sense. Its power is to be revered rather than exercised against persons within one's network of social relations'.[19] Nowadays extensive

---

[18] R Michaels, 'On the Comparability of Law' (2022) 12 *Ancilla Iuris* 19, 40 (www.anci.ch/articles/Ancilla2022_18_Michaels.pdf).

[19] F Koichiro, 'Changing Values and the Legal Culture in Japan' (1992) 4 *Japanstudien* 209, 211.

cultural generalisations continue to be part of the explanatory arsenal of comparative law, but the emphasis of cultural differences has clearly decreased compared to the twentieth century. Legal culture is referred to when explaining in a more subtle way sectors or certain special features instead of aiming at a comprehensive explanation by lumping everything under the phenomenon of Japanese legal culture. Comparative law has learned to be more open towards subtle variations and internal legal pluralism. Today it should be understood that labelling a whole system Asian or African tells us very little if anything about the actual legal systems situated in those vast geographical areas. Accordingly, for example, saying that South Korean law is 'Asian' or that the Egyptian system is 'African' does not reveal anything relevant about the legal systems of those countries.

Through culture it is also possible to understand and explain, for instance, gender linkage in the legal systems studied, which is visible in, for example, the history of legal ideas. There is quite a surprising similarity between Western and non-Western legal systems related to the latent gender ideology where division into public and private spheres of life is to be seen. Women (and children) have been considered to belong to the private sphere while men have been considered to belong to the public sphere, ie politics and economy.

Originally also in the West, civil and political rights were created for men only. The difference between Western and non-Western law today is, however, found in the fact that in Western countries women have been guaranteed formal equality between sexes in the sphere of formal law. In practice differences have remained to an extent, but by means of the international agreements on human rights it has been possible to balance the situation.

> The position of women and the regulation of their rights and obligations have been difficult areas for Western comparatists and jurists. Discussion has crystallised around a few questions, such as whether the obligation to cover one's hair (ie Islamic veil, *hijab*) is oppression or something else. Here legal cultures are talking past each other: from the Western perspective a veiled Muslim woman seems to be a subordinated victim of patriarchal power. On the other hand, a Muslim jurist can perceive that for example a Nordic woman is unprotected if not a victim of sexual rapacity. Both approaches are clearly extreme and cling to extremities – comparative law does not necessarily have anything to offer in a situation where different ideologies seem to consciously seek conflict. Yet, it is in the intellectual fabric of comparative law to understand and learn about different legal cultures, and this normally speaks for a conciliatory attitude and the attempt to tone down the extremities.

Political thinking is an expression of mentality. The political system of a State has a strong influence on the form and content of its legal system particularly in constitutional law, criminal law and administrative law. The political and economic system of a country is, on the other hand, influenced by the dominant ideology (conscious or unconscious). In general, the nature of the economic and political system of a country is designated in accordance with the prevailing ideology. For example, the nature of the legal system of the People's Republic of China can be seen to depend on the prevailing ideology in connection with many fundamental assumptions about law and the legal system (eg the role of the State). This is reflected for example in the legal status of a citizen in relation to the State and in possibilities of citizens to influence the decisions taken by the public administrative apparatus or in their opportunities to have effective protection provided by the law against public administrative apparatus.

On the other hand, law in China has developed at an amazing pace in the twenty-first century and simultaneously the differences compared to Western law – at least on the level of statutory law – have decreased in many sectors of law. Legal-cultural differences can all the same still exist as can be concluded on the basis of several individual issues.

> For example, the concept of the *rule of law*, which continues with the expression *not of men*, conflicts with traditional Chinese political and legal philosophical ideology where the emphasis is on the rule by men/people, ie *rénzhì*. It is literally a question of combining the word *rén* (人), which means a human being, with the word *zhì* (治), which means a rule; therefore, the meaning literally is *rule of man* and not *rule of law* or *control of law*. It is a kind of (Chinese) utopia of social control where the people who exercise power are thought to derive the right and entitlement to power through their own virtuousness, which is greater than the virtue of others (*control based on virtue: yǐ dé zhìguó*, 以德治国). Virtuousness can vary between the classical Confucian virtuousness and the presently dominating communistic virtuousness. However, this ideal of virtuousness is no less mythical or exaggerated than the Western versions of legal virtuousness, as an example of which the polysemic concept of *constitutionalism* can be mentioned. On the other hand, this kind of virtue ideal is an upside down ideal if it is compared to the rule of law instead of the rule of man.[20]

> It is hardly a surprise that the *rule of law* does not easily translate into Chinese, particularly if it refers to a constitutional State or a State where the foundation and limits for the exercise of power are set by law. *Fǎzhì* (法治), however, is a potential legal language translation because it combines the expression *fǎ*, which means law, and the expression *zhì*, which here means rule or power over someone. *Fǎzhì* actually means *rule that is carried out by law* where the main idea is also in the fact that law is a medium for a rule, not so much the basis and limitation for a rule, which it is generally thought to be in Western constitutional law and legal theory. Legal architectures differ from one another even though there are clearly similar elements in the building materials. Importantly, Chinese debates on key notions like the rule of law are more subtle and refined than comparatists tend to realise.[21]

It is also worth noting that ideological explanations by no means need to be related to systems of a distant legal culture, such as in China, or to systems that have been influenced by Islamic law. For example, the French and Italian

---

[20] For more detailed discussion, see eg R Peerenboom, *China's Long March Toward Rule of Law* (Cambridge, Cambridge University Press, 2002).
[21] S Seppänen, *Ideological Conflict and the Rule of Law in Contemporary China* (Cambridge, Cambridge University Press, 2016).

systems, which are legal-culturally close, have a shared legal inheritance in respect of how they treat the right of ownership. In both countries the right of ownership is based on the originally Roman law concept of *dominium*, which meant more or less virtually sovereign power based on ownership. In the age of the Enlightenment the theorists of natural law ignited a process whereby the idea of total ownership was transformed as a matter that involved obligations to the idea of ownership as a basic right of an individual. The individual became a central actor; the right of ownership existed ultimately for the benefit of an individual. Later on, in the nineteenth and twentieth centuries, this kind of thinking was called into question and more communal functions for ownership were sought.

From here Italy and France went in different directions: in France ownership is a fundamental right that is protected as a fundamental freedom, while in Italy ownership is not considered such an important value for the individual that it should be protected as a fundamental right. In Italy the approach in principle still is that ownership shall not be protected as a fundamental right that is constitutionally guaranteed – it is, nonetheless, guaranteed by civil law in various different ways, but not as a constitutional fundamental value.[22] However, there is no need to mystify legal mentality as an explanation for differences. As Blankenburg has noted the clear differences between, otherwise culturally very close, Germany and the Netherlands in litigation activity is not a question of mentality but rather there are different 'incentives their respective legal systems offer'.[23]

IV. ECONOMIC FACTORS

Normally economy refers to the process by which goods and services are produced and sold – this process or system has close connections with law. The basic structures of the legal system and the solutions adopted reflect the nature of the economic system of the society. This basic observation is general, and it does not mean commitment to a certain economic theory or over-emphasis of the significance of the economy when it comes to law. The study of the relation between law and economy came up particularly in the 1990s, with Posner as one of the leading figures. The tendency was born already in the 1960s, but it still took a while to rise to the forefront of research. The approach has gained ground by stressing the study method that attempts to observe the interactive connections between law/legal systems and the economy better than before. The trend is known by the name *Law and Economics*. The core idea in the movement is to

---

[22] Sabrina Praduroux, *The Protection of Property Rights in Comparative Perspective* (Groningen, Europa Law Publishing, 2013).
[23] E Blankenburg, 'The Infrastructure for Avoiding Civil Litigation: Comparing Cultures of Legal Behavior in the Netherlands and West Germany' (1994) 28 *L & Society R* 789, 807.

analyse legal norms by means of economic tools and by doing so it is hoped to be able to predict the economic effects of legal sanctions on human behaviour.[24]

In the economic analysis of law the content of legal norms is taken into consideration as the law in force and the main attention is in the first place paid to the economic efficiency/inefficiency of the norms. In this approach the areas of study and use have been laws on competition, companies and contracts. The *legal origins* theory, law and economics in comparative law, can be seen as a direct continuation development for this theory in the field of micro-comparative legal study. The theory has sought to explain the effectiveness of the economy with the inheritance of law from either common law or Continental European law.

> In legal economics the interest is focused on the law in force so that the analysis is carried out with tools developed in the sphere of micro-economics. While legal economics emphasises the significance of the law in force in the allocation of resources, the *legal origins* theory concentrates on the macro-level study. These approaches are however interested in common questions, the most central of which is economic efficiency. Legal origins theory has caused heated debate and discussion within comparative law and also within legal history.

To begin with, the idea of the interaction between law and economy seems sensible in all ways. A considerable part of the legal system has in fact been created to serve the needs that the economic activity in the society presumes. It would appear that an economy that favours free competition needs for example strong protection of property, which makes the competition between individuals for economic resources, as a guarantee for well-being and wealth, meaningful. The binding legal validity of contracts is an important principle for Western legal ideology. On one hand, in an economic system where the economy is controlled by the State the protection of the economy of individual citizens is not in an equally central position because a planned economy is not based on the competition between citizens over the economic resources. Albeit, the validity of contracts is an important basic idea also in a State-run economic system, as the example of modern China clearly shows.

In the former socialist countries the constitutional protection of property has been weaker while in Western market economy countries it has traditionally been quite strong. When such differences are explained, it becomes obvious that the different natures of the economic systems adopted have an obvious influence on the differences found in comparison. However, China in its present state is an interesting example of a hybrid legal system, which tries to combine private ownership and a socialist public law system (so called State-capitalism).

> From the end of the 1970s, a market economy and a centrally planned economy have been combined in China. In the eyes of a Western comparatist the tension between these two elements is inscribed in the Constitution of the People's Republic of China

---

[24] R Cooter and T Ulen, *Law and Economics*, 6th edn (Berkeley, Berkeley Law Books, 2016) 2–3.

according to which China is a socialist State under the people's democratic dictatorship led by the working class and based on the alliance of workers and peasants. On the other hand, in 2004 an amendment to the Constitution was made, according to which private property is protected. In China one speaks of Chinese socialism, which combines certain elements of Western law with certain elements of socialist law: the expression is *socialist market economy*. It is difficult for a Western comparatist to understand such a hybrid variation of legal culture although it seems to be an empirical fact. Difficulties are obvious: property rights and contract enforcement are weak, courts are not really applying law independently, and there is no Western style separation of powers or constitutionalism. Notwithstanding, China is undoubtedly an economic development success – notwithstanding its authoritarian government, which hardly fits into any Western definition of the rule of law or democracy. Tantalisingly, China seems to prove that there can be significant and even legal progress without the Western style rule of law.[25] All this may be difficult to digest if one is a Western comparatist.

The economic resources of a country might have an influence also on the differences and similarities of socio-legal solutions adopted in certain fields of law. If the economic system of an economically undeveloped country is to a great extent dependent on for example natural resources, it is natural that limitations set by environmental law (such as emission reductions, logging limits, protection of species or landscape, and pollution prohibition etc) are not as strict at the level of legal reality as in an economically developed post-industrial country.

In countries where there is wealth and economic resources it is also possible to direct resources to better observation of the environment as part of the economic activity. Here the question is specifically one of legal practice because the positive law of two countries can greatly resemble one another, but despite this there can be vast differences in the effectiveness of the regulation. In addition we have to pay attention to the integration of the Member States of the European Union in the field of commerce. Also the activity of the World Trade Organisation tends to reduce differences between the regulatory systems of different States although the effects on the level of legal culture might follow more slowly. Moreover, there is also competition between different legal systems and that may also have an impact on legal development.

V. HISTORICAL FACTORS

It has become obvious above just how close the connection is between comparative law and legal history. On the one hand, law and history are substantively intermingled, while on the other hand, it is almost impossible to fully separate

---

[25] J Husa, *Advanced Introduction to Law and Globalisation* (Cheltenham, Edward Elgar, 2018) 55–59.

comparative legal history from comparative law. The essentiality of history does not, however, mean that law would not be dynamic and that law would not change. But the change of law is rarely, if ever, a great leap, not even in a revolution. A good example of the inherent features of law is the division of Continental European law into private and public law, which is reflected everywhere in the legal system. Socialist law tried hard to shake off the division, but it was only partially successful and socialist law remained as an odd variant of civil law and socialist ideas about law.

The division already existed, though vaguely, in Roman law. Later the division between private and public law has been made on the basis of the definition of *Corpus iuris civilis* (the 'Body of Civil Law', a name which this collection received in the 1500s), which was done on the orders of East Roman Emperor Justinian (circa 482–565 CE) in the book *Institutiones* (1,1,4): 'publicum ius est, quod ad statum rei Romanae spectat, privatum quod ad singulorum utilitatem pertinent'. In other words 'public law concerns the State of Rome and private law is connected to private benefits'. Similar basic systematics are lacking from the sphere of the Anglo-American common law tradition, which has received considerably less Roman influence than civil law. The same type of permanent feature is also how the system produces legitimately new legal norms: is it done by means of the legislative body (statutory law-making) or by precedents of higher courts (judicial law-making)? In short, these kinds of basic distinctions are due to the historical processes. In other words, law is a highly path-dependent phenomenon.

So, history is important. However, because it is so important and so overarching, it is also rather difficult to perceive in a structured manner in the comparative study of law. It is, though, possible to present a certain number of typical historical factors to which it is possible to refer in the explanatory phase of comparison. For example, political history has a great impact on what form the legal system of each country takes. As a scholarly field political history typically deals with political decision-making, social power structures, political ideologies and the decision-making by the State. Factors that are most obviously political historical are found in the field of public law. For example, the most central features of constitutional law, such as the question of the form of government, can in most cases be explained by means of historical factors. For instance, the dominance of the President in the 1958 Constitution of France is explained by the influence of de Gaulle on its content. Likewise, the Japanese Constitution of 1947 bears a strong imprint of the US General MacArthur. And several features of common law in the US can be explained by colonialism and the cultural impact of English law, which is still ongoing albeit in a transformed and mutated form. The legal system of today's Iran would be difficult to grasp without taking into account the Islamic Revolution of 1979.

A. Colonialism

The explanation for the similarity of several Third World and Western legal systems is in most cases due to the colonial history of these countries. In addition to the substantive provisions of law, old colonial countries have inherited from their previous colonial rulers legal-cultural ideas of a fundamental nature, such as their doctrine of the sources of law as well as legal terminology and concepts. Anyone approaching the legal system of, say, New Zealand or Canada must inevitably observe the influence of English common law. In a similar fashion, it would be difficult to understand Latin American or North African systems without taking into account the long-lasting colonial impact.

> *Colonialism* refers to the imperialistic policy of colonisation where the greatest possible economic and military benefit from colonies was sought. The term is derived from the Latin word *colonia*, which refers to a settlement. Colonialism is closely related to imperialism in which several nations were brought under the control of the Western colonising States so that the ruler was able to govern the property and resources of the area under its power. Decolonisation, ie the dismantling of the colonial power, was at its strongest in the 1950s and 1960s, which was when the majority of African States became independent. Colonialism created an opportunity to exercise power and control over the colonial countries and enabled trade. In the field of law, colonisation meant transporting the European legal models to colonies. Decolonisation has not dismantled the legal-historical effect of colonisation, which continues to be seen today in all the States that were under the colonial power. On the other hand, scenarios vary and processes are multiple because the effect of legal colonisation has in many places also been positive – at least when seen from the point view of Western Countries.
>
> Most of the non-European world was colonised by means of public international law where it was called the Doctrine of Discovery. According to this doctrine, European colonial powers regarded themselves as 'better' than the people in other places. While the Europeans hoisted flags and built churches in the areas of the Indigenous peoples, they also made legal claims for the ownership of the new land, which according to their doctrine had been found (sic!). The doctrine was supported with a racist and ethnocentric way of thinking, which was supported by Christian belief: European white Christians were imagined as superior to others. Comparative law was not saved from colonial thinking, and the first part of the twentieth century was accordingly devoted to the attempt of comparatists to wriggle away from colonialistic thinking. Today colonialism has moved more into the twilight of methodologies and epistemologies; it can be glimpsed in such schools of thought and programmes as law and development. Comparative law is also in the process of decolonising itself as it struggles to take global legal diversity into account without imposing an implicit normative Western point of view.

However, the voluntary receptions of foreign law cannot be explained directly by colonialism, which is illustrated by the civil codification of Turkey that was earlier referred to in the book as well as by the reasons that are connected with the reception of European law by Japan. In fact colonialism is connected with these cases too, but in a way that is different from the general pattern: it was a question of the anticipatory rejection of colonisation by means of legal copying and transfer.

> The period of codifications in Japan was the 1890s when the fear of Western colonisation was real. Codifications had to come into force for the State to be able to build a new industrial Japan and to demand full sovereignty (in the eyes of Western powers). It was important for Japan to prove that it was an equal actor in relation to other sovereign States. In the opinion of the Japanese the codifications of Western Europe were the most refined models for laws, and therefore they were suitable for reception if and when they otherwise fitted the political agenda of the Meiji Empire.
>
> In the same way in Turkey the aim was to prevent the involvement of Western countries in the Turkish agenda in the 1920s, which for its part explains the quick renunciation of the tradition of Islamic law in the Osman (Ottoman) Empire and the desire to move over quickly to Western legal models. The Turkish (Kemalist) Republic embraced the Western code of law (also) in order to prevent the interferences of Western States in legal matters of the country which sought to question the sovereignty of the successor of the Ottoman Empire.

In hindsight, the question of colonialism is in fact considerably more versatile than the mere distinction between Western and non-Western legal traditions reveals. For example, present-day Australia is a product of British colonialism. Although English precedents no longer have a formal position after the 1986 Australia Act, it is not uncommon to see Australian courts referring to English precedents. Colonialistic structures nevertheless continued to have a significant place in legal thinking; as late as in 1992 the High Court in its *Mabo* decision ruled that the native people had title to land as against the immigrant population in cases that were related to natural resources and minerals.[26] In the *Mabo* case, the High Court rejected the Terra Nullius doctrine that had earlier been followed according to which the white immigrant population had entered land 'void' of laws or governance at all, stating that 'native title exists and is recognised by the common law of Australia'. The process of decolonisation of law is still, however, in the making in Australia as the Uluru Statement proves. The Statement calls for structural reforms in the system of governance in order to establish an aboriginal voice in public decision-making.[27]

For the modern comparatist it would be a grave mistake not to take the impact of colonialism into account. Importantly, it is not only about studying

---

[26] *Mabo and Others v Queensland* High Court of Australia [1992] HCA 23 ('the rejection of the notion of terra nullius clears away the fictional impediment to the recognition of indigenous rights and interests in colonial land' at [46]).

[27] D Larkin and K Galloway, 'Uluru Statement from the Heart: Australian Public Law Pluralism' (2018) 30 *Bond L R* 335.

post-colonial legal systems but also becoming aware of the impact of colonialism on the discipline of comparative law itself.

B. Understanding Institutions and their Adoption

Crucially, we must understand that history is not always 'only' history when it comes to law and legal matters. The execution of the comparative point of view in the doctrinal study of the law can also require the historical dimension. Frequently, understanding foreign law (why do they do what they do) presumes profound knowledge of its history, which means that comparison between the present and past of the system is also carried out. Clearly, the more significant a legal concept or institution is, the harder it is to understand its present role if something is not also known of its past that remains amongst us in the legal-culturally laden expressions and concepts of legal language.

The comparatist of the Continental European legal sphere in particular should make use of the historical dimension when they try to understand different kinds of law, such as the common law for example. When it comes to civil law and common law, as Samuel says, 'what differentiates these two traditions is primarily history'.[28]

A good example of the significance of legal history is the still visible remnants of the earlier *forms of action* of the judicial process. They developed as part of the common law over hundreds of years, ever since the early Middle Ages.

> It was a question of each legal problem being handled in a certain specified form. All in all the emphasis of the common law was and is in the court proceedings, even to the extent that content issues (law) were occasionally considered almost trivial. Here we have a significant difference of principle from the Roman-Germanic civil law concept of law, which is illustrated by an aspiration to justice (*cf* Roman *iustitia*). The forms defined for centuries what was admissible and what was not admissible to present by using a certain form of process, what could be referred to and what could not be referred to. One remnant of the forms of action is that even today in the common law the judge expressly controls the process by defining (ie judge applies the rules of evidence in the case at hand) what it is *admissible* and what is *inadmissible*.

> The idea behind the *forms of action* was that the question was not what was the correct decision in legal problem Z but what the correct form was for dealing with problem Z. Those forms were rejected ages ago, but their legal-cultural effect is still detectable (they were finally discontinued in 1873 by the Judicature Act). Forty years after the rejection of the forms the English authority of modern legal history FW Maitland (1850–1906) said as follows: 'The forms of action we have buried, but they still rule us from their graves'.[29] In common law *tort* (a delict, infringement of law) is

---

[28] G Samuel, *A Short Introduction to the Common Law* (Cheltenham, Edward Elgar, 2013) 1.
[29] W Maitland, *The Forms of Action at Common Law*, first published 1909 (Cambridge, Cambridge University Press, 1936) 1.

one of the legal offspring of the forms of action that have survived to the present day: an action brought is an *action of tort* (civil proceedings providing relief for persons who have suffered harm because of the wrongful acts of others).

Occasionally in comparative law, legal influences are thought to have travelled mainly by means of force. This, however, is not the whole truth. Sources of legal influence are by no means always to be explained by colonial history or the country's internal political history. It is also a question of which legal system has been ideologically valued (admired) to an extent that it has been seen proper to transplant/transfer its regulation models, institutions and concepts into one's own legal system. It can also be a question of idealisation of law of which the new coming of Roman law that spread from Germany in the nineteenth century is an indication. Idealisation of legal ideologies (eg admiration of the so-called classical Roman law) has its own role although it is rarely openly admitted to have been a central motive for adopting foreign law. In the case of Roman law admiration played, nonetheless, an important role.

However, why was Roman law adopted in the first place? Roman law has entered Europe several times: in Antiquity (*usus antiquus*), in the Early Middle Ages (*Karolings*), the Bolognian school of law in the Middle Ages, the Humanists (at the turn of the Middle Ages and the Modern Age) and later in the modern era (*usus modernus pandecratum*) and in the nineteenth century by means of the Pandectistic school of law (eg Bernhard Windscheid 1817–92). However, transplanting and other kinds of copying and learning take place and it is not simply about legal history.

For example, after the turmoil in the Eastern Europe at the beginning of the 1990s, several countries copied the US and German legal models and adopted from them often uncritically various regulation models without paying much attention to their applicability to their own legal culture. The German model of the Constitutional Court and US presidentialism have been especially frequently copied (applicably). For quite a while the *Ombudsman* institution of Swedish origin has also been popular around the world as part of different partial or total constitutional reforms. As an example from the sphere of Finnish law we can mention the adoption of principles concerning discretionary power relating to administrative law from the French and German legal systems that took place mainly in the 1950s through Finnish scholars. Later on those administrative principles were first entered in the Act on Administrative Procedure in 1983 and in the Act of Administration in 2004. The world of law is full of these kinds of examples. Watson puts it fittingly: 'Borrowing from another system is the most common form of legal change'.[30] This seems to be the case although it is not often openly admitted that comparative learning (by the legislator, courts or scholars) has taken place and foreign models have been utilised. A similar type of phenomenon can be seen in the use of comparative law by courts: foreign law is used but there is an absence of citation in published judgments.

---

[30] A Watson, *Legal Origins and Legal Change* (London, Hambledon Press, 1991) 73.

Sometimes legislative innovations are introduced not with a voluntary acceptance but by force. Coercion is a significant factor in particular in cases after a war when the winning party is able to dictate changes in the central features of the legal system of the losing party. A good example is the central role of MacArthur in the process of drafting the Constitution for Japan in 1947. The aim of the US was to make a constitution of a Western type, which would prevent attempts to assume an aggressive attitude in foreign policy. Several features in the Japanese constitutional system can be explained by this influence. In the same way, only historical factors can explain the provisions concerning the right to warfare of States that have been included in the constitutions of the States that lost in World War II. For example, the Constitution (actually the Basic Law of the Federal Republic of Germany, German *Grundgesetz für die Bundesrepublik Deutschland*) of Germany contains an express provision which forbids activities that are aimed at preparing aggressive warfare (Grundgesetz § 26 *Verbot der Vorbereitung eines Angriffskrieges*). This rule can be fully understood only against its historical background.

No one really denies the weight of history in comparative law. However, to take history into account is no small feat. Albeit, historical explanations are not always simple because, for example, in Israel the common law has been referred to in several cases although to start with its judiciary was almost singularly trained in Continental Europe. The substantive law of Israel seems to contain plenty of influence from Continental European systems while the procedural law is to a great extent in accordance with common law. This is due to the fact that jurists who had lived through the Nazi persecution saw in the adversarial common law process protection for civil liberties and human dignity, which the suppression mechanism of the Nazis had grossly and cruelly held in derision. The plural layers of the Israeli legal system are explained by legal history: general commercial law is Continental while maritime law is of a common law type.

> The Israeli law and Jewish law or *halakhah* are separate systems although they have many points of contact. *Halakhah* is literally translatable as 'the path'. The regulation covers the spiritual life and certain parts of the corporeal life. The norms consist of the main source *Torah* (*Pentateuch* with five books, and oral *Torah* consisting of orally transmitted legal tradition) in addition to the literary corpus of rabbinic legal texts and the overall system of religious law. *Halakhah* is about norms that are based on several written sources and in which there is material from the written law that consists of the five books of Moses and the compilation called *Talmud* where the texts of the *Torah* are explained. Like Islamic law, *halakhah* is based on the exposition of the divine law when the *Torah* and the *Talmud* were given to Moses at Sinai. The norms are likely to have been born over time acquiring different layers during its history.[31]

---

[31] For more detailed analysis from *Talmud* to modern Israeli law, see NS Hecht et al (eds), *An Introduction to the History and Sources of Jewish Law* (Oxford, Clarendon Press, 1996).

In the same way as Islamic law, the *halakhah* also takes a stand on religious issues related, for example, to praying and eating. Following it is in practice based on voluntariness, and the *halakhah* experts do not hold a similar stance to that of the Muslim *qâdi*. This legal tradition does not have one centralised or official interpretation; instead it gives scope for different interpretations. In Israel there are groups according to which no other law is needed, but there are also plenty of people who support a secular State. Curiously, Israel does not have a uniform constitution since the *Torah* has been considered as sufficient for that purpose. The modern legal world meets here the ancient legal tradition within the same legal system creating tensions and internal legal pluralism (hybridity). And, the pluralism is not due only to the *halakhah* but also due to the multilayered legal system that reflects its historical background: Ottoman law, British Mandatory (common law) and Israeli law. For an outsider, such as the comparatist, it is not easy to conceive what the relation between the Talmudic law and the law of Israel actually is.[32]

It is important for the comparatist to realise that the same external influences, such as the European Human Rights Convention, may cause different results in different receiver systems as the systems operate in different ways: a human rights obligation that in the Nordic Countries is carried out with hardly any problems can cause results that are completely unforeseeable in the legal systems of, say, Albania or Turkey. We can talk about a *mutation* of the source law in a foreign legal culture. An external influence that is adopted from somewhere else is not copied at the receiving end in exactly the same form as it had been in the source system: texts may be similar, but practices differ.

Mutation, in terms of evolution, is an unforeseeable alteration in the central features of the legal rule or legal institution borrowed. Mutation is not due to natural selection; instead, it is caused by the legal culture, ie a legal loan is adapted to the legal context that has changed (adaptation to the environment). Here we can perhaps talk about *evolution of law*, ie the slow alteration in the permanent features of law through legal systems adapting (or they are made to adapt by *refining* law) to their social environments. In short, law and its surroundings are interacting with one another.

It is also useful to notice that foreign models are hardly ever completely slavish imitations. It is typical that the national legislation attempts to combine its own legal culture and the foreign one to be adopted. Mutation is not always spontaneous. For example, the civil law book of Korea is to a great extent a copy of German civil codification and is divided into five books according to the German model: the first parts are the general part, the law of property and the law of obligations. The contents of the fourth and the fifth parts are formed so that they correspond to Korean customs and practices in the fields of family law and the law of inheritance.

Up to 2005 the civil codification gave the head of the family/household master (a male) priority in the law of inheritance (traditional 'head of the family' system

---

[32] HP Glenn, *Legal Traditions of the World*, 4th edn (Oxford, Oxford University Press, 2014) 122–30.

hojuje, Korean, 호주), but the system was found to be against the constitutional law. Therefore, the civil law book had to be renewed for it to satisfy the obligation of equality in the way required in the Constitution. At the basis of this is the classical Confucian style Korean idea according to which a family should have a head. Some of the Korean features of the system had been renewed earlier in the 1989 reform, but the *hojuje* model was still preserved at that time.[33] This could be regarded as an indication which speaks of the Westernisation of Asian law and the weakening role of Confucian ethics in the legal culture.

C. The Presence of the Past

The significance of history in explaining legal similarities and differences is hard to overestimate. As Gordley states: 'Legal rules acquire their structure over time. Thus even if comparative law scholars were only interested in the structure of modern rules, they would still need the help of history'.[34] If and when the intention is to carry out comparative research in a demanding way, from the point of explaining and understanding the observations ie differences and similarities, the time dimension is impossible to ignore. The significance of time, and in particular of time passed, is emphasised not only in common law but also in Islamic law.

> The relation of Islamic law to time and history is peculiar; it exceeds the respect for the conservatism and permanency that are characteristic of the common law. The traditional Islamic law Shari'a is based on certain sources and interpretations. The most important sources are the Koran and the established traditional knowledge (*Sunna*) that are related to the prophet Muhammad. On the basis of text sources an entity that was interpreted and aimed at systematicalness was created by means of Muslim legal scholars as early as in the eighth and ninth centuries. There are some differences between different schools of law, but they are all based on primary sources and on the system of Islamic law that is recorded in the basic works and commentaries of the schools.[35] *Fiqh* in its basic parts is based on the Koran and Sunna but there are, however, differences in emphasis. Essentially, 'the Quran is the most important source of law, but it is not the source of most law in Islam'.[36]

Basically Shari'a does not change because its basic sources do not change any more. If the system in general changes, it happens by means of reinterpretations

---

[33] See J Park, 'The Judicialization of Politics in Korea' (2008) 10 *Asian-Pacific Law & Policy Journal* 62.
[34] J Gordleys, 'Comparative Law and Legal History' in Reimann and Zimmermann, *Oxford Handbook* (n 7) 754, 773.
[35] As such, Islamic law is a very interesting subject for modern comparative law research; see H Harasani, 'Islamic Law as a Comparable Model in Comparative Legal Research' (2014) 3 *Global J Comp L* 186.
[36] A Black, H Esmaeili, N Hosen, *Modern Perspectives on Islamic Law* (Cheltenham, Edward Elgar, 2014) 11.

(*ijtihad*) of the same legal basic sources – the system is in other words more rigid than the common law because in the common law occasionally there is a completely conscious withdrawal from aged precedents. In Islamic law, on the other hand, the view is that to a great extent *the gates for reinterpretation* have been closed. Reformist Muslim legal scholars have been demanding for 100 years that *the gates should again be opened*. In connection with the common law in England, the House of Lords decided in the 1960s that the gates were again open for changing earlier precedents (to depart from a previous decision, 'When it appears right to do so').[37]

It seems to be a question of different degrees of legal conservatism. From the point of view of a comparatist it is a question of the same phenomenon but in different legal-cultural contexts. And, whereas Islamic law enshrines immutability, the common law is distinctly aware of the risks involved: 'too rigid adherence to precedent may lead to injustice in a particular case and also unduly restrict the proper development of the law'.[38] Curiously, the German Constitution (like that of some other States such as the Czech Republic, Greece and Turkey) has a so-called eternity clause (German *Ewigkeitsklausel*) which ensures that certain parts of the Constitution cannot be changed or amended. It has been noted in the comparative constitutional law that the eternity clauses forbidding changing the constitution's identity and core values have become more common than they previously were.[39]

Law as a cultural phenomenon builds on its past: the pastness is important for anyone wishing to understand and explain law. The law's quality of being in the past is, however, mixed with its presentness, ie law's quality of being in the present. Law is in force, but somehow its past is also part of its presence: layers rest upon other layers. So, the idea according to which law has the *presence of the past* makes sense. It refers to the significance of historical development and the specific legal mentality of law. Path dependence, the idea that past events influence future events, is an important factor for the comparatist who tries to explain differences and similarities.

VI. GEOGRAPHY AND CLIMATE

The influence of geography was for quite a while a popular theme in comparative law. As late as in the nineteenth century and early-twentieth century comparatists stupefied by colonialism might have considered that a certain climate and a certain geographic environment resulted in a certain kind of legal culture. It is

---

[37] The Practice Statement [1966] 3 All ER 77.
[38] ibid.
[39] Y Roznai, *Unconstitutional Constitutional Amendment* (Oxford, Oxford University Press, 2017).

hardly surprising that the northern environment was seen to create a vigorous and rational legal culture and the southern and eastern ones create something quite different. In fact Montesquieu commented on the influence of geography for comparative law in his classical work *The Spirit of the Laws* (*De l'esprit des lois*, 1748), the third book of which begins with an analysis of the effects of the climate. According to Montesquieu, the climate was the *first reason* for the development of nations.

> According to Montesquieu: 'In different climates there are different needs on the basis of which the different ways of life have been formed; these differences in the way of life have resulted in different laws!'[40] He stated it as a natural historical fact although this was just a prelude to his view according to which there were also important *physical* (climate, wind, temperature, soil) and *moral reasons*. He saw that such factors influence the *general spirit* of nations and the development of the forms of government and legislation, which are its expressions.

On the other hand, Montesquieu understood that the climate and other physical factors of the living environment do not directly determine the development of a nation. Such factors were only partially involved in the complicated process where the significance of moral reasons could over time turn out to be more significant than the physical reasons. Owing to such factors – which are still today used for explaining differences and similarities – Montesquieu underlined trade, production apparatus, finances, different moral habits and customs, religion and political institutions, among others. In his optimistic vision and belief in progress the developed nations were not fatally *at the mercy of nature* in the same way as the primitive communities. The lasting contribution of Montesquieu has been the insight into the significance of the context of law.

How about the situation today? There can be hardly any doubt that the content of the legal system is influenced among other things by geographical factors, such as the soil, natural conditions, climatic factors and neighbouring States. In countries where the risk of big natural catastrophes is considered to be great, the facts that are related to the soil have an impact on the legal system too. For example, in Japan a central field of operation for public officials is involvement in actions, such as advanced planning and readiness training, that aim at decreasing the effects of earthquakes. In practice, factors related to the soil have in such cases an effect on the legal power of the authorities in emergencies and on the fact that citizens are obliged to participate in the civil rescue rehearsals organised by the authorities or to follow strict rules concerning building.

Climatic factors have their impact on how the public authority regulates for the production and use of foodstuffs. In countries where climatic factors have an adverse effect on the self-sufficient production of victuals, authorities (or in

---

[40] 'Ce sont les différents besoins dans les différents climats, qui ont formé les différentes manières de vivre; et ces différentes manières de vivre ont formé les diverses sortes de lois!', C Montesquieu, *L'Esprit des lois* (Paris, Gallimard, 1995) pt 3, bk XIV, ch X.

some cases non-governmental organisations) must take care of, for example, collecting emergency stores and their storage. In countries where the degree of self-sufficiency is high in connection with food production, the existence and nature of such legislation differs from that of countries where the degree of self-sufficiency is low and the dependence on the import of foodstuffs is high. Attempts to ensure self-sufficiency can also explain, for example, the extent and content of legislation regulating agricultural subsidies. For instance, the agricultural subsidy system of the European Union largely explains the complex nature of the regulation of agriculture in Member States. In turn, the marked position of agriculture in integration is connected to the history of the Union. The context and historical path of law is important for the law itself but also for the comparatist who tries to understand it from an epistemic point of view of an outsider. More generally, due to the global climate change the role of future comparative law is being discussed against the backdrop of growing ecological concerns.[41]

A. Neighbourhood

English writer and poet GK Chesterton (1874–1936) once said that, 'The Bible tells us to love our neighbours, and also to love our enemies; probably because generally they are the same people'.[42] This quote fits well the world of law too. Ideologies prevailing in a State and the political systems adopted in it have an influence on the legal systems of the neighbouring countries. In this respect the geographical location of a State in relation to others is one explanatory factor in comparative law. The talk about the Nordic legal family is a good example – there would be no family without physical proximity.

Nearby countries that are included (or are thought be included) in the same cultural sphere are often the sources of legal ideas and socio-legal solutions. Many legal innovations have spread from one or another legal system to others. Geography and communications can sometimes have a significant role in the observation and charting of development trends. One example is the spreading of majority parliamentarianism, the so-called *Westminster* system that is of British origin, to several countries as a direct consequence of colonialism. On the other hand, the British system spreads far further than the neighbouring areas because of the seaways. Also Nordic legislative cooperation has resulted in considerable similarity of the legal systems of the Nordic countries; it has been a question of cultural unification of legal systems using legal-political measures, which has been facilitated by geography and carried out in several fields of law.

---

[41] M Nicolini, 'Methodological Rebellions' (2021) 16 *J Comp L* 487.
[42] GK Chesterton in *Illustrated London News* 16 July 1910.

The influence of neighbours can be detected, for example, in Belgian law, where French law has traditionally been an extremely strong influence. The Belgian Constitution divides the country administratively and regionally into four sectors, which are Brussels, Flanders (Dutch-speaking), Wallonia (French-speaking) as well as a small German-speaking part (French *Communauté germanophone*, Dutch *Duitstalige Gemeenschap*). All these areas have considerable autonomy. Official languages follow the division so that they are Dutch, French and German.

> For most of the nineteenth century the French and Belgian systems were almost identical, particularly in private law, because Napoleon's civil law codification was imported into Belgium in connection with the French occupation in 1804. In the same way, Belgian legal study was under the influence of France. In addition, the contributions of French legal scholars and French court judgments were used in Belgium as if they had always been part of Belgian law. Up until 1930 all university education was in French until the University of Ghent decided to use Dutch as its language of teaching. Other Dutch universities later followed suit, some as late as in the 1960s. Dutch-speaking legal study started developing as late as in the 1960s at the time German and Dutch legal doctrine in particular established a footing in Belgium (especially in Flanders).
>
> Most French-speaking jurists today no longer learn Dutch, and Dutch-speaking jurists have started to lose their knowledge of French. As an example we can mention the German concept for a loss of a right (*Rechtsverwirkung*), which came into Flemish legal study from Holland by means of the concept *rechtsverwerking* but was never rooted in the French doctrinal study of law in Belgium. It was partly a linguistic problem because the concept was difficult to translate into the legal French of Belgium. In Flanders the cultural effect of French law is diminishing at present, and in practice considerably more legal doctrine is being written in Dutch and English than in French, which was the dominant language of legal study up to the 1960s. The fall of legal scholarship in French in the bilingual and culturally divided Belgium led to the rise of legal scholarship in Dutch; also the influence of other countries other than France has increased.[43] In the same way it is possible to detect in Finnish legal science the sceptical and evasive attitude that has continued for over 200 years in regard to the law and legal doctrine of the neighbouring Russia. The attitude of Finland to Swedish (or other Nordic) study of law on the other hand has always been of a positive nature.

The role of geographical factors as explanatory actors in comparative law are often also related to history through which it is possible to answer why legal innovations have transferred from one country to another. For example, the long-lasting Finnish tradition of transplanting from Sweden is partly explained by historical factors and partly by geographical ones (indeed Sweden clearly used

---

[43] For a more extensive discussion, see D Heirbaut and ME Storme, 'The Belgian Legal Tradition' (2006) 14 *Eur R Priv L* 645.

to have better resources for drafting legislation before Finland did). Yet, legal-cultural models can be transplanted also from countries that are geographically far away. In such cases the legal system of the source country is often idealised – at least to some extent – in the receiving country. Sometimes geographical proximity can have an effect on what is appreciated. After a period of great changes in Eastern Europe, several countries took in many aspects of the German legal system to be their model for private law. To take another example, in East Asia it is not possible to disregard the impact of Confucianism. For instance, in constitutional law the general cultural values, customs and traditions are based on Confucianism and this fact is relevant when it comes to the applicability of Western constitutionalism.[44]

A well-known example is also the abovementioned Belgium, which for a long time followed French models in the development of its legal system: this was explained by geography and shared language (in Wallonia; the language of Flanders being Dutch). Geography and language explain also the influence of the Dutch and German legal cultures in Belgium, and in particular in Flanders.

VII. OTHER FACTORS

Other factors that can influence the contents of a legal system, or in a broader sense the legal culture, can include things that it is difficult to take into account because of their unexpected nature or because the case is of an unofficial but normatively significant arrangement, which is difficult to find on the basis of formal legal sources. Legal-cultural practices (living law) are not often based on written law or written precedents by courts. For the comparatist, being an outsider, finding such factors is likely to be difficult (eg customary law, internal traditions, legal mentality, professional practices). On the other hand, being an outsider can also be a methodological benefit because the comparatist looks at the foreign law from the outside and can grasp something that does not even occur to the lawyers operating within the system.

> Being an epistemic outsider is generally seen as negative when it is a question of research, but in comparison even this cognitive setting can be turned upside down. In the autumn of 2012 scholars in the field of psychology published a study according to which human beings make better decisions using a foreign language because the foreign language reduces decision-making bias.[45] This is due to the fact that a foreign language is ideal for removing deeply rooted fixed ideas embedded in one's own culture – by means of foreign language latent factors that have an emotional influence on attitudes can be surpassed. By means of comparative law a similar effect

---

[44] N Son Bui, *Confucian Constitutionalism in East Asia* (London, Routledge, 2017).
[45] B Keysar, SL Hayakawa and SG An, 'The Foreign-Language Effect' (2012) 23 *Psychological Science* 661 ('The reduced fluency in a foreign language could therefore lead to more analytic decision-making processes', 661).

can be achieved even more efficiently because there is a question of not only a foreign language of law but also foreign law. Thus, the foreign elements are double: rules and their legal-cultural context are unfamiliar as is the legal language. Foreign law and foreign legal culture may provide greater cognitive distance and emotional distance than one's own law and legal mother-tongue. What is lost with foreignness may be gained in creating epistemic distance from one one's own law.

There is not a shadow of doubt that constructing explanations and understanding foreign law is challenging. The legal system (or equivalent organised large-scale normativity) is so complicated as to its nature and interdependency that explaining it even partly is not possible if reference is made to only a limited number of explanatory factors. Even if the explanatory factors are almost the same in two countries, it is more than likely that the legal systems differ from one another. Unfortunately, there is an almost limitless number of different haphazard factors that are difficult to explain by means of the above-discussed general factors. Giving scientifically exact explanations and exact predictions is not often possible in comparison; therefore, in comparative law explaining is *interpretive explaining*, which is based on the (hermeneutical) understanding of foreign law. Thick description may lead to deep understanding and, finally, to explaining the reasons for differences and similarities.

> If the comparatist for example wants to explain the strong position of the president in the Finnish governmental system, they would have to get acquainted with the factors and events that had an influence on the birth of the Constitution in 1919. In the same way, the comparatist must be acquainted with German history from the period preceding World War II if the intention is to give an explanation for why certain parts of the Constitution of Germany have been defined as permanent (§ 79[3] *Eine Änderung ... in den Artikeln 1 und 20 ... ist unzulässig*). This eternity clause rejects changing certain fundamental principles of the German Constitution.

> Political scandals, the collapse of the value of money, historical events (eg declaration of independence, civil war, entering into the European Union and dissolution of State etc), environmental disasters or other types of major disaster can also be of significance when the reasons that have affected the adoption of legal decisions and the differences in legal systems are explained. For example, the structure and legal mentality of the European Union has from 2008 been influenced more by the financial crisis than by any other factor. Brexit has, no doubt, added another complicating layer in the EU governance.

> The inflexible formalities of the German civil code *Bürgerliches Gesetzesbuch* (BGB) caused major problems in economically difficult times. At that time the rigidity of the codification was dealt with by dismantling it on the basis on paragraph 242, which provides that, 'An obligor has a duty to perform according to the requirements of good faith, taking customary practice into consideration'. Basically, the rule contains a principle that requires the payment to be in accordance with honest and fair trade/exchange (*Treu und Glauben*) and trading practice (*Verkehrssitte*). This article provided a window for interpretation where good faith was given a much wider interpretation than the legislator had originally intended. The explanation is not legal-theoretical but is due to the fact that the BGB had been drafted in the

atmosphere of the Pandects of the nineteenth century, which favoured small enterprises and liberalism. Without interpretation the rules of the codification would not have adapted to the changing demands of different economic times: the aim was to avoid (economic) excess in legal practice and simultaneously to advance economic activity – without having to amend the BGB. So, the change of context normally changes living law. For instance, understanding the constitutional significance and role of the Supreme Court of the United States would be difficult without understanding the polarised political background. Similarly, understanding the African tradition of the strong-man style of presidency requires us to take into account colonialism and its aftermath in the post-colonial countries.

Among various unexpected factors there can also be various quasi-legal arrangements that complicate the comparatist's attempts to make out the content of a foreign legal system. The point is that not even within the Western legal cultural sphere do legal problems need to be solved only by means of legislation. One example to be mentioned is the labour market negotiations and the collective bargaining involved. The collective agreements partly replace actual legislation on labour law and actually (de facto) surpass the legal (de jure) legislative organs. In cases where such practices are included in the statutory law (ie arrangements can be based on written provisions) it is not difficult to detect them, but in cases where written law contains none or very few references, finding them is very complicated for the comparatist who examines the system from an outsider's perspective.

> For example, *guanxi* (关系) prevails in the Chinese cultural sphere. *Guanxi* is difficult to perceive but appears to be legal-culturally a significant factor. It seems that there is no universal consensus on how to explain or define the concept in either Chinese or English. Basically, it is a question of a confidential relationship between parties where reciprocity between parties prevails in relation to service provision. Furthermore, it is a question of kind of a friendship where parties have committed themselves to an ongoing social chain of exchanging services. The influence of the *guanxi* network can in some cases be more effective than the formal legal system. Here is the thing for the comparatist: it is difficult to tell it apart from actual corruption although *guanxi* is not directly identifiable with what in the West is called corruption. For the Western comparatist it is difficult to make the distinction between corruption (eg things like favouritism, nepotism and clientelism) and *guanxi*. In fact, *guanxi* is not corruption as such, rather it refers to a system of relationships that create a basis for various forms of social interaction and the development of trust and cooperation.[46]

VIII. DIFFERENCES BETWEEN EXPLANATORY FACTORS

Not all the explanatory factors that were discussed above have a similar influence on law and legal systems. They can occur either on their own or in different

---

[46] See eg B Kwock, MX James and AS Chuen Tsui, 'Doing Business in China' (2013) 4 *J Business Studies Q* 56.

combinations. The comparatist cannot just make a general reference (eg 'this is because of history', 'culture causes these things', 'mentality is the cause' etc) to different explanatory factors, but more structured explanations ought to be attempted in comparison. If the aim is to construct (for similarities and differences) explanations that are credible for the scholarly community of legal studies, it is useful to try to limit the factors that influence the study object so that the role of each explanatory factor can be evaluated separately. It might be useful to separate:

— *primary explanatory factors* (what is the primary explanation),
— *secondary explanatory factors* (what else is there in addition to the primary explanation); and
— *potential explanatory factors* (what explanations seem credible although there is no actual 'proof').

It might also be sensible for the comparatist to reject the aim to find perfect and all-inclusive scientific explanations. It is probably more rewarding to concentrate on the explanation of such differences and similarities between legal systems/cultures that appear to be the most central and interesting. One should follow the clues that appear to be most promising when getting acquainted with the data and during the study process and settle for the mere mentioning of the rest. Seldom does it make any sense to try to construct comprehensive scientific explanations. Not even a legal-culturally dense description is sufficient, but concentration and trimming is required. The process gives scope for creativity and different research emphases. On the other hand, a challenge is the spice of comparison for it gives extra excitement to the whole endeavour. This applies, of course, to quantitative comparative approaches too.

Explaining each detail would probably take so much time and trouble that making an attempt is not sensible. Because the comparatist studies legal systems that are unknown to them, it is not very wise for them to expect to be able to understand and explain everything. From the point of feasibility of the results of the comparative study, it is better justified to concentrate on factors that can with good reason be considered as essential new observations or surprises. Also the attempt to provide global hypotheses is likely to be too ambitious an aim for common sense comparative law, which is aware of its inborn weaknesses as a field of legal research.

In addition we must note the simple fact that in practice things in legal cultures usually tend to get intermingled. Not even within a single legal culture is it always obvious what kind of legal norms are really resorted to. There may also be regional differences within one country. Otto offers a fitting description: 'Anthropological research shows that people in local communities often do not distinguish clearly whether and to what extent their norms and practices are based on local tradition, tribal custom, or religion'.[47] In Turkey, for

---

[47] JM Otto, *Sharia and National Law* (Leiden, Leiden University Press, 2008) 30.

example, the traditions of Islamic marital law are widely followed and overlap with legislation that follows the Western model. In Turkey, this hybrid overlapping is, however, unofficial while, for example, in Ghana it is institutionalised by the official system.

> In Turkey, a customary habit is to give a dowry, a so-called *mahr* that is a payment to the bride as presumed by Islamic law. The civil codification of Turkey does not forbid *mahr*, but from the point of view of formal law the arrangement is based on voluntariness. The legal system of Turkey does not presume or demand such a gift. So, it seems that the traditional and religious feelings of people do not necessarily coincide with the formal legal system. Practices can be considered as normatively significant although they would not be based on officially recognised law. In Ghana, the customary laws of marriage can be based on the tribal laws or Shari'a, and both the forms of marriage can be polygamous. The marital gift is part of such marriages while common law marriages do not recognise a corresponding marital gift, and the common law marriage is monogamous.[48]
>
> The difference between Islamic and positive law is curious. According to, for instance, Article 26 of the Moroccan family law codification, 'Le fondement légal du Sadaq consiste en sa valeur morale et symbolique et non en sa valeur matérielle' ('The real value of the marital gift [Sadaq] is based on its moral and symbolic value, not on the material value'). Yet, the bride price is a condition for the legal validity of a marriage contract. The Moroccan marriage law seems to be somewhat patriarchal (as is typical for Islamic law). However, after the amendment of 2004 adult Moroccan women can enter into a marriage autonomously, although they may still opt for assistance by a male guardian.

For the comparatist it remains a great challenge to understand the subtle connections and interaction between social norms, Islamic rules and positive law. And, it is this subtlety which also tells why comparative study of law must often be genuinely multi-disciplinary: legal history, sociology of law, legal anthropology, law and development studies, law and economics, legal linguistics and political and governance studies belong to the methodological toolbox of the modern legal comparatist. However, for the comparatist it is crucial to be able to understand what is going on in other disciplines. Being able to understand and to apply does not transform the comparative lawyer into a sociologist, but it means that the comparatist may benefit from sociology. Despite the unavoidable difficulties related to interdisciplinarity it is part of the modern comparative study of law.

IX. THE PRESUMPTION OF SIMILARITY?

In comparative law certain natural law speculations have occasionally been presented according to which there would be a specific original law (French

---

[48] See J Bond, 'Pluralism in Ghana: The Perils and Promise of Plural Law' (2004) 10 *Oregon R Int'l L* 391, 402–03.

protodroit, German *Urrecht*), which would explain the similarities between legal systems. Natural law refers to a body of laws that is considered to be derived directly from nature, right reason or religion and which ethically binds all human societies. Right reason refers to Cicero's idea according to which, 'True law is right reason in agreement with nature; it is of universal application, constant and everlasting'.[49] For comparative law it is a question of the same thing as in early linguistics where the imaginary 'original language' of human beings was sought in a biblical spirit (ie language spoken before the Tower of Babel). According to linguistic monogenesis hypothesis there was a single proto-language of humankind. Now, it is true that at the basis of comparative law there are ideas of some sort of universalism, ie a belief in such concepts and theories that would be applicable to almost all people and things at all times. Importantly, comparative law's universalism is related to knowledge and not knowing the substance of law. Epistemic universalism does not require substance universalism as the latter does not embrace the global diversity of law.

Actually in modern comparison only a few scholars are committed to strong natural law universalism. The diversity of legal cultures and the peaceful coexistence of legal traditions are preferably emphasised. Pluralism is understood as a basic condition of the world of law in the twenty-first century. Besides, the existence of some sort of an *original law* does not seem credible since there can in fact be practices that differ from each other in the context of similar legal basic solutions, concepts or institutions. Accordingly, it does not pay to invest in the discovery of the Legal Atlantis or any other mythical original source of all law. But, of course, there are similarities in peoples' legal systems (or organised large-scale normativities), but it is more important to study the relation of law to its context than to the dream of the original law. Modern comparative law embraces diversity.

It is not possible to underestimate the contextual elements of legal systems without falling into ethnocentrism. It is hardly possible to explain any part of a legal system detached from its social context, irrespective of whether it is a question of economy, religion, culture or politics. The universalism of modern comparative law is of a milder form and emphasises that law ought to be studied without paying attention to the borders between States or any other formal distinctions. We can learn from each other while we perhaps learn to understand why other legal cultures differ from our own. It is a question of the forms of the normativity existing in different cultures and social practices, which we in one way or another find *legal*, ie there is normativity meaning that something *ought* to be done according to a normatively fixed position. Be that as it may, this has not always been sufficient for all comparative legal scholars.

---

[49] 'Est quidem vera Lex recta Ratio, naturae congruens, diffusa in omnes, constans, sempiterna', Cicero, *De Re Publica*, bk 3, ch 22.

190 *Comparing – Differences and Similarities*

In particular the functional comparative law that was further developed in the twentieth century by Zweigert and Kötz took as its driving force the assumption of similarity.[50] Their assumption has received due criticism, and in the theory of modern comparative law there is no longer a strong fundamental assumption of similarity. On the other hand, the assumption of similarity (Latin *praesumptio similitudinis*) cannot, however, be completely rejected because legal solutions in social problems are often surprisingly similar at the level of the *standard models* – at least if the systems compared belong to the same cultural sphere. When cultures change, there is also alteration and mutation in the legal approaches and socio-legal solutions.

The differences detected might in many cases be due to the circumstances rather than different basic ideas. Therefore, so-called common sense also seems to support – to a certain extent – the idea of the similarity of the contents of legal rules and principles. Perhaps the fundamental functions of the established social rules that guide human behaviour are not in the end so very different even if the technical solutions differ from one another. On the other hand, expectations have grown modest compared to what they were over 100 years ago in the days of the Conference in Paris and before the devastating world wars. The belief in the common law for the civilised world (French *droit commun l'humanité*) is no longer as strong as it was then. Pioneer Saleilles' dream of 'une sorte de droit commun de l'humanité civilisée' no longer really exists.[51] Comparatists have become more aware of differences when the theoretical straitjacket of private international law has been slackened and detached and the committed enthusiasm about normative harmonisation has subsided. Today, there is no longer an obsession towards similarity between legal systems – on the contrary, ideas of legal diversity have been on the rise at least in comparative law academia.

Here we are also close to the ethical questions of comparative law. Among the basic ideas of comparison, there is a belief that ultimately the people who create and use legal rules are pretty similar creatures. Independent of their field, comparatists often share the basic philosophical idea according to which people in spite of their cultural differences have similar patterns of behaviour, which result in regularities of the systems under study. On the other hand, today we have become more conscious than before of the fact that there are also differences between legal systems that have a close connection. We cannot stretch the assumption about similarity very far. For instance, in Nordic law we can, for example, easily tell apart the Eastern Nordic law of Finland and Sweden from the Western Nordic law of Denmark, Norway and Iceland; the law of Scotland

---

[50] K Zweigert and H Kötz, *An Introduction to Comparative Law*, 3rd edn (Oxford, Oxford University Press, 1998) 34.
[51] R Saleilles, 'Conception et objet de la science du droit comparé – Rapport présenté au Congrès international de droit comparé' (1900) 29 *Bulletin de la société de législation comparée* 383, 397. See also B Fekete, *Paradigms in Modern European Comparative Law* (Oxford, Hart Publishing, 2021) 74–75.

differs from the law of England and Wales; there are differences between the system of Hong Kong and Mainland China; the law of Louisiana differs to some extent from the rest of the US, etc.

Generalisations that are too rough do not serve well modern comparative law that aims at a balanced research frame: the scholar should not decide in advance whether they will emphasise differences or similarities. The assumption of similarity should not be stretched too far and often, frankly, it should not be assumed at all. It is also worth noting that legal terms and concepts that are seemingly identical (so-called *homonyms*) might result in considerable misconceptions in comparative law even within the same legal-cultural sphere. Even the exact same legal rule or institution can function in a considerably different way when placed in a different environment. The context of law is of importance especially for an outsider who lacks the internal legal-cultural embedding.

A. Diffusion and Similarity

In connection with the adoption of foreign law, changes in the rules of etiquette caused by the alteration of the internal procedures and decisions within the new legal system are involved. *Legal irritant* is one of the terms that today is preferred to legal transplant among other concepts such as legal transfer, legal transposition and legal translation. Although external influence has an effect on national and international law, each system leaves its own mark on the originally foreign influences and doctrines independent of whether they are inherited, forcefully introduced, borrowed or copied (directly or with modification). The context is of utmost significance. As pointed out by Tamanaha: 'Law cannot deliver in and of itself because it swims in the social sea with everything else'.[52]

The assumption of similarity can sometimes be connected to a problematic idea according to which all legal innovations would have only one genuine common source, and the occurrence of an innovation in different places could be explained by diffusion, ie the intermingling of various constituents. Watson in particular supported the view, according to which almost all that has ever been discovered in private law in one way or another originates in Roman law. This assumption is, however, not essential because it is also possible to think that similar situations can result in solutions of the same type, the application of which is attempted by means of similar socio-legal solutions. Yet, the general significance of Roman law can hardly be dismissed and in this sense Watson has a strong argument.

As an example of the versatility of diffusion, here legal diffusion, we can take the fact that although the fundamental features of the legal system of the

---

[52] BZ Tamanaha, 'The Primacy of Society and the Failures of Law and Development' (2011) 44 *Cornell Int'l L J* 209, 247.

US originate in the English common law legal culture, the Constitutions of these countries differ in form and content. The same applies to Germany and Japan in particular in connection with civil law: codifications of civil law are of a similar type, but the systems differ significantly at the levels of legal reality and attitudes to the legal-cultural climate. The civil codification of Switzerland also differs from the Turkish civil codification at the level of written law, although to begin with the Swiss regulation was copied almost word for word. There is an abundance of examples in legal history. Even though one would not support (as many do not) the views of Watson, his basic argument carries an undeniable force: 'Law develops mainly by borrowing'.[53] However, it is important to realise that borrowed law and that of the source system will most likely end up working differently. Different contexts of law produce different outcomes even if formal law would appear identical.

Of the basic interests of comparative law, the integrative interest seems to be built on the assumption of similarity, but strictly speaking it is not quite true. The assumption of similarity appears to be supported by Article 6 of the Treaty on European Union, according to which, 'The Union is founded on the principles of liberty, democracy, respect for human rights and fundamental freedoms, and the rule of law, principles which are common to Member states.' In addition, according to the article:

> The Union shall respect fundamental rights, as guaranteed by the European Convention for the Protection of Human Rights and Fundamental Freedoms signed in Rome on 4 November 1950 and as they result from the constitutional traditions common to the Member States, as general principles of Community law.

However, it is not a question of looking for any original law but rather that the national legal approaches in force in one Member State do not exhaust the body of potential alternatives for a socio-legal solution. The same applies to the mention in Article 38(1) of the Statute of the International Court of Justice: *the general principles of law recognised by civilised nations*, which does not presume an assumption of similarity but instead concentrates on the common features that exist (not stretching the assumption any further). What is more, the relationship between general principles and comparative law is complicated and not very satisfactory.[54]

To conclude, the assumption of similarity can perhaps be taken as a heuristic principle for the preliminary hypothesis of comparison in particular when the socio-legal solutions compared are written and are technical in nature. In the same way the assumption of difference can act as a hypothetical starting point for comparison when systems are culturally far apart, such as for example Iranian and Dutch matrimonial law or the Swedish law on consumer protection

---

[53] A Watson, *The Making of the Civil Law* (Cambridge MA, Harvard University Press, 1981) 181.
[54] J Ellis,' General Principles and Comparative Law' (2011) 22 *Eur J Int'l L* 949.

and the corresponding American law. Some sort of diffusion is very common in the world of law, but this does not result in general similarity. The fact that there is more and more legal transplants and diffusion does not mean that differences would disappear as long as there are differences in the contexts of law. Globalisation has not changed this as legal globalisation does not necessarily produce only similarities: there are always local social, political and economic complications. In other words, the comparatist should not be surprised to find *both* similarities and differences. At the end of the day, what really counts is to render similarities and differences comprehensible to one's readers.

8
Comparison – Obstacles and Difficulties

COMPARATIVE LAW THEORY is sometimes a curious thing to read; there are so many warnings and endless lists of difficulties one may encounter. Some of the writing seems to have but one purpose: scaring other scholars away from comparing laws. But this theoretical negativity hides the obvious: to practise comparative law is not only challenging but also very interesting and intellectually highly rewarding. Notwithstanding, it is often laborious enough to examine a single legal system, and study results that are unambiguous or directly applicable often remain a dream in cultural and social science studies including many kinds of legal studies.

When the number of legal systems increases and comparison is included, the number of problems increases many times over. Comparison in practice means wrestling with these problems and obstacles. Accordingly, comparative legal research is challenging but certainly *not impossible* or meant only for the Hercules-Scholar, ie the ideal comparatist, immensely wise and with full knowledge of various legal materials, cultures and languages. Being a real life comparatist is, luckily, more practical.

I. COMPARATIVE RESEARCH – BETWEEN THE FAMILIAR AND THE FOREIGN

The number of problems has made some scholars think that in comparative law foreign legal systems should not be studied in order to truly increase knowledge but instead in order to understand one's own legal system better. This is true, but only partly. There is no reason in comparative law to give up even when the study of foreign legal systems and cultures – just like one's own – is difficult and laborious. In the comparative law research process it is in practice impossible to avoid mistakes and misinterpretations: we make intuitively false assumptions based on our own culturally conditioned experience of law. It is, however, possible to reduce the number of mistakes and misunderstandings the longer and deeper comparison proceeds. Comparative law does not offer easy and quick profits for the impatient. This reveals the hermeneutic nature of comparative law; foreign law can be understood by studying individual parts against whole legal culture and the whole legal culture by reference to the individual parts (so-called hermeneutic circle).

On the other hand, it is not impossible to make decent legal comparisons, either. If and when there is commensurability there is also comparability and that is the lifeline of the comparative law endeavour. Epistemic commensurability, not similarity, is the quintessential thing.

Only a comparatist dedicated to full relativism (ie conceptions of law and legal principles are necessarily and totally relative to the persons and groups holding them) can end up regarding systems as so different that comparing them would simply not be possible. This extreme conclusion would mean the death of all kinds of comparative studies about humankind and human societies. However, human experience and our ability to communicate through language and cultural barriers do not support the idea of a complete lack of epistemic commensurability and full relativism.[1] A good example is comparative law in itself because international literature produced in its sphere is read despite borders between States and systems, languages and cultures. Moreover, even doctrinal legal scholars read and have always read legal literature in foreign languages – and have understood these texts at least to some degree. Looking over the borders enriches all sorts of forms of legal scholarship and in a globalising world looking over borders has become increasingly relevant.

In comparative law the significance of international publishing is great because the audience that the comparatist is attempting to reach through a deeper analysis of legal culture needs to be convinced of the conclusions and arguments based on comparison. It remains for a scholar's colleagues to rectify faulty ideas. And it remains for the comparatist to take the corrective feedback into consideration in later work. Many comparatists stress publishing in international languages – English, French and German – because otherwise getting critique and feedback is difficult in practice. As for Masters' theses, the aims, resource questions and capabilities/facilities have an influence on the fact that it is not sensible to attempt to draw up such works primarily in international languages – naturally there must not be many mistakes and any gross misunderstanding in these works either, and it is advisable to delimit the study topics as clearly as possible. And when the knowledge-interest is related to domestic legislation or the judicial function, it is natural to use the domestic language in publishing. Yet, seriously performed, comparative law should be published *mainly* in English because English is the main language of international legal study today. On the other hand, by means of German, French and even Spanish it is possible to reach a considerably wider readership than in smaller local languages, such as Icelandic, Finnish, Estonian, Irish (*Gaeilge*) or the Basque language (*Euskara*). This may also concern big languages which have internal

---

[1] HP Glenn, 'Are Legal Traditions Incommensurable?' (2001) 49 *Am J Comp L* 133.

variation, for instance, publishing in Cantonese Chinese reaches a smaller audience than publishing in Mandarin Chinese or English.

An inalienable part of comparative law is feedback and criticism, the purpose of which is not to suffocate the enthusiasm to study but to serve as necessary feedback for the comparative learning process. The significance of feedback is due to the fact that the comparatist investigates foreign legal systems from the epistemic viewpoint of an outsider. On the one hand, the outsider can make observations and perceptions, which those within the system are not able to make. But of course, being an outsider sets certain limits epistemologically and institutionally. Thus, the central incentive of the whole theory of comparative law and methodology is to offer tools and ideas for crossing borders in research. To that end, this is the sole purpose of this book too.

> Naturally it is not only a question of language but also of the internationality of the publication fora used. Language does not have a decisive importance if the study is published on a forum that is only known in one's own country: in such a case the study is out of reach of international review, but owing to its language even domestic jurists can miss it (if it is not in domestic lingua). On the other hand, it has to be emphasised that publishing in English does not mean that publishing in national languages is not necessary: national legal languages are by no means dying out and we must not abandon them and publish only in English. Nevertheless, in today's world a serious comparatist can hardly avoid publishing in English: it is the best (meaning the most widely understood) linguistic vessel for conveying non-national study of law.

However, one should not exaggerate because it is not always necessary to engage in demanding academic comparison. If we were to be content with just observing foreign legal systems without the comparative element, there would still be at least three benefits. First, there would be the more profound understanding of one's own legal system mentioned above. Secondly, there would be the activity in solving judicial problems and, thirdly, comparative information assists legislative drafting by providing examples and sometimes legal transplants. However, if the comparative dimension is included the aim is to create new knowledge that crosses the boundaries of national legal systems and can, in addition to its practical aims (drafting of legislation, judicial decision-making), also be directed to theory formation and the understanding of law as a cultural phenomenon. Different attempts to classify legal systems and to master the knowledge of their diversity form a central part of knowledge acquisition in comparative law. For example, constructing legal families and debating about them cannot be characterised only as an activity that aims at a better understanding of one's own legal system (more of this later).

In the following text, problems that the comparatist may come across in their work are discussed while simultaneously an attempt is made to chart some answers to those problems. The main problem bundles in comparative law are related to study material (or data if you prefer), handling and analysis of the study material, the concept of law and comparative law in itself. In practice these problem clusters are interrelated, which reflects the hermeneutical and interdisciplinary character of studying law comparatively.

II. RESEARCH DATA RELATED PROBLEMS

It is an indisputable requirement that in comparison that is aimed at the present (law in force is in focus) the study material used by the comparatist should be as up-to-date as possible. The freshness of the material does not have any intrinsic value, but it is a question of the nature of legal study according to which one has to be familiar with changes in legislation and one has to know what rules are in force. However, the fundamental characteristics of a legal system do not change quickly. For example, from the point of view of theoretical (macro-) comparative law, the freshness of the source material is not so essential. The rate at which the cultural deep structures of law change is considerably slower than the surface changes in black-letter law. The existence and continuing value of legal history, Roman law in particular, as a discipline stands as a testimony of the slowness of legal change.

And yet, the scholarly comparatist has to keep an eye on what kind of amendments in legislation or what kinds of precedents emerge concerning their study topic. The modernity and accuracy of the material presumes that the comparatist has a chance to get their legal study material (legislation, preparatory legislative material, court decisions etc) from sources that are as reliable as possible; browsing the Internet is certainly not always sufficient even though googling may provide a starting point.

Basically, it is recommended to get the primary sources from official legal materials (statute books, case registries and preparatory material for legislation) of the countries that are included in the comparison. In most cases sufficient knowledge of the foreign language in question is required by either the researcher or those assisting them. The situation is improved by the fact that nowadays provisions from the main areas of the legal system are to a great extent available as official translations in best known languages (mostly in English). It is possible to get material through the various legal servers available on the Internet, some of which are free of charge and others not (the latter has unfortunately been gaining more and more ground). Also different databases can be highly useful.

> Databases contain concentrated data that has been collected from legal literature. They perform the same function as printed bibliographies or libraries. Databases come in several formats. They can be classified into text, fact and reference bases. Both text databases and reference databases can be available separately or they can be included in a data bank that consists of different databases. The same database can be available in different data banks and in different forms. Some articles can be included as full text databases whereas some only reference information, like in the open SSRN database where there are a huge number of abstracts and full texts. For the comparatist, the most frequently used and most useful are, for example,

Westlaw International and *HeinOnline*. The increasing amount of open access publishing is slowly diminishing the problem of 'behind paywall' as the growing number of peer reviewed books and articles are appearing in Open Access form. For the comparatist the growth of open access publishing is a particularly welcome development.

Secondary sources are, for example, printed bibliographies, encyclopaedias, scholarly monographs and introductory works (textbooks), commentaries and journal articles and case comments published in legal periodicals. Secondary sources often help to locate the primary source (statutory rule, case). It would be irrational to try to directly locate the object of one's interest only on the basis of official material. Information contained by primary sources becomes accessible far more easily if the opinions of the national legal doctrine are also resorted to. By means of the literature and source references included in articles and books, it is easier to identify the relevant primary source material: it is like following the footsteps of national doctrinal study (or other authoritative internal formation of legal knowledge) because comparatists are not in a position to deduce for themselves which primary sources are relevant and which are not. Furthermore, in terms of time it is efficient to first get acquainted with secondary sources and, assisted by these, with the primary sources. The availability of both types of source material is assisted by the comparatist's personal contacts with scholars in the countries compared or other lawyers, such as judges, solicitors or civil servants. Email and social media like Twitter are handy tools in creating and upholding contacts with scholars all around the world.

> We may also find a technically developed Western law in which the most important legal-cultural sources are not legal cases or statutory law but jurisprudential (scholarly) texts. One example is Scottish legal culture which has assimilated Roman law, customary laws of local nature, feudal laws, canon law and English common law. The Scottish system has significantly absorbed case law and legislation from the neighbouring countries (England and Wales) and thus created a mixed legal system. While the English common law was for a long time under some kind of legal-cultural isolation, *ius commune* covered Scotland where it was also taught in universities. Both before and after 1707, when the Treaty of Union created the UK, Scottish jurists studied in Continental European universities and brought to Scotland law that differed from the common law. The consequences of this legal-cultural work can still be seen today in the works of great Scottish jurists: Thomas Craig (1538–1608), James Dalrymple, Viscount Stair (1619–95) and John Erskine (1695–1768). Their writings still have an authoritative legal position in Scottish legal culture: their texts are permitted to be used as complementary sources of law.[2]

Multilingual legal dictionaries are also useful for the comparatist who wrestles with the problems of legal translation. In different language areas legal dictionaries that are compilations of legal terminology have been published. Some of

---

[2] See DM Walker, *The Scottish Legal System*, 8th edn (Edinburgh, W Green/Sweet & Maxwell, 2001).

them are monolingual, and originally were meant to be used within a particular legal culture – this means that they are particularly good sources of knowledge for the comparatist, too. Renowned monolingual dictionaries are, for example, the French *Vocabulaire juridique* and the American *Black's Law Dictionary*. On the other hand, several legal dictionaries serve especially the interaction between language areas. There are also extensive bi- or multilingual legal dictionaries, in which each language in its turn is the source language. Within the framework of the European Union there has been formed an extensive multi-language database IATE (*InterActive Terminology for Europe*), which contains plenty of legal vocabulary in the languages of the Member States.

The task of legal translation in the EU is complex and it requires constant use of a comparative approach. IATE (iate.europa.eu) is useful for comparatists because it helps in translating many European legal terms and shows equivalent terms in EU legal languages. For example, the English term *legal act* (as an act intended to produce legal effects) is given equivalents in EU languages like *Rechtsakt* (German), νομική πράξη (Greek), *acte juridique* (French), *gerechtelijke handeling* (Dutch) and *oikeustoimi* (Finnish) etc. Also, the EuroVoc (eurovoc.europa.eu), which is a multilingual thesaurus, is useful for the comparatist. Yet, as the example above shows legal terminology is far from easy: *gerechtelijke handeling* does not really seem like the proper equivalent Dutch term (ie *rechtshandeling*).

The following list shows the general journals on comparative law that are worth keeping up with. From this list it is possible to grasp the current state of the comparative law debate and research. There are so many specialised journals that are available traditionally or via the Internet that a more comprehensive list here is not worthwhile. The relevance of the special journals depends on the interests of each comparatist.

Journals and Reviews on Comparative Law

AJCL/*American Journal of Comparative Law* (US). Published since 1952.
CJCL/*Chinese Journal of Comparative Law* (UK). Published since 2013.
GJCL/*Global Journal of Comparative Law* (The Netherlands). Published since 2012.
ICLQ/*International and Comparative Law Quarterly* (UK). Published since 1952.
JCL/*Journal of Comparative* Law (UK). Published since 2006.
MJ/*Maastricht Journal of Comparative and European Law* (The Netherlands). Published since 1993.
RabelsZ/*Rabels Zeitschrift für ausländisches und internationales Privatrecht* (Germany, in three languages: German, English, French). Published since 1927, and since 1961 under the present name.
RIDC/*Revue internationale de droit comparé* (France, bilingual: French, English). Published since 1949.

ZfRV/*Zeitschrift für Rechtsvergleichung* (Austria). Published since 1960.
ZvglRW/*Zeitschrift für vergleichende Rechtswissenschaft* (Germany, bilingual: German, English). Published since 1878.

The development of net-based networks now offers more and more extensive opportunities to study foreign law. Social media is also a great help these days (eg Facebook, Twitter, Mastodon). Some blogs are of particular interest like the American Society of Comparative Law Blog (ascl.org/blog). Courts and Ministries of Justice have web pages through which plenty of information and original documents, including as PDF files, are sometimes available. The problem with online sources can sometimes be their reliability, and the homepage addresses can change (with no forwarding instructions) or maintenance can be lacking. In many cases problems are also caused by the fact that information is not updated regularly. There can also be inaccuracies and variation in translations of the official legal languages (of the system) in a multilingual system. Sometimes translations cause more difficulties than they solve. Google translate is helpful but not always reliable.

In spite of the problems, the Internet is a great help in the acquisition of comparative and international study material. On the other hand, the Internet is no miracle worker: while we earlier suffered from a scarcity of sources, the present-day comparatists in most cases suffer from a monstrous oversupply of sources. Skills in comparative law are needed when information from different sources must be evaluated and made proportionate to other information. Bare documents need information about contexts if they are to be understood. Screening of sources presumes advance information, and googling alone does not take one very far – the Internet is filled with aberrations intermingled with correct information, and the trick is to separate these from one another. Moreover, this is important when reading national doctrinal texts as mainstream information is not always to be found on the Internet, whereas more obscure material seems to find its way into the cyberspace with no problems. Twitter, for example, is filled with information – some is very useful and some is nonsense – the trick is to tell these apart.

III. PITFALLS IN RESEARCH-MATERIAL PROCESSING AND ANALYSIS

The famous quote by Oliver Wendell Holmes expresses the special relation between law and language nicely: 'A word is not a crystal, transparent and unchanged; it is the skin of a living thought and may vary greatly in color and content according to the circumstances and time in which it is used'.[3] This quote underlines the living nature of legal language; a nature that causes difficulties for any comparatist.

---

[3] OW Holmes writing for the majority in the case of *Towne v Eisner* [1918] 245 U.S. 418.

A. The Problem of Legal Language

The difficulty of understanding foreign and even native law is partly due to the legal language itself. Even within a single legal language there can be problems with comprehension. This has its reasons, which are connected to the relation between law and language. Arntz described the relation fittingly: 'Everyone working on questions of legal language quickly becomes aware of the fact that language and law are closely bound up together. Law comes to life through language'.[4] More specifically, law comes to life in the legal language that is a language for specific purposes (LSP) which differs from standard language (eg common law English is not the same as standard English). In fact, legal language is a sublanguage, which means that it is a particular language used in a body of texts dealing with law/legal matters. In this sublanguage the creators of the documents containing rules, principles, judgments etc share a common vocabulary and common habits of word usage. Thus, it is not only a question of the unfamiliarity of legal language in comparison but its particular nature even within one's own system.

> It is a question of the nature of legal language as an LSP. Legal language is often deceptively easy because it resembles normal language, which is not very technical. But as Poscher states: 'despite the familiarity of the language used, lay people still get the impression that they do not really understand the legal texts'.[5] The situation is twice as hard for the comparatist who studies foreign law: comparatists can think that owing to their expertise they understand the foreign legal language better than they actually do (imagined familiarity). In terms of methodology this produces a kind of *triple hermeneutics*: (1) the lawyer ought to understand social reality (facts; the social dimension); (2) the lawyer ought to understand law/legal system (norms; normative dimension); and (3) foreign law/legal system ought to be interpreted through the comparatist's own (reconstructed) vision of foreign law (foreign norms: other normative dimension).

It may be argued that (Western) legal language is conceptual and abstract – the abstract formal concepts are its core. The concepts and how they are expressed are the result of a long historical process. They can also be thought to reflect the legal thinking, progress and operating logic of each legal language. The legal language used in English-language jurisdiction differs from standard English in a number of ways. Translating and understanding the language of English law also presumes knowledge of the common law and its history. The same can apply to all developed legal languages. Mattila has quite correctly emphasised that 'legal linguistics requires support from legal doctrine: it is the latter that shows the meaning of legal terms'.[6] So, legal language is difficult to understand

---

[4] R Arntz, 'The Roman Heritage in German Legal Language' in H Mattila (ed), *The Development of Legal Language* (Helsinki, Kauppakaari, 2002) 33, 33.
[5] R Poscher, 'The Hand of Midas' in J Hage and D von der Pfordten (eds), *Concepts in Law* (Dordrecht, Springer Verlag, 2009) 99, 99.
[6] H Mattila, *Comparative Legal Linguistics* (Aldershot, Ashgate, 2006) 15.

also from within the system because it typically contains words and linguistic features for which there is no need in everyday language. It has been pointed out that 'all legal systems develop certain linguistic features that differ from those of ordinary language'.[7] Hence, it is no wonder that the branch of linguistics researching LSPs has also shown an interest in legal language.

> *Legal linguistics* is a special field where legal language and its development, characteristics and use are studied. Legal language is studied from the point of view of linguistics. The field can be described as a synthesis of legal study and applied linguistics, which has several constituent parts: (1) *morphology* refers to the part of linguistics that studies inflections of words, their formation and derivation as well as how compounds are formed of different words; (2) *syntax* refers to the constituent part of linguistics that is related to the structure and constituent parts of a sentence and studies word order for example; and (3) *semantics* is the branch of linguistics that studies the meaning of the expressions of a language. These fields are not as relevant to the study of comparative law as they are to legal linguistics, even though sometimes it is difficult to see any distinction or to tell comparative law apart from comparative legal linguistics. As de Groot says: 'Interesting, relevant differences should not be "lost in translation": those differences have to be explained'.[8]
>
> In legal linguistics the focus is often on the study of legal language that takes place within one legal language or one legal culture. When the challenge offered by foreign legal languages is added to this, one of the greatest challenges met by the comparatist is to clear the obstacles presented by foreign legal languages. *Comparative legal linguistics* developed by Mattila is an interesting answer to this challenge of understanding as it combines linguistics, comparative law and even legal history.[9]

The comparatist has to translate text in a foreign LSP; that is often the prerequisite for understanding unless there are reliable translations available. Problems with translation are basically caused by the fact that legal language differs from the standard language both in its grammar and its style. It contains plenty of special vocabulary, its sentence structures are more complicated than those of the standard language and the terms and concepts usually have an exact legal meaning. Sometimes the legislator uses *legal definitions* and orders/dictates directly in the statute text how a certain term shall be understood in the context meant in the statute. Significant differences with the everyday language can be found in spite of the semantic similarity. Same challenge, in turn, concerns legal translators who need to identify relevant features of legal systems and relevant differences between them.[10]

---

[7] P Tiersma, 'History of the Languages of Law' in P Tiersma (ed), *Oxford Handbook of Language and Law* (Oxford, Oxford University Press, 2012) 13.
[8] G de Groot, 'The Influence of Problems of Legal Translation' in CJW Baaij (ed), *The Role of Legal Translation in Legal Harmonisation* (Alphen aan den Rijn, Kluwer, 2012) 139, 159.
[9] H Mattila, *Comparative Legal Linguistics*, 2nd edn (Abingdon, Routledge, 2016). French edition *Jurilinguistique comparée* (Montréal, Yvon Blais, 2012).
[10] J Engberg, 'Comparative Law for Legal Translation' (2020) 33 *Int'l J Semiotics L* 263.

All the factors mentioned above emphasise the need to resort to material in the original language or at least in key issues to examine the contents of the foreign law (also) directly in the original language. If the aim is to reach the legal-cultural level in comparative law a basic ability of some sort to read and perceive foreign legal language is necessary. Naturally this does not mean knowledge comparable to that of one's native language is necessary: one should master the foreign legal language to the extent that independent use of sources in that language becomes possible. To be sure, full command is not required as the research objective dictates the level of linguistic knowledge required. Moreover, if the number of systems is great it would not make any sense to require language skills in all the languages of the studied systems.

So, must the comparatist be a linguistic genius? The answer is: no. It is not a question of the simple command of a language but of the challenge offered by the special legal terminology of the foreign language. Understanding legal language involves problems of its own. Understanding legal language as an LSP requires more than understanding the text; knowledge of institutions, systematics, norms, processes as well as of legal culture and legal history is also required. Knowledge acquired specifically by means of comparative law is needed for the *legal-cultural context of foreign legal language* to become comprehensible. In practice the comparatist has to translate (and simultaneously interpret) from one language to another even if it is not done on paper or with a computer. As noted by Galdia: 'Legal speech acts that form the legal discourse in one legal language are transformed into equivalent legal speech acts of the target language'.[11]

B. Multilingualism

Owing to legal-cultural differences we can say that linguistic and conceptual terminological problems as such are only a part of the problem. Pozzo gets to the point: 'Legal languages have their own stories: they reflect the evolution and the architecture of a given legal system'.[12] *Legal encyclopaedias* are extremely useful when crossing these linguistic barriers is attempted: by means of them it is possible to get assistance for orientation in the foreign legal architecture. The need especially applies to legal dictionaries as standard language dictionaries are not sufficient to fill the need of specialised legal language. The technical terminology of legal language is only partly included in general dictionaries, and such translations are not always reliable because often they have not been checked by an expert in law. Problems are also caused by the fact that there are

---

[11] M Galdia, *Legal Linguistics* (Frankfurt am Main, Peter Lang Verlag, 2009) 224.
[12] B Pozzo, 'English as a Legal Lingua Franca' in Baaij (ed), *The Role of Legal Translation in Legal Harmonisation* (n 8) 183, 186.

certain systems where several official legal languages are used side by side, such as in Switzerland.

> The Swiss Confederation (Latin *Confoederatio Helvetica*) consists of 26 cantons, which have considerable autonomy. At the federal level the legislative power is vested in the Federal Assembly (German *Bundesversammlung*, French *Assemblée fédérale*). The administrative power is vested in the Federal Council (German *Bundesrat*, French *Conseil federal*), which is elected by the Federal Assembly. It is possible to challenge a law passed by the Federal Council and have a referendum if required by 50,000 or more citizens entitled to vote or at least eight cantons. The multilingual and multicultural structure of the country is also demonstrated in the number of legal languages because statutes are published in three languages, namely German, French and Italian. (Romansh spoken in some areas is not an official legal language.)

On a more profound level, it is a question of the legal-ideological climate and the different ways of perceiving legal institutions and concepts that are reflected by legal language. The more significant and essential the concept, the greater the danger of confusion and misinterpretation. In other words, the problems with legal translation are caused by the differences between systems because legal languages are *system specific*: the language and concepts used in medicine, chemistry and economics are not system specific in the same way. Moreover, a language does not necessarily constitute one legal language only: German legal language is, apart from Germany, found also in Switzerland and Austria; there are versions of legal English in, for example, England, Ireland, Scotland, the US, Canada, Australia, South-Africa, India, Hong Kong, Singapore and the European Union. There can also be systems where there are two versions of the same language within a country (Norway: Bokmål and Nynorsk, mutually intelligible) or administrative region (Hong Kong: Cantonese and Mandarin, not mutually intelligible in speech, intelligible in writing). A special case is formed by States where there are two or more legal languages (eg Belgium, Canada, Finland and Switzerland). The European Union is a case of its own kind as there are 24 official languages within it.

> The citizens of the Union have a right to send documents to the institutions of the European Union in any of the official languages of the Union. In addition, citizens have a right to get the answer in the same language. In the same way all directives, statutes and other EU legislation are published in all official languages. The members of the European Parliament have a right to express themselves in the official EU language of their choice. *Multilingualism* is based on the EU treaties. It reflects the cultural and linguistic variety of the Union. On the other hand, it is also a huge challenge. Almost all legislation and the most important political documents and judgments are translated into all official languages. This system is legally, comparatively and linguistically quite complex: EU legal concepts are often transferred from the national systems or from international law. However, these transplanted concepts now have autonomous EU legal meanings. Moreover, the EU has three procedural languages (English, French, German) that function as internal working languages.

The European Union is not, however, completely alone with its multilingualism because, for example, in South Africa there are 11 official languages. According to Article 6, Item 1 of the Constitution: 'The official languages of the Republic are Sepedi, Sesotho, Setswana, siSwati, Tshivenda, Xitsonga, Afrikaans, English, isiNdebele, isiXhosa and isiZulu'. All these languages can at least in theory be used in courts although English in practice is by far the strongest legal language. The position of Afrikaans has not completely disappeared, although English has overtaken it as the language of law.

> Afrikaans is a language that developed from Dutch and is spoken in both South Africa and Namibia. There are now about six million speakers of the language, of which about one half are white. Legal Afrikaans (*Regsafrikaans*, *reg* as Dutch *recht* and German *Recht*) has been in decline since 1994 but is still the second most significant legal language after English in South Africa. It is, for example, possible for a person knowing Dutch to understand Afrikaans in the same way as it is for a person knowing Swedish to understand other Nordic legal languages. Moreover, owing to the Roman-Dutch legal tradition (*Romeins-Hollandse reg*) it is possible to indirectly perceive legal Afrikaans on the basis of the concepts of legal Latin and legal German.[13]

C. The Significance of Context

One of the typical causes for translation problems is found in the difference between legal systems that are based on Roman-Germanic codified civil law and the common law tradition. For instance, in the sphere of both legal cultures Latin legal expressions are used, but those expressions mean different things. Finding corresponding direct translations is not always possible. Partly due to this, presentations on foreign law are usually overflowing with foreign words or at the very least there are expressions in the original language in brackets after the translations made by the comparatist; they are not there simply for decorative reasons are but due to the problems with translating the concepts. If a fitting translation is missing, it is possible to invent a *neologism* that is functional in the language of the publication and to place the expression in the original language in brackets after it. The rarity of the languages of Indigenous peoples presents its own additional challenges if the aim is to understand their legal cultures. For example, the Sámi language (any of its forms) did not originally have legal terms of its own, but they have since been developed when needs have arisen. Similar problems appear when a country seeks to make its native language legal language and abandons the language of the former coloniser. In Tanzania the Parliament passed a law in 2021 that declares Kiswhali as the official legal language, with English to be used 'as an exception'.[14]

---

[13] See L Meintjes-van der Walt (ed), *Introduction to South African Law*, 3rd edn (Cape Town, Pearson, 2018).

[14] Written Laws (Miscellaneous Amendments) Act, No. 3 of 2020 [United Republic of Tanzania].

When legal concepts have direct counterparts in the reality surrounding us, it is usually relatively easy to conceive the meaning of the terms: individual, family, fixed assets, murder, judge and so on. When legal terms do not have a counterpart that it is possible to observe by means of the senses, the situation becomes more complicated. It is, for example, hard to see an administrative procedure with one's senses although constituent activities related to it are easy to observe (by handling of documents, hearing, final act etc). For example, fundamental concepts such as a *legal act* or *legal capacity* cannot be directly observed by means of the senses.

Legal language like law itself is heavily *context related* by nature, which means that the technical translation of it by means of a dictionary does not necessarily produce an optimal result even if special law dictionaries are used. And, when comparison crosses cultural borders difficulties become more severe as, for example, when translating between a Western language and the language of Islamic law, ie Arabic. As Karakira notes:

> The difficulty arises when a translator's exposure to the cultural and legal environments of his working languages is unbalanced. This could lead a translator to misunderstand not only the significance of the specialised terms used, but also the distinctive features of syntax and register of the original language text. The other, and more significant, difficulty arises from the lack of equivalence at the term level in the two languages.[15]

Clearly, comparative law requires knowledge of the legal-social and linguistic contexts. Within the sphere of the EU the recognition of this problem is demonstrated by a special professional group of *jurist-linguists*, who are expected to be specialised in both translation and law. For example, jurist-linguists (or legal translators) in the Court of the European Union translate into all official languages the Court's judgments and the Opinions of the Advocates-General for publication in the European Court Reports. Jurist-linguists also translate requests from national courts for preliminary rulings as well as other documents required for the procedural purposes of the EU Court. In the European Union the variety of legal languages is a significant factor that often requires a comparative law approach for its support.

> The official and working languages of the EU's institutions are Bulgarian, Croatian, Czech, Danish, Dutch, English, Estonian, Finnish, French, German, Greek, Hungarian, Irish, Italian, Latvian, Lithuanian, Maltese, Polish, Portuguese, Romanian, Slovak, Slovene and Swedish. Legislation is legally valid in all 24 official languages. The jurist-linguist acts as a mediator in the legal praxis of the EU Court. The Court is the highest court in the European Union in matters of EU law. The role of the EU Court as a judicial organ is also based on the multilingualism applied

---

[15] S Karakira, *Lexis versus Text: The Case for Translating English Legal Texts into Arabic* (University of Western Sydney, 1997), researchdirect.westernsydney.edu.au/islandora/object/uws:19.

by it. The role of the translation service of the EU Court, and the jurist-linguists working there as mediators of legal praxis, is therefore crucially important for legal certainty.[16]

The fact that legal concepts and terms are tied to the context is again erecting obstacles for the study of legal systems *in their entirety*. Basically, it is a question of the risk that the comparatist (unintentionally) may assume that the object of their study is found in legal systematics in the same place as in their own legal system (the trap of assumed familiarity). Conceptual correspondence should be treated with benevolent suspicion and the same applies to legal concepts and terms that appear to be the same or similar (*faux amis*, ie false friends).

From the point of view of a case-oriented comparatist this means that, even though they would be interested in one special question only, at least to some extent they have to acquire knowledge of the entire legal system. If the study techniques in such a case are variable-oriented, the extent of the material makes studying whole legal systems difficult. It is, however, possible in such cases to engage more thoroughly in the *exceptional cases* (something that stands out from the data) that have emerged from the research material. Naturally, gathering variable-oriented material assumes knowledge of where and how the material is gathered, and this too presumes to some extent a command of the entirety of the legal system. And not just any statistics will do; critical evaluation of sources is required at this point too. Or to put it another way, quantitative methods do not offer freedom from independent and creative thinking. For instance, measuring the rule of law requires one to think carefully what kind of indicators one can and should use.[17]

IV. SIDE-STEP TO THEORY: COMPARING LAWS BUT WHAT LAWS?

When we speak of comparative law, then, what law are we actually referring to? Are comparatists referring to Latin *ius*, German *Recht*, French *droit*, Italian *diritto*, Spanish *derecho*, Greek *δίκαιο*, Finnish *oikeus*, Afrikaans *reg*, Islamic *Sharia*, Chinese *fǎ* (法), or perhaps Inuit customary law in Nunavut (eg *tirigusuusiit*; things one should refrain from, *maligait*; things that have to be followed)? There is, unfortunately, no simple answer terminologically or, far more importantly, theoretically.

Law is a complex normative entity that lives and changes along with the dynamics of human culture and society. It is never reduced into a mere statutory or even written law. To find for comparison an actual legal rule (of living law) that is actually in force can be quite difficult for an outsider because of the

---

[16] See E Paunio, *Legal Certainty in Multilingual EU Law* (Farnham, Ashgate, 2013).
[17] M Versteeg and T Ginsburg, 'Measuring the Rule of Law' (2017) 42 *L & Social Inq* 100.

nature of law as a living law. Living law consists of the rules of conduct that people in fact obey and which dominate collective human life; sometimes the rules of living law are the same as positive law, but sometimes they differ from each other. The comparatist must take into account not only the official (State) law but also other kinds of organised large-scale normativities, which are part of a given legal culture. A rule can be unwritten and yet still can be a living and legally significant factor in a legal culture. This is one of the central observations in the comparative law theory of the twentieth century: do not believe everything that is in writing, ie go beyond the positive law and take account also of the context(s) of law. This means, at the same time, openness towards information and methods of non-legal disciplines.

> The big name in American legal realism Roscoe Pound (1870–1964) presented the idea in his classic article in 1910: *law in books* can to a great extent differ from *law in action*.[18] In interesting court cases, the legal solutions provided by statute books and the legal reality of applying them do not always meet. What remains hidden from the formal legal point of view (stressing the positive law) can, however, be demonstrated in legal culture, which includes the education and professional attitudes of the jurists and overall the attitudes to law held by people in the community. Law is in interaction with its surroundings and cannot be separated from its context. In the same way another proponent of the realist movement Karl Llewellyn (1893–1962) took as a starting point an idea according to which 'rules alone, mere forms of words, are worthless'.[19] These realist insights are well absorbed in the intellectual fabric of comparative law although not necessarily taken into account in actual comparative law research.

The fact mentioned above can also impede the comparatist's work in at least two ways. On the one hand, the comparatist can come across a socio-legal solution model, which is not included in the statutes and is not based on the decision given by any court. A rule can be based, for instance, on a doctrinal legal construction or the professional ideology upheld by the courts, which has not necessarily been recorded in any written document. There are some normatively significant practices that have not been recorded anywhere in spite of their significance, which is often the case in connection with customary law. If the comparatist resorted to official sources only, they would go astray and might end up claiming that the legal answer to certain socio-legal questions is not included at all in the legal system under study. On the other hand, the comparatist can find a provision that includes a rule that is no more followed or a practice that is downright contrary to what the positive law presumes (Latin *contra legem*).

> For example, according to Article 3 of the Constitution of Norway, the executive power is with the King ('Den udøvende Magt er hos Kongen'), although in

---

[18] See R Pound, 'Law in Books and Law in Action' (1910) 44 *Am L R* 12.
[19] K Llewellyn, *Bramble Bush: On Our Law and Its Study* (New York, Oceana Publications, 1930) 3.

the constitutional practice the Norwegian Government uses the executive power. In exactly the same way, in Denmark the executive power is with the Government although the Constitution of the country does not acknowledge the organ. Surprises can be unexpected: the German *Bürgerliches Gesetzesbuch* (BGB), which aims at complete and coherent coverage in everything, does not define in any clause (a direct legal definition simply does not exist) what is meant by such a core concept as the manifestation or declaration of intent (*Willenserklärung*). Yet, the BGB uses this expression. Disputes between supporters of the doctrine of the declaratory effect of an Act and the theory of will prevented the formulation of the provision. So, the content of the declaration of intent is defined by means of the other provisions of the BGB, legal praxis and legal interpretation. This is yet one indication of law's nature as a living law, ie even highly formal and technically complicated rules interact with other parts of legal culture: law does not exist in a void but is a part of the surrounding society's fabric.

A. Validity of Law

The comparatist who concentrates on the present inevitably needs some kind of idea of what for them is the law in force, ie valid law (from the internal point of view) or living law (from the external point of view). Here they have to follow the national doctrinal study of law, reconstructing the situation taken in the system studied to the matter examined by the comparatist. Naturally the comparatist is not expected to, say, formulate normative recommendations for the interpretation of foreign law, yet they have to be able to somehow answer the question of how problem Y is dealt with in legal system X. This is inevitably akin to keeping up with the national mainstream interpretation of law as a normative and official creature. We can ask if this setting leaves any space for a normative approach in comparative legal studies. The answer is without a doubt affirmative. On the basis of comparison, support material can be produced for normative comments on one's own law, or proposals for systematisation can be presented and inspiration can be drawn. However, customary law and oral legal traditions are more problematic to approach, particularly from the point of view of systematisation, but even they can be used to support normative interpretative comments (ie how the legal question *ought* to be answered on the basis of formal legal materials). An interesting illustration is a Swedish case in which Indigenous Sámi were able to overturn a three-decade long law-based policy that had restricted their hunting and fishing rights.[20]

In the legal theory at least two opposed basic views can be distinguished: they can be called *formal* and *realistic*. Owing to its nature, comparative law

---

[20] Swedish Supreme Court, Case No: T 853-18. See C Allard and M Brändström, 'Girjas Reindeer Herding Community v. Sweden' (2021) 12 *Artic R L & Policy* 56.

mainly follows the realistic view but cannot completely ignore the formal one either. Because of its study setting, comparative law often finds itself between legal formalism (internal view) and legal realism (external view); the emphasis, however, being more on realism to which is added cosmopolitan legal pluralism.

According to the view of formal validity developed by Hans Kelsen (1881–1973), the best-known legal theorist of the previous century, law is in force in accordance with formal criteria. When a statute had been given in accordance with proper formal requirements and was technically sound, it was to be regarded as the law in force (expressly the domestic law). The validity of the statute in this context means that it was not in conflict with the rules in the norm hierarchy. In this way the ultimate basis for the law to be in force could be traced back to the constitution, the foundation for the legal order. The final basis for law was the *Grundnorm*, ie a hypothetical norm presupposed by Kelsen's theory, from which in a hierarchy all lower rules in a system, beginning with the constitution, are understood to derive their 'bindingness' (the normative authority).

The view of formal validity does not pay attention to whether the norm regarded as being technically in force is also de facto efficient. The validity is not related to the (empirical) legal reality; instead it is decided by means of factors connected to the form. The comparatist who is committed to this approach – consciously or unconsciously – prioritises in their source material official provisions and the law-drafting material. In such cases the potential alternative approaches offered to comparative law by non-legal disciplines (eg sociology, history, linguistics, economics, political science, anthropology) are ignored. Accordingly, legality, not legitimacy, is in focus.[21] On the other hand, this kind of approach might work in a Germanic legal culture and in countries where the legal culture resembles it – but even there *only* to a certain extent. There is a risk here; comparison of laws (broadly understood) may become reduced into comparison of legislation or precedents (law narrowly understood).

As an antithesis for the thought pattern that emphasises the form of law (positive law as an antithesis of natural law), different realistic trends in legal thinking have occurred. The representative of Scandinavian realism Alf Ross (1899–1979) from Denmark emphasised as the validity criterion the actual observance of law and particularly the fact that the rules of law are considered as psychological-socially binding ('the norms are effectively complied with, because they are felt to be socially binding'.[22] According to Ross, when a legal scholar describes a norm as a valid law, it is simultaneously a question of the description of the social reality, ie the content of a normative idea, which is effective and viable. Validity was for Ross a psychological fact.

In American realism, Pound and Llewellyn emphasised the significance of legal practice when they wanted to make American legal study more scientific.

---

[21] See L Vinx, *Hans Kelsen's Pure Theory of Law* (Oxford, Oxford University Press, 2007).
[22] A Ross, *On Law and Justice* (Berkeley, University of California Press, 1959) 34.

Both forms of realism are characterised by a certain desire to get rid of the strait-jacket of formal law (legal positivism) although there are also big differences between the trends of realism. They shared the desire to restore the ultimate foundation for the existence of law in human behaviour (renouncing the natural law theories) or human attitudes in behaviour. For the modern comparatist, these views make sense as the epistemic point of view to foreign law is that of an outsider. For the doctrinal legal scholar the situation is different as their epistemic point of view is internal.

A realistic and moderate way to understand validity is something that belongs to comparative law study as a natural constituent part. In the question of the mere practical comparison of the rules of positive law, a formal approach can sometimes be sufficient when looking for technical regulation models or stimuli for legislation. This may have curious ramifications: the comparatist may support formalism in their capacity as (internal) doctrinalists in their own system but cannot do the same in their capacity as (external) comparatists. When a closer look at foreign law is taken, it is, however, not possible to systematically only settle for statute texts and the preparatory material or precedents. On the other hand, comparison does not assume that one should accept all the ideas of legal realism or renounce practising the normative study of law (doctrinal study) that is based on the internal point of view of one's own system. Normativity of some sort is a natural part of all legal study, and this applies as well to the comparative study of law. Law is, even when understood broadly, a normative phenomenon.

Law can be created – as we know from several examples – without the support of written law or in case of a written law *contra legem*. In spite of this, law born through practice is no less normative than the law found by the comparatist from the law book. If people in a community regularly give their practices normative significance (Kelsen's bindingness), then the comparatist cannot ignore it on the basis that those practices when applied are not found in the rules of positive law. There is a deeper legal-theoretical insight involved here: because of the study setting that crosses borders the comparatist has to swallow a more extensive and open idea of what law is than colleagues who concentrate on the domestic system – the comparatist has not been granted the blessing of a shared (internal) concept of law. Accordingly, comparative law methodology requires one to combine the main aspects of legal realism and legal pluralism even though these two movements are not scholarly connected to one another.

Because modern comparative law relies on the idea of a toolbox of methods and not on the idea of one-size-fits-all, taking both realism and pluralism on board is not a problem.

B. Pluralism and Law

A frequent observation in comparative law is that rules and principles that have been created neither through legislation nor from precedents operate normally like the other legal rules, although the way they are created differs from the statutory law or the law based on precedent. Normative rules can be introduced from the sphere of religion or customary culture, and they can be effective. For instance, Islamic law works in the area of family law in countries with a Muslim majority where family law is regulated by an officially enacted positive legal order. In practice, different elements are intermingled creating a space that can be called *legal pluralism*.[23] In general, legal pluralism is associated with African systems or overall with systems where the legal orders are technically less developed than Western systems. Importantly, attributing legal pluralism only to Africa is way too restrictive as there are many examples of legal pluralism within Western legal culture as, for instance, Canada demonstrates.

> The Canadian system reflects both English and French influence. To a great extent the common law is applied in Canada, but in the Province of Quebec a civil law system of the French style is used. In addition, the Canadian system has dimensions of the rights of Indigenous peoples and their own legal traditions. There are also two official legal languages in the country, ie French and English. The entity can be characterised as a mixture of legal cultures and in this respect as pluralistic of its legal constituent parts. Moreover, in Canada there are also Indigenous legal traditions (First Nations, Inuit and Métis) which are partially recognised by the formal Canadian law.
>
> Further, there are good examples of the Canadian legal system and Indigenous legal systems living side-by-side and also partially colliding as is the case with the Islands of the Haida People (*Haida Gwaii*, commonly known as the Queen Charlotte Islands). The Haida Nation has always resisted colonisation, and it still has an ongoing dispute with the Canadian State over ownership (matters related to uses of land and sea) and jurisdictional matters. In *Kunst'aa Guu – Kunst'aayah Reconciliation Protocol* (2009) the pluralism is uniquely carved in a written form (Article A): 'The Parties hold differing views with regard to sovereignty, title, ownership and jurisdiction over Haida Gwaii'. First, the Haida Nation asserts the following: 'Haida Gwaii is Haida lands, including the waters and resources, subject to the rights, sovereignty, ownership, jurisdiction and collective Title of the Haida Nation who will manage Haida Gwaii in accordance with its laws, policies, customs and traditions'. Then comes the position of British Columbia: 'Haida Gwaii is Crown land, subject to certain private rights or interests, and subject to the sovereignty of her Majesty the Queen and the legislative jurisdiction of the Parliament of Canada and the Legislature of the Province of British Columbia'. However, the Protocol continues by stating that 'the Parties seek a more productive relationship and hereby choose a more respectful approach to co-existence by way of land and natural resource management on Haida Gwaii through shared decision-making'. So, the collision does not prevent reconciliatory cooperation and mutual recognition of competing legal systems.

A moderate realistic view of living law validity does not exclude the use of written law and other official material as a source, but it does make the comparatist suspicious, in a healthy way, so that they no longer settle only for *official texts*.

---

[23] Classical text on legal pluralism is J Griffiths, 'What is Legal Pluralism?' (1986) 18 *J Legal Pluralism* 1.

This is also the basic idea of functional comparative law: the written material on foreign law has to be treated with friendly suspicion and must be opened not only by means of a doctrinal approach but also through contexts beyond the law. Going beyond positive law requires looking at the social practices with distinct normative value in their own contexts. If comparative law rejects its colonial heritage and recognises other types or normativity than Western ones, then, its scope needs to be necessarily 'realist' so that it includes living law.

The realistic emphases of legal theory inevitably come across here: it is difficult to speak of foreign law in a sensible way if there is no reference to human behaviour (politics, history, economy, culture, mentality, language etc).

In comparative study, where the epistemic viewpoint on foreign law is that of an outsider, the normative *ought* perspective of the doctrinal study of law, emphasising rules, is an untenable idea. An outsider can never really reach an insider's epistemic viewpoint. The outsider stays outside, even if they simulate the intrasystemic (epistemologically) point of view in acquiring source material and in their analysis. Even at its best the reconstruction of foreign law done by an honest comparatist is not a genuine internal construction (in contrast to how it would be done by a domestic lawyer) but a *reconstruction*, which necessarily contains both external elements and an external point of view. As has become clear, there are various pluralisms in comparative law: methodological, legal, linguistic and jurisprudential. Crucially, this plurality is richness not a problem that needs to be weeded out.

V. LEGAL COMPARISON – A PARTICULARLY RISKY BUSINESS?

Comparative law is sometimes seen as a specifically risky field of study, and a particular risk of failure is supposedly attached to it. Frankly, one sometimes reads authors who have made it their business to underline the immense difficulties and obstacles involved in the comparative study of law. These scholars stress the risk of failure, thus, the picture painted by them is extremely gloomy. This book, on the contrary, seeks to encourage legal scholars to do all sorts of comparisons. Comparative law may be a bumpy ride but at least it is fun and one learns a lot during the research process.

The relatively tender age of systematic comparative law is one factor that causes a certain fragmentarism in the methodological and theoretical development. Yet, arguments presented in the discussion are far apart: some emphasise a strictly scholarly approach (comparative law as science); while for others its usefulness is a sufficient goal (comparative law as a meaningful practice). However, there are also signs of some agreement, which are indicated by the emphasis on functionality as the basic theory of comparative law. Certainly, a field of study of this kind offers plenty of meaningful challenges and leaves scope for creative thinking: in the doctrinal study of law genuinely new theoretical and methodological insights are exceptionally rare while the multitude of systems included in comparative law open many doors to surprises and new revelations. This, in fact, is both a boon and a bane.

A completely different question is that, due to the nature of comparative law, it is possibly never likely that a genuinely shared view is reached concerning its content, problem setting and approaches. The problems met in connection with comparative legal research are ultimately the factors that determine the approaches and hypotheses taken in the study. A kind of *study hunch* that the comparatist has probably developed during the process can in some cases be the only thing that makes the comparison and its results sensible and interesting. We may talk about the methodological toolbox of comparative law, not of the only right tool, ie as a research field comparative law is necessarily methodologically pluralistic.

However, it is important not to dramatically overestimate the difficulties and offer a view of a hopelessly difficult way to study law: pluralism and heuristic methodology are not only exacerbating factors but also sources of sheer academic enjoyment. Simply, it is enchanting and intellectually awarding to look for clues, to work for a thick description of foreign law and to have an open mind in the study of different legal contexts. Legal-cultural immersion is also intellectually rewarding. A *thick description* in comparative law involves looking at the rich details of systems compared, sorting out the complex layers of understanding foreign law (rules, principles, institutions, doctrines, customs etc) that structure the world of law in a system. The comparative study of law is a process of paying close attention to the contextual detail of law in observing and interpreting legal meanings when conducting research of foreign law. For a legal scholar comparative law's ability to work as an eye-opener is valuable as it offers a rich and nuanced view of law as a border-crossing phenomenon. In short, comparative law cultivates one's legal mind.

The theory and methodology of the field is not systematic or approved by all, and different schools are fighting with each other. All the same, heuristically useful ideas and examples *can be* presented in a reasonably systematic way, as attempts made above hopefully prove. Comparative law can also develop into a methodologically more disciplined and systematic activity only in the choppy seas of concrete study problems met in practice and the different attempts to solve them. Trial and error is indeed necessary; comparative learning means *learning by doing*. Learning by doing comparative law involves acquiring knowledge of foreign law or research skills through the direct experience of carrying out a comparative study (experiential learning). All this, in turn, keeps the movement going in the hermeneutic circle of research process.

Part of the fascinating challenge offered by comparative law is that owing to its nature it is against ethnocentrism, which means that comparatists have to the best of their ability to detach themselves from the context that their own legal system has created for their legal comprehension (the internal point of view of the lawyer). A small qualification is needed here. Rejecting the bias can, unfortunately, never completely succeed, but many barriers can be crossed by having contacts with foreign scholars, visiting countries under study, developing and maintaining an international colleague network, learning foreign languages and by acquiring as comprehensive study material as possible. Paradoxically, sometimes it can even be useful to stray from the straight path and let surprises and unexpected learning take place. An open mind is of the essence while a fixed one-size-fits-all method does not exist.

The main obstacles to comparative legal study and its most distinctive nature are found in bridging the gap between different legal cultures and in frequently falling into the gap as well as the ongoing attempt to climb out of it. Unfortunately, there are clues that do not lead anywhere. Failures are part of the everyday life of the comparatist, but over the years the comparatist should lessen both their frequency and impact, even if they cannot be completely avoided. To conclude, comparative law as a field of study is no more prone to risks than other members in the family of legal disciplines because all members have their weak spots.

VI. COMPARISON AS A LEARNING PROCESS

Learning by doing comparative law (*cf* John Dewey's 'experiential learning') is an interactive chain of processes where the comparatist embraces the experiences gained in the study of foreign law in a way that results in changes in their legal knowledge, skills and legal-cultural attitudes. Comparison in comparative law does not mean operating with watertight research results and exact methods but instead it is a *continuous learning process*. Part of the intellectual appeal of comparative law is specifically due to this *incompleteness*. Here we can quote Watson: 'Comparative law as an academic discipline is a very personal subject, giving its proponents great liberty to choose their interests'.[24] We can add to the list its delightfulness: getting to know international colleagues and establishing an educational *dialogical interaction* with them is one of the best ways to promote international legal study and the peaceful coexistence between different legal cultures and the mentality of *inquisitive cosmopolitanism*. And it is only reasonable to argue that when there is no competition over the same university posts, international cooperation remains easy; there are no internal conflicts with colleagues.

It is also justified to criticise comparative law due to the fact that its potential has remained at quite a low level in law-drafting, judicial application and legal policy. Those who utilise comparative legal knowledge are partly to blame, but comparatists themselves are also partially responsible for the state of affairs when they stay in their own small academic circles and only discuss matters with other comparatists. Modern comparative law is bound to rub shoulders

---

[24] A Watson, 'From Legal Transplants to Legal Formants' (1995) 43 *Am J Comp L* 469, 469.

with other disciplines instead of standing alone in a crowd of other fields of knowledge.[25]

Yet, there are also good examples of comparative law being applied in practice, such as the operation of the European higher courts and many informal projects on the harmonisation of law initiated by the European Union. For instance, in Europe there is the Network of Supreme Judicial Courts of the European Union.[26]

In spite of hindrances, comparative law is at present a well-known and acknowledged constituent part of legal disciplines, which in different fields of law is used as an auxiliary approach. It has its own legitimate objects, distinctive methodologies and a distinctive epistemology which differ from that of other legal studies (mixing internal and external viewpoints). When international relations increase and become more profound, travelling is easy (2020–22 COVID-19 restrictions were an exception) and in general the availability of legal knowledge improves, and hence the cultural divide that hinders comprehension gets broken down. On the other hand, the strengthening of Asia and the rise of the Islamic world can bring new barriers to replace the old ones if the approach is distinctively Western. Globalisation, it seems, does not produce only similarity.

In many respects the *McDonaldisation* of the world is a threat to cultural variety, but from the point of view of the comparatist, the trend is not completely unfortunate in all respects. *Juridiversity* is still to be seen although the situation is changing. Juridiversity refers to the degree of variation of different forms of law and organised large-scale normativities within a given system or even in relation to the entire globe. Juridiversity means acceptance of the cultural diversity in law and also protects different forms of law against unnecessary uniformisation.

The Western cultural sphere is inevitably increasing its influence on the citizens and cultures of the Asian and African States in particular, not only through political and commercial contacts but also by means of the Internet, television and the international media. Social media can also be a force for change in society. It is hardly possible that these developments would not be reflected in the sphere of law. And yet, embracing the whole of the unbelievable variety of law found in the world seems to be a very fit ideology for the non-ethnocentrist comparative law endeavour. As Twining points out, comparative law 'has diversified, developed and become more interesting and important, largely in response to accelerated globalisation'.[27]

Dimensions to which this book refers with expressions such as globalisation, pluralism, hybridity and transnational law are examples of events, phenomena and discussions that break new ground in legal study that is not as restricted

---

[25] J Husa, *Interdisciplinary Comparative Law* (Cheltenham, Edward Elgar, 2022) 1–8.
[26] www.network-presidents.eu.
[27] A Vereshchagin, 'An Introduction with William Twining' (2021) 16 *J Comp L* 445, 457.

by national borders as previously. But the development is not one-way, and the West learns from other cultural spheres through interactive processes. At the risk of being banal, we can state that all legal cultures are in the same boat and therefore are forced to interact with each other – whether they want to or not. Understanding this does not require the assumption of a common goal or other pompous achievements; it is a question of tolerating the legal-pluralistic state of affairs. Importantly, comparative law helps one to grasp legal contradictions and live with them without the overpowering urge to weed out diversity.

Finally, as reminded by Glenn in his seminal book about law's cosmopolitanism, comparative law teaches that dreams of legal unity or exclusivity of 'one's own law' can be complemented by softer notions of commensurability, multivalence, compatibility and interdependence. Glenn actually abandons the nation-State as an empirically impossible creation and replaces it with the notion of a cosmopolitan State which, according to him, corresponds to socio-legal reality.[28] No matter what one thinks of Glenn's contribution it is clear that he offers insights which fit well with the state-of-art comparative law methodology of today. Reducing comparative law into a tool of uniformity should be a thing of the past.

---

[28] See HP Glenn, *Cosmopolitan State* (Oxford, Oxford University Press, 2013) ('state is a modern, post-renaissance structure', 8).

9
Macro-comparison

As became clear at the beginning of the book, one constituent part of comparative law as an academic practice is macro-comparison. In it, whole systems (as organised large-scale normativities), legal cultures or traditions, which can be even more extensive than legal systems, are discussed and analysed. It is a question of the theory developed within comparative law and the generalising study that is not practised in other branches of legal disciplines. In the traditional generalisations of comparative law different systematisations and classifications of legal systems are presented as part of the comparative law theory. Their aim is to master the global plurality of the different legal systems in terms of knowledge, ie the motive is mainly epistemic. The aim is to create an at least reasonably reliable general panorama of the entity that is as rich and versatile as the law is in the world. Of course making taxonomies, models and typologies can be a part of any comparative law scholarship but the scale is typically not macro-level.[1]

All States have legal systems, as do many units that are smaller than States, such as cantons and different autonomous territories. But Indigenous peoples also have their own legal traditions, which are not systematically or legal technically similar or as comprehensive as the legal systems of States or communities that correspond to the State (eg the EU). Indigenous traditions do not coincide with national borders, which is exemplified for example by the Sámi law. The Sámi law consists not only of the national norms of Finnish, Swedish, Norwegian and Russian States and the relevant international norms concerning the Sámi people, but also of the traditional rules that are followed (internally) in Sámi communities because these rules are felt to have significant normativity (they are felt as binding norms).

Other non-Western normative entities based on, say, customary law can, in other words, form entities that are sensible from the point of view of comparative law as objects of research. In spite of this, comparative law has for a long time concentrated on the so-called legal families that are based on the State-centric

---

[1] Eg one can make taxonomies and typologies of constitutional justice, see M Nicolini and S Bagni, *Comparative Constitutional Justice* (The Hague, Eleven, 2021) 14–16. From the viewpoint of choosing units of comparison, see M Siems, *Comparative Law*, 3rd edn (Cambridge, Cambridge University Press, 2022) 419–21.

classification of formal legal systems that originate from Western law. In these classifications macro-constructions based on different theoretical backgrounds have been built; these constructions have over the course of time been given different names and definitions. Above there has been reference to common law, Roman-Germanic law, ie civil law, mixed law and religious or traditional law. Their content has already been referred to in this book, but a concise compilation of the basic blocks of macro-comparison has been lacking. In the following, these epistemic basic blocks will be presented in a more detailed manner but still in a compressed form.

I. BASIC BLOCKS OF MACRO-COMPARISON

A. Common Law

The term 'common law' is used in comparative law to refer to Anglo-Saxon or Anglo-American law. In such a case reference is to common law as a legal family. However, legal historically Anglo-Saxon law refers also to the law of ancient England before the Norman Conquest. Anglo-American law can sometimes refer only to the legal systems of English origin that are in force in North America. In the English law the term 'common law' refers to a body of legal precedents to distinguish it from statutory law. For macro-comparative law the key quality of common law is that is based on case law.[2]

In the discussion within comparative law, reference is not made to the internal historical systematics of the common law; instead, the aim is typically the more extensive sphere of the common law as a legal family. In other words, it is a question of a legal culture whose historical roots originate in England. On the other hand, it is important to note that the deep cultural roots of the idea of law were originally based on the legal tradition of North European customary law as it was before the reception of Roman law. This is still to be seen by the fact that according to the view the common law courts have of their role, there is no need to explain or clarify the law, since finding and applying it is sufficient. To simplify a great deal, common law seeks to *solve legal problems*. Unsurprisingly, there are historical reasons that explain why this is different from civil law.[3]

As a family, the common law is quite large and global. Common law has spread to former colonies via the colonial power. The voluntary reception of the common law has not been possible because its legal-culturally significant

---

[2] 'The specificity of English law is that it is case law' ('La spécificité du droit anglaise es d'être un droit jurisprudentiel'), G Cuniberti, *Grands systèmes de droit contemporains*, 4th edn (Paris, LGDJ, 2019) 89. Common law systems are not identical though. For example, differences between England and the US, see Siems (n 1) 74–77.

[3] For a concise introduction to the common law with helpful comparative references to civil law, see G Samuel, *A Short Introduction to Common Law* (Cheltenham, Edward Elgar, 2013) chs 1–2.

parts are not based on statutory law but on legal practice. It is a question of law that emphasises the significance of precedent and is applied in England and, for example, in the US, Canada (except Quebec), Ireland, New Zealand, and Australia. But the reach of common law does not stop there, as India, Jamaica, Hong Kong, and Singapore show. These systems form a legal family to the extent that their legal cultures differ from the civil law. They are connected by colonial history. In the comparative law usage common law in the legal technical sense is roughly a synonym for case law, ie legal precedents. Legal-culturally the *stare decisis* doctrine has been regarded as the most typical feature of the common law.

According to the *stare decisis* doctrine, it is the obligation of courts to adhere to past decisions made by higher courts in cases where the facts correspond with sufficient analogy. According to the definition in *Black's Law Dictionary*, a precedent like this refers to a legal rule that is 'established for the first time by a court for a particular type of case and thereafter referred to in deciding similar cases'. Basically such a precedent differs from a Continental precedent to the extent that the precedent in the common law is legally binding on a lower court.

We can summarise some legal-cultural generalisations of the common law as follows:

1. The legal system is mostly understood by lawyers (internal view) to be *based* on precedents. In codified/positive law the norms of the statutes are considered to obtain their legally-correct content when a higher court has established a precedent: the judicial application deciphers the actual legal content of 'a paper rule'.[4] The precedent formed in this way acts as a model for decisions in subsequent cases with sufficiently similar facts. The core of such a precedent, ie *ratio decidendi* (the judicial reason for the judgment) is binding in making future decisions (the so-called *stare decisis* doctrine) even on the very same court that has established the precedent.

    It is important to realise that the ratio is not an abstract norm or principle but concerns the *facts* of the case in question. The ratio has to be kept apart from the casual *obiter dicta* statement that concerns minor matters and does not have the effect of a precedent. In order to be able to decide what is ratio and what is obiter, a lawyer needs to distinguish material facts (having to do with the ratio) from unimportant facts (having to do with the obiter). Normally, the dicta are various statements from the court, and they do not have to be followed in future cases. However, one can separate two types of dicta: *judicial dicta* and *obiter dicta*. The judicial dicta obviously have a greater authority than what are commonly referred to as dicta.

2. Courts have a significant role in the formation of legal systems, and in a way a legal system consists legal-culturally of a great number of precedents given.

---

[4] However, this certainly does not mean that there would not be statutory laws. Rather, it is a question of legal mentality which Samuel (ibid 78–79) calls 'spirit of non-codification'.

Higher courts in particular are in a central position in this respect. It is crucial to understand that not all courts create precedents (and the ones that do not separately indicate that a precedent has been formed, but recognition takes place in later legal practice). Even though there is a huge amount of positive law in common law countries (and more coming every year), the role of precedent is regarded legal-culturally as the key feature of common law legal systems. Regardless, it is important to keep in mind that the amount of legislation in common law systems does not differ from that of civil law systems – the difference is the legal cultural weight lawyers give to precedent and legislation.

3. Owing to the important role of courts, the role of academic legal study has remained less significant than it is in Romano-Germanic legal systems. It would appear that respect for the legal discipline is not especially high if compared to the Romano-Germanic law. It is also usual to teach law by reference to cases, ie as a network of arguments and counter-arguments, not as a systematically organised whole that contains general doctrines and relies heavily on systematic considerations and general concepts. Yet, legal doctrine is also practiced in common law systems too and it would be wrong to exaggerate this difference.

4. The systematics of the legal system have not traditionally been based on the separation of public law and private law. More recently, within the common law of England, and related to the development of court practice, a field has formed that can be characterised as public law. In the US, public law became a recognised part of legal systematics considerably earlier because the country is a federation of States and it has a written Constitution. Yet, the differences are becoming fewer because, for instance, a new UK Supreme Court that seems to imitate Continental models, was founded in 2009. Furthermore, European integration has caused much pressure towards a unifying direction although there is also clear resistance in English common law against too much Europeanisation. Undoubtedly, the difference between EU law and the UK law will grow in the future as a result of the withdrawal of the UK from the EU. Or as Micklitz lamentingly puts it: 'The EU after Brexit leaves more room for French intellectualism and German legalism.'[5]

B. Continental Law aka Civil Law

Romano-Germanic law refers to the legal culture that has developed in Continental Europe and spread to other continents and emphasises more

---

[5] H-W Micklitz, *The Politics of Justice in European Private Law* (Cambridge, Cambridge University Press, 2018) 402.

than the common law the position of learned legal doctrine and codified law. Continental law has spread not only via colonial power but also through voluntary reception. As distinct from common law, the systems that have received civil law do not necessarily have a shared history. Unlike common law, civil law can be transplanted and copied in the form of legal texts rather easily (although the transplanted/copied rules or institutions work differently in different legal-cultural surroundings).

The two-part expression 'Romano-Germanic' refers to the fact that both the Romance countries (in the Middle Ages, Italy and, later on, France) and the Germanic countries (Germany in particular) had a significant influence on the development of law. Romano-Germanic law can be historically located in Continental Europe because of geography. In English literature, and indeed in this book, the Romano-Germanic law is referred to by the expression '*civil law*' (*civil law legal family*). This habit of international legal English is based on the fact that in the Middle Ages the Latin phrase *ius civile* (of which *civil law* is a direct translation) referred to *ius commune*, on the legal-cultural basis of which Continental law has been developed. The problem from the point of parlance is that 'civil law' in English has two meanings: in legal language it can also refer to another field of law with the name civil, ie certain areas of *private law*. In comparative law, 'civil law' refers to legal culture that has been influenced by the tradition of Roman law and which has spread to South America and Asia and also partly to Africa.

Typical features of Continental European legal culture are extensive private law codifications that generally follow either the German *Bürgerliches Gesetzesbuch* (BGB) or French (*code civil*) models. In a broad sense also Nordic countries belong to this legal family but, importantly, they have also their own special features that entitle the reference to a separate Nordic legal family situated between the great Western legal families. Now, if the common law seeks to solve legal problems and civil law seeks to *build learned conceptual systems*, then, Nordic law tries to do bit of both at the same time.

We can recognise certain basic legal-cultural features of civil law.

1. The overriding principle is the coverage of statutory, ie positive law. The idea is that for all legal problems there should be an existing positive law regulation the application of which causes the legal problem to be solved. 'One of the essential features of the continental tradition is that the law [legislation] is the main source of law'.[6] The content of the legal system is to be found in the norms of positive law – administrators of law *apply* law instead of actively creating it by precedents. In practice, nevertheless,

---

[6] 'L'un des traits essentiels de la tradition continentale es que la loi est la source principale du droit', Cuniberti (n 2) 55.

the role of superior courts in civil law systems is important as these courts create *de facto* precedents through their case law.
2. The significance of the case law created by courts for Romano-Germanic legal systems is usually regarded as less significant in a normative sense (ie courts *ought* not to give too much normative weight to precedents). When lines for solutions are established, an attempt is made to transfer them to positive law by means of applicable regulations. (Characteristic are massively extensive codifications in the field of private law, which, however, are lacking in the Nordic countries.)
3. The role of courts in creating law is officially seen to be small or it is seen as an exception to the rule. The quintessential idea is that courts solve concrete individual cases and that judgments and/or decisions do not create norms for future application of law. Continental Constitutional Courts, however, clearly deviate from this basic practice.
4. Historically, the role of academic legal study ('legal dogmatics' or legal doctrine, ie *Rechtsdogmatik*), and consequently the role of universities and learned law, in the development of the legal system has been significant. This is demonstrated both in the development of the structures and systematics of legal systems and the effects of study on the decisions in the interpretation of norms. The role of academic legal studies at universities continues to be an important part of legal culture. The German legal culture in particular is proud of its top specialist lawyers whose task it is to guarantee *Rechtsstaat* – even though it was specifically this legal culture that suffered a catastrophic decline in Hitler's Germany. The same type of domestic pride is easily seen, if looked at from the outside, in the French '*la doctrine*' which seems to hold perhaps an unreasonable conceit of its own superiority and academic quality.
5. The structure of a legal system is built on the separation between public and private law (following the tradition of Roman law and *ius commune*). Because of this, the general administration of law and application of administrative law are usually organised separately. In the Nordic countries in fact only Finland and Sweden follow this model.

Continental European law is perceived roughly, by comparatists at least, as a negation of the common law.[7] A feature of a fundamental nature is that in spite of precedents the written law is in principle the most important source of law in the Romano-Germanic system. At present there is as much enacted law in countries in the sphere of the common law as in the sphere of Romano-Germanic law. In spite of this the difference is important in principle: the common law lawyer approaches law through the prism formed by the cases not through statutory texts.

---

[7] There are, however, differences in civil law legal family. For diversity in Continental Europe, see Siems (n 1) 73–74.

In the Romano-Germanic law, statutory law forms the legal-cultural frame and the structure for the whole system. According to the traditional common law, the system is constructed of precedents, which means that statutory law in a sense corrects and completes the precedent law. The difference is legal-culturally significant although the consequences or practical applications are not necessarily so very dramatic. However, comparatists cannot miss the great weight given to doctrine: *die Lehre* (German), *la doctrine* (French) in civil law, which seems to regard itself as a special knowledge of law which is as to its nature logical and driven by the power of deduction. As defined by critical Jestaz and Jamin: 'legal science may be inexact as a science, but, it is a hard science'[8] ('une science inexacte, mais dure').

C. Mixed Legal Systems

Mixed legal systems (or *hybrid legal systems*) refer to systems that contain simultaneously key characteristics of other legal families. There have been different routes to hybridity of the legal system. For example, together with British imperialism, the common law spread also to areas where other types of law (Indigenous, traditional and religious) had earlier been used. If the law that had preceded the common law was legal-culturally strong, little by little systems were formed where there were features of both local law and the common law. In some cases, like Louisiana and Quebec, mixed systems are mixes between civil law and the common law. Today, arguably, it is possible to regard Hong Kong as a mixed legal system as socialist-civilian law has a stronger grip of the former common law system. Such systems are quite commonly called mixed legal systems. Unlike earlier, mixed legal systems are nowadays seen by some as an independent legal family, which are by no means dying out but are equal to common law and Continental law. The best example of this novel epistemic move can be seen in the book edited by Palmer called *Mixed Jurisdictions Worldwide*.[9] According to Palmer, the third legal family is 'conceived for purposes of convenience, utility, and explanatory power' and it can be used 'only if it provides better insights than comparative analysis has provided in the past'.[10] Yet, many comparatists leave mixed law out or deal with it in passing.[11]

---

[8] P Jestaz and C Jamin, *La doctrine* (Paris, Dalloz, 2004) 174.
[9] VV Palmer (ed), *Mixed Jurisdictions Worldwide*, 2nd edn (Cambridge, Cambridge University Press, 2012).
[10] Palmer, 'Introduction' in ibid 3, 16.
[11] Eg Cuniberti (n 2) deals with civil law, English law, American law, Chinese law, Japanese law, Islamic law, Indian law, and African law but stays silent about mixed law. Zweigert and Kötz distinguished Romanistic, Germanic, Anglo-American, and Nordic legal families. Besides these they distinguished law of the Far East and religious systems. K Zweigert and H Kötz, *An Introduction to Comparative Law*, 3rd edn (Oxford, Oxford University Press, 1998). Siems (n 1) speaks of 'disregard of hybrids', 99.

The oldest of the classical mixed systems is probably that of Scotland because it was independent for a long time before it formed a Union with England named Great Britain (1707). Scotland had had connections with Continental law and, thus, assumed many Roman law/*ius commune* influences. Also, in the law of the Province of Quebec in Canada there are similar features of mixed legal systems where the common law was mixed with the civil law elements implanted earlier: branches like property law and civil law are of a French type (civil law), but public law and criminal law are of a common law type. In Africa, the common law was mixed with the customary law of the tribes and in Asia with a legal tradition that could owing to its predominant cultural features be characterised as Confucian. This must be taken with a pinch of salt as describing Asian systems as Confucian is a strong generalisation indeed.

In the same way there are systems that belong to the family of Continental European law, for example in Latin America, Africa and Asia where Romano-Germanic law has intermingled with the traditional/Indigenous law of these countries. European integration has brought the common law and Romano-Germanic civil law closer to each other within the region of the European Union so that some comparatists these days classify the EU law as a kind of mixed law. Some of the former socialist countries, too, are in fact in a state of mixed law although in Europe they mainly belong to the sphere of Continental law.

> For example, Czech law is legal-culturally a complicated entity where remnants of socialist law are still to be found in civil law, labour law and family law. On the other hand, in the Czech system commercial law is clearly Romano-Germanic. The earlier picture has also been mixed by later legal transplants from Western law due to which the system is legal-systematically fragmented and contains inconsistencies. Today it is part of the European Union which has a huge impact on the law and legal culture of the Czech Republic.[12] Yet, it is quite possible to argue that some legal cultural remnants still exist in former socialist law countries.

Examples of hybrids or mixed systems are the Canadian law that has features of the common law and French Continental law (in the Province of Quebec) or the numerous African systems in which there is simultaneously influence of Western law brought by colonialism and traditional tribal law. Included in the same sphere of mixed law are also South Africa where the common law and Romano-Germanic law are combined and Malta, which combines the common law and Italian Continental law. Similar examples are the Philippines and Puerto Rico, which combine law of Spanish origin and the common law. In practice also all Islamic systems are hybrids mixing Western and Muslim ingredients (simply because Islamic law covers a relatively small area of the modern legal system.)

Different ingredients are mixed into different legal-pluralistic entities depending on schools of thought and local applications. What results is

---

[12] See B Havel, 'The Czech Republic' in J Smits (ed), *Elgar Encyclopedia of Comparative Law*, 2nd edn (Cheltenham, Edward Elgar, 2012) 279.

226 *Macro-comparison*

normally a mix between various legal-cultural ingredients combining Western and Non-Western, modern and traditional etc.

> It may be useful to note that the condition of being 'mixed law' or 'hybrid law' is not necessarily immutable, but there are differences between systems: some systems seem able to retain their constituent *mixité* whereas others have a more endangered status as hybrid systems. These differences are well presented and analysed in *A Study of Mixed Systems*.[13] This book shows that many mixed systems are in danger of losing their *mixité*. This, as such, is no surprise as law is always in a slow process of transformation.

D. Religious-traditional Law

To begin with, religious-traditional law is basically an antithesis of legal positivism which regards laws as commands of human beings without there necessarily being any links between law and morality. Religious-traditional law refers to various forms of traditional law, which are in many cases based on religious teachings and ideas (eg Christianity, Judaism, Islam and Hinduism) or some philosophical world-views. Essentially, law's key source is the divine will.[14]

Crucially, religious law is openly linked with ethical and moral codes taught by religions or long-established philosophical-religious traditions like Buddhism (which does not contain worship or allegiance to a supernatural being, ie Buddha is rather like the great teacher). However, the way in which Buddhist law is incorporated in a legal system of a country is very similar to that of other forms of religion-based normativities that have found their way to formal legal systems of States.

> Tibetan legal culture is probably the best example of living Buddhist legal thinking and legal tradition. Legal anthropologist and comparatist French distinguishes five major sources behind the Tibetan legal concepts.[15] The first sources are religious materials (eg the *Vinaya*, which is a canonical text outlining the rules for the monks to follow as outlined by Buddha). The second type is extant official documents (including administrative law books, edicts, decision documents, treatises, public contracts, estate record books etc). The third group consists of various documents issued by non-governmental institutions (eg monastic constitutions, private leases and private contracts). The fourth type is law codes and the fifth contains written and oral statements which describe the legal system.

---

[13] S Farran, E Örücü and SP Donlan (eds), *A Study of Mixed Systems* (Farnham, Ashgate, 2014).
[14] Cuniberti (n 2) speaks of Islamic law and points out that 'Islamic law is religious law. Its source is in the divine will' ('Le droit islamique est un droit religieux. Sa source est dans la volonté divine') 296.
[15] See R French, 'The Case of the Missing Discipline: Finding Buddhist Legal Studies' (2004) 52 *Buffalo L R* 679.

Although the religious type of law refers also to Christian law (by definition) various forms of Christian canon law are normally not included, curiously, by comparatists in the class of religious legal systems. The reason for this exclusion is probably that canon law is not generally thought to bind in the same general manner as does Western law. This can be seen in the law of the Vatican (The Holy See) which relies in many areas on Italian law: where canon law is absent, the law of the City of Rome (Italian law) is applied. Yet, this exclusion of religious law says something about the epistemic blindness of Western comparatists to their own law's link to Christianity – a link that is customarily and paradigmatically overlooked by Western comparatists themselves. This, if nothing else, tells us how deeply Western comparatists are embedded in the State-centred and legal positivistic thinking of modernism, which banished competing forms of customary and religious law into the private sphere. Regardless, Western law's close relation to Christianity is impossible to deny.

Religious law is normally regarded as not based on man-made law but on religion, traditional knowledge or cultural patterns and deeply embedded social institutions. The macro-comparatist tends to argue that there is a legal sphere covering several different traditional legal systems where it is typical that the norms lead to religion and its dogmata or cosmological ideas about the human kind and their place in the world. It can also be a question of a cultural tradition as is often the case with Indigenous peoples: they do not necessarily have organised religions, but on the other hand they have shared cultural views of the relation of humankind to nature and other human beings, for example.[16] Some of these views have constituted norms, the direct application of which is attempted or which have an indirect effect on the formulation of the material content of statutory law, ie traditional/customary laws and legal systems may be partially recognised by formal State law.

This group of laws contains legal systems/organised large-scale normativities in which law and religion or some other philosophical religious traditions have not been separated. Secularisation permeating legal systems that has taken place in Western law has not occurred there. Into this heterogenic legal group we can include different sub-groups: (1) systems of Islamic law (with its different schools); (2) systems influenced by Hindu law; (3) systems with so-called Asian mentality to law and society stressing collectivism or systems with the Confucian tradition (Confucianism influences legal discourse and legal thinking because legal meaning depends on cultural signs and narratives), and (4) Indigenous laws. In addition to legal professionals, these systems usually include social groups (such as Islamic priests, learned rabbis, tribal elders etc)

---

[16] Glenn spoke of 'chtonic legal traditions' that include normativities of 'aboriginals', 'natives', and 'Indigenous peoples'. HP Glenn, *Legal Traditions of the World*, 4th edn (Oxford, Oxford University Press, 2014) 61 et seq.

who can have a significant influence on the norms guiding the behaviour of individuals. Different versions of Christian canon law – Orthodox, Catholic, or Protestant – should also be included.

Legitimation of law that is related to religion is different from other law because the arguments can come directly from religion (eg the Koran and Islamic teachings or *Talmud*) or other arguments that are not within formal law; such as harmony that is of Confucian origin and social peace that is demonstrated in the desire to avoid conflicts and in the individual's responsibility to their family and the family's responsibility to the individual. The weight of traditional law can vary even within the same system (urban v rural, North v South etc) or between fields of law (private law v public law). For practical reasons, the religious systems are often of a mixed legal type in the sense that they include the influence of Western law and loans that are mixed with religious and traditional norms. Today we can see the rise of neo-Confucianism in China as it has become evident that Chinese law is not able to disregard traditional Chinese culture.[17]

Earlier it was believed that traditional and religious law would disappear, giving scope to the secular Western law, but this view has not proved to be correct. Traditional law has – if anything – overlapped with the more recent legal material often forming a mixed legal system. Instead of clear Westernisation we have more hybridity, ie legal composition such as rules, institutions and doctrines whose elements are derived from different legal cultures and from secular as well as from religious or customary spheres. As a result, Eurocentrism is becoming challenged as comparative law seeks to decolonise itself as a form of legal scholarship willing to look beyond the limits of formal law.

E. What about the Socialist Legal Family?

The fate of socialist law as a legal culture is not as simple as it may appear at first glance. In the 1990s, socialist law was declared to be deceased by many prominent comparatists and legal historians. Of course, socialist law as a legal family containing legal systems that uphold ideas of socialist law in their legal orders is minimal in comparison to the situation prior to the 1990s. However, the idea that socialist law would be dead and buried (à la Zweigert and Kötz) is clearly premature if socialist law is regarded as a legal tradition. Mańko points out that the dissolution of the socialist legal family cannot be identified with the disappearance of the socialist legal culture. Mańko says that, 'The Socialist Legal Family may well be dead and buried, but the same cannot be said of the Socialist Legal Tradition'.[18]

---

[17] See J Qing, *A Confucian Constitutional Order*, trans E Ryder (New Jersey, Princeton University Press, 2013).
[18] R Mańko, 'Survival of the Socialist Legal Tradition?' (2013) 4 *Comp L R* 1.

Today there are comparatists who actually regard the former socialist law countries as forming a specific Central European legal family that is based on the legal-cultural vitality of socialist law and that is much more legal positivistic and formalist than Western European systems. Uzelac underlines that socialist legal culture simply refuses to fade away, so, according to him 'two decades after the beginning of the "transition", some features of the "old" tradition have proven to be surprisingly resilient and unaffected by change'.[19] The main dividing factor between Western European legal culture and Continental European legal culture is, according to these analyses, the instrumentalist approach to law, which is upheld by elites which are accustomed to using legal processes and law in general as a tool for protecting their own interests. We can see traces of the socialist legal culture in the form of an instrumentalist approach in illiberal developments around the globe. Hungary and Poland are mentioned as illustrations of this development.[20] There are also clearer and more visible manifestations of socialist legal culture.

> The Constitution of the Peoples Republic of China (art 1) defines China as 'a socialist State' which follow 'the socialist system' although socialism is to be understood 'with Chinese characteristics'. Vietnam's Constitution (art 2) defines the State as 'a socialist rule of law State'. A similar type of idea is in the Cuban constitution (art 1) which describes Cuba as a 'socialist State of law and social justice'.

II. BUILDING MACRO-CONSTRUCTIONS

Some comparatists may think that systematisation of legal systems as such is an important activity that gives similar pleasure to comparatists as the classification of plants and the creation of taxonomies offers to a botanist. According to this view, the taxonomic classification and systematisation of legal systems alone would be a sufficient scientific motive. Hence, it would be a question of legal botany in an encyclopaedic spirit. Legal encyclopaedism had high epistemological ambitions for totality, coherence and order, just like other versions of encyclopaedism. These kinds of macro-comparatist still pose the eighteenth century style question: how much is there in the world of law to know? For these macro-comparative botanists the legal systems and legal cultures of the world are (paraphrasing Linnæus) 'like living libraries of law'. If it was so that, 'God created, Linnæus organised' (*Deus creavit, Linnæus disposuit*), then, the equivalent calling for the comparatist was to organise the world of law created by the Ancient Greek goddess of justice Dike (Δίκη) into scientific taxonomy.

There might be some truth in this approach, but a more rational basis for building macro-constructs might be found elsewhere. Put plain and simply:

---

[19] A Uzelac, 'Survival of the Third Legal Tradition?' (2010) 49 *Supreme Court L R* 377.
[20] T Drinóczi and A Bie-Kacała, 'Illiberal Constitutionalism' (2019) 20 *German L J* 1140.

a global mastery of all law is too tall an order for anyone. The most natural approach to the definition of, for example, the concept of legal family or legal culture is through the fact that macro-constructs are of their nature Max Weber's (1864–1920) *ideal types* (German *Idealische Typus*). It is typical of these ideal types that they are analytical information constructs that contain both empirical and theoretical elements. Construct refers here to a noun (not verb) which is an idea or theory that is formed in the minds of comparatists.

> Weber, who is one of the founding fathers of modern sociology, developed an approach of his own that is called interpretative sociology (*verstehende Soziologie*). Here the question is the same as in social-scientific hermeneutics, ie an explanation is aimed for in an attempt to understand the social-cultural object under study. It is a case of *interpretative explanation*. Weber's method of sociology tried to explain the reasons for what is being done as well as the different effects and consequences of the process.
>
> The approach is associated with the concept of an ideal type, which does not refer to anything that is ideal (idealistic, worth aiming at) but rather to something that is abstracted from a real phenomenon by means of reduction and is idealised in this sense; it is reduced by generalisation. The basic starting point is that the aim should not be to attain an ideal state, nor is there in the real perceptible world necessarily an accurate empirical counterpart for the ideal type. The ideal type is a conceptual construction to which reality is compared. The ideal type helps us to understand what is the hidden rationale of the social-cultural phenomenon that is analysed. In other words, ideal types are conceptual constructs to which the *true* (in an empirical sense) reality is compared. By means of an ideal type (such as feudalism, bureaucracy, capitalism etc) it is also possible to open up new research issues.[21]

By means of macro-constructs the comparatist can organise the reality of any given legal system (or other organised large-scale normativity) under study into a comprehensible entity (sources of law, use of the sources of law, interrelationship between rules, systematics, key concepts etc). In the comparative law theory, an individual legal family or legal culture or a more extensive entity formed by them is a theoretical construct by means of which it is easier to perceive existing legal systems in all four corners of the world. When the central features (eg use of legal sources, role of customary law, methods of legal argumentation, relation between religion and law etc) belong to the same legal family or legal culture, it is possible to explain and analyse rationally the legal system existing in reality. Macro-constructs like common law or civil law offer conceptual devices with which the comparatist can measure law and clarify the most important elements of unfamiliar legal systems.

By means of macro-constructs, explanation and analysis take place even if the content of a legal system is not described by means of overwhelming detailed

---

[21] See D Käsler, *Max Weber: An Introduction to his Life and Work* (Chicago, University of Chicago Press, 1988) 180–84.

information or if the knowledge basis offered by one's own legal system is abided by. As an ideal type, ie a type that has been refined by removing detailed characteristics (a huge amount of detailed qualitative data), a macro-construct as such is not to be reduced to any real existing legal system. It is the culmination of the typical features of its empirical models. Therefore, for example, a description of common law does not specifically tell us about Canadian law, and a description of civil law does not accurately represent Spanish law.[22] Yet, they provide an overview of those legal systems.

David, who is probably still the best-known macro-comparatist, understood well that the legal families he had constructed were not completely identifiable with the global legal reality. David was of the opinion (*Les grands systèmes de droit contemporains*, 2002, with Camille Jauffret-Spinosi) that: 'The concept of legal family does not correlate with the biological reality'.[23] On the other hand, macro-constructs have other reasons and grounds for their existence than the fact that they would be exact results of research. Macro-constructs serve the basic idea according to which it is useful for the comparatist after the preliminary acquaintance with foreign law to become detached from the details of the legal system studied and to conceive it as if from a more distant perspective (epistemological distancing, epoche-approach). In particular, this concerns the preliminary phases of the comparative process. As the comparatist gains more knowledge, the significance of macro-concepts diminishes.

A. Mastering Complexity by Means of Generalisations

The point of legal families, if there is one beyond teaching, and other similar macro-constructs is actually a simple one. The point is to get the nuanced object of study under epistemic preliminary control by detaching oneself from the immediacy and abundance of legal (and other) sources by resorting to the *pure type* specified in the first instance. Into such a type (eg common law, civil law, Nordic law, Islamic law, Maori law) most characteristic features of similar legal systems have been reduced. Only research that has detached itself from the maintenance of national law is capable of detaching itself in terms of knowledge. It is very difficult for the doctrinal study of law to detach itself from the national legal system (internal-normative view) and in terms of epistemology from the internal view on law. On the other hand, as appeared above, in the doctrinal study of law and the other fields of legal study it is possible to make use of comparative study settings and foreign law in other ways. Yet, it should

---

[22] For a more detailed discussion (with references), see J Husa, 'Family Affair – Comparative Law's Never Ending Story?' (2014) *Annuario diritto comparato* 25.
[23] 'La notion de "famille de droit" ne correspond pas à une réalité biologique', R David, *Les grands systèmes de droit contemporains*, 11th edn by C Jauffret-Spinosi (Paris, Dalloz, 2002) 16.

be kept in mind that the epistemic frameworks for the national and comparative approach are different.

It would seem to be comparative law wisdom that concrete and existing legal systems as such are not to be identified with any of the basic types constructed in the theory of comparative law. When we characterise, say, the legal systems of Austria and Italy as belonging to civil law, we do not simultaneously present an empirically exact description of these systems; we just describe the shared general legal-cultural and historical features typical of them. And at this point the names of macro-constructs are of no importance. Their functions are the same independent of whether we call these legal-cultural macro-constructs legal families, legal spheres, legal cultures or legal traditions. In all of these macro-constructs it is a question of generalisations on the macro-level and approximations, like fuzzy pictures or shadow images cast on the wall by the comparatist.

> What is said above can be illustrated by taking one concrete system under study. Focusing makes the picture more complicated. For example, New Zealand is without exception classified in comparative law literature as a member of the common law family or legal culture. There are solid grounds for this, because the legal system of the country is by and large based on the English common law, ie the system that New Zealand inherited as a colony of Great Britain. There is no written constitution in the country, and the law that was in force in England before 1840 is still formally part of the law of New Zealand in so far as more recent legislation or legal praxis has not changed it. Unlike in the UK, the position of the common law has been strengthened also by formal statutes, which are The English Law enactments from 1854, 1858 and 1908. On the other hand there are features in the New Zealand system that differ from the common law because even at a reasonably early stage fairness as a kind of meta-principle of law rose to the level of the common law of English origin. It was considered a more flexible aim that built on general principles more clearly than did the English common law as such.
>
> In New Zealand courts have for a long time applied the principle of fairness and the common law in interaction. They are seen as complementary parallel systems with the common law having the upper hand. In addition, there is Maori law in New Zealand and special courts (Maori Land Court, Maori Appellate Court and the Waitangi Tribunal) where questions are handled that are related to the rights of the Maori. Before the arrival of the British, the Maori had their own customary law (Maori *tikanga Māori*) system that has been revived over the last 40 years. Albeit, legal terminology is difficult to translate because the closest Maori equivalent to concepts of law and custom is *tikanga*, but it is 'not completely accurate' because Maori concepts do not really correspond exactly with the Western concepts which they appear to resemble on the surface.[24]
>
> The Maori language has been a legal language for a long time since the most significant agreements between what was originally the colonial power and the Maori are

---

[24] See *Māori Custom and Values in New Zealand Law* (Wellington, The Law Commission, 2001).

in both English and Maori. Therefore, although it is possible to get a good general picture of the operation and basic ideas of the law of the country by perceiving it as a common law system, in practice, nevertheless, there are other types of internal influences and Indigenous emphases that other common law systems do not have. In the grouping of legal systems of the world it is however sensible – at least for the time being – to place New Zealand in the sphere of common law. For example, the core significance of the judge that is lacking from Continental law is typical for New Zealand just as it is in the English common law culture. And, of course, the legal language of English is a common feature. English is the legal language that binds common law systems together and, what is more, it has also the ability to function as a lingua franca even between civil law systems.[25]

We have now given a certain explanation for macro-constructs, but there are still some questions. One of the key questions concerns the utility of macro-constructs in modern comparative law. Indeed, how does the research process in comparative law function and what is the role of macro-constructs in it?

In an early stage of a study, an individual legal system can be understood when comparing it to the theoretical-hypothetical models or macro-constructs that have been constructed in the macro-comparative law. The first stage ideas that are formed in this way of the objects under study are in essence preliminary hypotheses. Accordingly, they give references to the subsequent formation of a hypothesis. In other words, there is a kind of *hermeneutical spiral* in action which is movement between the macro-construct and foreign legal text (micro-dimension) which draws the comparatist nearer and nearer the constructed legal meaning of text – yet, getting close to this meaning is placed ultimately in the comparative framework, and not in the internal web of legal (normative) meanings.

As pointed out above, macro-constructs are the theoretical concepts or *ideal types* that the comparatist needs and the special features of which represent certain generalised features of legal systems. As such, the macro-construct is the conceptual-theoretic tool of comparatists, by means of which they can group the content of a real legal system and demonstrate the special quality (structure, central institutions and concepts) and central principles of operation in the legal systems, which in a way resemble each other. We could speak of *distinctive features* of law, ie the characteristics and features by means of which the system can be recognised and demarcated from the others. We can also speak of legal style of a system that is, in essence, a kind of a collective statement of legal-cultural identity.[26] Basically, any macro-construct fundamentally does one thing: it reduces the empirical complexity of foreign law.

---

[25] G Bell, 'The Civil Law, the Common Law, and the English Language' (2019) 14 *Asian J Comp L* S29.
[26] C Valcke, 'Comparing Legal Style' (2019) 15 *Int'l J L Context* 274.

In mastering the information of foreign law, the macro-construct has significance in levelling and reducing difficulties with knowledge. The legal family, legal culture, legal sphere or legal tradition is a crudely sketched roadmap for the comparatist or anyone else who examines foreign law in order to find information as well as a guide for subsequent and more specific planning of the route. But, even a micro-comparatist too can benefit from a legal macro-map, despite its obvious restrictions. The more specific and detailed the research questions are, the smaller is the significance of a fuzzy map. A parallel is offered by art: a large landscape painting looks quite different depending on whether you look at it from the distance of a few metres or a foot away. To put it another way, nobody wants to look at Vincent Van Gogh's paintings close up because the brushstroke is so rough, but from a distance one realises that one is actually looking at masterpieces. Perspective matters in general but especially it matters in comparative study of law.

III. GROUPING LEGAL SYSTEMS

Apart from building macro-constructs, comparatists have for a long time also systematised and organised them in order to create a global panorama of law. In spite of the differences, several macro-comparatists have all the same presented a rather reasonable number of suggestions for classifying them. Above (section I) a condensed general presentation was made of the current basic groups in which a majority of present systems can be placed either completely or at least in part.

It is likely that there are a limited number of different typical key questions related to the classification of legal systems: can legal systems or legal cultures of the world be classified into entities belonging to only a few large legal groups? Which are the large legal families/legal cultures of the world? On which criteria can the inclusion of an individual legal system in a specific legal culture or family be decided? Before these questions can be answered, the nature of the concept *legal family* has to be explained further. In addition, the other ways to organise and conceptualise the variety of different legal cultures and traditions of the world ought also to be investigated. One should realise that these macro-constructs are to a great extent overlapping although their authors (comparatists who created these constructs) themselves might emphasise the differences between the different macro-constructs. Ironically, the claim of the originality of a classification is the least original of the claims made by macro-comparatists. On closer inspection each of these classifications resembles each other.[27]

---

[27] J Husa, 'Macro-Comparative Law – Reloaded' (2018) 131 *Tidsskrift for Rettsvitenskap* 410.

A. Legal Family

In *Introduction to Comparative Law* by Zweigert and Kötz, which was for a long time the most influential work in comparative law and has been translated into several languages, the concept of legal family is used. Zweigert and Kötz listed in their work Roman, Germanic and Nordic laws, the common law and the Far Eastern systems, Islamic systems and the Hindu law.[28]

Curiously though, Zweigert and Kötz did not themselves start the terminological tradition (in the original work, reference is made to *legal sphere* or *Rechtskreis* – in the translation to *legal family*) where the large constructs in macro-comparison are called families. Nevertheless, their work has conveyed to the twenty-first century this epistemological tradition that is based on the theoretical and conceptual foundation of European legal history. Also in the French tradition the phrase *familles de droit* has been and still is used when reference is made to the so-called large modern legal systems (*grands systèmes de droit contemporains*). In short, *family* has been a metaphor favoured by many a macro-comparatist.

> The history of the concept of legal family is not quite clear, but it appears that in the French tradition it was first used by Adhemar Esmein (1848–1913) at the beginning of the twentieth century: 'Il faut classer législations (ou coutumes) des différent peuples, en les ramenent á un petit nombre de familles ou de groupes, dont chachun représente un système de droit original' ('The laws of nations – or the customary law should be classified by decreasing their number to a few families or groups so that each of them would form one original legal system').[29]

In the classic work by David *Les grands systèmes de droit contemporains* (first edition 1964) Romano-Germanic law, common law and socialist law were presented as the genuine legal systems. As other non-Western legal systems David mentioned Islamic, Hindu and Jewish law and the laws of the Far East, Africa and Madagascar.

A significant change in macro-classifications has been the fact that socialist law has been dropped in Europe after the developments of the early 1990s. Furthermore, no return to the previous Slavic legal system has taken place. It seems to have been replaced by Islamic law as the *Other law* (main form of non-Western law; representing legal otherness) and not only in a limited sense. It appears also in the form of different mixed law combinations with secular law in various systems in which the aim is to observe Islamic law.

A more recent example of classification that concentrates on legal families is in the work about 'grand' legal systems by Cuniberti.[30] His systematisation has three

---

[28] See Zweigert and Kötz (n 11) pt I B.
[29] A Esmein,' Le droit comparé et l'enseignement du droit' (1900) 45 *Nouvelle revue historique de droit Français et étranger* 488.
[30] Cuniberti, *Grands systèmes* (n 2).

parts. He distinguishes between Western law (*droit occidental*), Eastern/Oriental law (*droit orientaux*) and African law (*droit africain*). Cuniberti resolves the inclusion in Eastern law mainly on the basis of geography although he finds that criterion coincidental (*coincidence géographique*). On the other hand, he is of the opinion that Eastern systems have certain typical features on the basis of which they can be lumped together for macro-comparison. Cuniberti, however, states that there is no special general *Eastern* feature in the systems of these countries because Australia too, with its common law, is geographically included in Eastern law. He presents two facts as the actual cause for this classification, which are related to the foundation of the legitimacy of the State's power and the significance of (already existing) personal relations (ie social network). Cuniberti's macro-comparison seems to be based on David's work on everything that is essential although his classification differs in its contents from the (outdated) classifications of David.

Further, the novel epistemic move that came in the twenty-first century of mixed legal systems as the third big legal family between civil law and common law has strengthened the use of the family concept in comparative law carried out after the twentieth century as well. The *World Society of Mixed Jurisdictions of the World* that was founded in 2002 has been very active and mobilised new scholars to support the *mixed legal systems* thinking. This movement seems to have strengthened the desire to keep speaking of legal cultures using the family concept. But what does the concept *family* include in this respect? Why has it become so important a part of the intellectual fabric of scholarly comparative law?

Basically it is a question of the relations – kinship between systems. Bogdan uses the Swedish expressions *släktforskningen* (genealogy or family history) and *släktskap* (kindred, kinship).[31] In the first place the family metaphor makes it possible to speak of family members, like sisters and brothers and also of the father and the mother. Legal historians have also been fond of the family metaphor because it brings up the significance of legal history. Secondly it makes possible the use of a more extensive family concept, ie the fact that it is meaningful to speak of legal families belonging to the same family. Legal systems can be more or less related. We can also talk about a close relative or a distant relative.

By means of the family concept it is possible to speak of the relations (kinship) between different legal systems. For example, Nordic law can be described as a close relative of civil law, which however has some distinctive features. The author of this book has in another connection characterised Nordic law as the country cousin of Continental law. The country cousin might lack conceptual-logical refinement, but it has legal vitality; an ability to make creative decisions and has a cultural and democratic proximity to the people. We may speak of a common Nordic legal mentality or Nordic legal mind. As Letto-Vanamo and

---

[31] See M Bogdan, *Komparativ rättskunskap* (Stockholm, Norstedts, 2002) 76–77.

Tamm say, 'There is no such thing as Nordic law, but you may talk of a Nordic legal mind'.[32]

The question of being *Nordic* is not, perhaps surprisingly, limited to the Nordic Countries in the geographical sense if it is approached from the legal-cultural point of view. As a result, it is possible to regard, for example, the legal culture of the Netherlands as Nordic to some extent although there are no legal-historical or notable geographical ties. The Netherlands can be described as a legal culture that is in between the German and French tradition, which is illustrated, for example, by the 1992 civil codification (*Burgerlijk Wetboek*) that is based more on German abstract conceptual legal thinking than on the French one.

On the other hand, it is typical of the Dutch codification that there are several regulations that have been enacted openly that leave courts a reasonable scope for interpretation. In addition, the Supreme Court (Hoge Raad, literally 'High Council' which is the Court of Cassation) occasionally deviates from the regulations of written law on the basis that it is in the interest of justice to do so. In the Nordic countries, for example, so-called realistic arguments (in Swedish '*reella överväganden*', in Norwegian '*reelle hensyn*', ie '*real considerations*') are sometimes referred to instead of justice. These kinds of arguments are related to various substantive considerations concerning the case at hand, and normally urge the judge to take into account not only the written law but also the practical consequences of the judgment, ie fairness in a practical legal sense.[33]

B. Nordic Legal Family?

Where should we place the Nordic legal culture? In spite of the fact that the Nordic legal family has been greatly influenced by German legal culture (mostly by means of legal doctrine and legal theory), it cannot be automatically placed with civil law. However, broadly understood and compared to, for example, Islamic law or the law of Indigenous peoples, Nordic law should in general be placed with civil law. However, in comparative law we ought to distinguish Nordic law as a legal family of its own. This is owing to the fact that between the legal mentalities prevailing in the Nordic countries there are very obvious similarities, as well as historical and geographical connections, that make it justifiable to speak of the Nordic legal family. Notwithstanding, not all comparatists have recognised this.

Among the legal cultures of the world, common law and Nordic law are perhaps the ones that it is most convenient to place under the concept of legal family based on kinship. Clearly, family members have their distinctive

---

[32] P Letto-Vanamo and D Tamm, 'Nordic Legal Mind' in P Letto-Vanamo, D Tamm, BO Gram Mortensen (eds), *Nordic Law in European Context* (Cham, Springer, 2019) 1, 1.
[33] In the context of Nordic legal culture, see J Husa, K Nuotio and H Pihlajamäki, 'Nordic Law' in Husa, Nuotio and Pihlajamäki (eds), *Nordic Law* (Antwerp, Intersentia, 2007) 1.

connections that are related to history and the way of legal thinking: reference to family relations is sensible both historically and in relation to law (eg substance and the doctrine of sources of law). The same could, no doubt, be said about common law.

> Wilhelmsson considers that the Nordic legal family exists owing to the value base that has developed from historical factors, ideas of the same kind about the role of law and the legal method as well as of the similarity relating to substantive law and mutual interaction (Nordic legal cooperation). In spite of this, Wilhelmsson remarks fittingly that 'it does not however mean that all the children of the family look alike'.[34] With this he refers to the fact we can distinguish two sub-groups of Nordic law, which are the Western and the Eastern law group. The Western group consists of Denmark, Norway and Iceland while Sweden and Finland are included in the Eastern group. By means of the legal family metaphor, Wilhelmsson perceived Finland and Sweden as legal twins whose development since 1809 has to some extent gone in different directions. In this respect it is not a question of identical twins, but twins all the same, ie creatures that are connected by family relations.

Nordic legal scholars have emphasised the legal-cultural unity of Nordic law in that although there are differences in the positive law and legal praxis, the Nordic legal thinking is characterised by a similar type of legal mentality, which distinctly differs from civil law and common law.[35] They see that Nordic law can on the basis of legal culture, legal history (kinship) and legal content be considered a kind of legal family. This is the case in spite of the fact that the European Union has had an effect on it and has complicated the internal family relations of Nordic law.

> At the moment three Nordic countries belong to the European Union, but the other two are members (Norway and Iceland) of the European Economic Area. However, the Nordic legal culture has not fully identified with the legal culture of the Union. According to the conclusions of Bernitz, 'Scandinavian law is characterised by its specific legal method, its mixture of statutory and case law and its, in relation to most continental EU countries, less theoretical and conceptualised approach to legal problems'.[36] This also means that the Nordic legal culture differs from that of the EU in general even though the EU has had a unifying impact on the Nordic legal culture.

C. Legal Culture

It is useful to note that although legal culture is important for this book and that it also plays an increasingly significant role in the comparative study of law, it may have different meanings. In its most general sense it is 'one way of

---

[34] Public Speech '*Oikeusperhe ja epäidenttiset kaksoset*' ('Legal Family and Unidentical Twins') delivered 23 October 2008 at University of Helsinki.
[35] See Husa, Nuotio and Pihlajamäki (n 33).
[36] U Bernitz, 'What is Scandinavian Law? (2007) 50 *Scan Stud L* 13, 30.

describing relatively stable patterns of legally oriented social behaviour and attitudes' as defined by Nelken.[37] Now, in comparative law the concept of legal culture can be used in at least two ways. On the one hand, it refers to a group of factors (eg language, mentality, politics, and history) that are outside the formal legal system but are connected to the actual operation of the legal system in a broad sense. In such cases reference is made to system-specific cultures, such as litigious American, non-litigious Japanese or semi-litigious French legal culture. The degree to which a society is litigious is a question of legal culture: what kind of appetite for judicial solutions a society has involves much more than mere statutory law. For instance, Americans are quite accustomed to expressing their claims in legal dispute resolution whereas in Japan this has not traditionally been the case.

On the other hand, in comparative law literature legal culture is used as a macro-level concept with which reference is made to entities larger than one system, such as Western legal culture, Asian legal culture or Islamic legal culture. It is also possible to speak about German or common law legal culture. In practice, legal culture competes with the concept of legal family, and it has been influenced mainly by macro-level legal sociology, rather than by legal history. One renowned way to classify different legal cultures is the classification of big legal-cultural formations by Mattei. Although Mattei did not himself speak of a classification of legal cultures (*legal patterns* or actually *legal-cultural patterns*), it was precisely the point of his proposal: the division of the world of law into macro-constructs on general legal-cultural grounds.

> Mattei presented the best-known version of his suggestion for forming classifications of legal cultures in 1997 in his article 'Three Patterns of Law', the original version of which was published in Italian.[38] To begin with, Mattei developed his suggestion on the basis of the experiences he had from his international teaching, when he realised that he needed a new pattern that would facilitate the mutual understanding of the future jurists who came from different legal cultures. The aims were at least partly pedagogical just like they were with David and also Zweigert and Kötz. Unlike the other macro-comparatists, Mattei did not aim at a meticulous and *empirically* adequate description of all the systems in the world; instead, he continued with the basic approach by aiming at general control, ie forming Weberian ideal types. Yet, Mattei clearly wanted to go, as Nelken says 'beyond the tired categories so often relied on comparative law and incorporate the attention to the "law in action" and "living law" which is usually missing from comparative lawyers' classifications and descriptions'.[39]

As a starting point there was an observation that old classifications were not really holding water any more. Mattei considered that there was an obvious need

---

[37] D Nelken, 'Using the Concept of Legal Culture' (2004) 29 *Australian J Legal Phil* 1. See also ch 1 of this book.
[38] U Mattei, 'Three Patterns of Law' (1997) 45 *Am J Comp L* 5.
[39] Nelken (n 37) 2.

to create a new classification. He called his classification a taxonomy that was aimed at replacing the old classifications and mending their deficiencies both empirically and theoretically. The aim was also to simultaneously get rid of the earlier dominant position of the West. In a sense, Mattei's attempt can be seen as an early pursuit to decolonise comparative law scholarship. The basic idea was to get started with the notion that there are (in the sense of an ideal type) three kinds of norm types that are adhered to in the social context and which have an effect on the behaviour of individuals. The main sources of the norms are politics, law and the philosophical or religious tradition. The theoretical starting point of the classification criteria was not Western law/legal because the norm types distinguished on those grounds were – maintained Mattei – culturally neutral. For example, the Western system contains all norms but their mutual significance is different from that in Oriental law, for instance. In actual fact Mattei distinguished between the Western legal culture and the two sub-types of non-Western law.

> Mattei did not claim that any real legal system would be like one of the basic norm types. In all or at least most systems it was possible to separate one feature that was decisive (*hegemonic pattern*). This means that even within the same legal system there could in different fields of law be dissimilar legal-cultural typical features, which were characteristic considering the entity of the legal system. Classification was based on the legal-theoretical assumption according to which there are norms, which have basically been created by three ideal-type sources of norms and by means of which it is possible to evaluate the principal nature of legal systems. In the classification three basic types of legal system were separated: (1) professional law; (2) political law; and (3) traditional law.

Mattei was of the opinion that classification of this kind was rigid in nature. Over time a system that at present belongs to another class can change its place in the classification if its dominant feature changes (hence legal systems 'never are, they always become'). If for example a system that belongs to a class is transformed so that either professional or traditional law rises to a dominant position, this alteration also has to be observed in the classification. Like all the other suggestions for classification, the suggestion of Mattei was also – as he, too, admitted – a rough analysis that was based on generalisations. Albeit, he emphasised the macro-nature of his legal-cultural constructs by saying that classifications were not an aim as such but the means by which the entity of the legal systems in the world can be conceptualised and mastered by comparison.

i. Professional Law

The traditional classification into common law and Romano-Germanic law is a sub-classification of the professional family of law. Its starting point is the idea that Western law is – from the macro-comparative point of view – a rather homogenous group. The main representatives of the group are the US and English versions of common law, French law and Germanic law, Nordic law and the hybrid systems of both common law and Romano-Germanic law (eg Scotland and Quebec). In this connection Mattei brought up two dominating core features of Western law: (1) the separation of the forums where legal and political decision-making takes place, and (2) the extensive secularisation of law, ie separation from norms with religious origin.

Law and politics are not separate in professional law, but to a great extent they have been separated; the point is that the legislator or government or other institution wielding political power cannot directly influence legal processes in courts. Part of the norms can also be of traditional origin, but this does not apply to the majority of norms, ie it is not a dominant or decisive feature.

The legitimacy of the system that is based on professional law is argued by the fact that it is a professionally specialised profession (an undertaking which requires special education and skill). Overall, the situation is such that the field of law is controlled by trained specialists (jurists), the field of politics by politicians, and the field of religion by priests. Different sectors of life have become specialised and differentiated. It is this demarcation that informs the discussion on professional law.

ii. Political Law

In this group of law, law and legal processes are to a great extent defined by political relations. The government in its operations is not restricted by law; instead, it can to a great extent define both the limits and content of its operation. In systems that belong to this group there is also professional law and professional specialists in law (jurists), but the decisive characteristic of these systems is political law although it does not exclude the existence of other norm types. (Mattei in fact was of the opinion that all systems are partly hybrid, ie to some extent they contain norms from all norm types.)

> At that time Mattei included in the group of political law two different sub-groups: (1) a majority of the ex-socialist countries excluding Poland, Hungary and Czech Republic and (2) the least-developed States of South America excluding, however, the States where Islam had a dominant position. Cuba too belonged to the group of political law although it is situated in the Western hemisphere, while China, Mongolia, Vietnam, Laos and North Korea as well as the republics of the former Soviet Union that were in Asia belonged to traditional law, to the sphere of Asian legal culture.

> As far as Europe goes, this group has changed radically due to European integration, and the classification is no longer timely from the point of view of individual systems. On the other hand, it is clear that China has not simply broken loose from some ideas of socialist law although it has borrowed plenty of legal decision models and legislative ideas from Western countries. Notwithstanding, describing China's law as 'traditional' does not make much sense as it has developed its legal system in the recent decades. Similar development is also to be seen in Vietnam and recently also (perhaps) in Cuba. North Korea continues to differ from all the others, and its legal system is still very peculiar and from the comparative law point of view a real oddity

with an appalling and shocking record of serious human rights breaches. Russia, on the other hand, seems to have gone backwards in its legal development as it has been evolving into an authoritarian system under the rule of Vladimir Putin (1952–).

Political law is legitimated by arguments that to a great extent are similar to the ones used in connection with professional law (eg democracy or common good). The members of the legal culture in political law are connected by a certain kind of general social and/or economic instability, and therefore Mattei called these systems alternatively by the name *law of development and tradition*.

iii. Traditional Law

This legal group included legal systems in which law and religion, or some other philosophic-religious tradition, have not been separated, ie the secularisation that has passed through legal systems has not occurred as in political law and professional law. Mattei included in this group three different sub-groups: (1) systems of Islamic law (different versions); (2) systems of Hindu law; and (3) systems of Asian or Confucian tradition. In addition to the professional jurists these systems include social groups (such as Muslim priests) who have a significant impact on the norms that guide the behaviour of individuals. Systems that belong to this legal family have the institutions and other formal characteristics recognised by Western law with the exception that their operation is in fact different from that of Western systems.

> On the other hand, it has to be noted that law in books and law in action do not differ only in connection with borrowed Western law, but frequently also the traditional-religious law is affected. Dupret has observed in his studies a distinct difference between the learned upper-level Islamic law and the Islamic law that is applied in practice. On the basis of his research he does not define Islamic law by means of upper-level abstractions but states as follows:
>
> 'My contention is that Islamic law is what people consider as Islamic law, nothing more, nothing less, and that it is up to theologians, believers and citizens, not social scientists, to decide whether something does conform or not to some "grand tradition".'
>
> Baudouin's article presents an interesting approach to Islamic law, which he has coined as *praxiological* (realistic internal view).[40]

Mattei's classification is intriguing because it broke the earlier legal family division, left aside the historical connections between systems and emphasised certain legal-cultural general features. Although classification aroused discussion among comparatists, and there are plenty of references to Mattei's article in the study of comparative law, it has not threatened the position of legal families

---

[40] B Dupret, 'Legal Pluralism, Plurality of Laws, and Legal Practices' (2007) 1 *Eur J Legal Stud* 1.

as the most central conceptual-theoretical tool in the macro-comparative analysis.

D. Legal Tradition

In the comparative law scholarship legal tradition has been used in different contexts for a long time, but at the beginning of the twenty-first century the concept has been specifically connected with a particular comparatist. The first edition of the work *Legal Traditions of the World* by Patrick Glenn (1940–2014) was published in 2000, and the fourth edition saw daylight in 2014. In the field of macro-comparison the book has become a classic that has in general been received rather positively among comparatists. From the sphere of critical comparative law, however, there has been criticism of Glenn, saying that the era of building macro-constructs is a thing of the past. The majority of comparatists have, however, given Glenn's opening a somewhat warm welcome in spite of the fact that the arguments were perhaps not totally understood. The book has also stirred considerable criticism, and one need only look at the first issue of *The Journal of Comparative Law*, which was dedicated to Glenn's *opus magnum*, ie *Legal Traditions of the World*.[41]

Glenn's work has partly replaced the earlier paradigmatic analysis by Zweigert and Kötz. The work, the manuscript of which received the Grand Prize awarded by the International Academy of Comparative Law in connection with the international conference organised in Bristol in 1998, suits modern comparative law well with its new orientation and its general legal-cultural emphases. In the general comparative law context, the work continues the more general changes in direction; this has meant the turning of the comparative law emphasis towards that of culture, an emphasis that was first seen almost 30 years ago. Glenn's approach represents modern macro-comparison where the orientation is legal-cultural and has a modern anthropological and legal-pluralism friendly touch.[42] The fact that macro-comparison was earlier stuck in the scholarly trench war between civil law and common law or Western and non-Western law injected into the discussion on comparison Europe-centric emphases that had a belittling tone towards other legal cultures.

For Glenn the most significant legal traditions in the world are the following: the Jewish, civil law, Islamic, common law, Hindu and the Far East legal traditions and the oral traditions of the Indigenous peoples (*chtonic legal traditions*). Glenn not only deals with each tradition in its separate box but puts them in a

---

[41] The issue was entitled 'A Fresh Start for Comparative Legal Studies? A Collective Review of Patrick Glenn's Legal Traditions of the World' (2006).
[42] Glenn's comparative law scholarship and legacy is discussed in H Dedek (ed), *A Cosmopolitan Jurisprudence* (Cambridge, Cambridge University Press, 2021).

parallel position with each other, exposing also the interaction (present and past) between different traditions. The idea of the national character or autonomy of one's own law appears to stand on shaky ground in the light of Glenn's work if and when the perspective is stretched over centuries. The interaction between traditions is outlined in the work via long processes, not so much by means of individual cases of foreign law adoption. Glenn concentrated on the broad lines and did not pay attention to the forms of concrete legal loans or transplants or their travel from one system to another.

Glenn managed to show the interaction between different traditions while simultaneously efficiently muffling the Siren song of relativism, which aims at emphasising the distinctiveness of different traditions and their incapability of becoming involved in a genuine dialogue. The book's subtitle *Sustainable Diversity of Law* describes the aspiration for the preservation of a polyphonic legal culture. Glenn's argument is a powerful point for diversity and cultural pluralism while simultaneously avoiding being naïve or patronising in connection with non-Western traditions. However, Glenn's volume is certainly not without its problems that are typical to all macro-comparative law endeavours.

According to Glenn's theoretical ideas, there has been a desire in Western legal cultures to denounce the relation to the past while simultaneously Western legal cultures have refused to admit that Western law (civil law and common law) too is a form of traditional law, the rationality of which is part of the self-understanding of that particular tradition (it regards itself as a rationalistic form of law). For a European or American jurist, the expression *traditional law* referred as late as in the twentieth century to law which was inferior and irrational (ie non-Western) and left behind or surpassed in development by their own legal culture. Glenn's approach was not evolutionary but hermeneutic and prone to pluralism.[43]

By tradition Glenn refers to the part of the past that is still present at this time and has a chance to be transmitted even further. Also the expression *the presence of the past* used by Legrand fittingly describes the thinking that emphasises continuity and the significance of tradition. It is a question of the impact of the past and of how the past stays alive and reaches the present; *pastness* is conveyed in the information contained in tradition. Family classifications and the different groupings of legal culture presented above hardly contain dynamic interaction between legal families or cultures while Glenn's basic idea is a continuous dynamic relation. Different legal traditions interact with each other, which means that between them information (concepts, institutions, solution models, principles etc) is on the move.

In the sphere of Western law the traditionalism of law is particularly clearly visible in the common law, whose relation to the past differs from that of Continental law,

---

[43] For a discussion of Glenn's argument in a concise form, see J Husa, 'Emancipation or Deprivation for European Legal Mind?' (2006) 13 *Maastricht J Eur & Comp L* 81.

which emphasises the present. In part the common law is reminiscent of the Islamic law tradition. Sir Edward Coke (1552–1634) emphasises the source of law of the past generations almost poetically:

> 'our days upon the earth are but as a shadow, in respect of the old ancient days and times past, wherein the laws have been by the wisdom of the most excellent men, in many successions of ages, by long and continued experience (the trial of right and truth) fined and refined'.[44]

According to Glenn, the lines of demarcation do not follow legal history or geography or legal-cultural taxonomies. The distinction is drawn by the internal attitude, which traditions have to themselves (ie how they see themselves in comparison to other legal traditions) and others. According to some traditions, the truth is embedded in them, while it is not present in other traditions. The truth can be religious, and it can be based for example on divine intervention. On the other hand, the truth can be *rational* by its nature, and it can be based on the belief that one's own legal culture is the most sensible one and best suited to the modern way of life (civil law and common law). Moreover, such traditions are a threat to others because they want to dominate other legal traditions; there is an element of legal imperialism (legal-cultural control over other countries and cultures). However, because they in their own understanding are basically 'right', this universalism is not conceived (looking at it from the inside of the Western hemisphere) as being a problem.

Traditions that are based on allowing other parallel traditions are tolerant by nature, and they do not directly threaten other traditions (eg Hindu or Asian legal culture). According to Glenn, if we want to promote dialogue and cultural coexistence, it would be a good idea to get acquainted with what these traditions themselves teach us. The point is important for the comparatist as it conveys the fundamental message of *epistemic modesty* that means awareness of the limits of the comparatist's own knowledge and awareness of the limits of the ability to independently acquire knowledge about foreign law.

Glenn made an interesting observation, according to which in addition to different identifiable *vertical* legal traditions, it is possible to distinguish within them different *horizontal* legal traditions that occur simultaneously within different traditions. Casuistry and analogical case-based reasoning (Jewish, Islamic and common law) among others are mentioned. In addition, there are considerable similarities in traditions concerning legal professions and their role (eg the village elder, judge, theologian-judge, *qâdi*).

Glenn aimed most criticism in his work at a thesis according to which different legal traditions would be *incommensurable*, ie it would not be possible for them to engage in a shared dialogue, instead either one should be chosen, not both. But, if there is interdependence, and hence sharing, there is commensurability.

---

[44] In *Calvin v Smith*, 77 Eng Rep 377 (KB.1608).

Rejection of the incommensurability thesis does not, however, presume the fusion of different legal cultures; instead, it rather emphasises the significance of an equal dialogue. Yet, it is highly unlikely that legal traditions would ever find full agreement – in a pluralistic world there are always differences and colliding understandings about law. Globalisation has not and probably will not change the basic situation even though similarities seem to be growing; local adaptations will always differ as they work in their own legal cultural contexts.

Learning from other legal cultures can also be involved in the dialogue, which we can mention as examples of the legal cultures of Indigenous peoples and the environmental legal and philosophical discussion on the inherent value of nature or animal rights that has an interesting link to their thought pattern. Importantly, the direction of learning is not necessarily automatically in favour of Western models (the West teaching others, ie civilising the 'ignorant'). It is possible to keep one's eyes open and to learn something new while simultaneously sticking to one's own set of legal values. We may conclude by noting that Glenn's approach actually follows many of the traditional virtues of comparative law: willingness to learn from others, openness and ability to tolerate *Other* law. Epistemic openness lies at the heart of modern comparative law scholarship.

IV. MACRO-CONSTRUCTS AND METHODOLOGY

Some things seem obvious. Macro-constructs, such as legal family, are not absolutely necessary: the comparatist can do without macro-constructs. So, if comparative law is practised out of a practical interest with an intention to carry out objectives of a practical origin, the question of the classification of the world's legal systems or the results of the classification is hardly very interesting. The unavoidable question here is: does micro-comparison benefit from macro-comparison?

A court looking for inspiration in foreign law is hardly interested in the legal family classification when the aim is to solve the legal case at hand. A court applying EU law does not study the interpretations of the EU norms made by other Member States for the sake of macro-comparison but in order to look for support in the interpretation of the EU law. The same applies probably also to civil servants working with the drafting of legislation; although from the point of legislative benefit, legal family classifications could have some (unconscious) significance when it is decided which legal systems are sensible from the point of view of the (national) State's legislation to adopt legal ideas from other countries. This is demonstrated in the practical legislative work when the law-drafting civil servant looks for ideas and models for regulation from foreign systems. The law drafter tends to stick to systems and legal cultures with which they are familiar (and which they think to be significant) and where their knowledge of languages and their legal-cultural literacy is considered sufficient.

In the comparative study of law it is more difficult to fully avoid such macro-notions as civil law and common law. For instance, Smith's study of the law of loyalty illustrates this well. The study concern micro-comparative law, ie situations in which person holds powers not for themselves but for and on behalf of others. Smith elucidates different justificatory principles that are used in these situations. When studying these principles he crosses the boundaries between private and public law and between common law and civil law. Macro-notions are embedded in the fabric of Smith's study even though they are not separately addressed anywhere in the book.[45]

A. Change in the Knowledge Environment

When the aim is to construct theory for comparative law or to otherwise serve the attempts to produce general knowledge through comparative law (eg how law interacts with the society in different legal cultures), the situation is epistemically more demanding than in law-drafting. The difference between these two comparison-interests should not be overly emphasised as has become clear above. The construction of macro-constructs and the classifications and groups formed are not useless for the practical comparatist either. With the help of classification the problem of the multiplicity of the legal systems in the world diminishes, and the approachability of foreign legal systems improves as a result of the typification and classification of legal systems. By means of legal families and other macro-level classifications it is possible to lower the *initial knowledge threshold* when foreign law is examined. At best, macro-constructs may reveal something general about how jurists in the legal culture in question are usually inclined to think and act.

> One example is the attitude to judges. In Continental legal culture judges are respected, but legal-culturally they do not have a similar status to that in the English common law, which in the words of Cuniberti is 'un droit jurisprudential qui glorifie ses juges', ie case law that glorifies its judges.[46] In the same way within Islamic law it is possible to note that a *qâdi* is a respected person with whom not only the Islamic administration of law but also societal respect is associated. *Qâdi*'s respected position is easy to understand as *qâdi* is a mediator between parties seeking to establish a momentary peace between parties before reaching an agreement on how divine law of Koran is to be applied. Beyond that, *qâdi* may also utilise local customs in his decisions.[47] However, this does not mean that judges would not be respected; it is a question of how they are envisaged – as administrators of law, hero judges or highly learned but bland authorities.

---

[45] L Smith, *The Law of Loyalty* (Oxford, Oxford University Press, 2022).
[46] Cuniberti, *Grands systèmes* (n 2) 127.
[47] L Rosen, *The Justice of Islam* (Oxford, Oxford University Press, 2000) 4–23 (focuses on the system of Morocco).

One of the biggest challenges that the comparatist can meet is the knowledge environment attached to foreign law that is different from one's own law. Siems is spot on when he says that 'as soon as lawyers leave the borders of their own country, they may feel as if they are stranded on a foreign planet. Learning about comparative law aims to address this problem'.[48] Foreign planet refers to the change of legal environment, ie the sum of legal surroundings in which lawyers are accustomed to operating. The epistemic change in the knowledge environment coming with the foreign law becomes easier to control if it is possible to analyse the world outside one's own legal system and to perceive it by means of features that are common and typical to it. This is difficult as lawyers are, by and large, trained in and for their domestic jurisdiction and in this sense lawyers tend to be parochial.

In other words, the classification of legal systems into legal families or other macro-constructs may have an influence on the preparedness to acquire information and the ease or difficulty related to knowledge seeking. It is the question of the knowledge level in the preliminary phase of study to decide at which point it is possible by means of macro-constructs to soften the epistemic chaos that follows when facing a foreign legal world. A macro-construct can operate as an epistemological preliminary analysis and result in a *hermeneutical preliminary comprehension* of the foreign law under study. In practice, this means that law's components work as a whole: the components (rules, principles, cases, customs etc) cannot be understood without some preliminary understanding of the whole legal system/culture, and the whole cannot be understood without comprehending its legal components (ie hermeneutic circle as a model of the process of understanding). The epistemic benefit of macro-constructs is maximal when the systems differ from each other radically and is minimal when the systems are legal-culturally very close. For example, for a Nordic jurist it is not particularly useful to read general comparative law works on what a Nordic legal family is like; instead, it would be preferable to concentrate directly on the study of one's own specific topic (eg how the legal issue X has been solved in different Nordic countries). Or, for the common law lawyer it would hardly be greatly beneficial to read about the common law legal family when studying the law of another common law country in regard to a specific legal problem. A Dutch comparatist does not benefit much from macro-comparative law when studying German law, nor does an Australian comparatist when studying Canadian law etc.

The benefits from the macro-constructs formed are mainly of two kinds. On the one hand, the benefits can have a direct link to actual comparative law study. On the other hand, the benefits can be instrumental in their nature and establish an initial connection with pedagogical objectives. In a globalising world, comparative law's value for educating lawyers has become more relevant as it trains legal minds for a transnational world.[49]

---

[48] Siems (n 1) 1.
[49] J Husa,' Comparative Law in Legal Education' (2018) 52 *The Law Teacher* 201.

What about the comparative research process in micro-comparison and macro-comparative law? There are in fact at least two kinds of comparison taking place. First, a legal system is compared to a pure type, ie a macro-construct built in the comparative law theory. *Double comparison* of this kind enables two different things. The comparatist can approach a legal system that is unknown to them on the basis of an organised preliminary hypothesis. The macro-level preliminary idea makes the later acquisition of material easier and creates a foundation for the explanation of differences and similarities. Organisation of the knowledge material gathered in accordance with the *style and spirit* of the legal system studied *presumes* some sort of understanding of the legal family or more extensive legal culture. In short, this means that the comparatist does not start from level-zero but relies on some form of prior understanding.

Secondly, the knowledge acquisition gets easier for the comparatist because they can compare the legal system under study via some other hypothetical context than their own legal system (unfamiliarity element). The construct built into macro-comparison at the early stages of research provides the starting point for the comparatist instead of their own legal culture and legal system. The role of legal families or legal cultures may be part of the process of knowledge acquisition and to facilitate the management of the versatile information in the early stages of the study. The transfer from one's own legal system to the foreign legal system becomes easier when the comparatist can exploit organised ready-made macro-constructs as a preliminary fuzzy map of law.

B. Concentration on Basic Matters

By means of macro-constructs it is possible to describe and approach reasonably rationally legal systems whose material content resembles the content that is in accordance with a specifically constructed theoretical macro-construct. A legal family or legal culture offers the comparatist a conceptual tool for preliminary comprehension. Such a preliminary tool (the macro-construct) is in terms of knowledge better than resorting to one's own preconceptions and possibly false presumptions about the content, characteristics, structure and legal praxis of the foreign law or legal culture. In other words, a macro-construct is the first timid step away from the ethnocentric conception of what is 'law' and what is 'legal'. For example, without sufficient basic knowledge of Islamic law a Western comparatist can easily end up reinforcing their misguided preconceptions. Legal orientalism is another example as the comparatist may conceive Chinese law through culturally conditioned implicit assumptions.

> Many comparatists at present have a rather critical attitude to macro-constructs, but in practice everyone admits that they have at least a pedagogical significance. For example, Bogdan comments on legal families saying that they are 'a rather crude pedagogical instrument' although he simultaneously devoted about 65 per cent of his

book to the macro-level study of different systems.[50] The pedagogical benefit from legal families is related to the epistemic first-aid they offer for the study of foreign law and comparative law. The macro-level forces one to concentrate on general structures, general doctrines and general principles. However, In 'New approaches' to comparative law, like that of Siems in his *Comparative Law* and in this book, macro-comparative law has a role, but legal families/cultures do not consume the majority of the text.[51]

One may wonder, however, whether we are placing too much weight on macro-constructs and their possible benefits. It has been argued above that macro-constructs are not merely for pedagogical purposes. And yet, fundamentally there certainly is pedagogical thinking involved. In short, it is not essential to learn an unreasonable amount of the content of material law in order to be able to operate with foreign law in the capacity of a comparatist. In the same way, it would not be sensible to teach the content of the national legal system by requiring the learning of huge numbers of statutes or cases by rote. Different legal rules, precedents and the statutory law in particular can sometimes change quickly, but parts of law and particularly part of the knowledge concerning the legal system are much slower to change by nature. Such knowledge includes, for example, the concept of the source of law, the rules concerning the use of the sources of law and the core content of legal concepts and terminology: the lock, stock and barrel of an organised large-scale normativity. It is precisely the sustained knowledge of these types of *typical characteristics*, such as legal interpretation, that are focused on when legal systems are classified into different macro-constructs.

If a person who studies foreign law or otherwise has to be in contact with it and has in advance been acquainted with the general legal and legal-cultural knowledge contained in a macro-construct, it is easier for them to understand the concrete (culturally distant) legal systems included. However, the further one gets into the comparative study of foreign law, the smaller the significance of macro-constructs becomes. In the classification, the significance of individual legal families or legal cultures is greatest in the first stages of comparison when foreign law is approached for the first time and an overall picture of it is being built. When the study becomes more detailed, the significance of macro-constructs becomes smaller and the original roughly sketched roadmap becomes more nuanced and more specific. This is, unavoidably, when generalisations become far less useful than a detailed and accurate knowledge of law.

Macro-constructs are epistemic scaffolding that need to be dismantled after the building is ready. This seemingly simple idea is deeply philosophical in the

---

[50] 'Ganska grovt pedagogiskt instrument', Bogdan (n 31) 79.
[51] Siems (n 1) chs 3 and 4.

sense that one uses macro-constructs as a ladder which needs to be thrown away after one has climbed up it as the ladder itself proves to be, in a way, nonsensical.[52]

V. FINALLY

Today the challenge of macro-comparison is the interaction between legal cultures and the fact that they penetrate each other. There is clear hybridity and plurality if one conceives law globally. It is not possible to completely ignore normatively significant organised systems even if they seem foreign. An idea of a culturally 'pure' or 'national' legal system has virtually always been dubious, but now its disintegration is more visible than before: the economy, the Internet, communication and supranational interests link legal cultures and overlapping normativities with one another.

Along with migration, smaller parts of foreign legal cultures and normativities travel, while on the macro-level integration and globalisation form new hybrids by mixing together different large-scale legal-cultural ingredients. If and when old mixed systems transform into 'pure' ones, then old 'pure' ones transform into mixed ones leading to what we label an *elusive global mixité of laws*. For example, in Europe such culturally foreign normativities as Islamic marriage norms of immigrants (external dimension) have to be faced. Furthermore, we can see how China has developed its own version of the rule of law 'with Chinese characteristics' or how Maori law has gained ground in New Zealand. Finally, macro-constructs have to be changed too, but is it possible to speak of *global evolution* of law in connection with them? Do legal systems or cultures evolve?

---

[52] L Wittgenstein, *Tractatus Logico-Philosophicus* (London, Kegan Paul, 1922) 6.54 ('My propositions are elucidatory in this way: he who understands me finally recognises them as senseless, when he has climbed out through them, on them, over them. (He must so to speak throw away the ladder, after he has climbed up on it. He must surmount these propositions; then he sees the world rightly.')

10

Legal Evolution?

IN MACRO-COMPARATIVE LAW the conceptual basic blocks have for a long time been the same tripartition: common law, civil law and other systems or legal cultures. This seems, if nothing else, to demonstrate the fundamental conservatism and permanence of law. On the other hand, if we glimpse at present-day macro-comparison and the theoretical basic concepts used in it, change can also be seen. This is of course natural because despite its rigidity law does change and evolve. In his multi-layered view of law Tuori makes the point that law is a historically changing phenomenon. However, different parts of law (broadly understood) change with varying paces. In this sense, we can speak of *legal dynamics* in which in which deeper layers of law (legal cultural basic assumptions) create preconditions for and impose limitations on the changes at the surface level of law (legislation).[1]

On the surface the change is quite obvious: new Acts are enacted; old Acts are abrogated or amended, new precedents override old precedents, new normative customs are developing in international business communities etc. Also, the objects governed by law change: while the Romans regulated the use of slaves (as property with no legal personhood), today for example the ownership, renting or leasing of a car is regulated. In those common law countries where high courts create precedents with their decisions, it is no longer acceptable to refer to, say, the eighteenth-century decision on a case concerning the master's right over subordinates although it is possible to refer to the same case (similar type of factual situation) when evaluating how to legally define *master*, ie foreman. But can this kind of inevitable change in law be conceived or even described as the *evolution of law*? There are many possible answers, and we will look at some of them from the point of view of macro-comparative law.

A legal historian who knows the law of Antiquity might insist the opposite and describe how the essential features of our system have a surprising resemblance to the features of Ancient Rome or at least a great resemblance to the later *ius commune*, which was a combination of Catholic canon law and secular learned Roman law. Or an expert on Islamic law on the other hand might emphasise the lack of change (closing the gates of *ijtihad*) and hold that jurists of our time are all bound to the unquestioned acceptance of their respected early

---

[1] K Tuori, *Critical Legal Positivism* (London, Routledge, 2002) ch 7.

predecessors as the authoritative doctrinalists of Islamic law. So, all that present Islamic lawyers can do is to issue legal opinions based on or drawn from established early precedents, which are regarded as classical Islamic jurisprudence (*fiqh*). However, there are Muslim legal scholars who would like to reinterpret Islamic law for modern needs, and they claim that the practice of *ijtihad* (as legal interpretation and reasoning based on sacred texts) ought to be revived. The key point of the Neoijtihadist movement is to argue that despite the Koran's divine and immutable text, application of its verses is contingent on the conditions and needs of the times.[2]

On the other hand, the question of the evolution of law is legal-culturally sensitive (does it also mean development?), and there is a danger that the comparatist is alienated from the research-ethical foundation of comparative law and begins to put different legal cultures in a ranking order according to economic efficiency or how legal cultures uphold the rule of law, liberal constitutionalism etc. This is by no means a novelty in the world of comparative legal research. In the nineteenth century and at the beginning of the twentieth century, different legal systems of the world were referred to and classified because of their state of development or the lack of it. In the early 1900s, scholars believed by and large that the development of law went through a series of stages, ie from a non-Western uncivilised form towards Western civilised forms. Classifications of that time also used the concept of evolution, but in them the evolution (understood as an improvement) of law was associated with race or culture. On that basis, the 'underdeveloped law' of undeveloped races and the developed law of developed races were analysed. Undoubtedly, the Congress in Paris in 1900 reflected in many ways this ethnocentric thinking, which white European men deigned to maintain in their arrogance concerning law.

One of the key motives of the scholars of that time was not only to create an autonomous discipline of comparative law but also to order, describe and understand the complexities of the world of law.[3] Despite these noble motives the 1900 Congress is a part of the colonial heritage of comparative law, now considered (and rightly so) as a dubious heritage.

As late as during the twentieth century, race, nationality and culture were concepts used for ranking legal systems and played a key role in the classification and systematisation of different legal cultures and systems. But if the earlier racist approaches are rejected – as is right and proper – and the emphasis is placed on macro-level evolution, we are entitled to ask whether the concept of evolution at all is suitable for conceptualising the evolution of different legal systems and cultures of the world and for giving them a comprehensible form. Can we speak of legal evolution in macro-comparative law? Is the transfer of

---

[2] L Takim, 'Islamic Law and the Neoijtihadist Phenomenon' (2020) 12 *Religions* 1.
[3] See D Bonilla Maldonado, *Legal Barbarians* (Cambridge, Cambridge University Press, 2021) 100–13 (discusses legal taxonomies and families).

a system from one legal culture to another, either completely or partly, evolution of law or just commonplace alteration? If customary systems transform into hybrid and from hybrid into, say, civil law, is evolution in the full sense of the word a fitting conceptualisation? If so, then can we also have legal cultures which are endangered, ie forms of law that will likely become extinct?

Another key thing to keep in mind is that the following discussion on the evolution of the law is not about assigning value to legal systems and their alteration but simply to talk about the conceptualisation of macro-level transformation.

I. IS THERE EVOLUTION IN LAW?

Legal evolution – if we adapt the evolution theory that Charles Darwin (1809–82) developed – refers to alteration of the permanent features of legal systems over time. In evolution, legal systems adapt to their environment gradually. It is a series of (social) events that cannot be controlled and the alteration of the permanent characteristics of legal systems. Through evolution that has already taken place, the law in the world has developed into its present state of a diversity of different legal cultures. The mechanisms of legal evolution are the *descent* of legal systems (the receiving system adopts features of the donating system), *mutation* (receiving systems are not alike) and *selection* of law (a kind of natural selection, ie different receiving systems operate in different ways – degrees of functionality and dysfunctionality vary).[4]

In the world of law, permanent features mean features that go deep into the system, such as legal systematics, the doctrine of the sources of law or the nature of law (divine v secular), which change considerably, slowly over sometimes very long historical periods.[5] Also deeply rooted legal institutions, like the *trust* or *jury*, underline the permanency of law. Change in law rarely, if ever, takes place in a leap, not even in connection with a revolution.

> An example of these deep cultural features of law is the division of Continental law into private and public law, which is reflected everywhere in the legal system. This distinction can be detected in Roman law. The same systematics is lacking in the sphere of the Anglo-American common law tradition, which has received considerably less Roman influence. A similar permanent characteristic is also the way in which a system produces new legal norms in an acceptable way: does it happen by means of a legislative organ, through precedents of higher courts or through divine revelation? Systematics is also reflected in legal professions, like in the UK, where jurists working as lawyers are separated into two main categories: *solicitors* (working in law offices) and *barristers* (working in courts). In Continental law the division used in the

---

[4] The underlying ideas here are *natural selection* and *adaptation*. See eg DJ Futuyma, *Evolution*, 2nd edn (Sunderland MA, Sinauer Associates, 2009) ch 11.

[5] Tuori (n 1) ch 6 speaks of 'deep structure of the law' ('The deep structure is the most stable layer in the law.')

common law is not recognised but instead there is a different division into *notaries public* and *jurists* – in the lay-character legal tradition of Nordic countries both classifications are unknown even though the distinction between private law and public law is upheld. And, for instance, in Islamic law there is the distinctive institution of *qâdi*.

Sometimes, these permanent legal-cultural features introduce unexpected parallels at the macro-level. At the core of the common law there has always been the judge, and the common law has been described by the emphatic expression *judge-made law*. Thinking of a similar type can also be detected in Islamic law where the judge *qâdi* is functionally akin to the judicial foundation of the system. Decisions made by the learned Muslim judge must of course be based on the sources of Islamic law, but ultimately the judge is institutionally independent. A Muslim judge can through prestige attain a prominent position as a distinguished administrator of law. In the same way, the statements of a senior common law judge are more significant than those of other less respected judges. This legal-cultural characteristic seems to be lacking in Continental and Nordic law: judges seem (or they are assumed) to speak *with the words of law* and not with words of their own. Broadly speaking, we may detect the ideas of Montesquieu reflected in these non-common law legal mentalities. Montesquieu in his *Spirit of the Laws* famously argued that judges should be but 'a mouthpiece of law'.[6] Now, even though this is clearly an exaggeration in the reality of civil law, it seems to encapsulate some of the basic legal mentality concerning the role of a judge in civil law. Dawson called western judges, in his classic book, *oracles of law* arguing that judge-made law is a component of all modern legal systems even though judicial methods are different.[7] In general, Dawson's point clearly makes sense.

Adaptation to the environment and the gradual change of permanent features seem to be interrelated. In the long run changes in the social environment lead sooner or later to the alteration of the permanent features of law in a series of events, which overall is not controlled by anyone or any goal-oriented actor. European integration has, for example, resulted in a situation where in the UK legal thinking that is against the common law tradition and supports the separation of public law and private law has gained ground. The role courts play as the creators of legal rules has also diminished in England over the past 100 years. Partly the pressure for change has been endogenous (internal environment), like the expansion of the public sector and statutory law, but partly it is due to the unintentional integration process (external environment). But even here we can detect evolution because the systematics of classical civil law have gradually converged with the systematics of English law and the systematics of

---

[6] 'Mais les juges de la nation ne sont, comme nous avons dit, que la bouche qui prononce les paroles de la loi', ch VI. C Montesquieu, *De l'Esprit des Lois* (1748) bk XI.
[7] JP Dawson, *The Oracles of the Law* (Ann Arbor, University of Michigan Press, 1968).

EU law seem to continue to be a hybrid between the common law and civil law models. Brexit, nevertheless, most likely diverts this development back towards English common law.

Adaptation to the environment can also occasionally have taken place not voluntarily but because of external coercion. In the world of law *colonialism* has had special significance. By means of colonialism Western countries introduced by force their own legal traditions and methods in numerous places in the world. For example, in Africa European law was introduced in several forms: the French version, Belgian version and English common law version and the Spanish, Portuguese or Roman-Dutch (Rooms-Hollands recht) versions. The local customary law was overtaken or supplanted by the new imported law, and local customary law was applied only in exceptional cases. This situation left behind by colonialism legal-culturally still largely prevails, because law of European origin seems to form a yardstick for the local customary law: these days, local legal customs are being revived in many African States, but the resurrected customary law is examined and rediscovered through European legal-cultural spectacles. In some places, colonial law developed into a new field of law that was specifically created for the colonies. *Derecho indiano* (Spanish colonial law) is an example of this kind of a field of law.[8]

However, the fact that hybrid law is handled and understood with more respect than before has changed the intellectual atmosphere: the aim towards *pure* law now enjoys considerably less popularity than it did before. It is easy to see that an interest in today's legal hybridity has become very popular in comparative law research, but it is not actually a new phenomenon at all as Donlan has pointed out: 'In place of forcing plural and dynamic traditions into discrete, closed legal families or systems, the complexity of Western legal history suggests a new, admittedly complex and challenging study of hybridity and diffusion'.[9] In any case, as Siems puts it, 'Diffusion of law has been a core element of legal evolution.'[10]

The reluctant adoption of Continental systematics in England can be described as a choice of transplant to the extent that English common law at the receiving end has inherited one permanent deep feature, ie the way to perceive and systematise the legal norm material of the donor system, ie civil law. On the other hand, the evolutionary process of law has moved in the other direction, too, as integration has introduced to civil law a central feature of English common law, ie the strengthening of the position of the highest courts as creators of law. Global south is finding its voice, and this means that the idea of the supremacy of Western law also needs to be discussed by the comparatists.

---

[8] See M Bastias Saavedra, 'The normativity of possession' (2020) 29 *Colonial Latin Am* R 223, 224–26.
[9] SP Donlan, 'Remembering: Legal Hybridity and Legal History' (2011) 2 *Comp L R* 1, 23.
[10] M Siems, *Comparative Law*, 3rd edn (Cambridge, Cambridge University Press, 2022) 111.

Common law sometimes proves to be problematic for civil law lawyers and even geography may be difficult to conceive. From the point of view of macro-comparison, the UK and England must be distinguished. The UK in fact consists of four countries: England, Wales, Scotland and Northern Ireland. From the point of jurisdiction three areas are distinguished; they are the system shared by England and Wales, and the independent systems of Scotland and Northern Ireland, which have their own legal professions and court systems. Scotland and Northern Ireland have naturally received plenty of influence from English common law, but there are also differences in relation to England and Wales.

In addition, the Channel Islands still have their own legal traditions that are based on the old customary law of the Normans. Jersey, for example, has its own French-English legal tradition, which is a hybrid. Jersey is in fact a separate *Crown dependency*, which is known by the name *The Bailiwick of Jersey*. In the Crown dependency of Jersey, the Norman history in general is strongly visible, which is demonstrated by its minority language (*Jèrriais*), which is the Jersey version of the Norman language. There are, though, not many speakers of this tongue because the main language is English and the second language French.[11]

The external environment to which the permanent features of law have adjusted is that of Europeanisation, which has tied the national systems to an unintentional legal-cultural process of alteration. The process can be called uncontrollable, because the official aim of integration has not been to change national legal cultures or cause mutual interaction that in the end results in their permanent features becoming more and more alike. Importantly, the declared aims have been the increase of peaceful cooperation, the creation of common markets and the removal of obstacles to free the mobility of goods, services, labour and capital. Harmonisation has mainly been of a technical nature, but it has also included quite significant cultural influence. Today we talk not only of the economic aims but also of human rights and democracy. Further, more and more doubt is openly expressed concerning the limits of legal integration in Europe. Brexit being the case in point on limits of legal integration.

Yet, in certain respects, we have started to recall the innate hybridity or our own national laws – much of the legal positivistic dream and the normative fiction of the centrality of the State has now started to evaporate. Comparative law's contribution is to help native lawyers to find themselves in the other, ie to find 'legal', 'law' or 'organised normativity' in places that at first seem foreign, unfamiliar, or even incomprehensible. Comparative law's role in studying the non-familiar has not been, contrary to what some might believe, diminished due to legal globalisation. Graziadei concludes that: 'New perspectives on the vocation of comparative law as a means to know how the law unfolds in the various

---

[11] See eg TVR Hanson, 'Comparative Law in Action: the Jersey Law of Contract' (2005) 16 *Stellenbosch L R* 194.

places have emerged' as the 'exclusive attention to national dimension of the law is a thing of the past'.[12]

II. PROBLEMS IN MACRO-COMPARISON

Although European integration and, more extensively, globalisation have caused plenty of unification, the long transformation processes in the different legal systems of the world have on the one hand resulted in the diversity of legal cultures: the law of Indigenous peoples is being recognised better than in the past, Islamic law is spreading with Muslims immigrating, Chinese law is spread through initiatives like the New Silk Road. Laws are seemingly quite alike *in parts*, but there are also significant differences between them. Differences are emphasised when attention is not paid to positive law or the outcomes of precedents (or equivalent judgments), but instead law beneath the surface is inspected as living law and cultural phenomena. Contexts of laws differ; hence, laws tend to be different even if they would appear similar at first glance. A good example is the notion of rule of law that is understood differently in different places even though the concept looks semantically similar.[13]

On the other hand, if we go deep enough, we notice that the historical roots of Western and Islamic culture are the same: at the basis of both there is a monotheistic religion that was born in the Ancient Middle East and which is based on the Book, which is regarded as holy, the doctrinal development of which has been promoted by classical Greek philosophy and scientific thinking. From the point of evolution, the desynchronisation of social and economic development stands out if we focus on Islamic and Western legal cultures. Because of this, the different versions of Islamic law in different countries and the different versions of Western law in different countries seem to exist in different periods formulated by the special quality of their own cultural and social frameworks. Crucially, it is easier to grasp hybridity in legal systems other than one's own. Moreover, if we delve deep enough into legal history, we can also cast doubts over the classical narrative of Roman law's superiority in the ancient world and conceive legal pluralism or multiculturalism based on Western law.[14]

---

[12] M Graziadei, 'What Does Globalisation Mean for the Comparative Study of Law? (2021) 16 *J Comp L* 511, 535.

[13] M Burnay, *Chinese Perspectives on the International Rule of Law* (Cheltenham, Edward Elgar, 2018) 11–44 (distinguishes the English Rule of Law, the German *Rechtsstaat*, and the French *Etat de Droit* and then discusses the distinction between formal ('thin') and substantive ('thick') versions of the rule of law).

[14] PG Monateri, 'Black Gaius: A Quest for Multicultural Origins of the "Western Legal Tradition"' (2000) 51 *Hastings L J* 479.

It is easy to observe the variety of legal cultures when the differences between English common law, the German legal culture or the legal culture of Nordic countries are compared in regard to their reaction to the role of courts as creators of legally binding norms. The most adverse attitude to judges as creators of law prevails in Nordic countries, and Germany is somewhere between England and the Nordic countries. Ever since the (French) Revolution, France has been suspicious of the creation of law by the courts, but in the twenty-first century the legal-cultural attitude has been gradually changing.

It has also to be observed that differences in the recipient systems result in differences even when the influences assumed are identical – processes speak for interaction and change, but it is futile to predict any actual *end of history* in the field of legal modification because the versatility of legal cultures is so obvious. This is also due to legal mutation, which ensures that even exactly identical external influences (such as the European Convention on Human Rights, for instance) have different ramifications in different legal cultures – systems operate in different ways and in different contexts. For example, a human rights obligation that can be carried out without a problem in Finland can cause unpredictable consequences in the legal systems of, say, Moldova or Turkey. When borrowed elsewhere, American plea-bargaining is different from what it is in the US. Legal transplants easily end up as irritants and, what is more, it may be that societies have such different values that there is no way of judging what works well in a particular society. Without extending the argument on cultural relativism too far it seems likely that there are legal incompatibilities which are revealed when societies are developed by imported legal ideas and institutions.[15]

Therefore, it seems that it is possible to talk about the macro-level change of law on a general level by resorting to evolutionary concepts. John Henry Wigmore (1863–1943) distinguished between three different comparative approaches to law. *Nomoscopy* described foreign legal systems and *nomothetics* analysed the strong and weak points of systems. *Nomogenetics* paid attention to the chronological development and the influences the systems had on each other. Wigmore applied his nomogenetic approach to the idea of evolution: according to it systems influence each other, which again results in the creation of interaction between systems.[16] Importantly, legal systems and cultures influence each other whether lawyers conceive and identify the influences or not.

Long-lasting interaction, on the other hand, shapes systems so that they acquire features that they did not have before. In interaction influences are given and received. It is crucial to understand that even those legal cultures (mostly Western) that regard themselves as donors also implicitly receive. This can be seen, for example, in the English common law where the UK became the first

---

[15] See MJ Trebilcock and MM Prado, *Advanced Introduction to Law and Development* (Cheltenham, Edward Elgar, 2014) 3–16.
[16] See JH Wigmore, *A Panorama of the World's Legal Systems* (Saint Paul, West Publishing, 1928) 1120–21. Deriving first part of the terms *nomos* from the Greek νόμος for 'law'.

non-Muslim country to sell bonds that can be bought by Islamic investors. This was done to encourage large-scale Muslim investment into the UK. The legal outcome is a Shari'a compliant finance: this is clearly peaceful interaction between different legal cultures.

A. Changing of Law

Macro-comparison has been, in certain respects, close to botany in its classification and creation of taxonomies of the legal systems and legal cultures of the world. This is, most likely, a remnant from an era when comparative law was being developed into a 'true' science. The idea of macro-comparative law has been to produce a picture of what kind of systems there are and what are their core features. An answer has been searched for to the question of whether based on their core features they can be classified into various bigger groups (legal families or legal cultures). This type of operation is sensible and needed, as was explained in the previous chapter, but it is frequently confronted by the main problem: mutations that are going on make the global perception of law challenging; the field studied is in slow motion like a slowly flowing legal magma of rules, institutions, customs and doctrines. Not even the most conservative legal cultures are stable – even though they may themselves think that their most fundamental feature is immutability.

> Islamic law is seen as a basic example of conservatism. However, for example in 2009 in the West Bank, Palestinians nominated two female *qâdi* judges. Also, in Indonesia there are female Muslim judges with full legal authority. On the other hand, in Malaysia the authority of female Muslim judges is restricted to divorce and criminal cases. Yet, there are divided opinions on the matter of appointing women to judicial positions in the Sharia courts.[17] For its part, the common law experienced a big cultural change when in the autumn of 2009 the new Supreme Court of the United Kingdom, which was organised according to Continental models, started its work. The Court replaced the judicial function previously performed by the House of Lords (ie the Appellate Committee of the House of Lords), and the judges are no longer Lords but *Justices* of the Supreme Court. This legal evolution tells us about changes in the common law legal mentality because it was felt that there needed – in response to pressure from the European Court of Human Rights – to be a sharper distinction between the courts and the Parliament. But as the discussion on the European human rights in the UK shows some parts of the UK are quite suspicious about European human rights.

Notwithstanding this, evolution and macro-comparison are not completely compatible. It is difficult to include in the same theoretical framework both the slow motion of the legal-cultural magma and strict classifications. Any taxonomy is rigid and static while legal evolution makes the system being

---

[17] A Muneeza, 'Appointment of Female Judges in Muslim Countries' (2014) 16 *Eur J L Reform* 317.

classified dynamic. There are at least two answers to the problem. On the one hand, attempts are made to keep the *list of macro-constructs* up to date by making systematic observations and correcting classifications from time to time. On the other hand, any classification concentrates only on the essential and dominating features. By concentrating on structures and legal-cultural basic features, macro-constructs become less prone to change. For example, Japan and Turkey demonstrate well the significance of the upkeep of the list of categories.

> While Japan at the beginning of the twentieth century was classified as a member of the Asian legal family, by the 1950s it was seen partly as a member of the Western legal family; one which had strong Asian features such as the willingness to compromise and a very small relative number of professional jurists. By the 1970s and 1980s several fields of law were quite prepared to consider that Japan was largely Westernised. Today, the law of Japan is classified as Asian mainly on geographical grounds. In most evaluations Japanese law is considered practically a Western system that mostly follows the Continental European model, which however has influence of American law in places and some patches that might still be described as in accordance with the so-called Asian legal culture.
>
> Another example of evolution and mutation involved in the legal family thinking is Turkey, which to begin with as an Ottoman State (from the fourteenth century onwards) was in the sphere of Islamic law but started to undergo a transformation in the nineteenth century due to the weakening of the State. One of the areas that was reformed was the legal system, which was Westernised in accordance with European models. Later, in the 1920s and 1930s when the Ottoman State had collapsed and modern Turkey was born from its ruins, law was more strongly modernised according to European models, and as part of the reform policy, attempts were made to completely destroy the old model. The most curious and massive reformation was the almost word-for-word copying of the Swiss Civil Code for Turkey by simply translating it straight into Turkish (the Western alphabet had replaced the Arabic one). In Turkey, evolution has, however, not resulted in a situation where it would be classified as a 'full' member of the Western legal family. However, when we turn our eyes from written law (what it is supposed to be) towards legal practices and legal culture (what it actually is in an empirical sense), we can observe that dysfunctional features keep slowing down the mutation. In addition, there are major political forces in Turkey wishing to turn the direction of legal evolution – partly – back towards the Islamic legal culture. Under the political rulership of Recep Tayyip Erdoğan (1954–) Turkey seems to have taken many steps back to the pre-westernisation period.

The cases of Japan and Turkey at least prove how difficult it is to classify whole systems – they are continuously in slow motion. On the other hand, as was indicated by the collapse of socialism at the beginning of the 1990s, radical changes in the environment are also important and can lead to significant change. Socialist law, which earlier has been one of the core families of global law, became almost extinct. States like Cuba, Vietnam and China are little by little giving up many ideas that were valid in socialist law (eg private ownership of the means of production being disallowed). On the other hand, China has by no means in all sectors of its law given up some basic ideas of socialist law, as the one-party system and limited political rights prove. The general picture of Chinese law is in the eyes of comparative law legal-culturally a system of mixed law or at least a mixture of laws. And, as such a hybrid it is a legal culture that is very difficult to place into any of the old categories of macro-constructs. For the constitutional comparatist, on the other hand, the problem is whether to classify the Chinese system as authoritarian or totalitarian.

III. LIMITS OF LEGAL EVOLUTION?

Against the backdrop of the above discussion, it seems that it is possible to describe or at least attempt to understand the global change of law by means of evolutionary concepts. It seems obvious that this can be done as long as the previous cultural and racial discrimination is clearly renounced. The evolutionary perception and understanding of the change in the legal systems and cultures of the world seems in fact somewhat workable. Problems, however, start to accumulate if the aim is to apply the evolutionary concepts in a very exact and detailed way to the change in the world of law. It is obvious that the comparatist's hermeneutic research methods and grounds used for classification are not very precise and there is serious disagreement about them – instead of a uniform taxonomy, macro-comparison offers a fuzzy picture of the main features and changes of global law.

On the other hand, it is worth noting that even a fuzzy picture is better than no picture. It is quite close to the picture about which philosopher Gottfried Wilhelm Leibniz (1646–1716) dreamt when he wrote in the seventeenth century about the legal map of the world, which he called in Latin *theatrum legale mundi*.[18] It is telling that not even Leibniz managed to finish his project to compose a map of the entire global law – and in his time the world of law was technically not as complicated as it is today. Accordingly, it is not easy to describe in a sensible way by means of any theoretical concepts how complete legal systems and legal cultures change. The situation reminds us of what GWF Hegel (1770–1831) meant when he wrote that 'the owl of Minerva takes its flight with the falling of the dusk'; macro-comparative law comes to understand law globally only as it passes away. To put it another way, the global view of legal systems is possible only in hindsight after legal systems have already changed.[19]

Evolutionary theory provides certain tools for perceiving law on a global level more successfully than legal theories (legal realism, legal positivism, natural law theory) that are attached to individual legal systems or cultures: they are

---

[18] GW Leibniz, *Nova Methodus discendae docendaeque Jurisprudentiae* (1667). In English 'A New Method for Learning and Teaching Jurisprudence'. For a concise analysis see JH Wigmore, 'Nova Methodus Discendae Docendaeque Jurisprudentiae' (1917) 30 *Harvard L R* 812.

[19] GWF Hegel, *Elements of the Philosophy of Right*, trans TM Knox (Oxford, Oxford University Press, 1952) 13 [Grundlinien der Philosophie des Rechts, 1820].

troubled by permanent geographic shackles because, to start with, they have been connected with a particular legal system. The advantage of the evolutionary theory is that it is neutral in relation to macro-level change: it is possible by means of it to dispassionately register both the transformation of law into something more religious and more professional without involving subjective evaluations of the scholar on the good–bad axis based on the idea of ethical superiority. Perhaps this is its toughest problem from the perspective of the Western study of law, which is committed to liberalism, humanism and human rights. It is difficult for the Western comparatist to have a neutral attitude to opposition inflicted on their own deep-seated legal values even though such difficulties must not prevent the comparatist from studying law that radically differs from their own law. Then again, it is problematic if the comparatist makes value judgements while sitting on their culturally embedded moral high horse. It is, indeed, difficult to combine the roles of the comparatist and the legal activist in a balanced manner.

It is essential to take legal evolution into consideration although we cannot speak of the irrelevance of legal history. After the Cold War Fukuyama sketched the end of history in his famous argument:

> What we may be witnessing is not just the end of the Cold War, or the passing of a particular period of post-war history, but the end of history as such: that is, the end point of mankind's ideological evolution and the universalisation of Western liberal democracy as the final form of human government.[20]

In other words: everything of significance would have been done already. The development of the legal history of humankind and the battle between legal ideologies (socialist v middle-class/bourgeois, secular v religious, professional v amateur) would have ended in the victory of liberal democracy, ie civil law and common law. These visions were clearly premature as we now know.

The developments of the twenty-first century have considerably reduced the popularity enjoyed by Fukuyama's thesis although Western law has spread efficiently all over the world. All the same, the result has not been unity but different local applications and legal pluralism, ie novel forms of legal hybridity have emerged. Islamic law has experienced a resurgence, and States have been forced to acknowledge the existence of regions (eg Scotland, Catalonia and Quebec) and Indigenous peoples and their legal traditions (eg American Indian peoples, the Māori, the Sámi, aboriginals, the Inuit etc). Moreover, it has been noted that the legal relations between Indigenous peoples and States have developed towards an asymmetric and pluralistic model which has eroded the idea of a unitary State and the exclusiveness of positive law.[21]

---

[20] F Fukuyama, 'The End of History' (1989) 16 *The National Interest* 3.
[21] See J Uimonen, *From Unitary State to Plural Asymmetric State* (Rovaniemi, Lapland University Press, 2014).

But all change is not useful or wished for. For instance, Russia developed into an autocracy, attacked Ukraine in early 2022 showing that globalisation and the victory of liberalism has been but a dream. Once again Europe sees a war on a large scale raging on its soil causing huge suffering and loss of life. To that end, Russian law has taken huge steps backwards. Calling that development evolution of law does not, however, feel like a proper conceptualisation.

11
Groupings, Classifications, Categories

U P UNTIL THE last few years, mainstream textbooks on comparative law have been constructed in a typical form: first, some theory and methodology, followed by classification where the big legal families or major legal systems of the world are (to varying extents) descriptively introduced, and finally selected private law issues might be discussed. Macro-comparative law and the attempt to create a taxonomy of the world's legal systems has occupied a key role in comparative law literature throughout the last hundred years.[1] Typically these classifications have mainly been constructed for private law. In addition, they have earlier been characterised by an emphasis that is clearly Western, which for example Bogdan has defended with practical reasons by saying that 'it is pedagogically justifiable'.[2] Regardless, the Western ethnocentrism has deep roots in the comparative law pedigree as an academic field. There are still traces of colonial epistemology left in macro-comparative law.

> In the work by Arminjon, Nolde and Wolff, French, German, Scandinavian, English, Russian, Islamic and Hindu legal families were introduced.[3] In the work *Les Grands systèmes de droit contemporains* (running to more than 10 editions) by David, the Romano-Germanic (civil law), common law and socialist families were introduced as genuine legal groups. As in other, non-Western legal systems David mentioned Islamic, Hindu and Jewish law as well as the law of the Far East, Africa and Madagascar. Germans Zweigert and Kötz presented in their influential mainstream work *Einführung in die Rechtsvergleichung* Roman, German, Nordic, common law and socialist legal families as well as the Far Eastern and Islamic systems and Hindu law.[4]
>
> In more recent books, for example, Peter de Cruz has continued the tradition in his textbook *Comparative Law in a Changing World*, which naturally contains some updated ideas and struggles to fit in also European Union law.[5] Moreover, *Annuario di diritto comparato 2013* entitled 'Diritto comparato e sistemologia: le nuove sfide'

---

[1] See M Pargendler, 'The Rise and Decline of Legal Families' (2012) 60 *Am J Comp L* 1043.
[2] 'den är enligt min mening pedagogiskt försvarlig', M Bogdan, *Komparativ rättskunskap* (Stockholm, Norstedts juridik, 2003) 81.
[3] P Arminjon, B Nolde and M Wolff, *Traité de droit comparé I* (1950); R David and C Jauffret-Spinosi, *Les grands systèmes de droit contemporains*, 11th edn (Paris, Dalloz, 2002).
[4] *Einführung in die Rechtsvergleichung auf dem Gebiete des Privatrechts*, vol 1 (Tübingen, Mohr, 1971), English versions 1987, 1992 and 1998.
[5] P de Cruz, *Comparative Law in a Changing World*, 3rd edn (London, Routledge-Cavendish, 2007).

('Comparative Law and Systemology: New Challenges') offers articles in several languages concerning the new challenges of systematising legal systems and/or legal cultures.[6] Even though comparative law has developed towards diversity embracing the field of legal study, legal families are still discussed and this will most likely not change in the foreseeable future.[7]

The fact that private law has been stressed in the classifications, groupings and categorisations is not necessarily an insurmountable problem. Even these kinds of classifications are not useless because they describe not only private law but also general legal-cultural features (eg legal mentality manifested in private law) that have created the context where the entire legal system operates. Even if the public law of an individual system had features which cannot be regarded as being part of the main classification of the whole legal system, it does not mean that from the point of view of public law the classification would have necessarily been different. It is a question of legal culture and tradition that is on a different abstraction level compared to legal systematics. For example, in several European countries legal thinking has historically developed in the various sectors of private law, and public law has been included later on. In other words, in many cases public law is in a legal-cultural sense rather like the little sister of the much older private law. In macro-comparison the question has always been of the differentiation made between macro-level factors, which has meant that details have inevitably remained in the background (see chapter nine, sections II and III). Macro-comparison places all details, whether they be private law or public law details, in a less crucial role and concentrates on overall features.

Since there are several kinds of classifications of legal families, legal cultures and legal traditions, it is justifiable to ask how one can grasp the entity of macro-constructs. To begin with, one will notice that classification suggestions are in fact quite similar and there is surprisingly little variation. Similarity is not that surprising because macro-constructs have been built by looking for the typical and permanent characteristics of legal systems. That is why they are not overly vulnerable to historical changes and changing legislation.

In spite of their similarity, it is difficult to estimate the superiority of individual classification suggestions, because they have been constructed from somewhat different starting points and at different times. In connection with different classifications it is important to know the criteria on the basis of which the suggestion has been built. At least two major different classification criteria can be distinguished. In the first type, attention is paid to the technique of legal systems, and in the other comprehensive factors. It is not, however, possible to keep these two approaches completely separate.

---

[6] 'Diritto comparato e sistemologia' (ed) B Pozzo, *Annuario di diritto comparato e di studi legislativi 2013* (Naples, ESI, 2013).
[7] J Husa, 'The Future of Legal Families' in *Oxford Handbook Topics in Law*, online edn (Oxford, Oxford University Press, 2016) doi.org/10.1093/oxfordhb/9780199935352.013.26.

I. TECHNICAL CRITERIA

The technical classification criteria for macro-constructs are related to the formal characteristics of the legal system. In other words, these are distinctively Western criteria. When grounds like these are used for demarcation, often the bonds that legal systems have with the cultures and social orders to which they belong are more or less ignored. The use of technical differentiation criteria presumes commitment of some degree to the formal view of law (legal positivism). The use of technical criteria is interesting mainly from the point of view of comparative law with practical or non-academic aims. The judge, the legislator or the lawyer civil servant is seldom interested in legal families or cultures as such or the more general legal-cultural factors by means of which the similarities and differences can be understood and explained. Explanatory understanding and socio-legal engineering based on practical needs are founded on a different way of thinking. The same applies to the unravelling of the substance of foreign law in the court in a case where there is a difference between the laws of at least two jurisdictions, so that the outcome depends on which jurisdiction's laws will be used in resolving the legal issues at hand.

Attention can be paid to the technique in which *legal rules* are expressed, ie to the fact of whether the rules are enacted or case law based. More specifically it is a question of whether there is comprehensive official written information about the living law, which means that, for example, any system of an English origin tends to be based on judicial precedents (judge-made law) whereas systems with Continental European roots tend to be based on large-scale systematic codifications (positive law). Moreover, the systems of both written and unwritten law can be placed in different legal families (eg a Western legal family with written documentation and, say, a traditional Indigenous law that has been orally transmitted).

It is likely that pure types, which belong only to the systems of either enacted or case law, are quite rare because there are elements of both in most legal systems. For instance, the English law of today has a massive amount of statutory law even though the cultural attitude towards such legal material is that it is regarded roughly as the 'raw material of law'; in other words, it is the job of the courts to carve out the precise legal content of these 'paper rules'. Now, if the aim is macro-classification, the decisive factor is which one of the features can be considered more characteristic of the system in question. Also the point of view from which the classification is made has an effect. Occasionally classifications made on the basis of private law and public law may have a different end-result.

> For example, the system of German civil law can be called Germanic, but if the criterion is the control method of constitutionality the German system belongs to the same group as the USA. India, on the other hand, is mainly included in the sphere of common law, but from the point of view of certain core sectors it represents Hindu law and Islamic law. With regard to constitutional law, India could however be considered a Continental system although in its legal culture there is no civil law

heritage that would be based on historical contacts or adoption. English language has a significant position not only as *lingua franca* but also as the language of law. Japan has German-style civil and criminal law but a quite American constitutional system, which, however, works quite differently from the American constitutional culture. The Maltese system is a kind of synthesis of many legal cultures (eg Italian and British) inherited from layers of colonial rule. Louisiana mixes American common law and some elements of civil law. This list could go on and on.

Another technical distinguishing criterion (closely related to the previous one) concerns the *sources of law* and their use. It is a question of how different sources of law are recognised and how they are used as part of legal argumentation. David used as one of his criteria the sources of law, statutory law, precedents of certain higher courts or something else (eg religion). David was specifically interested in authority, ie where legal rules originated from. Paradigmatic classification that is built on this kind of classification of legal sources is carried out between *statutory law* (civil law) systems and systems that rely on the precedents made by courts. These are complemented by systems with a religious background such as Islamic law where the ultimate, and in the legal-cultural sense the most essential, source of law is the Koran.

> The *source of law* refers to the normative source material from which the organs applying law are seeking norms for decision-making in judgments. In comparative law, the concept *source of law* typically refers to statements in the descriptive doctrine of the sources of law on what the legal weight of different sources of law have in the sphere of a certain legal system. On the other hand, within legal theory and the doctrinal study of law normative ideas are presented of what the weight and capacity of different sources of law ought to be. Owing to the macro-nature of the classification of legal families and legal cultures, features of the lists of legal sources belonging to different systems are examined on a rather general level in comparative law. This leads to a rather fuzzy picture of those legal systems that are included in the groupings, classifications and taxonomies. Moreover, these lists tend to disregard sources of religious or Indigenous nature as the focus is typically on common law and civil law.

The descriptive distinctions concerning the use and recognition of the sources of law are essential criteria for distinction although in practice legal argumentation generally operates by means of statutory law and precedents. It is a question of what weight and order of priority they are considered to have in different systems. For example, the English common law system contains *Acts of Parliament*, ie *statutory law* and *case law with precedential value*. *Case law* here refers to the method (so-called *distinguishing* technique) that is used in the application of norms that have been created in previous legal praxis in connection with new cases, ie to a system that historically originates from England. This demonstrates how quickly one, by using technical grounds, can get to the realm of legal history. In fact, the explanations concerning the reasons of why legal systems are as they are, are virtually always historical. Accordingly, nothing else but history explains why Australia, Canada, New Zealand or Singapore belong to the common law legal family and nothing else but history explains why later Roman law (*ius commune*) had relatively little impact on the legal systems of Nordic countries. Nordic countries are legal-culturally the middle ground: the formal doctrine of the sources of law emphasise statutory law, but in the practical legal life precedents of higher courts have a central role in the system. In many systems where the doctrine of *stare decisis* (binding precedent) is not officially embraced, important judgments by superior courts have (*cf* Ehrlich's living law) at least a persuasive force as a source of law. This is one of the reasons why the comparatist needs to look beyond black-letter law.

II. GENERAL REQUIREMENTS

The weakness in most attempts to classify legal systems has been concentration on only one or two key factors on the basis of which the whole classification has been drawn. The advantage of such a classification is its unambiguousness and systematic clarity but the lack of a legal-cultural 'living law' view is its weakness. In many systems there are simultaneously several features, and it is not sensible to group them only on the basis of one criterion and one field of law. It is a question of the legal-culturally dominating features of the systems, as has above become clear. Global diversity of laws understandably complicates making classifications.

Instead of such separate factors, some comparative law theorists like Zweigert and Kötz wanted to bring up more extensive general concepts, such as *the style of legal systems* by means of which classification can be performed more fittingly.[8] The style can be determined by means of legal-culturally typical factors that are related to the sources of law, interpretation of law and legal argumentation as well as the education for legal occupations, and the relation of the legal profession to other learned professions.

> It is difficult to judge from any individual source what the characteristic style of an entire system consists of. The style is closely connected to legal culture and legal mentality. One example is the way in which the thinking of a jurist and a judge is sketched in legal disciplines. Continental thinking has been compared to mathematics, logics and geometry. Within the common law, thinking has been compared to visual thinking, ie to a situation where the event of application is perceived in the form of a photograph in which facts and the event of application are emphasised instead of the interpretative logic of written rules. It is of course a question of fuzzy large-scale metaphors, but from the point of macro-classification they describe the basic legal-cultural differences in legal thinking. In a similar way, the legal expert can in Islamic law be conceived as a *qâdi* judge with religious training, while in the West law is perceived with different legal-cultural links. There are also courts that combine

---

[8] K Zweigert and H Kötz, *An Introduction to Comparative Law*, 3rd edn (Oxford, Oxford University Press, 1998) 63–73.

Western law and Indigenous law as the tribal courts in the US show. Judges in these courts seek to incorporate tribal values, culture and perspectives into modern legal practice.[9]

The comparatist who aims at systematic macro-classification must, according to the legal style approach, try to find the characteristic style of each legal system that distinguishes it from other legal systems or organised large-scale normativities. The problem is that it is very difficult to say which features are characteristic of each legal system. This is particularly difficult in connection with the comparatist's own legal system because they have been epistemically integrated with it: seen from within, many factors that the national jurist finds self-evident can be all but self-evident when seen from the outside. Jurists all over the world have in a surprisingly profound way been conditioned legal-cognitively with their very own law and its implicit legal-cultural basic assumptions. This is one of the key difficulties for the comparatist.

It is probably easier to notice the stylistic features typical of foreign legal systems because the comparatist looks at the system through the eyes of an outsider: a Nordic jurist notices the existence of the *jury* in the common law criminal trial; the German jurist may wonder about the English wigs while simultaneously wondering about the lack of the cloak/robe in the Nordic countries; the Nordic jurist again is amazed by the loudness of a Greek Court of First Instance (Greek *Πρωτοδικείο*) or the rituality of a German Constitutional Court etc. A common law lawyer may be surprised to see a female New Zealand judge (ethnic Māori) wearing moko kauae, ie the traditional chin tattoo. The comparatist examining foreign law can be (legally and culturally) surprised in a way that is not possible within the sphere of their own legal system because of the epistemic embedding; of course there are internal surprises but they are very seldom of an 'eye-opening' nature.

In a way, being an outsider is a drawback. On the other hand, when classification of legal systems according to their style is in question, being an outsider is actually a prerequisite for being able to detect the special characteristics of style. This may sound, at first, paradoxical but it is not really the case. Namely, familiarity does not arouse questions and objections at an intensity that is anywhere close to that aroused by something new and strange. This is related to the pedagogical power of comparative law that is based on a (conscious) epistemic exit from within one's own legal limits. A Nordic jurist might be unaware of the significance of the notary institution in Central Europe in the same way as the Continental European jurist is surprised to see that it is lacking in the Nordic countries.

It is not, however, possible to consider just any factor as a factor of style; they concern important, longstanding, and characteristic features. Several stylistically

---

[9] 'Tribal Courts' (2020) 59 *The Judge's Journal*.

significant matters can be detected but at least the following can be mentioned as – partly overlapping – factors:
General criteria in classifying

1. Historical development
2. Nature of legal thinking
3. Social and legal ideology
4. Factors related to the cultural sphere

III. HISTORY-RELATED FACTORS

What has been written earlier in this book seems like a clear indication of the significance of history to a comparatist who is serious about the comparative endeavour. When it is assessed whether a legal system or other large-scale organised normativity belongs to a certain legal family or culture, historical factors constitute a crucial element on the basis of which it is possible to evaluate the position of the legal system in question in the genealogy of legal families. One of the central characteristics influencing the style of a legal system is its historical path; the style is formed over the course of history.

For example, the fact that common law countries belong to the common law family is only explained by historical factors. The fact that such different countries as Australia, Ghana, the UK, India, Kenya, Malaysia, New Zealand, Nigeria, Pakistan, Singapore, South Africa and Zambia belong to the common law family is only explained by the colonial history of the British Empire. There is no other explanatory factor (eg climate, culture, language or geography) for the considerable similarity of the legal systems of these countries. Plain and simple, the similarities in style are based on a common history – colonial past.

However, in connection with Continental legal systems historical factors do not offer one indisputable cause for classification. It is in fact not clear if we can speak of one big Continental legal family (civil law) or if we should further distinguish different sub-groups (Romano, Germanic and Nordic). When grounds for legal family classification are sought in history, it has to be understood that the purpose is not to present sophisticated legal historical explanations. Albeit, this is not as simple as it may sound. Gordley describes the situation well:

> The mistake of legal historians is to assume that the law of a given time and place can be studied without regard to how the law has developed elsewhere. The corresponding mistake for comparative lawyers is to assume that the law of each modern jurisdiction forms a coherent system rather than an amalgam of solutions developed over time.[10]

---

[10] J Gordley, 'Comparative Law and Legal History' in M Reimann and R Zimmermann (eds), *The Oxford Handbook of Comparative Law*, 2nd edn (Oxford, Oxford University Press, 2019) 762.

The aim is to look for explanatory factors to explain features that are characteristic of legal systems (distinctive characteristics of legal thinking) and that are found in a certain specific legal system. The aim is also to answer the questions of why within this legal system certain things are taken for granted, why the branch of legal systematics is what it is or why there are certain distinctive institutions not found in other legal families. For example: why are there separate administrative courts in Finland and Sweden according to the Continental model but in Denmark and Norway this is not the case even though all these systems recognise the distinction between private law and public law? Or why does Morocco have a court system based on French law even though its legal system can also be described as Islamic?

By means of legal history it is also possible to understand and explain why certain rules or institutions become established in another legal system while others do not. So, when we think about the classification, we must observe that most explanatory factor types are always historical in some respect. However, this does not mean that they are legal-culturally easy to grasp or easily explained.

It is very difficult for a Western comparatist to explain and understand Islamic law. The explanation, according to which this is due to the fact that Islamic law is based on religious factors and Western law on professional factors, remains unsettled: religious law is different because it is religious. It might be that differences are not so great because in both legal cultures there are norms and principles, a specific understanding of the order of priority (what happens when norms collide) and application of norms and legal study. If explanations are sought from below the surface, it can be observed that legal differences are also based on different legal-theoretical basic assumptions of law and the attitude to the individual and society. In the West, law has traditionally been associated with nation States with their own geographical areas and sovereignties, while in the Islamic world law is dominated by a personal dimension, and for example the applicable norms of family law are not defined by the law of the State but by religion and often even by the specific sect of religion to which the person in question belongs.

The classical aim of Western law is to be the same for all people and to neutralise the personal dimension while in Islamic law the choice of private legal norms applied to the person in certain situations depends on their religion. It is difficult to reconcile basic approaches that differ seemingly so radically, but of course there is no need for the comparatist to even try. However, the comparatist should be aware of these factors because they no doubt influence comparative study. Importantly, there are natural connections between comparative law and legal history and in many ways these fields overlap to a significant degree.[11] It is a question of the basic nature of legal thinking and, to be sure, there can be no assumption of similarity here. Yet, this does not exclude the possibility of similarities.

---

[11] H Pihlajamäki, 'Merging Comparative Law and Legal History' (2018) 66 *Am J Comp L* 733.

IV. NATURE OF LEGAL THINKING (LEGAL MENTALITY)

The characteristic basic nature of legal thinking is of significance when stylistic features of an individual legal system are discussed, such as what is *a rule of law* or a *source of law*. Civil law thinking is characterised by an attempt to use abstract legal norms, an attempt to divide the legal system into different exactly defined fields of law and the tendency to filter the evaluation of the reality at hand through legal concepts – the reality is in such cases evaluated via a network of legal concepts (deductive thinking). The approach is not exactly spontaneous or focused on facts but instead predetermined and focused on norms: reality is seen through norms and the legal mind works from general concepts towards facts.

In civil law thinking, legal rules are considered to be general abstract normative rules of behaviour that are situated on a different level from the application of law. In the same way the national legal disciplines and doctrinal study of law in particular are considered to be situated on a different abstraction level from that of practical legal decision-making and application. Furthermore, in civil law the idea of a hierarchy is respected to a great extent, which means that the constitution has the top position in the hierarchy. In civil law thinking the Constitution (Constitutional Act as German *Grundgesetz* or Swedish *grundlag*) that is above ordinary written laws (parliamentary Acts) is considered central to the whole legal system while, for example, in the UK, Israel and New Zealand this is not the case. Apart from the US, the common law has up till the last few years avoided strictly defined hierarchies of legal norms. Notwithstanding, the British Human Rights Act that came into force in 2000 and the Supreme Court that started work in 2009 have strengthened the features of internal hierarchy in the UK. However, British ongoing political debate revolving around the Human Rights Act may be catalysed by certain civil law features that the Act has transferred into common law.[12]

In common law thinking, the concept of a legal rule continues to differ from the view of the Continental tradition despite certain convergence. Formation of legal rules is considered to be due to the legal practice, ie *precedents* given by higher courts in their decisions. Legal rules are considered, in a way, to represent the same level of abstraction as court decisions. In the civil law system the basis of the legal system is considered to consist of legislation and the abstract rules included in it. In the common law, on the other hand, the basis of the legal system is considered to be in the specification of the factual state of the court decisions on the legal problem and in the decisive grounds for decision (*ratio decidendi*). In connection to such parts of judgments that are of a secondary nature (*obiter dictum*), the intention is not to flesh out an actual common law

---

[12] J Husa, 'Human Rights? No thanks We're English' (2016) 3 *Eur J Comp L & Governance* 229.

rule but only to make a passing remark on the matter.[13] Finding the ratio is not easy because there is no specific way to present it or no specific place for it in the decision, and at the moment of decision-making there is no knowledge of the future potential *ratio decidendi* effect. In short, common law seems to think inductively, ie it conceives norms through facts and not the other way round. This kind of 'common law mind' developed rather early in England consisting of various things forged by historical events.

When we speak of law on the macro-level, it is easy to make generalisations, to refer to civil law or Islamic law, for example. When non-Western systems are compared, such generalisation seems to be justified if seen from the Western legal sphere. On the other hand, if the object of study is European law, it is worth noting that there are also differences between Romanic law and Germanic law although at their basis is a shared legal history in the form of *ius commune*. The differences are clearly seen in the large and legal-culturally significant civil law codifications of Germany and France.

A. Differences Between the Basic Codifications of Continental Civil Law

In France, the preparation of codification ordered by Napoleon did not only rely on *ius commune*, but also on the material on the application of law that was created during the *ancien régime* and on other legal traditions, for example those customary law traditions that were born out of commercial practice. Before the Great Revolution (1789), France was divided: in Northern parts there was great influence of *droit coutumier* whereas in Southern parts the written Roman-influenced law (French *droit écrit*) prevailed. But there is more to it, since before the Revolution there were in the area of France several regional customary law norms such as *coutume de Normandie*, *coutume d'Orleans* and the best-known *coutume de Paris* that were applied also outside their own region.[14] In Germany, on the other hand, the drafters of codifications were permeated by Pandectism and the nineteenth century German law, and unlike in France the preparation of the *Bürgerliches Gesetzesbuch* (BGB) did not rely on the unwritten established customary norms. In the German area it could be said the Pandectist legal science replaced customary law because Pandectic ideas and doctrines were applied in German legal practice.[15] It is owing to Pandectism that in Germany the practice preceding civil law legal family codifications was more consistent than the situation in France before the *code civil*.

The end-result was two different codifications on the basis of which we can make the difference between these two basic members of civil law. The

---

[13] For a concise discussion, see G Samuel, *A Short Introduction to Common Law* (Cheltenham, Edward Elgar, 2013) 79–82.
[14] G Cuniberti, *Grands systèmes de droit contemporains*, 4th edn (Paris, LGDJ, 2019) 45–47 and Bogdan, *Komparativ rättskunskap* (n 2) 149–52.
[15] See Zweigert and Kötz, *Introduction* (n 8) 143–54.

systematic placement of commercial law was legal-technically one of the key distinguishing factors.

> According to the codification strategy selected in France *code civil*/Code Napoleon (1804) consisted of three books. It was meant to be all-inclusive so that the academic legal discipline and judge-made law were made useless once and for all. Commercial law was included in the codification on purpose. The 2,281 articles that the codifications contained were divided into several books/sections, subsections and articles. There is no separate general part in the codification, and *ius commune* had a commanding role, but the significance of the customary law (*droit coutumier*) of France that had preceded the codification can be seen. The codification was divided into three main books, which are: I the Book of Persons, II the Book of Property and III the Book of the Different Modes of Acquiring Property.
>
> According to the strategy that was selected in Germany, the BGB (1900) was to contain five books, and the codification was not to include commercial law. The aim was not so clearly, as was the case in France, to replace the science of law (ie legal doctrine). Instead, *as extensive and systematic a codification* as possible was the aim. The structure of sections and subsections in the BGB does not consist of as many phases as the French *code civil*. There is also a separate general part that is not included in the French codification. The significance of the *ius commune* tradition is clearly visible in the work as well as the attempt to return to genuine (as it was understood) *Roman law*. The Roman character was introduced into the codification through the Pandectic legal science (*Pandektenwissenschaft*), ie in the form that emphasised conceptual logical thinking. The German codification consists of: I the General Part, II Law of obligations, III Property law, IV Family law and V Inheritance law. The codification contains 2,385 sections.

There are also important commonalities. Both codifications are the result of the nineteenth century thinking and the ideology of liberalism is pronounced (particularly the freedom of contract); they contain lots of cross-references, legal definitions, a strong conceptual nature and all-compassing rigidity. Although they only apply in private law, their legal-cultural significance is stronger: they can be seen as *monuments* of the legal thinking and legal mentality of their own legal cultures. The *code civil* reflects the advantage that the legislator has over courts, and the regulation is in a more straightforward way than the BGB's downright hostility to judge-made law: Article 5 specifically prohibits making decisions on the basis of general – unregulated – principles ('Il est défendu aux juges de prononcer par voie de disposition generale et réglementaire sur les causes qui leur sont soumises'). The way in which codifications are structured is one method by which systems within Continental law can be classified into Roman or Germanic legal culture. It is not, however, the only way because often there are both elements in the system, as for example in Italy and also the Netherlands and other systems, which belong to civil law.

> In Italy the model for written civil legislation has been French regulations in particular, but law with a French influence has been interpreted by means of the doctrinal study of law that has been subjected – comparatively speaking – to a strong German

influence. At the start of the twentieth century it was a question of a kind of a hybrid between French positive law and German Pandectist legal science. The civil codification of 1865 followed closely the French model while in the 1942 civil codification a clear influence of German legal thinking is to be seen.[16]

Similar internal civil law legal family hybridity can be seen in the Netherlands where the 1992 civil codification (*Burgerlijk Wetboek*) is original in structure but in regard to its legal style much closer to the German abstract model than to French *code civil*. The previous civil codification of the Netherlands from 1838 had considerably more *code civil* influence. *Burgerlijk Wetboek*'s structure is as following: (1) Personen en familierecht (Individual and Family); (2) Rechtspersonen (Dutch Legal Persons); (3) Vermogensrecht in het algemeen (Assets); (4) Erfrecht (Succession); (5) Zakelijke rechten (Property); (6) Algemeen gedeelte van het verbintenissenrecht (Contracts and Obligations; (7) Bijzondere overeenkomsten (Specific Contracts I); (7A) Bijzondere overeenkomsten; vervolg (Specific Contracts II); (8) Verkeersmiddelen en vervoer (Resources and Transport); (10) Internationaal privaatrecht (Private International Law). Book 9, Intellectual property (De rechten op voortbrengselen van de menselijke geest) is still missing. Even though Dutch code follows German ideas it also has some influences from French law and, in general, Dutch understanding of law tends to be more flexible than the German understanding. It is accepted that 'The core concepts of Dutch Civil Code are continually in motion'.[17]

There are similar modern hybrid dimensions elsewhere, in Lithuania for example, where the 2001 civil codification (*Civilinis Kodeksas*) combines German and French civil law. There are also legal-cultural dimensions of the same type in Spain and other countries.

Occasionally the characteristic nature of legal thinking can also cause difficulties in the classification of legal systems. Problems are encountered when the written law system differs significantly from the legal reality prevailing in practice. For example, it is still typical in socialist law that the practical level of law and *law in books* have significant differences. Living law tends to complicate things. This is precisely why the inquisitive scope of a comparatist cannot be too formal. The comparatist must also view legal systems with the eyes of a legal sociologist or anthropologist and not simply compare *rules that are on paper* only. This is especially the case when the comparatist studies authoritarian or totalitarian systems.

For the comparatist, the context of law is important in two respects: it helps to understand the law of a foreign system and it helps in explaining similarities and differences. From the point of view of a practical comparatist it might be of some importance to compare rules that are on paper only, particularly if it is a question of routine-like extension of the knowledge base in the drafting of legislation. On the other hand, when customary law or the unwritten law of

---

[16] For a broader view, see MA Livingston, PG Monateri, F Parisi, *The Italian Legal System*, 2nd edn (Redwood City, Stanford University Press, 2015).
[17] CG Clementine Geertruida Breedveld-de Voogd et al (eds), *Core Concepts in the Dutch Civil Code* (Deventer, Kluwer, 2016) vii.

Indigenous peoples is examined, ethnographic and anthropological approaches are virtually the only ones that are possible to apply because the norms have probably never been in a written form. In any case, openness towards non-legal information and non-legal fields of knowledge is important.

When differences and similarities are studied and attempts are made to understand and explain them, it is not possible to rely on *rules that are on paper only* because mere legal texts do not normally reveal their context. Even though it is difficult, the comparatist should try to grasp the 'living law'. The rules, institutions and principles under study should always be placed in their contexts. An attempt has also been made to perceive legal thinking at the level of practices and legal-cultural basic assumptions, ie mentality. In this context mentality refers to attitudes, assumptions, prejudices, professional discourse and methods applied by lawyers of a country or other large-scale organised human community. Mentality links also with societal ideologies and political roots of a legal system. In the end, the modern comparatist needs to remain open to interdisciplinarity especially when factors like legal mentality are taken into account.

V. FACTORS RELATED TO IDEOLOGY

The ideological and societal views prevailing in the society of the legal system also have an effect on its style. In particular, the effect of such factors is seen in systems where the impact of the background ideology of religion or the political system is embraced. In Muslim countries certain characteristic stylistic features of their legal systems are explained by the close connection of these countries to the Islamic religion and the Holy book Koran, which is regarded as its central source of law. This is the case in spite of the fact that in the substantive sense Shari'a covers a relatively small part of modern law. The Hindu law and Jewish *halakhah* law have similar effects.

The impact of religious and/or ideological factors is usually at its strongest within certain parts of private law (eg family, inheritance) while many later developed fields of law (eg administrative law and constitutional law) may be surprisingly Western in style. It would seem to be advisable to place the stylistic features into their respective historical context because at different times the legal style of one and the same State can vary according to the tempo of the legal-cultural change. Sweden was a different State before and after 1809, while Finland held onto the old Swedish system (especially constitutional laws and traditions) for much longer although it formally was an autonomous part of the Russian Empire (1809–1917). Legal systems are, generally speaking, layered.

> When for example the legal styles of Turkey are evaluated, different periods have to be considered as well as the fact that earlier periods have by no means disappeared from the present system; instead, they have overlapped. Legal culture is multilayered and to a certain extent of a hybrid nature. We might argue that the past is also present in today's system. The law of Turkey can be divided into different layers, which are

the period of Islamic law in the Ottoman Empire (1299–1839), the intermingling of Islamic law and more modern law in the *Tanzimat* period, ie at the stage of reorganisation (1839–1923), the period of secularised law (1923–2001) and a period (2001–) that slightly rehabilitates certain dimensions of earlier Islamic legal culture but is mainly Western in nature.[18] Lately, however, Turkey's constitutional system has transformed toward an illiberal form of constitutionalism in the wake of neo-authoritarianism.

The influence of socio-ideological views on the style of legal systems, on the other hand, is clearly seen in countries such as China, Vietnam, North Korea (as an extreme example) and Cuba where legal culture of a socialist type still exists. In the Western view the worst part of the so-called socialist legal systems is considered to be their generally poor human rights situation. Weaknesses are particularly demonstrated in the narrowness of traditional freedoms, property rights and political rights. In the Western legal tradition the freedom of an individual from interference by governments in matters that are seen to belong to the sphere of individual freedoms (liberalism) has been emphasised. In any event, it has been thought in today's law and development movement that Western style law is most efficient in the economic sense. Paradoxically, it seems that China is doing well at least in regard to the economy although it has not abandoned all doctrines of socialist law. The Chinese Communist Party is a key factor and power in China and, importantly, the Party has adopted an understanding of law different from the liberal view.[19]

In the classification of families, ideological factors have a significant role when the style of legal systems is evaluated in connection with systems with religious emphasis and of socialist types. The same factors, however, have much less significance when an attempt is made to divide Western countries that are culturally relatively homogenous into different groups. In spite of this, Western industrial countries have their own ideological features: Christian ethics (underlying the surface of societies), the system of market economics with strong protection of property rights and liberal constitutionalism. The capacity of the last two to spread and be adopted has proved to be globally quite strong on the ideological level. All the same, we can detect differences between the Protestant North and Catholic South – every so often they appear, for example in the voting behaviour of the European Human Rights Court in decisions connected with the family and children. Catholic and Orthodox Europe is sometimes amazed at the liberal and individualistic attitude of the Netherlands to prostitution, euthanasia and soft drugs. Also, much of Dutch liberalism seems to apply to Nordic countries. The same applies to Africa which is a huge continent with lots of religious, linguistic, political and legal variation. Accordingly, labelling the legal systems of Mauritius, Sudan, Algeria and South-Africa as 'African' makes very little sense for the comparative study of law.

---

[18] See Ö Metin and O Gelbal, 'The Path to Modern Turkish Law' (2008) 1 *Ankara Bar R* 121.
[19] D Xiaodong, 'Law According to the Chinese Communist Party' (2017) 43 *Modern China* 322.

In the past few years the rule of law thinking has become a kind of normative mega-trend that Western States in particular expect of such big States as China and Russia. The requirement is actually directed to the harmonisation of law. However, as the repeated failures of law and development movement show, one cannot underestimate the significance of legal culture and the context of law. Also, the political ideology plays an important role even though the law and development movement used to be virtually blind to this.

A. Law and Development

During the 1960s and 1970s the law and development movement was rooted in the ideology of modernisation.[20] In practice, this meant that development was seen as something that should take place as State-led. The big issue that early law and development confronted was underdevelopment, which was understood as the product of local institutions, cultures and societies. The quintessential idea was straightforward: Western laws and legal institutions were needed in order to direct and shape economic behaviour in underdeveloped States. Typically, law and legal institutions were seen to serve the creation of modern frameworks for the governance of State industries. The State was seen as the driver of economic growth. Legal-theoretical thinking leaned heavily on the instrumental view of law, which was literally an instrument enhancing State-led development. What is clear today, however, is that the first generation of law and development failed and it did so quite spectacularly. The irritating problem of the first generation of law and development was the inability to recognise that the realities of developed Western countries and those of developing countries were too far removed from each other for the legal reforms to work in practice.

The second generation of law and development reforms brought about a new focus and new concepts. The shift moved to concepts of good governance or best practice in law and legal institutions. In this, various aspects were woven together so that in order to reach good governance legal reform was needed and, thus, the rule of law projects were also needed. According to the second-generation approaches, development was conceived mainly as a question of governance. This meant that legal and judicial reforms started to appear regularly at the top of the list of deep-reaching structural and institutional reforms in the policies set by various international financial institutions. The idea seemed and seems to be that reforms ought to work in such a manner that economic development becomes possible when, and only when, certain legal requirements are fulfilled: the rule of law, property rights and more recently human rights. Instead of singular large-scale projects the emphasis moved to more comprehensive thinking,

---

[20] Of law and development from the point of view of comparative law, see M Siems, *Comparative Law*, 3rd edn (Cambridge, Cambridge University Press, 2022) ch 13.

which underlined and underlines the importance of specific structural legal reforms. Albeit the ultimate justification behind structural reforms still seemed to be economic as to its nature.

In the 1990s, law and development started a new more active phase with the backing of such actors as the World Bank (third generation). As a result there was a huge growth of various legal reform projects in developing and transitioning post-socialist countries. Moneywise, the new phase was impressive because billions of dollars were spent on different kinds of rule of law projects since the beginning of the decade. This surge of interest seemed to assume that there was a broad consensus according to which it was necessary to create rule of law-based governments in the developing and transitional economies. The rule of law was taken as the basis of development policies and the key interest was placed on trying to find the best strategies to implement rule of law development objectives. However, as time passed the amount and significance of challenges became distinct and the early enthusiasm of the 1990s concerning the rule of law fell into decline. The latest turn of events has been an endeavour to elevate the role of law as the recent attempt 'has been more attuned to the idea that law has a value in and of itself'.[21] It became obvious that the seemingly coherent and unified concept of the rule of law was actually masking a plurality of visions and approaches, which were not necessarily compatible with each other.

The problem, well known in comparative law, was that the rule of law is not really a universal value nor is it easy to achieve because this concept has many meanings. Ideology and legal mentality play a role here. So, it is hardly a surprise that the results of such projects have been disappointing. There have been noteworthy implementation problems and it has been noted that one crucial factor behind the failures has been the inability of Western legal experts to recognise the role of local knowledge and the need to adapt to local conditions while promoting (well meaning) rule of law reforms. For the comparatist the continuing troubles of law and development efforts clearly indicate how important the cultural and ideological factors are for law. Yet, it is all but easy to distinguish clearly between culture and ideology because they are intertwined in much the same way as are language and culture.[22]

VI. CULTURAL FACTORS

One way to categorise legal systems into big packages is to consider that different countries belong to civilisations that are culturally different. As Van Hoecke and Warrington point out: 'by taking the perspective of "law as culture" this

---

[21] MJ Trebilcock and MM Prado, *Advanced Introduction to Law and Development* (Cheltenham, Edward Elgar, 2014) 46.
[22] See J Husa, 'Nordic Law and Development?' (2015) 60 *Scan Stud L* 15.

approach should be less biased than the "law as rules" approach of traditional comparative law'.[23]

Admittedly, any macro-classification is of a very general nature and is all but blind to the richness of detail and nuance. Regardless, attempts are made to explain some differences and similarities of legal systems by means of extensive cultural concepts and talking about different cultural spheres (German *Kulturkreis*). Mattei's classification that was discussed in the previous chapter is one example. Certain mental structures or epistemic structures are thought of as being typical constituent parts of a particular cultural sphere. This goes, undoubtedly, way beyond the study of the legal system although it certainly affects the legal style and legal-cultural identity. Van Hoecke and Warrington underline that it is 'important to take into account the cultural identity as perceived by the people and the lawyers'.[24]

Basically, professional law is seen as belonging to the West and religious law as belonging to the non-Western cultural sphere etc. Here the question is of explaining the differences and similarities between systems by means of different legal-cultural factors and the legal mentality. There are risks involved here because using these factors for explanation can at its worst turn to disguising ethnocentric prejudices as more acceptable – it can be a question of scholarly neo-colonialism. It can also be a question of something that is nastier: Kennedy has criticised comparative law for promoting the conservative political agenda under the cover of neutrality.[25] Unfortunately the criticism by Kennedy is not unfounded and especially with such comparative law-related movements like law and development one cannot help but to detect undeniable ethnocentric and neo-colonialist dimensions. Sometimes comparative law exercises are also implicitly ethnocentric as the cases of legal orientalism and law and development show.

The legal sphere (*Rechtskreis*) has been derived from the concept of the cultural sphere. Legal systems are classified on the basis of this by deriving from characteristics that belong to specific cultural circle explanations for the features that are stylistically typical of legal systems. According to this, among legal spheres there would be, for example, the Western countries, the Far East, Africa, Arab countries and India as well as different nomadic cultures. A legal sphere can be defined as an entity that is more extensive than a legal system and includes deeply rooted historical and established attitudes to what the nature of law is and what its role is in the society. In this more extensive division law is still roughly divided into Western and non-Western law although this division

---

[23] M Van Hoecke and M Warrington, 'Legal Cultures, Legal Paradigms and Legal Doctrine' (1998) 47 *ICLQ* 495, 502.
[24] ibid 536.
[25] See D Kennedy, 'The Politics and Methods of Comparative Law' in P Legrand and R Munday (eds), *Comparative Legal Studies: Traditions and Transitions* (Cambridge, Cambridge University Press, 2003) 345.

is inaccurate and does not work sufficiently, particularly with mixed or hybrid systems. In practice, it is a question of overlapping legal cultures and hybridity. The difficulty is that cultures are overlapping and that law travels over the borders; purity was but a dream of an outdated national doctrinalist.

> In Israel for example there are in marriage law different legal-cultural compartments depending on the religion of the person: Jewish law for Jews, Islamic law for Muslims and canon law for Catholics. The norms are applied by religious courts that apply different sets of rules depending on the religion of the person in question. Israeli's legal pluralism on this matter is based on the Ottoman Empire's personal status system (*millet*).[26] Similar statutory pluralism is represented by the constitutional system of Lebanon where according to the *Ta'if* agreement from 1989 (the agreement that ended the civil war) the President is Maronite Christian, the Prime Minister Sunni Muslim and the Spokesman in the Chamber of Deputies Shia Muslim. In addition, the Constitution of Lebanon (art 24) orders that in the legislative organ there has to be equal representation for both Christians and Muslims.

The problem with making divisions between cultural spheres is that owing to its own setting it seems to reject the original cosmopolitan and pluralist assumptions of comparative law that are against ethnocentricism and accepts the old prejudices between different cultures. Is the customary law of Indigenous peoples in this approach automatically primitive and less developed statutory law and judge-made law? The natural reaction of comparatist would be: I do not know, I will have to look into it before any answer can be given. In the biased views, the comparative framework is ethnocentrically based on own law which is automatically regarded as better than what is thought to be the law of the 'underdeveloped' people. Legal orientalism is, for example, a form of ethnocentriscism, a kind of epistemic racism. And, in some versions of law and development one can see similar unacceptable qualities based on predetermined implicit normative value judgements. The comparatist should be extremely careful when it comes to normative value judgements as they may have an impact on what the comparatist sees when they study foreign law. Western legal scholarship has for a long time disregarded Indigenous/primitive normativities as 'non-legal' from the basis of the civilising narrative.[27]

On the other hand, if the cultural and legal sphere division is to be used as part of matter-of-fact comparative law without epistemological racism, it ought not to uphold ethnocentric features. Cultural and ethnical factors can have real effects when explanatory factors are looked for between different legal systems. Such potential factors ought to be found and analytically described in a study that to start with is as free of prejudice (epoche-approach) as possible. One solution that has been suggested (by Patrick Glenn) for the problems connected to the 'culture' concept has been giving it up and speaking of the legal traditions

---

[26] See Y Sezgin, 'The Israel Millet System' (2010) 43 *Israel L R* 631.
[27] K Tuori, *Lawyers and Savages* (London, Routledge, 2015).

of the world (to which Western law too belongs) in a more neutral way.[28] Yet, the diversity of traditions makes them difficult for macro-comparison (and of course for micro-comparison too).

>Occasionally several factors meet within a hybrid cultural sphere, such as religion, business and law. Islamic banking is an example in which taking interest is a problem as it is forbidden (*haraam*) for Muslims. On the other hand, it is known that banking without taking interest is not profitable. In practice, Islamic banks invest in joint enterprises and distribute the profit to their shareholders; in other words, the operation is not based on interest but on profit sharing.
>
>On the basis of deferred profit, the bank takes from the investor/depositor the share of the expected profit that has been agreed in advance. In Western law this is perceived as de facto interest. In fact there are several models in *Islamic Banking*, of which the abovementioned *musharakah* is only one example of several interrelated solutions (it is a form of *sukuk*, ie a bond). In other words, there is within the Islamic cultural sphere a creative legal solution model that enables sensible banking business. Belonging to a given cultural sphere is not an obstacle here; instead the actor guides the formulation of their own legal institutions so that they are made to correspond with the form required in their own cultural sphere. In the West the battle against a corresponding ban for taking interest adopted in the sphere of Catholic Church went on for centuries. Before the Christian world renounced the ban, it had for a very long time evaded it by turning to Jewish bankers (who were not restricted by the interest ban). And, one should not overestimate the exotic nature of Islamic banking because, for instance, it has been accepted in the UK where it is regarded as a legitimate form of doing financial business.[29] In the UK, Islamic banks offer, simply, Shari'a-compliant financial service products to Muslims. Yet, the basic rules of Shari'a are not being broken: a Muslim is not allowed – strictly speaking – to benefit from lending money or receiving money from someone.

From the point of view of macro-comparative law, the advantage of legal families over legal spheres (or cultural families) is their smaller size and due to this the more illustrative and legal-historically nuanced picture is achieved. Legal spheres may, however, be useful when the stylistic features of legal systems are evaluated since the occurrence of certain special features as part of a legal system can cross the borders of legal families and in this respect be related to cultural or legal spheres (eg the views of human rights in China and Islamic countries v Western liberalist views).

VII. FINALLY

Macro-constructs are living systematisations, and they are not meant to be eternal. Legal systems are constantly in slow legal-cultural motion in the sluggish

---

[28] HP Glenn, 'Legal Cultures and Traditions' in M Van Hoecke (ed), *Epistemology and Methodology of Comparative Law* (Oxford, Hart Publishing, 2004) 7.

[29] For more detailed discussion, see eg R Wilson, 'Challenges and Opportunities for Islamic Banking and Finance in the West' (1999) 41 *Thunderbird Int'l Business R* 421.

stream of legal history. Classification into different legal families, traditions and cultures is not to any extent based on natural law thinking that searches for *unchanging law*. Any presentation of legal families, cultures or traditions is dependent on the period when it has been made. The comparatist's own legal-cultural background plays an important epistemic role. From the point of view of the comparatist, not even big alterations in legislation necessarily frustrate the idea of classification. The aim is not always to commit oneself to the present and to attempt to produce the latest knowledge especially if the aims of comparison are theoretical or pedagogical. Classifications, however, live with the legal systems of the world when changes are thorough and fundamental and not just on the surface. To be sure, the heartbeat of legal change is also the heartbeat of macro-comparative law.

However, certain caution is in order here. It is not possible to notice all changes in macro-comparison, and the images are always behind the times, *hazy pictures of the past*. This *is* natural. Comparative law cannot begin to compete with the national doctrinal study of law over who is more aware of the latest turn in legislative development or most recent case law. The national doctrinalists and the normative legal doctrine inevitably win this competition. Macro-comparison helps in the placement of legal cultures in their contexts and this is crucial because legal culture becomes comprehensible only when we place it against its contexts. The main task of macro-comparison can be considered to be the setting of legal cultures against their backgrounds, for them to become comprehensible to those who look at them from the outside.

There is no unanimous opinion among comparatists on how the legal systems or other large-scale organised normativities of the world should be classified. It is easy to criticise classification suggestions and their drawbacks. However, in spite of criticism, classifications that differ greatly from the existing ones have not been suggested. The various classifications are actually surprisingly similar. In comparative law theory innovations are scarce in connection with macro-classification and modified plagiarism is as strong as ever. This does not necessarily mean that comparative law is not capable of developing because this is to a great extent due to the multiplicity and complexity of legal systems and other organised normativities. This also manifests the creativity and kaleidoscopic nature of comparative law that, in turn, reflects the global diversity of law (juridiversity).

12
Conclusion

As an academic field comparative law in all its manifestations offers a remarkable amount of freedom. That much is clear. This liberty offers great temptations for any legal scholar. However, as Kahn-Freund has noted: 'On the professor of comparative law the Gods have bestowed the most dangerous of their gifts, the gift of freedom'.[1] Kahn-Freund stressed the fact that freedom does not come for free, but it comes with a responsibility to take foreign laws and legal cultures seriously. It is through an understanding of this author that this combination of freedom and responsibility concerns all those who engage in the quest of studying law comparatively and hope to exceed mere description of foreign law. There is a great deal of freedom when it comes to the choice of research questions, thematic areas and methods. At the same time, nevertheless, there is a scholarly responsibility to explain one's choices to others and try to make sure that the choices make sense to the readers. The obligation to explain oneself to others is important because, as Monateri says, 'Comparative law as well as other branches of legal analysis is a goal-oriented purposive process'.[2] It is not just a hobby of a legal scholar who does comparative law for leisure alongside the 'more serious' normative study of law. Reaching beyond a mere description of foreign law is not a walk in the park, as we have seen in the previous chapters.

This short conclusion is not a detailed summary of the book but, instead, it highlights five key features that are essential for the modern comparative study of law as it has been described in this book. These features are not methods as such, but they draw together the crucial qualities that are embraced by the modern comparative study of law.

First, *methodological openness* is important for studying law comparatively. This means simply that there is no one-size-fits-all method. Instead, the study of comparative law offers a toolbox of methods, but it is for the comparatist to choose which method they want to use. There is no single approach, theory or paradigm in the comparative study of law.[3] The fact that the comparatist needs

---

[1] O Kahn-Freund, 'Comparative Law as an Academic Subject' (1966) 82 *LQR* 40, 41.
[2] PG Monateri, *Advanced Introduction to Comparative Legal Methods* (Cheltenham, Edward Elgar, 2021) 111.
[3] *cf* G Samuel, *An Introduction to Comparative Law Theory and Method* (Oxford, Hart Publishing, 2014) 179.

to study law in context also means that the openness necessarily includes receptivity to interdisciplinarity. In other words, comparative law literature offers a lot of illustrations and inspiration, but in the end it is for the comparatist to make the methodological decisions and explain these choices to their readers. Openness of the comparatist simply means the quality of being receptive to new methods that, then, need to be tailored to the need of the comparatist. Furthermore, one should also be open to cooperation with other scholars as research questions may be impossible to answer by a lonely comparatist equipped with a limited set of skills.

Second, there is *epistemic sensitivity* that refers to the attempt of the comparatist to be impartial. It is, however, important to conceive that full objectivity is impossible to attain. Yet, the comparatist needs to do their best to mitigate the fact that they are embedded in their own law and that they may hold normative views on the issues they have chosen to study comparatively. In practice, for instance, this may mean seeking to abandon the colonial mindset. This also entails that the comparatist accepts the inborne epistemic limitations that the comparative study of law contains. In short, it is not about actually reaching absolute impartiality but, rather, to be sensitive when it comes to matters that impact on the comparatist's legal thinking and studying of foreign law. Importantly, sensitivity includes a desire to become aware of one's own epistemic bias. To put it another way, self-reflection is necessary for the comparatist.

Third, the endeavour to study law comparatively is based on the underlying *borderlessness of the scholarly mind* of the comparatist. This quality contains two key dimensions. There is an urge to look over the borders and broaden the study of law beyond one's own country and beyond international fields of law. Borderlessness also concerns the willingness to abandon the classical border between law and non-law as it has been understood in the Western legal traditions. In other words, this entails attempting to look beyond formal law based on legislation or case law by official courts of law. Consequently, borderlessness of the scholarly mind includes considering non-official normativities (practices, customs etc) if they are legally relevant for the research question that the comparatist seeks to answer. This, too, may require considering information and methods of non-legal disciplines.

Fourth, throughout the hermeneutic process of trying to understand foreign law and compare there is an *inquisitive humility* involved. This concerns the skills of the comparatist and being aware of the inherent limits there are. Humility also includes willingness to learn that may mean that the comparatist needs to go back to the assumptions of their study if it turns out that the assumptions or hypotheses are misguided and need to be reworked. There needs to be a mental flexibility that involves learning from one's mistakes and learning new skills if they are needed to provide answers to the research questions of the comparatist. All in all, inquisitive humility means that the comparatist stays open to surprises and learns by doing. This seems to require that the comparatist is capable of learning more about law (in a quite broad sense) when they undertake comparative research. To that end, humility is a kind of a reflectivity guided by the learning process offered by the comparative endeavour. Importantly, for the comparatist there is always something to learn, and the process of learning never really stops.

Finally, the attempt to study law comparatively requires a fair amount of *scholarly courage*. This may sound like a strange feature, but it is only realistic to accept that abandoning the epistemic safety provided by one's own law is no small feat. At the outset, it is clear that the comparatist will never understand foreign law from the inside like the legal professionals of that system do. Be that as it may, awareness of this inevitable fact should not demoralise the comparatist. On the contrary, the attempt to compare law and to discover differences and similarities (and then trying to explain them) is an intellectually inspiring way of trying to grasp what this thing we call 'law' is about when we abandon the narrow limits of our own legal system and our own legal culture(s). As it is virtually impossible to get everything right the comparatist needs to have scholarly courage both to face the challenge of understanding law beyond one's own system and to revise it when it is needed. This kind of courage is, it should go without saying, facilitated by the four abovementioned features. It is not about avoiding mistakes altogether but to avoid making the same mistakes over and over.

The above essential comparative law scholarship features have not changed much even though there have been various emphases during the last 200 years. One may, however, ask how these features do fare in the world where law is globalising. The answer lies in the direction of diversity and pluralism.

For the modern comparative study of law, pluralism is the lifeline of the common sense approach to comparative law that is advocated in this book. In the words of Sacco: 'the vision of the comparative law perspective is the pluralistic vision. It is the richness of pluralism in law'.[4] But, it is also the richness of law which poses challenges: this book is building on the twentieth century's comparative law tradition, but the challenge of today and especially that of tomorrow is how to adapt methodological insights to a situation where the nation-State is no longer the main defining entity. The manner by which we compare more fluid entities will require comparatists to keep their eyes open in the future. Globalisation of law, whatever it brings, will diversify and develop comparative law as it is a central instrument to understanding the legal phenomena and ideas of our time.[5]

---

[4] 'la visione del diritto nell'ottica comparatistica è la visione pluralista. É nel pluralismo la ricchezza del diritto', R Sacco, 'Quali scienze interessano il giurista?' in G Comandé and G Ponzanelli (a cura di), *Scienza e diritto nel prisma del diritto comparato* (Turin, Giappichelli, 2004) 27–32, 29.

[5] W Twining in A Vereshchagin, 'An Interview with William Twining' (2021) 16 *Comp L J* 445, 457.

Index

academic legal study and legal systems, 221, 223
acceptance theory (EU), 89
agriculture, comparative law research's effect on, 181–2
American:
  comparative law, 10–11
  legal realism, 208
Ancient Law (Sir Henry Maine), 8
Aristotle (384-322 BC), comparative study of constitutions, 7
Auslandsrechtskunde, 36, 64, 67, 94, 153
Australia, colonialism in, 174

before/past-now/present dimensions, 108–9
Begriffsjurisprudenz (German legal doctrine), 42
Belgium, French laws' influence on, 183
borderlessness of the scholarly mind (comparative law), 286
Buddhism, religious law based on, 226
Bürgerliches Gesetzesbuch (BGB), 25, 47, 185–6, 209, 222, 274, 275

Canadian legal system, legal pluralism in, 212
Chinese:
  court system, hybrid nature of, 145
  law, Western analysis of, 144–5
Christian law, canon law not included in, 227
civil codification (Greece), 25
civil law:
  countries, 29
  legal cultural features of, 222–3
  legal doctrine in, 224
  statutory law is principle of, 222–3
  thinking, 273
'Civil Marriage in the Antiquity and in the Principal Modern European Legislation, The' (Glasson), 108
'civilised nation' concept, 86
code civil (France), 275
codifications period (Japan), 174
colonial epistemology in macro-comparative law, 265–6

colonialism, 173–5, 256
  Australia, in, 174
  concept and definition of, 173
  derecho indiano, 256
  rejection of via legal copying and transfer, 174
commensurability, 154
common constitutional traditions (Europe), 79
Common European Sales Law (CESL) (EU), 84–5
Common Frame of Reference (CFR) (EU), 84–5
common law, 77
  development and legal history of, 177–8
  legal-cultural generalisations, 220–1
  legal family, as, 219–20
  negation of and continental European law, 223
  new (European), 81
  origin of, 62–3
  precedents and, 219, 224
  thinking, 273–4
  UK variations of, 257
comparability, functional approach to, 157–8
comparative:
  approach, restrictions on use, 27–8
  constitutional law, increase of (1990s), 16
  interest's connection with political objectives, 93–4
  international law, 88
  legal economics and linguistics, 50–2
  sociology of law and corporate law compared, 44
Comparative Administration Law (Goodnow), 8–9
comparative arguments:
  ICJ and ECtHR, used in, 92
  use of (US), 91–2
comparative criminal law:
  systemic macro-comparison example, 139–40
  Western criminal procedure regimes of, 139
comparative law, 9–11, 31, 33–4, 91 (case law), 96–8, 142, 189
  bilateral, 113
  case-oriented, 113

comparatists' role in, 21
comparison in, 27–8, 190–1
definitions of, 2, 3–4, 20
dynamic approach to, 132–8
functional law (Zweigert and Kötz), 190
methodological and theoretical standard of, 92–3
methodology, 29–31
multilateral, 114–15
pedagogy concept of, 96
teaching of, 98–9
Comparative Law in a Global Context (Menski, 2006), 48–9
comparative law research, 12–13, 121–2
  agriculture, effect of on, 181–2
  Dewey on, 100–1
  foreign language, effect of on, 184–5
  hermeneutic, 103
  historical and horizontal comparison of, 109–10
  interpretative explaining and, 185–6
  longitudinal comparison of, 109
  method, 12–13
  micro-comparison in, 105–6
  neighbouring states and neighbourhood, effect of on, 181, 182–4
  quasi-legal arrangements, 186
  reliability of sources assessed, 121–2
  sources for, 120–2
  time dimension, 108–13
Comparative Legal History (journal), 40–1
comparative legal studies, 31
  normative approach in, 209
comparative study:
  human knowledge and, 67
  intentional cover-up and, 150
  methodology, 148
  origins of, 7
  strategy, 104
comparative study of law, 17–18, 22–3, 34, 259
  Confucian thinking and, 164
  Islamic law and, 165–6
  mentality, 166–7
  religion and, 163–5
comparison:
  comparative law, in, 27–8, 190–1
  concept of, 65, 69
  examples of, 72–3
  first and second stages, 146
  tertium comparationis, of, 158
  third, fourth and fifth stages, 147
Concept of Law (Hart), 35–6

Confucian thinking and comparative study of law, 164
congress on international comparative law (Paris, 1900), 10
constitutions:
  Greek city states, study of in, 7
  literature on, 7–9
Continental civil law, French and German codification of, 274–5
Continental European:
  law and negation of common law, 223
  legal culture, features of, 222
contradictive comparative study and research, 76–8
copying and learning (legal history), examples of, 176
corporate law and comparative sociology of law compared, 44
courts:
  case law created for Romano-Germanic legal system, 223
  formation of legal systems, role in, 220–1
  international comparative law, treatment of, 13
  law created by, 223
  legal problems of and private international law, 53–4
  precedents established by, 41, 97, 116, 174, 220–1, 222
  private international law and, 102
  public international law, application of, 57
critical competence law (Legrand), 140–3
criticalness, types of, 140
cross-cultural comparison (Western legal systems), 119
cultural factors (legal systems), 280–3
  classification of, 280–1
customary international law, 87–8

David, R, on legal families, 231, 235
De l'esprit des lois (Montesquieu), 44
decision-making:
  ECtHR's and comparative law, 26
  hard cases, in, 36
Dessau, C, on comparative law, 48
Dewey, John, on comparative law research, 100–1
doctrine:
  Begriffsjurisprudenz, 42
  Discovery, of, 173
  legal *see* legal doctrine

stare decisis, 220, 269
Terra Nullius, 174
dominium, 169
double comparison (legal systems), 249
Draft Common Frame of Reference (EU, 2009), 84
Dupret, B, on Islamic law, 242

economic resources' effect on socio-legal solutions, 171
end of history, 259, 263
  Fukuyama on, 263
English law in statutory law, 267
epistemic:
  commensurability, 195
  modesty, 245
  sensitivity (comparative law), 286
  universalism, 23–5
epoche research technique, 126–7
ethnocentrism, 72–4, 189
Europe, integration in, 79–80
European Court of Human Rights (ECtHR):
  comparative arguments used in, 92
  comparative law used in decision-making, 26
  public international law and, 57–8
European federation, (2020s), 16–17
European Human Rights Court and comparative law, 57–8
European Union (EU):
  administrative law hearing procedure, 82–3
  comparative law applied in, 216
  fundamental law, legal system secured in, 82 (case law), 82
  fundamental rights, 81–3 (case law)
  internal market and harmonisation, 79–80
  official languages of, 204, 206
European Union law, 83–4
  comparative law and, 69, 109–10
  public international law and, differences between, 83
  Raitio on comparative law research, 109–10
  translation of, 206–7
evolution:
  law, of, 178
  legal *see* legal evolution
  macro-level, 253
  theory and global law, 262–3
Ewald, W, on comparative law, 47–8
experiential learning, 100–2, 152, 214
explaining foreign law, 160
  bias, avoidance of, 161–2
  comparative law factors and, 162

plot method, 160–1
thick description concept, 161
explanatory factors, differences between, 186–8
  types of, 187

false friends (functional comparative law), examples of, 124–5
feedback and comparative law, 196
Feuerbach, Anselm von (1775–1833), 23
Fisheries Jurisdiction (UK v Norway) (1951), 88
foreign languages, comparative law research, effect of on, 184–5
foreign law:
  comprehension of, 248
  explaining *see* explaining foreign law
  knowledge threshold lowered for, 247
  legal systems and, 63–4
  macro-constructs and, 233–4, 250
foreign legal culture, 162–3
  methodological sensitivity and, 150
foreign legal language and examination of material in original language, 203
foreign legal systems, 270
  academic comparison of, 196
  macro-comparison of, 108
formal law, comparative law confined to, 59–60, 137
forms of actions (judicial process), 175–6
French law's effect on Belgian law, 183
Fukuyama, F, on the end of history, 263
functional:
  counterparts, finding, 129
  equivalences, 124
functional comparative law, 122–4, 159
  criticism of, 158
  procedure of, 129
functional comparison, 124, 159
  purpose of, 126
  tertium comparationis and, 157–60
  translating legal language and, 130–2
functions, conceptual framework for, 125–6

gender and mentality, 167
general:
  legal knowledge and comparative law, 24–5
  principles of law in international law, 86–7
geography and climate, effect on law, 180–1
German civil code, 185–6
German Constitution 1919, 185–6
Germany, comparative law in, 24

gifts (comparative law), 129–30
    Hyland on, 106, 129–30
Glenn, H Patrick:
    legal tradition, on, 243–6, 283
    national legal systems, on, 71–2
global diversity, method and methodology for, 103
global law, 262
    evolutionary theory and, 262–3
    Hegal and Leibniz on, 262
    writing on, 262
guanxi, 186

halakhah, 177–8, 277
Haley, JO, on comparative law, 20
hard cases, decision-making in, 36
harmonisation, 75–6
    development of, 76–7
    EU internal market and, 79–80
    Nordic countries, in, 80
Hegel, GWF, on global law, 262
HELO (Finnish law-drafting guide), 93–4
hermeneutic circle, 194–5
heuristics, 151
Hindu law sources, 120–1
history:
    comparative law and, 70
    end of *see* end of history
    law, of, and comparative law, 30–1
horizontal comparison (legal systems), 116
human knowledge and comparative study, 67
human rights, application of, 178
humanities, comparative law is part of, 65–6
Hyland, R, on gifts, 106, 129–30

ideal types (Weber), 230
idiographic case studies, 113–14
    Inuit terminology, 114–15
    Lasser on, 113–14
indigenous peoples:
    legal languages of, 205
    macro-comparison and, 218
inquisitive humility (comparative law), 286–7
integration in Europe, 79–80
integrative interest, 75
intentional cover-up and comparative study, 150
international:
    humanitarian law, 87
    publishing and comparative law, 195–6

International Court of Justice (ICJ):
    comparative arguments used in, 92
    functions of, 86
    public international law and, 57
International Institute for Unification of Private Law (Unidroit), 90
international law:
    comparative, 12, 58, 88
    general principles of law and, 86–7
    tradition and, 88 (case law)
intracultural comparison, 119–20
Islamic law:
    comparative law's approach to, 18–19, 89
    comparative study of law and, 165–6
    Dupret on, 242
    legal history, relationship to, 179
    precedents in, 180, 253
    study of, 97
    transnational law and, 117–19
Islamic marriage contract, 136
Italy, legal codification in, 275–6

Japan:
    codifications period, 174
    keeping list of macro-constructs up to date, 261
Jhering, R von, 73–4
judges, attitudes to, 247
juridiversity, 216
jurist-linguists (EU), 206, 207

Kahn-Freund, O, on transplant criticism, 111
Kelsen, Hans, on formal validity of law, 210
knowledge:
    acquisition, 64–5, 249
    increase of and theoretical approach, 95–6
    interests, 74–5
    threshold lowered for foreign law, 247

language and law, 51
language for a specific purpose (LSP):
    foreign, translation of, 202
    legal language as, 201
Lasser, M de S-O-l'E, 113–14
law, 211, 254–5
    comparative study of *see* comparative study of law
    comparison of, 62, 142
    courts' creation of, 223
    diffusion of and legal evolution, 256
    discourse, as, and law as politics differentiated, 140

doctrinal study of, 35–6
Europeanisation of, 257
field of and private international law, 55–6
functional comparative and written
   material, 213
judge-made, 255
Kelson on, 210
language and, 51
legal research and, Universalist attitude to,
   70
legitimation of, 228
loyalty, of (Smith), 247
macro-comparatists on, 230–1
macro-comparative *see*
   macro-comparative law
social environment changes and, 255–6
society and, 63
validity of *see* validity of law
see also specific entries
law and development, 46–7
law and development movement, 279–80
   1960s, 1970s and 1990s, during, 279–80
   second generation reforms, 279–80
law and economy, 169–71
   origins and state control of, 169–70
lawyers, change of environment for, 248
learning by doing (legal comparison), 214, 215
legal:
   borrowing, 112
   codification in Italy and the Netherlands,
      275–6
   comparison, 20, 213–15
   concepts, translation of, 206
   conservatism, 180
   copying and transfer and rejection of
      colonisation, 174
   diffusion, 191–2
   disciplines, 33
   family concept and legal culture, 239–40
   formats, 137–8
   harmonisation (Europe), 79–80
   historical research, 39–40
   influence, spread of, 176
   intentions, study of, 159–60
   irritant (Teubner), 112, 191
   linguistics, 201–2
   mentality, 141–2
   norms intermingled in legal cultures, 187–8
   orientalism (Ruskola), 143–5
   problem functionalism, 128–9
   sociology and functionality of legal rules,
      43

   spheres, 281–2
   tapestry, 60–1
legal classification:
   private and public law basis, on, 267–8
   sources of law and, 268–9
legal-cultural, 27
   literacy, 146
   models, transplantation of, 183–4
   practices' influence on legal systems,
      184–6
legal cultures:
   comparative law, in, 238–9
   definition, significance and research
      role of, 45
   foreign and research ethics, 149–50
   legal family concept and, 239–40
   legal norms, intermingling of, 187–8
   macro-comparison of, 107
   Mattei on, 239–40
legal doctrine, 34–5
   civil law, in, 224
   comparative law and, 36–8, 98
   Flanders, in, 183
   legal theory and, 46
legal evolution, 253–4, 254–5
   diffusion of law and, 256
legal families 218–19, 235–7
   classification of (Cuniberti), 235–6
   common law as, 219–20
   David on, 231, 235
   definition, 235
   study of and research into, 232
   Zweigert and Kötz on, 235
legal history:
   common law development and, 177–8
   comparative law and, 39
   importance of, 38–9
   legal rules, interpretation of for, 179–80
   significance of, 175–6
legal history and comparative law, 171–80
   Roman law and, 172
legal language, 51, 201–3
   indigenous people, of, 205
   LSP, as, 201
   translating and fundamental comparison,
      130–2
'legal order', 23
legal origins theory, 42, 52, 113, 114, 170
legal pluralism, 60–1, 211–12
   Canadian legal system, 212
legal research and comparative law, 59
   Universalist attitude to, 70

legal rules:
  expression of, 267
  functionality of and legal sociology, 43
  functions of, 158–9
  legal history, reinterpretation of, for, 179–80
  written, 276–7
legal study materials:
  comparative law journals and reviews, 199–200
  databases, 197–8
  internet, 200
  multilingual legal dictionaries, 198–9
  net-based networks, 200
  primary and secondary sources, 197–8
legal system ideology, 277–80
  examples of, 277
  Turkey and Western legal tradition, of, 277–8
legal systems, 22–3
  academic legal study and, 221, 223
  characteristics of and macro-construct's technical classification, 267
  classification criteria, 270–1
  courts' role in formation of, 220–1
  differences and similarities explained, 249
  double comparison of, 249
  foreign *see* foreign legal systems
  foreign law and, 63–4
  formation of, courts' role in, 220–1
  legal family classification of, 271
  living law's influence on, 184–6
  mixed, 236
  precedents, based on, 220
  public law and, 221
  socio-legal contexts of, 135–6
  structure of and separation of public and private law, 223
  study of, 207
  style of (Zweigert and Kötz), 269–71
  systematisation of, 36
  transfer, 112, 191
  transposition, 112, 191
  understanding of and macro-constructs, 249–50
legal theory:
  comparative law and, 46, 47–8
  legal doctrine and, 46
legal traditions, 282–3
  chtonic (Glenn), 243–4
  Glenn on, 243–6, 283
  incommensurable, 245–6
  macro-comparison of, 107
  past, in the, 244–5
  vertical and horizontal, 245
  Western legal culture and, 244
Legal Traditions of the World (Glenn, 2014), 243–6
legal translation, 112, 130–2
  legal traditions, taking into account, 205
  problems of, 204
  socio-legal solution model, 208–9
legal transplant:
  research, 110–13
  Watson on, 110
legislative:
  comparative law, 9
  innovation via coercion, 177
Legrand, P:
  critical competence law, on, 140–3
  transplant criticism, on, 111–12
Leibniz, GW, on global law, 262
lex causae, 53, 54
Lex Dei quam praecepit Dominus ad Moysen, 8
lex fori, 53, 54
living law (Ehrlich), 42–3, 207–8
  legal systems, influence on, 184–6

macro-comparatists on law, 230–1
macro-comparative law, 260–1
  colonial epistemology in, 265–6
  examples of, 260
macro-comparison, 28–9, 106
  comparative criminal law as systemic example of, 139–40
  concept and extent of, 218–19
  foreign legal system, of, 108
  private law, in, 266
macro-constructs:
  benefits of, 248
  classification of, 266
  foreign law and, 233–4, 250
  generalisation of, 232–3
  keeping up to date, 261
  legal system characteristics and technical classification, 267
  legal systems, understanding of and, 249–50
  utility of, 233
Maine, Sir Henry, 8, 9, 10
marriage practices (Turkey and Ghana), 188
Mattei, U:
  legal culture, on, 239–40
  political and traditional law, on, 241–3
Mattila, HES, on language and law, 51

Menski, W, on comparative law, 48–9
mentality:
  comparative study of law and, 166–7
  definition of, 141–2
  gender and, 167
  political thinking and, 167–8
method and methodology (comparative law research), 101–4
  global diversity, in, 103
methodological:
  openness (comparative law), 285–6
  sensitivity and foreign legal culture, 150
methodology, theoretical choices of, 122
micro-comparison (comparative law research), 105–6
mixed legal systems, 225–6, 244–6
  former socialist countries have, 225
  history and concept of, 224
  Romano-Germanic law and, 225
  Scotland, in, 225
model shopping, 16
multilingualism, 203–5
  legal encyclopaedias and dictionaries, use of, 203
mutated loan, 111
mutation, 178–9
  legal, 259

Napoleonic *Code civil*, 93
nation-states (Glenn), 71–2
National Blood Case, The (2001, England), 56
national law, comparative law's contribution to, 257–8
national legal systems, development of, 71
  Glenn on, 71–2
natural law, 189
  comparative law and, 49–50
  universalism, 189
neighbouring states and neighbourhood and comparative law research, 181, 182–4
Netherlands, legal codification in, 276
nomogenetics and nomoscopy, 259
nomothetics, 259
  study approach, 113
Nordic:
  comparative law, 12, 47
  countries, harmonisation in, 80
  law, 238
  legal family and mind, 236–8

ordre public (private international law), 55
'ornamental' comparative law, 37

past, the, in legal tradition, 244–5
political:
  history, impact of, 172
  law (Mattei), 241–2
  thinking and mentality, 167–8
polycentric levels (normative systems), 116
polygamy, 165
post-colonialism, 143–4
practicality, 91–4
  comparative law approach and, 91 (case law)
precedents, 34, 135, 172, 220, 252
  Islamic law, in, 180, 253
  states', binding law, as, 60
Principles of European Contract Law (PECL) (EU), 84, 99
private:
  ordering (Thailand), 15–16
  ownership, socialist public law system (China), 170–1
private international law, 53–6, 77, 78–9
  comparative law and, 14, 54–6
  courts and, 102
  courts' legal problems and, 53–4
  field of law, as, 55–6
  Rabel on, 53
private law, 53
  comparative law and, 13, 14–15, 17
  literature on, 14–15
  macro-comparison, in, 266
  separation of and legal systems, 223
professional law, 240–1
proportion, significance of, 66–7
public:
  private law and, separation of and legal system structure, 223
  undertakings, 15–16
public international law, 56–61
  courts' application of, 57
  ECtHR and, 57–8
  EU law and, differences between, 83
  ICJ and, 57
  statute of the court regulates, 86
public law:
  comparative law and, 14
  legal classification made on, 267–8
  legal systems and, 221
  1989–90, developments after, 16
  separation of public and private law, legal systems built on, 223

Rabel, E, on private international law, 53
racist classification, macro-comparison of, 107

religion and comparative study of law, 163–5
religious law:
    Buddhism, based on, 226
    Christian canon law not included in, 227
    religion based on traditional knowledge or culture, 227–8
religious-traditional law, 226–8
research ethics:
    comparative law, in, 148–9
    foreign legal cultures, respect for and, 149–50
right of ownership (France and Italy), 169
Roman law and legal history and comparative law, 172
Romano-Germanic Law, 221–2
    mixed legal systems and, 225
    statutory law as legal-cultural frame of, 224
Romano-Germanic legal system and case law created by courts, 223
rule of law (China), 168
rules of law and legal concepts (Legrand), 141
Ruskola, T, on legal orientalism, 143–5

Sacco, Rodolfo, on dynamic approach, 137
Saleilles, Raymond (1855–1912), 23
Scalia, Antonin (US judge), 91–2
Schlesinger, Rudolf, on comparative law, 20
scholarly:
    comparative law, 9–10
    courage, 287
    mind, borderlessness of, 286
school of truth, comparative law known as, 25
science and comparative law, 65, 66
Scotland:
    legal culture (legal-cultural source), 198
    mixed legal system in, 225
similarity, 191, 192–3
social environment changes and law, 255–6
socialist countries, former, and mixed legal systems, 225
socialist law, 228–9
    scarcity of, 261–2
socialist legal systems, structural comparability of, 134–5
socialist public law system (China) and private ownership, 170–1
society:
    comparative law, and, 9, 145
    law and, 63
socio-legal solutions, country's economic resources' effect on, 171
sociology of law, 41
    comparative law's relation to, 41–3

sources of law and legal classification, 268–9
South Africa, official languages of, 205
Spirit of the Laws, The (Montesquieu), 8
stare decisis doctrine, 220, 269
State-capitalism, 170–1
state sovereignty, lessening of (2020s), 16–17
statistical comparative law, 43
Statute of the Court (EU) regulates public international law, 86
statutory law:
    civil law, principle of is, 222–3
    English law, in, 267
    legal-cultural frame of Romano-Germanic law is, 224
strict liability study (Cappelletti), 134
structural:
    comparability and dispute over socialist and Western legal systems, 134–5
    comparison, 132–3
structural comparative law, 133–4
    legal-culturally important contexts of, 135
study of law, 60–1
    comparative and formulation of theories, 25–6
supranational law (legal systems), 115
Swiss Confederation's official languages, 204
system-specific labels:
    Greek example, 127–8
    ignoring, advantages of, 127–8
systemic:
    comparison, 138–9
    macro-comparison, examples of, 139–40

technical methodological choices, 104–5
    alternatives for, 104
tertium comparationis, 154
    comparison of, 158
    definition and example of, 155
    functional comparison and, 157–60
    procedure of, 155–7
theoretical approach:
    concept of, 94
    increase of knowledge and, 95–6
    theoretical methodology choices, 122
theoretical research, 95
theories, formulation of, and comparative study of law, 25–6
theory of comparative law, 22
theory of state (Glenn), 71–2
thick description (legal comparison), 214
    concept, 161
time and space (Zeit und Raum), 109

traditional law, 242–3
  Mattei on, 242–3
  sub-groups of, 242
transnational law, 116–19
  definition and dimensions of, 177
  Islamic law and, 117–19
transnationality (legal systems), 115–19
transplant theory, criticism of, 111–12
Turkey:
  legal system of ideology and, 277–8
  macro-constructs kept up to date, 261
Twelve Tables (laws), comparative history of, 69
twentieth century comparative law, background and development of, 11–12
twenty-first century comparative law, 11–13

unification, 76
universal nature of law, 10
universalism and comparative law, 24

validity of law, 209–11
  format, 210
  living, and written law, 212
  methods of understanding, 211
  realistic, 210
variable-oriented study (comparative law), 114

vertical comparison (legal systems), 116
Visser, M de, on systemic comparison, 138

Watson, A, on legal transplants, 110
Western countries and states' legal systems' ideological features, 278–9
Western law, 78
  aim of, 272
  study of, 97
Western legal culture as legal tradition, 244
Western legal systems:
  cross-cultural comparison, 119
  structural comparability of, 134–5
Western legal tradition and legal system ideology, 278
Westminster system, 182
Wilhelmsson on Nordic legal family, 238
World Society of Mixed Jurisdictions of the World (2002), 236
World Trade Organisation (WTO), 88–9

Yntema, Hessel E, on legal science, 70–1

Zweigert and Kötz:
  functional law, on, 190
  legal families, on, 235
  style of legal systems, on, 269–71